The Aims of Argument

A Brief Guide

The Aims of Argument
A Brief Guide

Timothy W. Crusius
Southern Methodist University

Carolyn E. Channell
Southern Methodist University

McGraw-Hill
Higher Education

Boston   Burr Ridge, IL   Dubuque, IA   New York   San Francisco   St. Louis
Bangkok   Bogotá   Caracas   Kuala Lumpur   Lisbon   London   Madrid   Mexico City
Milan   Montreal   New Delhi   Santiago   Seoul   Singapore   Sydney   Taipei   Toronto

McGraw-Hill
Higher Education

Published by McGraw-Hill, an imprint of The McGraw-Hill Companies, Inc., 1221 Avenue of the Americas, New York, NY 10020. Copyright © 2009, 2006, 2003, 2000, 1998, 1995 by The McGraw-Hill Companies, Inc. All rights reserved. No part of this publication may be reproduced or distributed in any form or by any means, or stored in a database or retrieval system, without the prior written consent of The McGraw-Hill Companies, Inc., including, but not limited to, in any network or other electronic storage or transmission, or broadcast for distance learning.

This book is printed on acid-free paper.

1 2 3 4 5 6 7 8 9 0 DOC/DOC 0 9 8

ISBN: 978-0-07-340583-4
MHID: 0-07-340583-3

Vice president and Editor-in-chief: *Michael Ryan*
Publisher: *David S. Patterson*
Director of development: *Carla Kay Samodulski*
Sponsoring editor: *Christopher Bennem*
Developmental editor: *Joshua Feldman*
Marketing manager: *Allison Rauch*
Production editors: *April Wells-Hayes/Melissa Williams*
Lead production supervisor: *Randy Hurst*
Interior designer: *Maureen McCutcheon*
Cover designer: *Laurie Entringer*
Photo researcher: *Lou Ann Wilson*
Compositor: *Aptara, Inc.*
Typeface: 10.25/12 *Giovanni Book*
Printer and binder: *RR Donnelley & Sons*

Cover art © Tracy Melton

Text and photo credits appear on pages 727–728 at the back of the book and constitute an extension of the copyright page.

LIBRARY OF CONGRESS CATALOGING-IN-PUBLICATION DATA

Crusius, Timothy W.
   The aims of argument : a brief guide / Timothy W. Crusius,
Carolyn E. Channell.—Brief ed., 6th ed.
      p. cm.
   Includes index.
   ISBN 0-07-340583-3; 978-0-07-340583-4
   1. English language—Rhetoric—Handbooks, manuals, etc.   2. Persuasion (Rhetoric)—
Handbooks, manuals, etc. 3. Report writing—Handbooks, manuals, etc.   I. Channell,
Carolyn E.

PE1431.C778 2009
808'.042—dc22   2008003453

www.mhhe.com

For W. Ross Winterowd

As its first five editions were, the sixth edition of *The Aims of Argument* is different from other argumentation texts because it remains the only one that focuses on the aims, or purposes, of argument. That this book's popularity increases from edition to edition tells us that our approach does in fact satisfy the previously unmet need that moved us to become textbook authors.

NOTES ON THIS TEXT'S ORIGINS

With more than sixty years of teaching experience between us, we had tried most argument books. Many of them were good, and we learned from them. However, we found ourselves adopting a text not so much out of genuine enthusiasm but because it had fewer liabilities. We wondered why we were so lukewarm about even the best argumentation textbooks. We boiled our dissatisfaction down to a few major criticisms:

- Most treatments were too formalistic and prescriptive.
- Most failed to integrate class discussion and individual inquiry with written argumentation.
- Apart from moving from simple concepts and assignments to more complicated ones, no book offered a learning sequence.
- Despite the fact that argument, like narrative, is clearly a mode or means of discourse, not a purpose for writing, no book offered a well-developed view of the aims or purposes of argument.

We thought that these shortcomings had undesirable consequences in the classroom, including the following:

- The overemphasis on form confused students with too much terminology, made them doubt their instincts, and drained away energy from inventing and discovering good arguments. Informal argumentation is not formal logic but open-ended and creative.

- The separation of class discussion from composing created a hiatus between oral and written argument. Students had difficulty seeing the relation between the two and using insights from each to improve the other.

- The lack of a learning sequence—of assignments that build on each other—meant that courses in argumentation were less coherent and meaningful than they could be. Students did not understand why they were doing what they were doing and could not envision what might come next.

- Finally, inattention to what people actually use argument to accomplish resulted in too narrow a view of argument and in unclear purposes for writing. Because instruction was mainly limited to what we call arguing to convince, students took argument only as monologues of advocacy. They ignored inquiry.

We set out to solve these problems. The result is a book different from any other argument text because it focuses on four aims of argument:

Arguing to inquire, questioning opinions

Arguing to convince, making cases

Arguing to persuade, appealing to the whole person

Arguing to mediate, finding common ground between conflicting positions

COMMON QUESTIONS ABOUT THE AIMS OF ARGUMENT

Instructors have certain questions about these aims, especially how they relate to one another. Here are some of the most frequently asked questions:

1. *What is the relative value of the four aims? Because mediation comes last, is it the best or most valued?* No aim is "better" than any other aim. Given needs for writing and certain audiences, one aim is more appropriate than another for the task at hand. Mediation comes last because it integrates inquiry, convincing, and persuading.

2. *Must inquiry be taught as a separate aim?* No. It *may* be taught as a separate aim, but we do not intend this "may" as a "must." Teaching inquiry as a distinct aim has certain advantages. Students need to learn how to engage in constructive dialogue, which is more disciplined and more focused than most class discussion. Once they see how it is done, students enjoy dialogue with one another and with texts. Dialogue helps students think through their arguments and imagine reader reaction to what they say, both of which are crucial to convincing and

persuading. Finally, as with mediation, inquiry offers avenues for assignments other than the standard argumentative essay.

3. *Should inquiry come first?* For a number of reasons, inquiry has priority over the other aims. Most teachers are likely to approach inquiry as prewriting, preparatory to convincing or persuading. And commonly, we return to inquiry when we find something wrong with a case we are trying to construct, so the relationship between inquiry and the other aims is also recursive.

   Moreover, inquiry has psychological, moral, and practical claims to priority. When we are unfamiliar with an issue, inquiry comes first psychologically, as a felt need to explore existing opinion. Regardless of what happens in the "real world," convincing or persuading without an open, honest, and earnest search for the truth is, in our view, immoral. Finally, inquiry goes hand in hand with research, which requires questioning the opinions encountered.

4. *Isn't the difference between convincing and persuading more a matter of degree than kind?* Sharp distinctions can be drawn between inquiry and mediation and between both of these aims and the monologues of advocacy, convincing and persuading. But convincing and persuading do shade into one another so that the difference is clearest at the extremes, with carefully chosen examples. Furthermore, the "purest" appeal to reason—a legal brief, a philosophical or scientific argument—appeals in ways beyond the sheer cogency of the case. Persuasive techniques are submerged but not absent in arguing to convince.

   Our motivation for separating convincing from persuading is not theoretical but pedagogical. Case-making is complex enough that attention to logical appeal by itself is justified. Making students conscious of the appeals to character, emotion, and style while they are learning to cope with case-making can overburden them to the point of paralysis.

   Regardless, then, of how sound the traditional distinction between convincing and persuading may be, we think it best to take up convincing first and then persuasion, especially because what students learn in the former can be carried over intact into the latter. And because one cannot make a case without unconscious appeal to character, emotional commitments (such as values), and style, teaching persuasion is a matter of exposing and developing what is already there in arguing to convince.

Here are the central tenets of an approach based on aims of argument:

- *Argumentation is a mode or means of discourse, not an aim or purpose for writing;* consequently, we need to teach the aims of argument.
- *The aims of argument are linked in a learning sequence so that convincing builds on inquiry, persuasion on convincing, and all three contribute to mediation;* consequently, we offer a learning sequence for conceiving a course or courses in argumentation.

We believe in the sequence as much as the aims. We think that many will come to prefer it over any other approach.

Of course, textbooks are used selectively, as teachers and programs need them in achieving their own goals. As with any other text, this one can be used selectively, ignoring some parts, playing up others, designing other sequences, and so on. If you want to work with our learning sequence, it's there for creative adaptation. If not, the text is flexible enough for almost any course structure or teaching method.

A FINAL WORD ABOUT THE APPROACH

Our approach is innovative. But is it better? Will students learn more? Will instructors find the book more satisfying and more helpful than what they currently use? Our experience—both in using the book ourselves and in listening to the responses of those who have read it or tested it in the class-room or used it for years—is that they will. Students complain less about having to read this book than about having to read others used in our pro-gram. They do seem to learn more. Teachers claim to find the text stimulat-ing, something to work with rather than around. We hope your experience is as positive as ours has been. We invite your comments and will use them in the perpetual revision that constitutes the life of a text and our lives as writing teachers.

NEW TO THE SIXTH EDITION

The more important changes and additions to this edition are the following:

1. **A new chapter on plagiarism and ethical writing**   To have all of the advantages of computers and online research, we have paid a price—more intentional and unintentional plagiarism because students can so easily copy and paste from their research sources. This new chapter offers a focused and comprehensive explanation of the ethical and uneth-ical use of sources and advice on the ethics of receiving help on papers.

2. **A new appendix on fallacies and critical thinking**   Instead of a list of items often called fallacies, we've defined "fallacy" as the misuse of legitimate kinds of persuasive appeal. We think our treatment leads students to distinguish sound from unsound thinking better than tra-ditional approaches based on formal logic.

3. **Increased emphasis on visual persuasion**   This edition expands our already extensive coverage of visual arguments. Chapter 4, "Reading and Writing about Visual Arguments," has been significantly revised. Just as important, we have added new visual material to all parts of the book, so that arguments made through photographs, cartoons, graphics, and so on are integrated throughout.

In addition to these major additions and changes, those familiar with the fifth edition will detect many more: for instance, several new student essays, more process coverage in the persuasion chapter, and a much-needed updating of the research chapter. We think the year's work that went into this new edition of *Aims* was worth the effort and hope you will, too.

Revised Online Learning Center

In addition to the many changes the sixth edition offers in the text itself, this edition of *Aims* is accompanied by a newly revised Online Learning Center, accessible at www.mhhe.com/crusius. The site features all the tools of Catalyst 2.0, McGraw-Hill's award-winning writing and research Web site. You will find integrated references throughout the text, pointing you to additional online coverage of the topic at hand.

Online Course Delivery and Distance Learning

In addition to the Web site, McGraw-Hill offers the following technology products for composition classes. The online content of *The Aims of Argument* is supported by WebCT, Blackboard, eCollege.com, and most other course systems. Additionally, McGraw-Hill's PageOut service is available to get you and your course up and running online in a matter of hours—at no cost! To find out more, contact your local McGraw-Hill representative or visit <http://www.pageout.net>.

PageOut

McGraw-Hill's widely used click-and-build Web site program offers a series of templates and many design options, requires no knowledge of HTML, and is intuitive and easy to use. With PageOut, anyone can produce a professionally designed course Web site in very little time.

AllWrite! 2.1

Available online or on CD-ROM, *AllWrite!* 2.1 offers more than 3,000 exercises for practice in basic grammar, usage, punctuation, context spelling, and techniques for effective writing. The popular program is richly illustrated with graphics, animations, video, and Help screens.

Teaching Composition Faculty Listserv at <www.mhhe.com/tcomp>

Moderated by Chris Anson at North Carolina State University and offered by McGraw-Hill as a service to the composition community, this listserv brings together senior members of the college composition community with newer members—junior faculty, adjuncts, and teaching assistants—in an online newsletter and accompanying discussion group to address issues of pedagogy in both theory and practice.

ACKNOWLEDGMENTS

We have learned a great deal from the comments of both teachers and students who have used this book, so please continue to share your thoughts with us.

We wish to acknowledge the work of the following reviewers who guided our work on the first, second, third, fourth, and fifth editions: Linda Bensel-Meyers, University of Tennessee, Knoxville; Elizabeth Howard Borczon, University of Kansas; Joel R. Brouwer, Montcalm Community College; Lisa Canella, DePaul University; Mary F. Chen-Johnson, Tacoma Community College; Matilda Cox, University of Maryland–College Park; Margaret Cullen, Ohio Northern University; Dr. Charles Watterson Davis, Kansas State University; Amy Cashulette Flagg, Colorado State University; Richard Fulkerson, Texas A&M University–Commerce; Lynee Lewis Gaillet, Georgia State University; Cynthia Haynes, University of Texas at Dallas; Matthew Hearn, Valdosta State University; Peggy B. Jolly, University of Alabama at Birmingham; James L. Kastely, University of Houston; William Keith, Oregon State University; Lisa J. McClure, Southern Illinois University, Carbondale; Rolf Norgaard, University of Colorado at Boulder; Julie Robinson, Colorado State University; Gardner Rogers, University of Illinois, Urbana-Champaign; Judith Gold Stitzel, West Virginia University; Cara-Lynn Ungar, Portland Community College; N. Renuka Uthappa, Eastern Michigan University; and Anne Williams, Indiana University-Purdue University Indianapolis; John F. Barber, University of Texas, Dallas; Claudia Becker, Loyola University; Kathleen Bell, University of Central Florida; Richard Fantina, Florida International University; Lynne Graft, Saginaw Valley State University; Peggy Jolly, University of Alabama at Birmingham; Beth Madison, West Virginia University; Patricia Medeiros, Scottsdale Community College; Christine Miller, California State University, Sacramento; Sarah R. Morrison, Morehead State University; Angela Rhoe, University of Cincinnati; James Sodon, St. Louis Community College; Mary Torio, University of Toledo; Julie Wakeman-Linn, Montgomery College; Sandra Zapp, Paradise Valley Community College; and Tom Zimmerman, Washtenaw Community College; Jennifer Almjeld, Bowling Green State University; Richard Fantina, Florida International University; John C. Gooch, University of Texas at Dallas; Matthew Hartman, Ball State University; William Lawton, James Madison University; Cynthia Marshall; Wright State University; Sarah Quirk, Waubonsee Community College; Ana Schnellmann, Lindenwood University; Molly Sides, Rock Valley College; Effie Siegel, Montgomery College; Linda VanVickle, St. Louis Community College; Desiree Ward, University of Texas at Dallas; Joan Wedes, University of Houston–Downtown; and Sandra Zapp, Paradise Valley Community College.

April Wells-Hayes of Fairplay Publishing Service, our production editor, and Barbara Armentrout, our copyeditor, went far beyond the call of duty in helping us refine and complete the revised manuscript. Finally, Christopher Bennem and Joshua Feldman, our editors, showed their usual brilliance and lent their unflagging energy throughout the process that led to this new edition of *Aims*.

A special thanks to Marcella Stark, research librarian at SMU, for all her help with updating the research chapter.

Timothy Crusius
Carolyn Channell
Dallas, Texas

Our goal in this book is not just to show you how to construct an argument but also to make you more aware of why people argue and what purposes argument serves. Consequently, Part Two of this book introduces four specific aims that people have in mind when they argue: to inquire, to convince, to persuade, and to mediate. Part One precedes the aims of argument and focuses on understanding argumentation in general, reading and analyzing arguments, doing research, and working with such forms of visual persuasion as advertising.

The selections in Parts One and Two offer something to emulate. All writers learn from studying the strategies of other writers. The object is not to imitate what a more experienced writer does but to understand the range of strategies you can use in your own way for your own purposes.

Included are arguments made with words and images. We have examples of editorial cartoons, advertisements, and photographs.

This book concludes with two appendixes. The first is on editing, the art of polishing and refining prose, and finding common errors. The second deals with fallacies and critical thinking. Consult these references often as you work through the text's assignments.

Arguing well is difficult for anyone. We have tried to write a text no more complicated than it has to be. We welcome your comments to improve future editions. Write us at

The Rhetoric Program
Dallas Hall
Southern Methodist University
Dallas, Texas 75275

or e-mail your comments to

cchannel@mail.smu.edu

Timothy W. Crusius is professor of English at Southern Methodist University, where he teaches beginning and advanced composition. He's the author of books on discourse theory, philosophical hermeneutics, and Kenneth Burke. He resides in Dallas with his wife, Elizabeth, and their children, Micah and Rachel.

Carolyn E. Channell taught high school and community college students before coming to Southern Methodist University, where she is now a senior lecturer and specialist in first-year writing courses. She resides in Richardson, Texas, with her husband, David, and "child," a boxer named Gretel.

BRIEF CONTENTS

CONTENTS

CHAPTER 4

Reading and Writing about Visual Arguments   61

CHAPTER 5

Writing Research-Based Arguments   93

CHAPTER 8

Making Your Case: Arguing to Convince   209

CHAPTER 9

Motivating Action: Arguing to Persuade   247

BOXES BY TYPE

Concept Close-Up Boxes

Best Practices Boxes

Resources for Reading and Writing Arguments

RESOURCES FOR READING AND WRITING ARGUMENTS

CHAPTER 1

Understanding Argument

The Aims of Argument is based on two key concepts: argument and rhetoric. These days, unfortunately, the terms *argument* and *rhetoric* have acquired bad reputations. The popular meaning of *argument* is *disagreement;* we think of raised voices, hurt feelings, winners and losers. Most people think of *rhetoric,* too, in a negative sense—as language that sounds good but evades or hides the truth. In this sense, rhetoric is the language we hear from the politician who says anything to win votes, the public relations person who puts "positive spin" on dishonest business practices, the buck-passing bureaucrat who blames the foul-up on someone else, the clever lawyer who counterfeits passion to plead for the acquittal of a guilty client.

The words *argument* and *rhetoric,* then, are commonly applied to the darker side of human acts and motives. This darker side is real—arguments are often pointless and silly, ugly and destructive; all too often, rhetoric is empty words contrived to mislead or to disguise the desire to exert power. But this book is not about that kind of argument or that kind of rhetoric. Here we develop the meanings of *argument* and *rhetoric* in an older, fuller, and far more positive sense—as the language and art of mature reasoning.

WHAT IS ARGUMENT?

In this book, **argument** means *mature reasoning.* By *mature,* we mean an attitude and approach to argument, not an age group. Some older adults are incapable of mature reasoning, whereas some young people reason very well. And all of us, regardless of age, sometimes fall short of mature reasoning. What is "mature" about the kind of argument we have in mind? One meaning of *mature* is "worked out fully by the mind" or "considered" (*American Heritage Dictionary*). Mature decisions, for example, are thoughtful ones, reached slowly after full consideration of all the consequences. And this is true also of mature reasoning.

The second term in this definition of argument also needs comment: *reasoning.* If we study logic in depth, we find many definitions of reasoning, but for practical purposes, *reasoning* here means *an opinion plus a reason (or reasons) for holding that opinion.* As we will see in detail later in this chapter, good arguments require more than this; to be convincing, reasons must be developed with evidence like specific facts and examples. However, understanding the basic form of "opinion-plus-a-reason" is the place to begin when considering your own and other people's arguments.

One way to understand argument as mature reasoning is to contrast it with *debate.* In debate, opponents take a predetermined, usually assigned, side and attempt to defend it, in much the same way that an army or a football team must hold its ground. The point is to win, to best one's opponent. In contrast, rather than starting with a position to defend, mature reasoners work toward a position. If they have an opinion to start with, mature reasoners think it through and evaluate it rather than rush to its defense. To win is not to defeat an opponent but rather to gain insight into the topic at hand. The struggle is with the problem, question, or issue we confront. Rather than seeking the favorable decision of the judges, as in debate, we are after a sound opinion in which we can believe—an opinion consistent with the facts and that other people will respect and take seriously.

Of course, having arrived at an opinion that seems sound to us, we still must *make our case*—argue in the sense of providing good reasons and adequate evidence in support of them. But whereas debaters must hold their positions at all costs, mature reasoners may not. The very process of making a case will often show us that what we thought was sound really isn't. We try to defend our opinion and find that we can't—or at least, not very well. And so we rethink our position until we arrive at one for which we *can* make a good case. From beginning to end, therefore, mature reasoning is a process of discovery.

WHAT IS RHETORIC?

Over time, the meanings of most words in most languages change— sometimes only a little, sometimes a lot. The word *rhetoric* is a good example of a big change. As indicated already, the popular meaning of *rhetoric* is empty verbiage—the art of sounding impressive while saying

Defining Mature Reasoning

Argument as mature reasoning means

- Defending *not the first position* you might take on an issue *but the best position,* determined through open-minded inquiry
- Providing reasons for holding that position that can earn the respect of an opposing audience

---

little—or the art of verbal deception. This meaning of *rhetoric* confers a judgment, and not a positive one.

In contrast, in ancient Greece, where rhetoric was invented about 2,500 years ago, *rhetoric* referred to the art of public speaking. The Greeks recognized that rhetoric could be abused, but, for their culture in general, it was not a negative term. They had a goddess of persuasion (see Figure 1.1), and they respected the power of the spoken word to move

Figure 1.1

Peitho, the goddess of persuasion, was often involved in seductions and love affairs. On this piece (a detail from a terra-cotta kylix, c. 410 BCE), Peitho, the figure on the left, gives advice to a dejected-looking woman, identified as Demonassa. To the right, Eros, the god of love, stands with his hand on Demonassa's shoulder, suggesting the nature of this advice.

Defining Rhetoric

Rhetoric is the art of argument as mature reasoning. The study of rhetoric develops self-conscious awareness of the principles and practices of mature reasoning and effective arguing.

Bust of the great ancient Greek orator, Demosthenes (384–322 BCE). Louvre, Paris

people. It dominated their law courts, their governments, and their public ceremonies and events. As an art, the spoken word was an object of study. People enrolled in schools of rhetoric to become effective public speakers. Further, the ancient rhetoricians put a high value on good character. Not just sounding ethical but being ethical contributed to a speaker's persuasive power.

This old, highly valued meaning of rhetoric as oratory survived well into the nineteenth century. In Abraham Lincoln's day, Americans assembled by the thousands to hear speeches that went on for hours. For them, a good speech held the same level of interest as a big sporting event does for people today.

In this book, we are interested primarily in various ways of using *written* argument, but the rhetorical tradition informs our understanding of mature reasoning. Mature reasoning has nothing to do with the current definition of rhetoric as speech that merely sounds good or deceives people. The ancient meaning of *rhetoric* is more relevant, but we update it here to connect it directly with mature reasoning.

If argument is mature reasoning, then rhetoric is its *art*—that is, how we go about arguing with some degree of success. Just as there is an art of painting or sculpture, so is there an art of mature reasoning. Since the time of Aristotle, teachers of rhetoric have taught their students *self-conscious* ways of reasoning well and arguing successfully. The study of rhetoric, therefore, includes both what we have already defined as reasoning *and* ways of appealing to an audience. These include efforts to project oneself as a good and intelligent person as well as efforts to connect with the audience through humor, passion, and image.

AN EXAMPLE OF ARGUMENT

So far, we've been talking about argument in the abstract—definitions and explanations. To really understand argument, especially as we define it here, we need a concrete example. One thing mature reasoning does is to challenge unexamined belief, the stances people take out of habit without much thought. The following argument by a syndicated columnist would have us consider more carefully our notion of "free speech."

You Also Have the Right to Tell a Bigot What You Think

LEONARD PITTS

For the record, I have no idea who let the dogs out. I didn't even know the gate was open.

We Americans get hooked on saying some pretty silly things, you know? "Where's the beef?" "Make my day."

Generally, it is pretty harmless stuff. Granted, after the fifteenth time someone avows that he feels your pain, you probably are ready to inflict some of your own. But overall, yeah—pretty harmless.

There is, however, one expression that never fails to make me nuts. Truth be told, it is less a catchphrase than a cop-out, a meaningless thing people say—usually when accusations of racism, sexism, anti-Semitism or homophobia have been leveled and they are being asked to defend the indefensible.

"Entitled to my opinion," they say. Or "entitled to his opinion," as the case 5 may be. The sense of it is the same even when the words vary: People clamber atop the First Amendment and remind us that it allows them or someone they decline to criticize to say or believe whatever they wish.

It happened again just the other day, on the eve of the Grammys. One of the entertainment news programs did an informal poll of musicians, asking them to comment on the rapper Eminem's violently homophobic and misogynistic music. You would have sworn they all were reading from the same script: "He is entitled to say what he feels," they said.

In that, they echoed the folks who thought John Rocker was unfairly maligned for his bigotry: "He is entitled to his opinion," the ballplayer's defenders told us. And that, in turn, was an echo of what happened in 1993 when a reporter asked a student at City University of New York about Dr. Leonard Jeffries' claim of a Jewish conspiracy against black people. "He had a right to say whatever he chooses to say," the student replied.

As I said, it makes me crazy—not because the observation isn't correct, but because it is beside the point.

Anybody who is a more ardent supporter of the First Amendment than I probably ought to be on medication. I believe the liberties it grants are meaningless unless extended as far as possible into the ideological hinterlands. Only in this way can you preserve and defend those liberties for the rest of us. So, as far as I am concerned, every sexist, homophobe, communist, flag burner, Jew baiter, Arab hater and racist must be protected in the peaceful expression of his or her beliefs.

But after acknowledging the right of the hateful to be hateful and the vile to 10 be vile, it seems to me that the least I can do is use my own right of free speech to call those people what they are. It seems to me, in fact, that I have a moral obligation to do so. But many people embrace moral cowardice instead and blame it on the First Amendment.

It is a specious claim. The First Amendment is violated when the government seeks to censor expression. That didn't happen to Eminem. That didn't happen to

John Rocker, either. What did happen was that the media and private citizens criticized them and demanded that some price—public condemnation or professional demotion—be extracted as a penalty for the stupid things they said.

Friends and neighbors, that isn't a violation of free speech. That *is* free speech. And if some folks confuse the issue, well, that is because too many of us believe freedom of speech means freedom from censure, the unfettered right to say whatever you please without anyone being allowed to complain. Worse, many of us accept that stricture for fear of seeming "judgmental." These days, of course, "judgmental" is a four-letter word.

I make no argument for being closed-minded. People ought to open themselves to the widest possible variety of ideas and expressions. But that doesn't mean losing your ability to discern or abdicating your responsibility to question, criticize . . . *think*. All ideas aren't created equal. To pretend otherwise is to create a rush from judgment—to free a bigot from taking responsibility for his beliefs and allow him a facade of moral validity to hide behind.

So I could happily live the rest of my life without being reminded that this fool or that has the right to say what he thinks. Sure, he does. But you know what? We all do.

Leonard Pitts, "You Also Have the Right to Tell a Bigot What You Think," *Miami Herald,* March 1, 2001, p. 1E. Copyright 2001 by McClatchy Interactive West. Reproduced with permission of McClatchy Interactive West in the format Textbook via Copyright Clearance Center.

Discussion of "You Also Have the Right . . ."

Leonard Pitts's argument is an example of a certain type or *genre* of written argument, the opinion column we find in the editorial section of newspapers. Arguments of this genre are usually brief and about some issue of general public concern, often an issue prominent in recent news stories. Most arguments written for college assignments are longer and deal with academic topics, but if we want to grasp the basics of mature reasoning, it's good to begin with the concise and readable arguments of professional columnists. Let's consider both the argument Pitts makes and his rhetoric—the art he uses to make his argument appealing to readers.

Pitts's Reasoning

In defining argument as mature reasoning, we stressed the process of arriving at an opinion as much as defending it. Arriving at an opinion is part of the aim of argument we call **inquiry**, and it's clearly very important for college writers who must deal with complex subjects and digest much information. Unfortunately, we can't see how authors arrived at their opinions by reading their finished work. As readers, we "come in" at the point where the writer states and argues for a position; we can't "go behind" it to appreciate how he or she got there. Consequently, all we can do with a published essay is discover how it works.

Let's ask the first question we must ask of any argument we're analyzing: What is Pitts's opinion, or claim? If a piece of writing is indeed an argument, we should be able to see that the author has a clear position or opinion. We can call this the **claim** of the argument. It is what the author wants the audience to believe or to do.

All statements of opinion are answers to questions, usually **implied questions** because the question itself is too obvious to need spelling out. But when we study an argument, we must be willing to be obvious and spell it out anyway to see precisely what's going on. The question behind Pitts's argument is: What should we do when we hear someone making clearly bigoted remarks? His answer: We have the right and even the moral obligation to "call those people what they are." That is his claim.

What reasons does Pitts give his readers to convince them of his claim? He tells them that the common definition of freedom of speech is mistaken. Freedom of speech does not give everyone the right to say whatever he or she wants without fear of consequences, without even the expectation of being criticized. He thinks people use this definition as an excuse not to speak up when they hear or read bigotry.

In developing his reason, Pitts explains that this common definition is beside the point because no one is suggesting that people aren't entitled to their opinions. Of course they are, even if they are uninformed and full of hatred for some person or group of people. But freedom of speech is not the right to say anything without suffering consequences; rather, as Pitts says, it's a protection against government censorship, what's known in law as *prior restraint*. In other words, if a government authority prevents you from saying or printing something, that is censorship and a violation of the First Amendment in most cases. We should not feel that someone's rights have been taken away if a high price—for instance, "public condemnation or professional demotion" (paragraph 11)—must be paid for saying stupid things. The First Amendment does not protect us from the social or economic consequences of what we say or write. "All ideas aren't created equal," as Pitts maintains. Some deserve the condemnation they receive.

Now that we understand what Pitts is arguing, we can ask another question: What makes Pitts's argument mature, an example of the kind of reasoning worth learning how to do? First, it's mature in contrast to the opinion about free speech he criticizes, which clearly does not result from a close examination of what free speech means. Second, it's mature because it assumes civic responsibility. It's not a cop-out. It argues for doing the difficult thing because it is right and good for our society. It shows mature reasoning when it says: "People ought to open themselves to the widest possible variety of ideas and expressions. But that doesn't mean losing your responsibility to question, criticize . . . *think*." Finally, it's mature in contrast to another common response to bigotry that Pitts doesn't discuss—the view that "someone ought to shut that guy up" followed by violence or the threat of violence directed at the offending person. Such an attitude is neither different from nor better than the attitude of a playground bully, and the mature mind does not accept it.

In recognizing the maturity of Pitts's argument, we should not be overly respectful of it. Ultimately, the point of laying out an argument is to respond to it maturely ourselves, and that means asking our own questions. For instance, we might ask:

When we say, "He's entitled to his opinion," are we *always* copping out, or is such a response justified in some circumstances?

Does it do any good to call a bigot a bigot? Is it wiser sometimes to just ignore hate speech?

How big a price is too big for stating a foolish opinion? Does it matter if a bigot later retracts his opinion, admits he was wrong, and apologizes?

One of the good things about mature arguments is that we can pursue them at length and learn a lot from discussing them.

⊚⊚ FOLLOWING THROUGH

Select an opinion column on a topic of interest to your class from your local city or campus newspaper. Choose an argument that you think exemplifies mature reasoning. Discuss its reasoning as we have here with Pitts's essay. Can you identify the claim or statement of the author's opinion? The claim or opinion is what the author wants his or her readers to believe or to do. If you can find no exact sentence to quote, can you nevertheless agree on what it is he or she wants the readers to believe or to do? Can you find in the argument one or more reasons for doing so?   •

Other Appeals in Pitts's Argument

Finally, we ask, what makes Pitts's argument effective? That is, what makes it succeed with his readers? We have said that reasoning isn't enough when it comes to making a good argument. A writer, like a public speaker, must employ more than reason and make a conscious effort to project personality, to connect with his or her readers. Most readers seem to like Leonard Pitts because of his T-shirt-and-shorts informality and his conversational style, which includes remarks like "it makes me crazy" and sentence fragments like "But overall, yeah—pretty harmless."

We can't help forming impressions of people from reading what they write, and often these impressions correspond closely to how authors want us to perceive them anyway. Projecting good character goes all the way back to the advice of the ancient rhetoric teachers. Showing intelligence, fairness, and other signs of maturity will help you make an argument effectively.

Pitts also makes a conscious effort to appeal to his readers (that is, to gain their support) by appealing to their feelings and acknowledging their attitudes. Appreciating Pitts's efforts here requires first that we think for a moment about who these people probably are. Pitts writes for the *Miami Herald,* but his column appears in many local papers across the United States. It's safe to say that the general public are his readers. Because he is writing an argument, we assume he envisions them as not already seeing the situation as he sees it. They might be "guilty" of saying, "Everyone's entitled to an opinion." But he is not angry with them. He just wants to correct their misperception. Note that he addresses them as "friends and neighbors" in paragraph 12.

He does speak as a friend and neighbor, opening with some small talk, alluding to a popular song that made "Who let the dogs out" into a catchphrase. Humor done well is subtle, as here, and it tells the readers he knows they are as tired of this phrase as he is. Pitts is getting ready to announce his serious objection to one particular catchphrase, and he wants to project himself as a man with a life, an ordinary guy with common sense, not some neurotic member of the language police about to get worked up over nothing. Even though he shifts to a serious tone in the fourth paragraph, he doesn't completely abandon this casual and humorous personality—for example, in paragraph 9, where he jokes about his "ardent" support of the First Amendment.

But Pitts also projects a dead serious tone in making his point and in presenting his perspective as morally superior. One choice that conveys this attitude is his comment about people in the "ideological hinterlands": "every sexist, homophobe, communist, flag burner, Jew baiter, Arab hater and racist must be protected in the peaceful expression of his or her beliefs."

◎◎ FOLLOWING THROUGH

For class discussion: What else in Pitts's argument strikes you as particularly good, conscious choices? What choices convey his seriousness of purpose? Pay special attention to paragraphs 9 and 13. Why are they there? How do they show audience awareness? Which of Pitts's strategies or choices seem particularly appropriate for op-ed writing? Which might not be appropriate in an academic essay? One reason for noticing the choices professional writers make in their arguments is to learn some of their strategies, which you can use when writing your own arguments.   •

FOUR CRITERIA OF MATURE REASONING

Students often ask, "What does my professor want?" Although you will be writing many different kinds of papers in response to the assignments in this textbook, your professor will most likely look for evidence of mature reasoning. When we evaluate student work, we look for four criteria that we consider marks of mature reasoning.

Mature Reasoners Are Well Informed

Your opinions must develop from knowledge and be supported by reliable and current evidence. If the reader feels that the writer "doesn't know his or her stuff," the argument loses all weight and force.

You may have noticed that people have opinions about all sorts of things, including subjects they know little or nothing about. The general human tendency is to have the strongest opinions on matters about which we know the least. Ignorance and inflexibility go together because it's easy to form an opinion when few or none of the facts get in the way and we can just assert our prejudices. Conversely, the more we know about most topics, the harder it is to be dogmatic. We find ourselves changing or at least refining our opinions more or less continuously as we gain more knowledge.

Mature Reasoners Are Self-Critical and Open to Constructive Criticism from Others

We have opinions about all sorts of things that don't matter much to us, casual opinions we've picked up somehow and may not even bother to defend if challenged. But we also have opinions in which we are heavily invested, sometimes to the point that our whole sense of reality, right and wrong, good and bad—our very sense of ourselves—is tied up in them. These opinions we defend passionately.

On this count, popular argumentation and mature reasoning are alike. Mature reasoners are often passionate about their convictions, as committed

"I don't listen to the evidence. I like to make up my own mind."

This classic cartoon from the New Yorker *(1954) captures well the still-common attitude "don't confuse me with the facts." It also reflects gender stereotypes unquestioned in 1954 and sometimes still evident today.*

to them as the fanatic on the street corner is to his or her cause. A crucial difference, however, separates the fanatic from the mature reasoner. The fanatic is all passion; the mature reasoner is able and willing to step back and examine even deeply held convictions. "I may have believed this for as long as I can remember," the mature reasoner says, "but is this conviction really justified? Do the facts support it? When I think it through, does it really make sense? Can I make a coherent and consistent argument for it?" These are questions that don't concern the fanatic and are seldom posed in the popular argumentation we hear on talk radio.

In practical terms, being self-critical and open to well-intended criticism boils down to this: Mature reasoners can and do change their minds when they have good reasons to do so. In popular argumentation, changing one's mind can be taken as a weakness, as "wishy-washy," and so people tend to go on advocating what they believe, regardless of what anyone else says. But there's nothing wishy-washy about, for example, confronting the facts, about realizing that what we thought is not supported by the available evidence. In such a case, changing one's mind is a sign of intelligence and the very maturity mature reason values. Nor is it a weakness to recognize a good point made against one's own argument. If we don't listen and take seriously what others say, they won't listen to us.

Mature Reasoners Argue with Their Audiences or Readers in Mind

Nothing drains energy from argument more than the feeling that it will accomplish nothing. As one student put it, "Why bother? People just go on thinking what they want to." This attitude is understandable. Popular, undisciplined argument often does seem futile: minds aren't changed; no progress is made; it's doubtful that anyone learned anything. Sometimes the opposing positions only harden, and the people involved are more at odds than before.

Why does this happen so often? One reason we've already mentioned— nobody's really listening to anyone else. We tend to hear only our own voices and see only from our own points of view. But there's another reason: The people making the arguments have made no effort to reach their audience. This is the other side of the coin of not listening—when we don't take other points of view seriously, we can't make our points of view appealing to those who don't already share them.

To have a chance of working, arguments must be *other-directed,* attuned to the people they want to reach. This may seem obvious, but it's also commonly ignored and not easy to do. We have to imagine the other guy. We have to care about other points of view, not just see them as obstacles to our own. We have to present and develop our arguments in ways that won't turn off the very people for whom we're writing. In many ways, *adapting to the audience* is the biggest challenge of argument.

CONCEPT CLOSE-UP

Four Criteria of Mature Reasoning

MATURE REASONERS ARE WELL INFORMED

Their opinions develop out of knowledge and are supported by reliable and current evidence.

MATURE REASONERS ARE SELF-CRITICAL AND OPEN TO CONSTRUCTIVE CRITICISM

They balance their passionate attachment to their opinions with willingness to evaluate and test them against differing opinions, acknowledge when good points are made against their opinions, and even, when presented with good reasons for doing so, change their minds.

MATURE REASONERS ARGUE WITH THEIR AUDIENCES OR READERS IN MIND

They make a sincere effort to understand and connect with other people and other points of view because they do not see differences of opinion as obstacles to their own points of view.

MATURE REASONERS KNOW THEIR ARGUMENTS' CONTEXTS

They recognize that what we argue about now was argued about in the past and will be argued about in the future, that our contributions to these ongoing conversations are influenced by who we are, what made us who we are, where we are, what's going on around us.

Mature Reasoners Know Their Arguments' Contexts

All arguments are part of an ongoing conversation. We think of arguments as something individuals make. We think of our opinions as *ours*, almost like private property. But arguments and opinions have pasts: Other people argued about more or less the same issues and problems before—often long before—we came on the scene. They have a present: Who's arguing what now, the current state of the argument. And they have a future: What people will be arguing about tomorrow, in different circumstances, with knowledge we don't have now.

So most arguments are not the isolated events they seem to be. Part of being well informed is knowing something about the history of an argument. By understanding an argument's past, we learn about patterns that will help us develop our own position. To some extent, we must know what's going on now and what other people are saying to make our own reasoning relevant. And although we can't know the future, we can imagine the drift of the argument, where it might be heading. In other words, there's a larger context we need to join—a big conversation of many voices to which our few belong.

WHAT ARE THE AIMS OF ARGUMENT?

The heart of this book is Part Two, the section entitled "The Aims of Argument." In conceiving this book, we worked from one basic premise: Mature reasoners do not argue just to argue; rather, they use argument to accomplish something: *to inquire* into a question, problem, or issue (commonly part of the research process); *to convince* their readers to assent to an opinion, or claim; *to persuade* readers to take action, such as buying a product or voting for a candidate; and *to mediate* conflict, as in labor disputes, divorce proceedings, and so on.

Let's look at each of these aims in more detail.

Arguing to Inquire

Arguing to **inquire** is using reasoning to determine the best position on an issue. We open the "Aims" section with inquiry because mature reasoning is not a matter of defending what we already believe but of questioning it. Arguing to inquire helps us form opinions, question opinions we already have, and reason our way through conflicts or contradictions in other people's arguments on a topic. Inquiry is open minded, and it requires that we make an effort to find out what people who disagree think and why.

The ancient Greeks called argument as inquiry **dialectic;** today we might think of it as dialogue or serious conversation. There is nothing confrontational about such conversations. We have them with friends, family, and colleagues, even with ourselves. We have these conversations in writing, too, as we make notations in the margins of the arguments we read. Listserv groups engage in inquiry about subjects of mutual interest.

Inquiry centers on questions and involves some intellectual legwork to answer them—finding the facts, doing research. This is true whether you are inquiring into what car to buy, what major to choose in college, what candidate to vote for, or what policy our government should pursue on any given issue.

Arguing to Convince

We've seen that the goal of inquiry is to reach some kind of conclusion on an issue. Let's call this conclusion a **conviction** and define it as "an earned opinion, achieved through careful thought, research, and discussion." Once we arrive at a conviction, we usually want others to share it. The aim of further argument is to secure the assent of people who do not share our conviction (or who do not share it fully).

Argument to **convince** centers on making a case, which means offering reasons and evidence in support of our opinion. Arguments to convince are all around us. In college, we find them in scholarly and professional writing. In everyday life, we find arguments to convince in editorials, courtrooms, and political speeches. Whenever we encounter an opinion supported by reasons and asking us to agree, we are dealing with argument to convince.

Arguing to Persuade

Like convincing, persuasion attempts to earn agreement, but it wants more. **Persuasion** attempts to influence not just thinking but also behavior. An advertisement for Mercedes-Benz aims to convince us not only that the company makes a high-quality car but also that we should go out and buy one. A Sunday sermon asks for more than agreement with some interpretation of a biblical passage; the minister wants the congregation to live according to its message. Persuasion asks us to do something—spend money, give money, join a demonstration, recycle, vote, enlist, acquit. Because we don't always act on our convictions, persuasion cannot rely on reasoning alone. It must appeal in broader, deeper ways.

Persuasion appeals to readers' emotions. It tells stories about individual cases of hardship that move us to pity. It often uses photographs, as when charities confront us with pictures of poverty or suffering. Persuasion uses many of the devices of poetry, such as patterns of sound, repetitions, metaphors, and similes to arouse a desired emotion in the audience.

Persuasion also relies on the personality of the writer to an even greater degree than does convincing. The persuasive writer attempts to represent something "higher" or "larger" than him- or herself—some ideal with which the reader would like to be associated. For example, a war veteran and hero like John McCain naturally brings patriotism to the table when he makes a speech.

Arguing to Mediate

By the time we find ourselves in a situation where our aim is to **mediate,** we will have already attempted to convince an opponent to settle a conflict or dispute our way. Our opponent will have done the same. Yet neither side has secured the assent of the other, and "agreeing to disagree" is not a practical solution because the participants must decide what to do.

In most instances of mediation, the parties involved try to work out the conflict themselves because they have some relationship they wish to preserve—as employer and employee, business partners, family members, neighbors, even coauthors of an argument textbook. Common differences requiring mediation include the amount of a raise or the terms of a contract. In private life, mediation helps roommates live together and families decide on everything from budgets to vacation destinations.

Just like other aims of argument, arguing to mediate requires sound logic and the clear presentation of positions and reasons. However, mediation challenges our interpersonal skills more than do the other aims. Each side

Comparing the Aims of Argument

The aims of argument have much in common. For example, besides sharing argument, they all tend to draw on sources of knowledge (research) and to deal with controversial issues. But the aims also differ from one another, mainly in terms of purpose, audience, situation, and method, as summarized here and on the inside front cover.

	Purpose	Audience	Situation	Method
Inquiry	Seeks truth	Oneself, friends, and colleagues	Informal; a dialogue	Questions
Convincing	Seeks assent to a thesis	Less intimate; wants careful reasoning	More formal; a monologue	Case-making
Persuading	Seeks action	More broadly public, less academic	Pressing need for a decision	Appeals to reason and emotions
Mediating	Seeks consensus	Polarized by differences	Need to cooperate, preserve relations	"Give-and-take"

We offer this chart as a general guide to the aims of argument. Think of it as the "big picture" you can always return to as you work your way through Part Two, which deals with each of the aims in detail.

must listen closely to understand not just the other's case but also the emotional commitments and underlying values. When mediation works, the opposing sides begin to converge. Exchanging viewpoints and information and building empathy enable all parties to make concessions, to loosen their hold on their original positions, and finally to reach consensus—or at least a resolution that all participants find satisfactory.

A GOOD TOOL FOR UNDERSTANDING AND WRITING ARGUMENTS: THE WRITER'S NOTEBOOK

Argumentation places unique demands on readers and writers. One of the most helpful tools that you can use to meet these demands is a writer's notebook.

The main function of a writer's notebook is to help you sort out what you read, learn, accomplish, and think as you go through the stages of creating a finished piece of writing. A writer's notebook contains the writing you do before you write; it's a place to sketch out ideas, assess research, order what you have to say, and determine strategies and goals for writing.

Ways to Use a Writer's Notebook

Any entry that you may want to use for future reference is appropriate to add to your writer's notebook. It's for private exploration, so don't worry about organization, spelling, or grammar. Following are some specific possibilities.

TO EXPLORE ISSUES YOU ENCOUNTER IN AND OUT OF CLASS

Bring your notebook to class each day. Use it to respond to ideas presented in class and in every reading assignment. When you're assigned a topic, write down your first impressions and opinions about it. When you're to choose your own topic, use the notebook to respond to controversial issues in the news or on campus. Your notebook then becomes a source of ideas for your essays.

TO RECORD AND ANALYZE ASSIGNMENTS

Staple your instructor's handouts to a notebook page, or write the assignment down word for word. Take notes as your instructor explains the assignment. Later, look it over more carefully, circling and checking key words, underlining due dates and other requirements. Record your questions, ask your instructor as soon as possible, and jot down the answers.

TO WORK OUT TIMETABLES FOR COMPLETING ASSIGNMENTS

To avoid procrastination, schedule. Divide the task into blocks—preparing and researching, writing a first draft, revising, editing, final typing and proofreading—and work out how many days you can devote to each. Your schedule may change, but making one and attempting to stick to it helps avoid last-minute scrambling.

TO MAKE NOTES AS YOU RESEARCH

Record ideas, questions, and preliminary conclusions that occur to you as you read, discuss your ideas with others, conduct experiments, compile surveys and questionnaires, and consult with experts. Keep your notebook handy at all times; write down ideas as soon as possible and assess their value later.

TO RESPOND TO ARGUMENTS YOU HEAR OR READ

To augment the notes you make in the margins of books, jot down extended responses in your notebook. Evaluate the strengths and weaknesses of texts,

Why Keep a Notebook?

Some projects require extensive research and consultation, which involve compiling and assessing large amounts of data and working through complex chains of reasoning. Under such conditions, even the best memory will fail without the aid of a notebook. Given life's distractions, we often forget too much and imprecisely recall what we do manage to remember. With a writ-

compare an argument with other arguments; make notes on how to use who you read to build your own arguments. Note page numbers to make it easie to use this information later.

TO WRITE A RHETORICAL PROSPECTUS

A *prospectus* details a plan for proposed work. In your notebook, explore

Your thesis: What are you claiming?

Your aim: What do you want to accomplish?

Your audience: Who should read this? Why? What are these people like?

Your persona: What is your relationship to the audience? How do you want them to perceive you?

Your subject matter: What does your thesis obligate you to discuss? What do you need to learn more about? How do you plan to get the information?

Your organizational plan: What should you talk about first? Where might that lead? What might you end with?

TO RECORD USEFUL FEEDBACK

Points in the writing process when it is useful to seek feedback from other students and the instructor include

When your *initial ideas* have taken shape, to discover how well you can explain your ideas to others and how they respond

After you and other students have *completed research* on similar topics, to share information and compare evaluations of sources

Upon completion of a *first draft*, to uncover what you need to do in a second draft to accommodate readers' needs, objections, and questions

At the end of the *revising process,* to correct surface problems such as awkward sentences, usage errors, misspellings, and typos

Prepare specific questions to ask others, and use your notebook to jot them down; leave room to sum up the comments you receive.

TO ASSESS A GRADED PAPER

Look over your instructor's comments carefully, and write down anything useful for future reference. For example, what did you do well? What might you carry over to the next assignment? Is there a pattern in the shortcomings your instructor has pointed out?

er's notebook, we can preserve the ideas that come to us as we walk across campus or stare into space over our morning coffee. Often, a writer's notebook even provides sections of writing that can be incorporated into your papers and so can help you save time.

In the chapters that follow, we refer frequently to your writer's notebook. We hope you'll use this excellent tool.

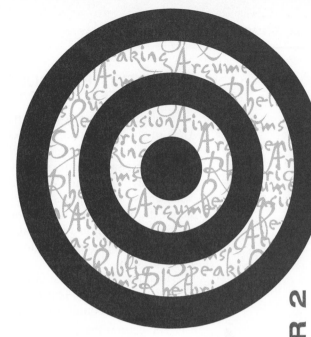

CHAPTER 2

Reading an Argument

In a course in argumentation, you will read many arguments. Our book contains a wide range of argumentative essays, some by students, some by established professionals. In addition, you may find arguments on your own in books, newspapers, and magazines, or on the Internet. You'll read them to develop your understanding of argument. That means you will analyze and evaluate these texts—known as **critical reading.** Critical reading involves special skills and habits that are not essential when you read a book for information or entertainment. This chapter discusses those skills and habits.

By the time most students get to high school, reading is no longer taught. While there's plenty to read, any advice on *how to read* is usually about increasing vocabulary or reading speed, not reading critically. This is too bad, because in college you are called on to read more critically than ever.

Have patience with yourself and with the texts you work with in this book. Reading will involve going through a text more than once, no matter how careful that single reading may be. You will go back to a text several times, asking new questions with each reading. That takes time, but it's time well spent. Just as when you see a film a second time, you notice new details, so each reading increases your knowledge of a text.

Before we start, a bit of advice: Attempt critical reading only when your mind is fresh. Find a place conducive to concentration—such as a table in the library. Critical reading requires an alert, active response.

THE FIRST ENCOUNTER:
SEEING THE TEXT IN CONTEXT

Critical reading begins not with a line-by-line reading but with a fast over-view of the whole text, followed by some thinking about how the text fits into a bigger picture, or *context*, which we describe shortly.

We first **sample** a text rather than read it through. Look at the headings and subdivisions. They will give a sense of how the text is organized. Note what parts look interesting and/or hard to understand. Note any information about the author provided before or after the text itself, as well as any publication information (where and when the piece was originally published). Look at the opening and closing paragraphs to discern the author's main point or view.

Reading comprehension depends less on a large vocabulary than on the ability to see how the text fits into contexts. Sampling will help you consider the text in two contexts that are particularly important:

1. *The general climate of opinion* surrounding the topic of the text. This includes debate on the topic both before and since the text's publication.

2. *The rhetorical context* of the text. This includes facts about the author, the intended audience, and the setting in which the argument took place.

Considering the Climate of Opinion

Familiarity with the climate of opinion will help you view any argument critically, recognize a writer's biases and assumptions, and spot gaps or errors in the information. Your own perspective, too, will affect your interpretation of the text. So think about what you know, how you know it, what your opinion is, and what might have led to its formation. You can then interact with a text, rather than just read it passively.

◎◎ FOLLOWING THROUGH

An argument on the topic of body decoration (tattoos and piercing) appears later in this chapter. "On Teenagers and Tattoos" is about motives for decorating the body. As practice in identifying the climate of opinion surrounding a topic, think about what people say about tattooing. Have you heard people argue that it is "low-class"? a rebellion against middle-class conformity? immoral? an artistic expression? a fad? an affront to school or parental authority? an expression of individuality? If you would not want a tattoo, why not? If you have a tattoo, why did you get it? In your writer's notebook, jot down some positions you have heard debated, and state your own viewpoint.   •

Considering the Rhetorical Context

Critical readers also are aware of the **rhetorical context** of an argument. They do not see the text merely as words on a page but as a contribution to some debate among interested people. Rhetorical context includes the author, the intended audience, and the date and place of publication. The reader who knows something about the author's politics or affiliations will have an advantage over the reader who does not. Also, knowing if a periodical is liberal, like *The Nation,* or conservative, like *National Review,* helps.

An understanding of rhetorical context comes from both external and internal clues—information outside the text and information you gather as you read and reread it. You can glean information about rhetorical context from external evidence such as publishers' notes about the author or about a magazine's editorial board or sponsoring foundation. You can find this information in any issue of a periodical or by following an information link on the home page of an online publication.

You may also have prior knowledge of rhetorical context—for example, you may have heard of the author. Or you can look in a database such as *InfoTrac* (see pages 108, 109–113) to see what else the author has written. Later, when you read the argument more thoroughly, you will enlarge your understanding of rhetorical context as you discover what the text itself reveals about the author's bias, character, and purpose for writing.

In sum, the first encounter with a text is preliminary to a careful, close reading. It prepares you to get the most out of the second encounter. If you are researching a topic and looking for good sources of information and viewpoints about it, the first encounter with any text will help you decide whether you want to read it at all. A first encounter can be a time-saving last encounter if the text does not seem appropriate or credible.

◎◎ FOLLOWING THROUGH

Note the following information about "On Teenagers and Tattoos."

When published: In 1997, reprinted fall 2000.

Where published: In the *Journal of Child and Adolescent Psychiatry,* published by the American Academy of Child and Adolescent Psychiatry, then reprinted in *Reclaiming Children and Youth.*

Written by *whom:* Andres Martin, MD. Martin is an associate professor of child psychiatry at the Yale Child Study Center in New Haven, CT.

Then do a fast sampling of the text itself. In your writer's notebook, make some notes about what you expect to find in this argument. What do you think the author's perspective will be, and why? How might it differ from that of a teen, a parent, a teacher? Do the subheadings give you any idea of the main point? Do you notice at the opening or closing any repeated ideas that might give a clue to the author's claim? To whom do you imagine the author was writing, and what might be the purpose of an essay in a journal such as the one that published his argument? •

Guidelines for Determining Rhetorical Context

To determine an argument's rhetorical context, answer the following questions:

Who wrote this argument, and what are his or her occupation, personal background, and political leanings?

To whom do you think the author is writing? Arguments are rarely aimed at "the general public" but rather at a definite target audience, such as "entertainment industry moguls," "drivers in Dallas," or "parents of teenagers."

Where does the article appear? If it is reprinted, where did it appear originally? What do you know about the publication?

When was the argument written? If not recently, what do you know about the time during which it appeared?

Why was the article written? What prompted its creation, and what purpose does the author have for writing?

AN ARGUMENT FOR CRITICAL READING

On Teenagers and Tattoos

ANDRES MARTIN

The skeleton dimensions I shall now proceed to set down are copied verbatim from my right arm, where I had them tattooed: as in my wild wanderings at that period, there was no other secure way of preserving such valuable statistics.

—Herman Melville, *Moby Dick*

Tattoos and piercing have become a part of our everyday landscape. They are ubiquitous, having entered the circles of glamour and the mainstream of fashion, and they have even become an increasingly common feature of our urban youth. Legislation in most states restricts professional tattooing to adults older than 18 years of age, so "high end" tattooing is rare in children and adolescents, but such tattoos are occasionally seen in older teenagers. Piercings, by comparison, as well as self-made or "jailhouse" type tattoos, are not at all rare among adolescents or even among school-age children. Like hairdo, makeup, or baggy jeans, tattoos and piercings can be subject to fad influence or peer pressure in an effort toward group affiliation. As with any other fashion statement, they can be construed as bodily aids in the inner struggle toward identity consolidation, serving as adjuncts to the defining and sculpting of the self by means of external manipulations. But unlike most other body decorations, tattoos and piercings are set apart by their irreversible and permanent nature, a quality at the core of their magnetic appeal to adolescents.

Adolescents and their parents are often at odds over the acquisition of bodily decorations. For the adolescent, piercing or tattoos may be seen as personal and

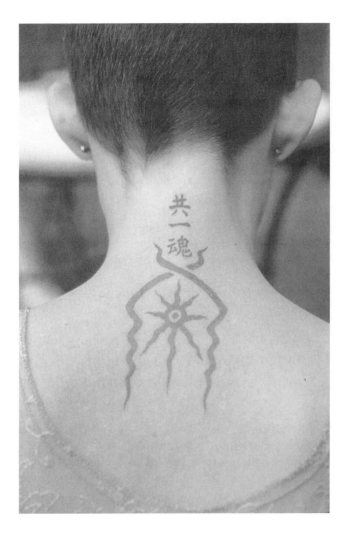

beautifying statements, while parents may construe them as oppositional and enraging affronts to their authority. Distinguishing bodily adornment from self-mutilation may indeed prove challenging, particularly when a family is in disagreement over a teenager's motivations and a clinician is summoned as the final arbiter. At such times it may be most important to realize jointly that the skin can all too readily become but another battleground for the tensions of the age, arguments having less to do with tattoos and piercings than with core issues such as separation from the family matrix. Exploring the motivations and significance [underlying] tattoos (Grumet, 1983) and piercings can go a long way toward resolving such differences and can become a novel and additional way of getting to know teenagers. An interested and nonjudgmental appreciation of teenagers' surface presentations may become a way of making contact not only in their terms but on their turfs: quite literally on the territory of their skins.

The following three sections exemplify some of the complex psychological underpinnings of youth tattooing.

IDENTITY AND THE ADOLESCENT'S BODY

Tattoos and piercing can offer a concrete and readily available solution for many of the identity crises and conflicts normative to adolescent development. In using such decorations, and by marking out their bodily territories, adolescents can support their efforts at autonomy, privacy, and insulation. Seeking individuation, tattooed adolescents can become unambiguously demarcated from others and singled out as unique. The intense and often disturbing reactions that are mobilized in viewers can help to effectively keep them at bay, becoming tantamount to the proverbial "Keep Out" sign hanging from a teenager's door.

Alternatively, feeling prey to a rapidly evolving body over which they have no 5 say, self-made and openly visible decorations may restore adolescents' sense of normalcy and control, a way of turning a passive experience into an active identity. By indelibly marking their bodies, adolescents can strive to reclaim their bearings within an environment experienced as alien, estranged, or suffocating or to lay claim over their evolving and increasingly unrecognizable bodies. In either case, the net outcome can be a resolution to unwelcome impositions: external, familial, or societal in one case; internal and hormonal in the other. In the words of a 16-year-old girl with several facial piercings, and who could have been referring to her body just as well as to the position within her family: "If I don't fit in, it is because I say so."

INCORPORATION AND OWNERSHIP

Imagery of a religious, deathly, or skeletal nature, the likenesses of fierce animals or imagined creatures, and the simple inscription of names are some of the time-tested favorite contents for tattoos. In all instances, marks become not only memorials or recipients for dearly held persons or concepts: they strive for incorporation, with images and abstract symbols gaining substance on becoming a permanent part of the individual's skin. Thickly embedded in personally meaningful representations and object relations, tattoos can become not only the ongoing memento of a relationship, but at times even the only evidence that there ever was such a bond. They can quite literally become the relationship itself. The turbulence and impulsivity of early attachments and infatuations may become grounded, effectively bridging oblivion through the visible reality to tattoos.

Case Vignette: "A," a 13-year-old boy, proudly showed me his tattooed deltoid. The coarsely depicted roll of the dice marked the day and month of his birth. Rather disappointed, he then uncovered an immaculate back, going on to draw for me the great "piece" he envisioned for it. A menacing figure held a hand of cards: two aces, two eights, and a card with two sets of dates. "A's" father had belonged to Dead Man's Hand, a motorcycle gang named after the set of cards (aces and eights) that the legendary Wild Bill Hickock had held in the 1890s when shot dead over a poker table in Deadwood, South Dakota. "A" had only the vaguest memory of and sketchiest information about his father, but he knew he had died in a motorcycle accident: The fifth card marked the dates of his birth and death.

The case vignette also serves to illustrate how tattoos are often the culmination of a long process of imagination, fantasy, and planning that can start at an early age. Limited markings, or relatively reversible ones such as piercings, can at a later time scaffold toward the more radical commitment of a permanent tattoo.

THE QUEST OF PERMANENCE

The popularity of the anchor as a tattoo motif may historically have had to do less with guild identification among sailors than with an intense longing for rootedness and stability. In a similar vein, the recent increase in the popularity and acceptance of tattoos may be understood as an antidote or counterpoint to our urban and nomadic lifestyles. Within an increasingly mobile society, in which relationships are so often transient—as attested by the frequencies of divorce, abandonment, foster placement, and repeated moves, for example—tattoos can be a readily available source of grounding. Tattoos, unlike many relationships, can promise permanence and stability. A sense of constancy can be derived from unchanging marks that can be carried along no matter what the physical, temporal, or geographical vicissitudes at hand. Tattoos stay, while all else may change.

Case Vignette: A proud father at 17, "B" had had the smiling face of his 10 4-month-old baby girl tattooed on his chest. As we talked at a tattoo convention, he proudly introduced her to me, explaining how he would "always know how beautiful she is today" when years from then he saw her semblance etched on himself.

The quest for permanence may at other times prove misleading and offer premature closure to unresolved conflicts. At a time of normative uncertainties, adolescents may maladaptively and all too readily commit to a tattoo and its indefinite presence. A wish to hold on to a current certainty may lead the adolescent to lay down in ink what is valued and cherished one day but may not necessarily be in the future. The frequency of self-made tattoos among hospitalized, incarcerated, or gang-affiliated youths suggests such motivations: A sense of stability may be a particularly dire need under temporary, turbulent, or volatile conditions. In addition, through their designs teenagers may assert a sense of bonding and allegiance to a group larger than themselves. Tattoos may attest to powerful experiences, such as adolescence itself, lived and even survived together. As with Moby Dick's protagonist, Ishmael, they may bear witness to the "valuable statistics" of one's "wild wandering(s)": those of adolescent exhilaration and excitement on the one hand; of growing pains, shared misfortune, or even incarceration on the other.

Adolescents' bodily decorations, at times radical and dramatic in their presentation, can be seen in terms of figuration rather than disfigurement, of the natural body being through them transformed into a personalized body (Brain, 1979). They can often be understood as self-constructive and adorning efforts, rather than prematurely subsumed as mutilatory and destructive acts. If we bear all of this in mind, we may not only arrive at a position to pass more reasoned clinical judgment, but become sensitized through our patients' skins to another level of their internal reality.

REFERENCES

Brain, R. (1979). *The decorated body.* New York: Harper & Row.
Grumet, G. W. (1983). Psychodynamic implications of tattoos. *American Journal of Orthopsychiatry, 53,* 482–92.

Andres Martin, "On Teenagers and Tattoos," *Journal of the American Academy of Child & Adolescent Psychiatry,* vol. 36, no. 6 (June 1997), pp. 860–861. Reprinted by permission of Lippincott Williams & Wilkins.

THE SECOND ENCOUNTER: READING AND ANALYZING THE TEXT

We turn now to suggestions for reading and analyzing. These are our own "best practices," what we do when we prepare to discuss or write about a written text. Remember, when you read critically, your purpose goes beyond merely finding out what an argument says. The critical reader is different from the target audience. As a critical reader, you are more like the food critic who dines not merely to eat but to evaluate the chef's efforts.

To see the difference, consider the different perspectives that an ant and a bird would have when looking at the same suburban lawn. The ant is down among the blades of grass, climbing one and then the next. It's a close look, but the view is limited. The bird in the sky above looks down, noticing the size and shape of the yard, the brown patches, the difference between the grass in this yard and the grass in the surrounding yards. The bird has the big picture, the ant the close-up. Critical readers move back and forth between the perspective of the ant and the perspective of the bird, each perspective enriching the other. The big picture helps one notice the patterns, even as the details offer clues to the big picture.

Because critical reading means interacting with the text, be ready with pencil or pen to mark up the text. Highlighting or underlining is not enough. Write comments in the margin.

Wrestling with Difficult Passages

Because one goal of the second encounter is to understand the argument fully, you will need to determine the meanings of unfamiliar words and difficult passages. In college reading, you may encounter new words. You may find allusions or references to other books or authors that you have not read. You may encounter metaphors and irony. The author may speak ironically or for another person. The author may assume that readers have lived through all that he or she has or share the same political viewpoint. All of this can make reading harder. Following are common features that often make reading difficult.

Unfamiliar Contexts

If the author and his or her intended audience are removed from your own experience, you will find the text difficult. Texts from a distant culture or time will include concepts familiar to the writer and original readers but not to you. This is true also of contemporary writing intended for specialists. College increases your store of specialized knowledge and introduces you to new (and old) perspectives. Accepting the challenge of difficult texts is part of college. Look up concepts you don't know. Your instructors can also help you to bridge the gap between your world and the text's.

Contrasting Voices and Views

Authors may state viewpoints that contradict their own. They may concede that part of an opposing argument is true, or they may put in an opposing view to refute it. These voices and viewpoints may come as direct quotations or paraphrases. To avoid misreading these views as the author's, be alert to words that signal contrast. The most common are *but* and *however*.

Allusions

Allusions are brief references to things outside the text—to people, works of art, songs, events in the news—anything in the culture that the author assumes he or she shares knowledge of with readers. Allusions are one way for an author to form a bond with readers—provided the readers' and authors' opinions are the same about what is alluded to. Allusions influence readers. They are persuasive devices that can provide positive associations with the author's viewpoint.

In "On Teenagers and Tattoos," the epigraph (the quotation that appears under the title of the essay) is an allusion to the classic novel *Moby Dick*. Martin alludes to the novel again in paragraph 11. He assumes that his readers know the work—not just its title but also its characters, in particular, the narrator, Ishmael. And he assumes his readers would know that the "skeleton dimensions" of a great whale were important and that readers would therefore understand the value of preserving these statistics. The allusion predisposes readers to see that there are valid reasons for permanently marking the body.

Specialized Vocabulary

If an argument is aimed at an audience of specialists, it will undoubtedly contain vocabulary peculiar to that group or profession. Martin's essay contains social science terminology: "family matrix" and "surface presentations" (paragraph 2), "individuation" (paragraph 4), "grounded" (paragraph 6), "sense of constancy" (paragraph 9), and "normative uncertainties" (paragraph 11).

The text surrounding these terms provides enough help for most lay readers to get a fair understanding. For example, the text surrounding *individuation* suggests that the person would stand out as a separate physical presence; this is not quite the same as *individuality,* which refers more to one's character. Likewise, the text around *family matrix* points to something the single word *family* does not: it emphasizes the family as the surroundings in which one develops.

If you need to look up a term and a dictionary does not seem to offer an appropriate definition, go to one of the specialized dictionaries available on the library reference shelves. (See pages 100–106 for more on these.)

If you encounter an argument with more jargon than you can handle, you may have to accept that you are not an appropriate reader for it. Some readings are aimed at people with highly specialized graduate degrees or training. Without advanced courses, no one could read these articles with full comprehension, much less critique their arguments.

⊙⊚ FOLLOWING THROUGH

Find other words in Martin's essay that sound specific to the field of psychology. Use the surrounding text to come up with laymen's terms for these concepts. •

Missing Persons

A common difficulty with scientific writing is that it can sound disembodied and abstract. You won't find a lot of people doing things in it. Sentences are easiest to read when they take a "who-does-what" form. However, these can be rare in scientific writing. Many of Martin's sentences have abstract subjects and nonaction verbs like *be* and *become:*

> *An interested and nonjudgmental appreciation of teenagers' surface presentations* may become a way of making contact not only in their terms but on their turfs. . . .

In at least one other sentence, Martin goes so far in leaving people out that his sentence is grammatically incorrect. Note the dangling modifier:

> Alternatively, *feeling prey to a rapidly evolving body over which they have no say,* self-made and openly visible decorations may restore adolescents' sense of normalcy and control, a way of turning passive experience into active identity.

The italicized phrase describes adolescents, not decorations. If you have trouble reading passages like this, take comfort in the fact that the difficulty is not your fault. Recasting the idea into who-does-what can clear things up:

> Teens may feel like helpless victims of the changes taking place in their bodies. They may mark themselves with highly visible tattoos and piercings to regain a sense of control over their lives.

Passive Voice

Passive voice is another common form of the missing-person problem. In an active-voice sentence, we see our predictable who-does-what pattern:

> *Active voice:* The rat ate the cheese.

In passive-voice sentences, the subject of the verb is not an agent; it does not act.

> *Passive voice:* The cheese was eaten by the rat.

At least in this sentence, we know who the agent is. But scientists often leave out any mention of agents. Thus, in Martin's essay we have sentences like this one:

> Adolescents' bodily decorations . . . *can be seen* in terms of figuration rather than disfigurement. . . .

Who can see them? Martin means that *psychiatrists should see tattoos* as figuration rather than disfigurement. But that would sound too committed, not scientific. Passive-voice sentences are common in the sciences, part of an effort to sound objective.

If you learn to recognize passive voice, you can often mentally convert the troublesome passage into active voice, making it clearer. Passive voice takes this pattern:

> A helping verb in some form of the verb *to be: Is, was, were, has been, will be, will have been, could have been,* and so forth.

> Followed by a main verb, a past participle: Past participles end in *ed, en, g, k,* or *t.*

Some examples:

> The car *was being driven* by my roommate when we had the wreck.

> Infections *are spread* by bacteria.

> The refrain *is sung* three times.

◎◎ FOLLOWING THROUGH

Convert the following sentences into active voice. We have put the passive-voice verbs in bold type, but you may need to look at the surrounding text to figure out who the agents are.

> A sense of constancy **can be derived** from unchanging marks that **can be carried** along no matter what the physical, temporal, or

geographical vicissitudes at hand. (paragraph 9) To edit this one, ask *who* can derive what and *who* can carry what.

The intense and often disturbing reactions that ***are mobilized*** in viewers can help to effectively keep them at bay, becoming tantamount to the proverbial "Keep Out" sign hanging from a teenager's door. (paragraph 4) To edit, ask *what* mobilizes the reactions in other people.

Using Paraphrase to Aid Comprehension

As we all know, explaining something to someone else is the best way to make it clear to ourselves. Putting an author's ideas into your own words, **paraphrasing** them, is like explaining the author to yourself. For more on paraphrasing, see Chapter 5, pages 125–127.

Paraphrase is often longer than the original because it loosens up what is dense. In paraphrasing, try to make both the language and the syntax (word order) simpler. Paraphrase may require two sentences where there was one. It looks for plainer, more everyday language, converts passive voice to active voice, and makes the subjects concrete.

Analyzing the Reasoning of an Argument

As part of your second encounter with the text, pick out its reasoning. The reasoning is the author's case, which consists of the *claim* (what the author wants the readers to believe or do) and the *reasons* and *evidence* offered in support of it. State the case in your own words and describe what else is going on in the argument, such as the inclusion of opposing views or background information.

If a text is an argument, we can state what the author wants the readers to believe or do, and just as importantly, *why*. We should look for evidence presented to make the reasons seem believable. Note claims, reasons, and evidence in the margins as you read.

Reading Martin's Essay

Complex arguments require critical reading. Two critical-reading skills will help you: **subdividing the text** and **considering contexts.**

Finding Parts

Critical readers break texts down into parts. By *parts*, we mean groups of paragraphs that work together to perform some role in the essay. Examples of such roles are to introduce, to provide background, to give an opposing view, to conclude, and so on.

Discovering the parts of a text can be simple. Authors often make them obvious with subheadings and blank space. Even without these, transitional

Guidelines for Paraphrasing

- Use your own words, but don't strain to find a different word for every single one in the original. Some of the author's plain words are fine.
- If you take a phrase from the original, enclose it in quotation marks.
- Use a simpler sentence pattern than the original, even if it means making several short sentences. Aim for clarity.
- Check the surrounding sentences to make sure you understand the passage in context. You may want to add an idea from the context.
- Try for who-does-what sentences.

expressions and clear statements of intention make subdividing a text almost as easy as breaking a Hershey bar into its already well-defined segments. However, some arguments are more loosely constructed, their subdivisions less readily discernible. Even so, close inspection will usually reveal subdivisions and you should be able to see the roles played by the various chunks.

We have placed numbers next to every fifth paragraph in the essays reprinted in our text. Numbering makes it easier to refer to specific passages and to discuss parts.

Martin helps us see the parts of his essay by announcing early on, in paragraph 3, that it will have three sections, each "[exemplifying] some of the complex psychological underpinnings of youth tattooing." Martin's essay can thus be subdivided as follows:

1. Epigraph
2. Paragraphs 1, 2, and 3: the introduction
3. Paragraphs 4 and 5: an example
4. Paragaphs 6, 7, and 8: another example
5. Paragraphs 9, 10, and 11: a third example
6. Paragraph 12: the conclusion

Using Context

Taking the larger view again, we can use context to help pick out the reasoning. While a quick reading might suggest that Martin is arguing that teens have good reasons for decorating their bodies, we need to recall that the essay appeared in a journal for psychiatrists—doctors, not parents or teachers. Martin is writing to other psychiatrists and psychologists, clinicians who work with families. Reading carefully, we learn that his audience is an even smaller portion of this group: clinicians who have been "summoned as the final arbiter" in family disputes involving tattoos and other body decoration (paragraph 2). Because journals such as the *Journal of Child and Adolescent Psychiatry* are aimed at improving the practice of medicine, we want to note sentences that tell these readers what they ought to do and how it will make them better doctors.

Identifying the Claim and Reasons

The claim: Martin is very clear about his claim, repeating it three times, using just slightly different wording:

> His readers should "[explore] the motivations and significance [underlying] tattoos and piercings. . . ." (paragraph 2)

> His readers should have "[a]n interested and nonjudgmental appreciation of teenagers' surface presentations. . . ." (paragraph 2)

> His readers should see "[a]dolescents' bodily decorations . . . in terms of figuration rather than disfigurement. . . ." (paragraph 12)

Asked to identify Martin's claim, you could choose any one of these statements.

The reason: The reason is the "because" part of the argument. Why should the readers believe or do as Martin suggests? We can find the answer in paragraph 2, in the same sentences with his claim:

> Because doing so "can go a long way toward resolving . . . differences and can become a novel and additional way of getting to know teenagers."

> Because doing so "may become a way of making contact not only in their terms but on their turfs. . . ."

And the final sentence of Martin's essay offers a third version of the same reason:

> Because "we may not only arrive at a position to pass more reasoned clinical judgment, but become sensitized through our patients' skins to another level of their internal reality."

Again, we could choose any one of these sentences as the stated reason or paraphrase his reason. Using paraphrase, we can begin to outline the case structure of Martin's argument:

> **Claim:** Rather than dismissing tattoos as disfigurement, mental health professionals should take a serious interest in the meaning of and motivation behind the tattoos.

> **Reason:** Exploring their patients' body decorations can help them gain insight and make contact with teenagers on teenagers' own terms.

Where is Martin's evidence? Martin tells us that the three subsections will "exemplify some of the complex psychological underpinnings of youth tattooing." In each, he offers a case, or vignette, as evidence.

> **Example and evidence** (paragraphs 4 and 5): Tattoos are a way of working out identity problems when teens need either to mark

themselves off from others or to regain a sense of control of a changing body or an imposing environment. The sixteen-year-old-girl who chose not to fit in.

Example and evidence (paragraphs 6, 7, and 8): Tattoos can be an attempt to make the intangible a tangible part of one's body. The thirteen-year-old boy remembering his father.

Example and evidence (paragraphs 9, 10, and 11): Tattoos are an "antidote" to a society that is on the run. The seventeen-year-old father.

THE THIRD ENCOUNTER: RESPONDING CRITICALLY TO AN ARGUMENT

Once you feel confident that you have the argument figured out, you are ready to respond to it, which means evaluating and comparing it with other perspectives, including your own. Only by *writing words* can you respond critically. As the reading expert Mortimer Adler says in *How to Read a Book,*

> Reading, if it is active, is thinking, and thinking tends to express itself in words, spoken or written. The person who says he knows what he thinks but cannot express it in words usually does not know what he thinks. (49)

Annotation Is Key

We suggest that you annotate heavily. **Annotation** simply means making a note. Use the margins, and/or writer's notebook, for these notes of critical response. Many writers keep reading journals to practice active interaction with what they read and to preserve the experience of reading a text they want to remember.

What should you write about? Think of questions you would ask the author if he or she were in the room with you. Think of your own experience with the subject. Note similarities and contrasts with other arguments you have read or experiences of your own that confirm or contradict what the author is saying. Write about anything you notice that seems interesting, unusual, brilliant, or wrong. *Comment, question*—the more you actually write on the page, the more the text becomes your own. And you will write more confidently about a text you own than one you are just borrowing.

The list in the Best Practices box on page 37 will give you more ideas for annotations.

A concluding comment about responses: Even if you agree with an argument, think about who might oppose it and what their objections might be. Challenge the views you find most sympathetic.

Following is an example of annotation for part of Martin's argument.

Sample Annotations

How is he defining "solution"? Do tattoos solve a problem or just indicate one?

It seems like there are more mature ways to do this.

Or would it cause parents to pay attention to them rather than leave them alone?

Is he implying that the indelible mark is one they will not outgrow? What if they do?

Tattoos and piercing can offer a concrete and readily available <u>solution</u> for many of the identity crises and conflicts normative to adolescent development. In using such decorations, and by marking out their bodily territories, adolescents can support their efforts at autonomy, privacy, and insulation. Seeking individuation, tattooed adolescents can become unambiguously demarcated from others and singled out as unique. The intense and often disturbing reactions that are mobilized in viewers can help to effectively <u>keep them at bay</u>, becoming tantamount to the proverbial "Keep Out" sign hanging from a teenager's door.

Alternatively, feeling prey to a rapidly evolving body   5 over which they have no say, self-made and openly visible decorations may restore adolescents' sense of <u>normalcy</u> and control, a way of turning a passive experience into an active identity. By <u>indelibly</u> marking their bodies, adolescents can strive to reclaim their bearings within an environment experienced as alien, estranged, or suffocating or to lay claim over their evolving and increasingly unrecognizable bodies. In either case, the net outcome can be a <u>resolution to unwelcome impositions</u>: external, familial, or societal in one case, internal and hormonal in the other. In the words of a 16-year-old girl with several facial piercings, and who could have been referring to her body just as well as to the position within her family: "If I don't fit in, it is because I say so."

What is normal?

Would he say the same about anorexia?

Does he assume this family needs counseling—or will not need it? He says the problem is "resolved."

WRITING ASSIGNMENT: A CRITICAL RESPONSE TO A SINGLE ARGUMENT

This assignment asks you to write an essay about your critical reading of an argument. Writing about your encounters with a text will make you more conscious about your critical thinking, exposing your habits and practices. Here, write for your classmates. The goal of your paper is to

Ways to Annotate

- Paraphrase the claim and reasons next to where you find them stated.

- Consider: Does the author support his or her reasons with evidence? Is the evidence sufficient in terms of both quantity and quality?

- Circle the key terms. Note how the author defines or fails to define them.

- Ask: What does the author assume? Behind every argument, there are assumptions. For example, a baseball fan wrote to our local paper arguing that the policy of fouls after the second strike needs to be changed. His reason was that the fans would not be subjected to such a long game. The author assumed that a fast game of hits and outs is more interesting than a slow game of strategy between batters and hitters. Not every baseball fan shares that assumption.

- Note any contradictions you see, either within the text itself or with anything else you've read or learned.

- Consider the implications of the argument. If we believe or do what the author argues, what is likely to happen?

- Think of someone who would disagree with this argument, and say what that person might object to.

- If you see any opposing views in the argument, question the author's fairness in presenting them. Consider whether the author has represented opposing views fairly or has set them up to be easily knocked down.

- Ask: What is the author overlooking or leaving out?

- Consider: Where does the argument connect with anything else you have read?

- Consider: Does the argument exemplify mature reasoning as explained in Chapter 1, "Understanding Argument"?

- Ask: What aim does the argument seem to pursue? One of the four in the box on page 17, or some combination of them?

- Ask: What kind of person does the author sound like? Mark places where you hear the author's voice. Describe the tone. How does the author establish credibility—or fail to?

- Note the author's values and biases, places where the author sounds liberal or conservative, religious or materialistic, and so on.

- Note places where you see clues about the intended audience of the argument, such as appeals to their interests, values, tastes, and so on.

help your classmates better comprehend and criticize an essay you have all read.

In Part One

The project has two parts. In Part One, explain the rhetorical context, including who the author is and his or her point of view, as well as the intended audience as you infer it from clues outside and inside the text. Describe what you see as the claim and reason. Comment on the organization, referring to groups of paragraphs and the role they play in the argument. Tell about your experience of reading the essay—whether you found it easy, difficult, or confusing, and why. Be specific, and refer to actual passages.

In Part Two

In Part Two, evaluate the argument. How effective might it have been for its target audience? Focus on the text of the argument, but talk about its strengths and weaknesses. Your point is not simply to agree or disagree with the author; instead, show your understanding of the qualities of mature argumentation. In developing Part Two, use the suggestions for annotation on pages 35–37 as well as the criteria for mature reasoning on pages 11–14. Although your responses may be critical in the sense of negative, we use the term here to mean "a careful and exact evaluation and judgment" (*American Heritage Dictionary*).

Other Advice for Both Parts

- Refer to paragraphs in the text by number.
- Quote exactly and use quotation marks. Indicate in parentheses the paragraph they come from.
- Use paraphrase when talking about key ideas in the essay, and cite the paragraph in which the idea appeared.
- Use first person.
- Refer to the author by full name on first mention and by last name only after.

STUDENT SAMPLE ESSAY: CRITICAL RESPONSE TO A SINGLE ARGUMENT

Here we have reproduced another argument on the topic of tattoos and body decorations. Following it is one student's critical response to this essay, which follows the structure laid out above.

Once outlawed, the tradition of tribal tattooing has undergone a recent renewal among the Maori people of New Zealand and other Polynesian cultures. Full facial markings, or moko, such as this Maori chief has, are the most common in New Zealand.

Called the Tribe, these men (gathered under the Golden Gate Bridge in San Francisco) are leaders of the local Modern Primitivism movement. The Tribe has a tattoo parlor that does only tribal marking. Several of the tattoo artists have traveled to Borneo and learned the craft from tribal masters.

The Decorated Body

FRANCE BOREL

Nothing goes as deep as dress nor as far as the skin; ornaments have the dimensions of the world.

—Michel Serres, *The Five Senses*

Human nakedness, according to social custom, is unacceptable, unbearable, and dangerous. From the moment of birth, society takes charge, managing, dressing, forming, and deforming the child—sometimes even with a certain degree of violence. Aside from the most elementary caretaking concerns—the very diversity of which shows how subjective the motivation is—an unfathomably deep and universal tendency pushes families, clans, and tribes to rapidly modify a person's physical appearance.

One's genuine physical makeup, one's given anatomy, is always felt to be unacceptable. Flesh, in its raw state, seems both intolerable and threatening. In its naked state, body and skin have no possible existence. The organism is acceptable only when it is transformed, covered with signs. The body only speaks if it is dressed in artifice.

For millennia, in the four quarters of the globe, mothers have molded the shape of their newborn babies' skulls to give them silhouettes conforming to prevalent criteria of beauty. In the nineteenth century, western children were tightly swaddled to keep their limbs straight. In the so-called primitive world, children were scarred or tattooed at a very early age in rituals which were repeated at all the most important steps of their lives. At a very young age, children were fitted with belts, necklaces, or bracelets; their lips, ears, or noses were pierced or stretched.

Some cultures have designed sophisticated appliances to alter physical structure and appearance. American Indian cradleboards crushed the skull to flatten it; the Mangbetus of Africa wrapped knotted rope made of bark around the child's head to elongate it into a sugar-loaf shape, which was considered to be aesthetically pleasing. The feet of very young Chinese girls were bound and spliced, intentionally and irreversibly deforming them, because this was seen to guarantee the girls' eventual amorous and matrimonial success.[1]

Claude Lévi-Strauss said about the Caduveo of Brazil: "In order to be a man, 5 one had to be painted; whoever remained in a natural state was no different from the beasts."[2] In Polynesia, unless a girl was tattooed, she would not find a husband. An unornamented hand could not cook, nor dip into the communal food bowl. Pink lips were despicable and ugly. Anyone who refused the test of the tattoo was seen to be marginal and suspect.

Among the Tivs of Nigeria, women called attention to their legs by means of elaborate scarification and the use of pearl leg bands; the best decorated calves were known for miles around. Tribal incisions behind the ears of Chad men rendered the skin "as smooth and stretched as that of a drum." The women would laugh at any man lacking these incisions, and they would never accept him as a husband. Men would subject themselves willingly to this custom, hoping for scars deep enough to leave marks on their skulls after death.

At the beginning of the eighteenth century, Father Laurent de Lucques noted that any young girl of the Congo who was not able to bear the pain of scarification and who cried so loudly that the operation had to be stopped was considered "good for nothing."[3] That is why, before marriage, men would check to see if the pattern traced on the belly of their intended bride was beautiful and well-detailed.

The fact that such motivations and pretexts depend on aesthetic, erotic, hygienic, or even medical considerations has no influence on the result, which is always in the direction of transforming the appearance of the body. Such a transformation is wished for, whether or not it is effective.

The body is a supple, malleable, and transformable prime material, a kind of modeling clay, easily molded by social will and wish. Human skin is an ideal subject for inscription, a surface for all sorts of marks which make it possible to differentiate the human from the animal. The physical body offers itself willingly for tattooing or scarring so that, visibly and recognizably, it becomes a social entity.

The absolutely naked body is considered as brutish, reduced to the level of [10] nature where no distinction is made between man and beast. The decorated body, on the other hand, dressed (if even only in a belt), tattooed, or mutilated, publicly exhibits humanity and membership in an established group. As Theophile Gautier said, "The ideal disturbs even the roughest nature, and the taste for ornamentation distinguishes the intelligent being from the beast more exactly than anything else. Indeed, dogs have never dreamed of putting on earrings."

So, it is by their categorical refusal of nakedness that human beings are distinguished from nature. The "mark makes unremarkable"—it creates an interval between what is biologically and brutally given in the animal realm and what is won in the cultural realm. The body is tamed continuously; social custom demands, at any price—including pain, constraint, or discomfort—that wildness be abandoned.

Each civilization chooses—through a network of elective relationships which are difficult to determine—which areas of the body deserve transformation. These areas are as difficult to define and as shifting as those of eroticism or modesty. An individual alone eludes bodily modifications; they are the expression of a homogeneous collectivity which, at a chosen moment, comes to a tacit agreement to attack one or another part of the anatomy.

Whatever the choices, options, or differences may be, that which remains constant is the transformation of appearance. In spite of our contemporary western belief that the body is perfect as it is, we are constantly changing it: clothing it in musculature, suntan, or makeup; dying its head hair or pulling out its bodily hair. The seemingly most innocent gestures for taking care of the body very often hide a persistent and disguised tendency to make it adhere to the strictest of norms, reclothing it in a veil of civilization. The total nudity offered at birth does not exist in any region of the world. Man puts his stamp on man. The body is not a product of nature, but of culture.

NOTES

1. Of course, there are also many different sexual mutilations, including excisions and circumcisions, which we will not go into at this time as they constitute a whole study in themselves.
2. C. Lévi-Strauss, *Tristes Tropiques* (Paris: Plon, 1955), p. 214.
3. J. Cuvelier, *Relations sur le Congo du Père Laurent de Lucques* (Brussels: Institut royal colonial belge, 1953), p. 144.

The Decorated Body from *Le Vêtement incarné—Les Métamorphoses du corps* by France Borel, translated by Ellen Dooling Draper. © Editions Calmann-Lévy, 1992.

A SAMPLE STUDENT RESPONSE

Analysis of "The Decorated Body"
Katie Lahey

Part One

"The Decorated Body" by France Borel addresses the idea of external body manipulation not only as an issue prevalent to our own culture and time but also as a timeless concept that exists beyond cultural boundaries. It was published in *Parabola*, a magazine supported by the Society for the Study of Myth and Tradition. Borel discusses the ways in which various cultures both ancient and modern modify the natural body. Borel, who has written books on clothing and on art, writes with a style that is less a critique than an observation of his populations. This style suggests an anthropological approach rather than a psychological one, focusing on the motivations of people as a whole and less on the specific individuals within the societies. It seems, therefore, that she may be targeting an academic audience of professional anthropologists or other readers who are interested in the similarities of both "primitive" and "modern" cultures and the whole idea of what it means to be human.

Borel makes the claim that "social custom" dictates that all humans manipulate their bodies to brand themselves as humans. She says in the first paragraph that "an unfathomably deep and universal tendency pushes families, clans, and tribes to rapidly modify a person's physical appearance." She restates the idea in paragraph 2: The body "is acceptable only when it is transformed, covered with signs." She believes that in all cultures this type of branding or decorating is essential to distinguish oneself as legitimate within a civilization. Man has evolved from his original body; he has defied nature. We are no longer subject to what we are born with; rather, we create our bodies and identities as we see fit.

Borel reasons that this claim is true simply because all cultures conform to this idea and do so in such diverse ways. As she says, "the very diversity . . . shows how subjective the motivation is . . ." (paragraph 1). She provides ample evidence to support this reasoning in paragraphs 3 through 7, citing various cultures and examples of how they choose to decorate the body.

Part Two

However, Borel does not provide a solid explanation as to why the human race finds these bodily changes necessary to distinguish itself as human. It serves her argument to state that the various specific motivations behind these changes are irrelevant. All she is interested in proving is that humans must change their bodies, and she repeats this concept continually throughout the essay, first saying that a man remaining "in a natural state was no different from the beasts" in paragraph 5 and again in paragraphs 9 and 10. Maybe some readers would think this reiteration makes her point stronger, but I was unsatisfied.

I found myself trying to provide my own reasons why humans 5 have this need to change their bodies. What makes this essay so unsatisfying to me is that, once I thought about it, it does in fact matter why cultures participate in body decoration. For example, why did the Chinese find it necessary to bind the feet of their young girls, a tradition so painful and unhealthy and yet so enduring? In such traditions, it becomes obvious that ulterior motives lie beneath the surface. The binding of the feet is not simply a tradition that follows the idea of making oneself human. In fact, it methodically attempts to put women below men. By binding the feet, a culture disables the young women not only physically but emotionally as well. It teaches them that they do not deserve the same everyday comforts as men and belittles them far beyond simply having smaller feet. Borel, however, fails to discuss any of these deeper motives. She avoids supplying her own opinion because she does not want to get into the politics of the practices she describes. She wants to speak in generalizations about body modification as a mark of being human, even though people in modern Western culture might see some of these activities as violations of human rights.

Borel barely touches on modern Western civilization. She really only addresses our culture in the final paragraph, where she alleges that everyday things we do to change ourselves, whether it be shaving, tanning, toning, dying, or even applying makeup, are evidence that we have the same need to mark ourselves as human. She challenges our belief that "the body is perfect as it is" by showing that "we are constantly changing it" (paragraph 13). But many people today, especially women, *do* doubt that their individual bodies are perfect and would concede that they are constantly trying to "improve" them. What does Borel mean by "perfect as it is"? Is she talking about an ideal we would like to achieve?

Her placement of this paragraph is interesting. I wondered why she leaves this discussion of our own culture until the very end of the essay so that her ideas of European and American culture appear as an afterthought. She spends the majority of the essay discussing other, more "primitive cultures" that yield many more examples of customs, such as the American Indian cradleboards, that clearly mark one as a member of a tribe. Perhaps Borel tends to discuss primitive cultures as opposed to our modern Western culture because primitive cultures generally back up her thesis, whereas American culture, in particular, veers from her claim that people decorate themselves in order to demonstrate what they have in common.

Borel ignores any controversy over tattoos and piercing, which people in Western culture might do to mark themselves as different from other people in their culture. In America, we value individualism, where everyone tries to be unique, even if in some small way. Other authors like Andres Martin, who wrote "On Teenagers and Tattoos," look at American culture and claim that we use body decoration as a means to show and celebrate our individuality. Martin says one good reason for teens to tattoo themselves is for "individuation"—to mark themselves as distinct from their peers and their families. This goes completely opposite from Borel's claim that "[a]n individual alone eludes bodily modifications; they are the expression of a homogeneous collectivity . . ." (paragraph 12).

Borel makes a sound argument for her claim that human existence is something more complex or more unnatural than simply being alive. But we know this already through humans' use of speech, social organization, and technology. Before I read her argument and even after the first time I read it, I wasn't swayed by Borel. I was looking for something more specific than what she is saying. In fact, all she is showing is that we decorate to symbolize our humanity. She does support this claim with good evidence. In this sense, the argument holds. But I cannot help but prefer to think about the other, more specific things we symbolize through our body decorations.

Analyzing Arguments:
A Simplified Toulmin Method

In Chapter 2, we discussed the importance of reading arguments critically: breaking them down into their parts to see how they are put together, noting in the margins key terms that are not defined, and raising questions about the writer's claims or evidence. Although these general techniques are sufficient for analyzing many arguments, sometimes—especially with intricate arguments and with arguments we sense are faulty but whose weaknesses we are unable to specify—we need a more systematic technique.

In this chapter, we explain and illustrate such a technique based on the work of Stephen Toulmin, a contemporary philosopher who has contributed a great deal to our understanding of argumentation. This method will allow you to analyze the logic of any argument; you will also find it useful in examining the logic of your own arguments as you draft and revise them. Keep in mind, however, that because it is limited to the analysis of logic, the Toulmin method is not sufficient by itself. It is also important to question an argument through dialogue (see Chapter 7) and to look at the appeals of character, emotion, and style (see Chapter 9).

A PRELIMINARY CRITICAL READING

Before we consider Toulmin, let's first explore the following argument carefully. Use the general process for critical reading we described in Chapter 2.

Rising to the Occasion of Our Death

WILLIAM F. MAY

> William F. May (b. 1927) is a distinguished professor of ethics at Southern Methodist University. The following essay appeared originally in *The Christian Century* (1990).

For many parents, a Volkswagen van is associated with putting children to sleep on a camping trip. Jack Kevorkian, a Detroit pathologist, has now linked the van with the veterinarian's meaning of "putting to sleep." Kevorkian conducted a dinner interview with Janet Elaine Adkins, a 54-year-old Alzheimer's patient, and her husband and then agreed to help her commit suicide in his VW van. Kevorkian pressed beyond the more generally accepted practice of passive euthanasia (allowing a patient to die by withholding or withdrawing treatment) to active euthanasia (killing for mercy).

Kevorkian, moreover, did not comply with the strict regulations that govern active euthanasia in, for example, the Netherlands. Holland requires that death be imminent (Adkins had beaten her son in tennis just a few days earlier); it demands a more professional review of the medical evidence and the patient's resolution than a dinner interview with a physician (who is a stranger and who does not treat patients) permits; and it calls for the final, endorsing signatures of two doctors.

So Kevorkian-bashing is easy. But the question remains: Should we develop a judicious, regulated social policy permitting voluntary euthanasia for the terminally ill? Some moralists argue that the distinction between allowing to die and killing for mercy is petty quibbling over technique. Since the patient in any event dies—whether by acts of omission or commission—the route to death doesn't really matter. The way modern procedures have made dying at the hands of the experts and their machines such a prolonged and painful business has further fueled the euthanasia movement, which asserts not simply the right to die but the right to be killed.

But other moralists believe that there is an important moral distinction between allowing to die and mercy killing. The euthanasia movement, these critics contend, wants to engineer death rather than face dying. Euthanasia would bypass dying to make one dead as quickly as possible. It aims to relieve suffering by knocking out the interval between life and death. It solves the problem of suffering by eliminating the sufferer.

The impulse behind the euthanasia movement is understandable in an age 5 when dying has become such an inhumanly endless business. But the movement may fail to appreciate our human capacity to rise to the occasion of our death. The best death is not always the sudden death. Those forewarned of death and given time to prepare for it have time to engage in acts of reconciliation. Also, advanced grieving by those about to be bereaved may ease some of their pain.

Psychiatrists have observed that those who lose a loved one accidentally have a more difficult time recovering from the loss than those who have suffered through an extended period of illness before the death. Those who have lost a close relative by accident are more likely to experience what Geoffrey Gorer has called limitless grief. The community, moreover, may need its aged and dependent, its sick and its dying, and the virtues which they sometimes evince—the virtues of humility, courage, and patience—just as much as the community needs the virtues of justice and love manifest in the agents of care.

On the whole, our social policy should allow terminal patients to die, but it should not regularize killing for mercy. Such a policy would recognize and respect that moment in illness when it no longer makes sense to bend every effort to cure or to prolong life and when one must allow patients to do their own dying. This policy seems most consonant with the obligations of the community to care and of the patient to finish his or her course.

Advocates of active euthanasia appeal to the principle of patient autonomy—as the use of the phrase "voluntary euthanasia" indicates. But emphasis on the patient's right to determine his or her destiny often harbors an extremely naïve view of the uncoerced nature of the decision. Patients who plead to be put to death hardly make unforced decisions if the terms and conditions under which they receive care already nudge them in the direction of the exit. If the elderly have stumbled around in their apartments, alone and frightened for years, or if they have spent years warehoused in geriatrics barracks, then the decision to be killed for mercy hardly reflects an uncoerced decision. The alternative may be so wretched as to push patients toward this escape. It is a huge irony and, in some cases, hypocrisy to talk suddenly about a compassionate killing when the aging and dying may have been starved for compassion for many years. To put it bluntly, a country has not earned the moral right to kill for mercy unless it has already sustained and supported life mercifully. Otherwise we kill for compassion only to reduce the demands on our compassion. This statement does not charge a given doctor or family member with impure motives. I am concerned here not with the individual case but with the cumulative impact of a social policy.

I can, to be sure, imagine rare circumstances in which I hope I would have the courage to kill for mercy—when the patient is utterly beyond human care, terminal, and in excruciating pain. A neurosurgeon once showed a group of physicians and an ethicist the picture of a Vietnam casualty who had lost all four limbs in a landmine explosion. The catastrophe had reduced the soldier to a trunk with his face transfixed in horror. On the battlefield I would hope that I would have the courage to kill the sufferer with mercy.

But hard cases do not always make good laws or wise social policies. Regularized mercy killings would too quickly relieve the community of its obligation to provide good care. Further, we should not always expect the law to provide us with full protection and coverage for what, in rare circumstances, we may morally need to do. Sometimes the moral life calls us out into a no-man's-land where we cannot expect total security and protection under the law. But no one said that the moral life is easy.

Dr. Jack Kevork-ian served a prison sentence for assist-ing with voluntary euthanasia.

A STEP-BY-STEP DEMONSTRATION OF THE TOULMIN METHOD

The Toulmin method requires an analysis of the claim, the reasons offered to support the claim, and the evidence offered to support the reasons, along with an analysis of any refutations offered.

Analyzing the Claim

Logical analysis begins with identifying the *claim*, the thesis or central con-tention, along with any specific qualifications or exceptions.

Identify the Claim

First, ask yourself, *What statement is the author defending?* In "Rising to the Occasion of Our Death," for example, William F. May spells out his claim in paragraph 6:

> [O]ur social policy should allow terminal patients to die, but it should not regularize killing for mercy.

In his claim, May supports passive euthanasia (letting someone die by withholding or discontinuing treatment) but opposes "regularizing" (making legal or customary) active euthanasia (administering, say, an overdose of morphine to cause a patient's death).

Much popular argumentation is sometimes careless about what exactly is being claimed: Untrained arguers too often content themselves with merely taking sides ("Euthanasia is wrong"). Note that May, a student of ethics trained in philosophical argumentation, makes a claim that is both specific and detailed. Whenever an argument does not include an explicit statement of its claim, you should begin your analysis by stating the writer's claim yourself. Try to state it in sentence form, as May's claim is stated.

Look for Qualifiers

Next, ask, *How is the claim qualified?* Is it absolute, or does it include words or phrases to indicate that it may not hold true in every situation or set of circumstances?

May qualifies his claim in paragraph 6 with the phrase "On the whole," indicating that he recognizes possible exceptions. Other qualifiers include "typically," "usually," and "most of the time." Careful arguers are wary of making absolute claims. Qualifying words or phrases are used to restrict a claim and improve its defensibility.

Find the Exceptions

Finally, ask, *In what cases or circumstances would the writer not press his or her claim?* Look for any explicit exceptions the writer offers.

May, for example, is quite clear in paragraph 8 about when he would not press his claim:

> I hope I would have the courage to kill for mercy—when the patient is utterly beyond human care, terminal, and in excruciating pain.

Once he has specified these abstract conditions, he offers a chilling example of a case in which mercy killing would be appropriate. Nevertheless, he insists that such exceptions are rare and thus do not justify making active euthanasia legal or allowing it to become common policy.

Critical readers respond to unqualified claims skeptically—by hunting for exceptions. With qualified claims, they look to see what specific exceptions the writer will admit and what considerations make restrictions necessary or desirable.

Summarize the Claim

At this point it is a good idea to write out in your writer's notebook the claim, its qualifiers, and its exceptions so that you can see all of them clearly. For May, they look like this:

(qualifier)   "On the whole"

(claim)   "our social policy should allow terminal patients to die, but it should not regularize killing for mercy"

(exception) "when the patient is utterly beyond human care, terminal, and in excruciating pain"

Analyzing the Reasons

Once you have analyzed the claim, you should next identify and evaluate the reasons offered for the claim.

List the Reasons

Begin by asking yourself, *Why is the writer advancing this claim?* Look for any statement or statements that are used to justify the thesis. May groups all of his reasons in paragraph 5:

The dying should have time to prepare for death and to reconcile with relatives and friends.

Those close to the dying should have time to come to terms with the impending loss of a loved one.

The community needs examples of dependent but patient and courageous people who sometimes do die with dignity.

The community needs the virtues ("justice and love") of those who care for the sick and dying.

When you list reasons, you need not preserve the exact words of the arguer; often, doing so is impossible because reasons are not always explicit but may have to be inferred. Be very careful, however, to adhere as closely as possible to the writer's language. Otherwise, your analysis can easily go astray, imposing a reason of your own that the writer did not have in mind.

Note that reasons, like claims, can be qualified. May does not say, for instance, that "the aged and dependent" *always* show "the virtues of humility, courage, and patience." He implicitly admits that they can be ornery and cowardly as well. But for May's purposes it is enough that they sometimes manifest the virtues he admires.

Use your writer's notebook to list the reasons following your summary of the claim, qualifiers, and exceptions. One possibility is to list them beneath the summary of the claim in the form of a tree diagram (see the model diagram in the Concept Close-Up box on page 53).

Examine the Reasons

There are two questions to ask as you examine the reasons. First, ask, *Are they really good reasons?* A reason is only as good as the values it invokes or implies. A value is something we think is good—that is, worth pursuing for its own sake or because it leads to attaining other goods. For each reason, specify the values involved and then determine whether you accept those values as generally binding.

Second, ask, *Is the reason relevant to the thesis?* In other words, does the relationship between the claim and the reason hold up to examination? For example, the claim "You should buy a new car from Fred Freed" cannot be supported by the reason "Fred is a family man with three cute kids."

Be careful as you examine whether reasons are good and whether they are relevant. No other step is as important in assessing the logic of an argument, and no other can be quite as tricky.

To illustrate, consider May's first reason: Those who know they are about to die should have time to prepare for death and to seek reconciliation with people from whom they have become estranged. Is this a good reason? Yes, because we value the chance to prepare for death and to reconcile with estranged friends or family members.

But is the reason relevant? May seems to rule out the possibility that a dying person seeking active euthanasia would be able to prepare for death and reconcile with others. But this is obviously not the case. Terminally ill people who decide to arrange for their own deaths may make any number of preparations beforehand, so the connection between this reason and May's claim is really quite weak. To accept a connection, we would have to assume that active euthanasia necessarily amounts to a sudden death without adequate preparation. We are entitled to question the relevance of the reason, no matter how good it might be in itself.

◎◎ FOLLOWING THROUGH

Now examine May's second, third, and fourth reasons on your own, as we have just examined the first one. Make notes about each reason, evaluating how good each is in itself and how relevant it is to the thesis. In your writer's notebook, create your own diagram based on the model on page 53.   •

Analyzing the Evidence

Once you have finished your analysis of the reasons, the next step is to consider the evidence offered to support any of those reasons.

List the Evidence

Ask, *What kinds of evidence (data, anecdotes, case studies, citations from authority, and so forth) are offered as support for each reason?* Some arguments advance little in the way of evidence. May's argument is a good example of a moral argument about principles; such an argument does not require much evidence. Lack of evidence, then, is not always a fault. For one of his reasons, however, May does offer some evidence: After stating his second reason in paragraph 5—the chance to grieve before a loved one dies—he invokes authorities who agree with him about the value of advanced grieving.

Examine the Evidence

Two questions apply. First, ask, *Is the evidence good?* That is, is it sufficient, accurate, and credible? Second, ask, *Is it relevant to the reason it supports?* The evidence May offers in paragraph 5 is sufficient. We assume his citations are accurate and credible as well. We would also accept them as relevant because, apart from our own experience with grieving, we have to rely on expert opinion. (See Chapter 5 for a fuller discussion of estimating the adequacy and relevance of evidence.)

Noting Refutations

A final step is to assess an arguer's refutations. In a refutation, a writer anticipates potential objections to his or her position and tries to show why they do not undermine the basic argument. A skilled arguer uses them to deal with any obvious objections a reader is likely to have.

First, ask, *What refutations does the writer offer?* Summarize them. Then, ask, *How does the writer approach each objection?* May's refutation occupies paragraph 7. He recognizes that the value of free choice lends weight to the proeuthanasia position, and so he relates this value to the question of "voluntary euthanasia." Because in our culture individual freedom is so strong a value, May doesn't question the value itself; rather, he leads us to question whether voluntary euthanasia is actually a matter of free choice. He suggests that unwanted people may be coerced into "choosing" death or may be so isolated and neglected that death becomes preferable. Thus, he responds to the objection that dying people should have freedom of choice where death is concerned.

Summarizing Your Analysis

Once you have completed your analysis, it is a good idea to summarize the results in a paragraph or two. Be sure to set aside your own position on the issue, confining your summary to the argument the writer makes.

Although May's logic is strong, it doesn't seem fully compelling. He qualifies his argument and uses exceptions effectively, and his single use of refutation is skillful. However, he fails to acknowledge that active euthanasia need not be a sudden decision leading to sudden death. Consequently, his reasons for supporting passive euthanasia can be used to support at least some cases of active euthanasia as well. It is here—in

Model Toulmin Diagram for Analyzing Arguments

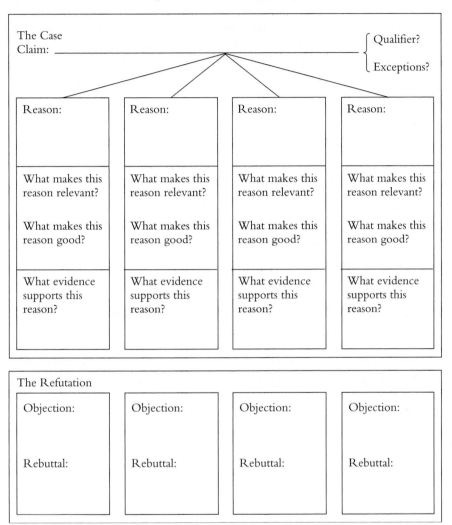

The Case
Claim: _____

Qualifier?

Exceptions?

Reason:	Reason:	Reason:	Reason:
What makes this reason relevant? What makes this reason good?	What makes this reason relevant? What makes this reason good?	What makes this reason relevant? What makes this reason good?	What makes this reason relevant? What makes this reason good?
What evidence supports this reason?	What evidence supports this reason?	What evidence supports this reason?	What evidence supports this reason?

The Refutation

Objection: Rebuttal:	Objection: Rebuttal:	Objection: Rebuttal:	Objection: Rebuttal:

the linkage between reasons and claim—that May's argument falls short. Furthermore, we may question whether the circumstances under which May would permit active euthanasia are in fact as rare as he suggests. Many people are beyond human care, terminal, and in pain, and many others suffer acute anguish for which they might legitimately seek the relief of death.

Toulmin Analysis

A. ANALYZE THE CLAIM

1. **Find the claim.** In many arguments, the claim is never explicitly stated. When it isn't, try to make the implied claim explicit by stating it in your own words. (Note: If, after careful analysis, you aren't sure *exactly* what the writer is claiming, you've found a serious fault in the argument.)

2. **Look for qualifiers.** Is the claim absolute? Or is it qualified by some word or phrase like *usually* or *all things being equal?* If the claim is absolute, can you think of circumstances in which it might not apply? If the claim is qualified, why is it not absolute? That is, is there any real thought or content in the qualifier—good reasons for qualifying the claim?

3. **Look for explicit exceptions to the claim.** If the writer has pointed out conditions in which he or she would not assert the claim, note them carefully.

Summarize steps 1–3. See the diagram on page 53.

B. ANALYZE THE REASONS

1. **Find the reason or reasons advanced to justify the claim.** All statements of reason will answer the question "Why are you claiming what you've claimed?" They can be linked to the claim with *because.* As with claims, reasons may be implied. Dig them out and state them in your own words. (Note: If, after careful analysis, you discover that the reasons aren't clear or relevant to the claim, you should conclude that the argument is either defective and in need of revision or invalid and therefore unacceptable.)

2. **Ponder each reason advanced.** Is the reason good in itself? Is the reason relevant to the thesis? Note any problems.

List the reasons underneath the claim. See the diagram on page 53.

C. ANALYZE THE EVIDENCE

1. **For each reason, locate all evidence offered to back it up.** Evidence is not limited to hard data. Anecdotes, case studies, and citations from authorities also count as evidence. (Note: Not all reasons require extensive evidence. But we should be suspicious of reasons without evidence, especially when it seems that evidence ought to be available. Unsupported reasons are often a sign of bad reasoning.)

2. **Ponder each piece of evidence.** Is it good? That is, is it accurate and believable? Is it relevant to the reason it supports? Note any problems.

List the evidence underneath the claim. See the diagram on page 53.

D. EXAMINE THE REFUTATIONS

If there are refutations—efforts to refute objections to the case—examine them. If not, consider what objections you think the writer should have addressed.

◎◎ FOLLOWING THROUGH

Following is a student-written argument on capital punishment. Read it through once, and then use the Toulmin method as described in this chapter to analyze its logic systematically.   •

STUDENT SAMPLE An Argument for Analysis

Capital Punishment: Society's Self-Defense
Amber Young

Just after 1:00 a.m. on a warm night in early June, Georgeann, a pretty college student, left through the back door of a fraternity house to walk the ninety feet down a well-lighted alley to the back door of her sorority house. Lively and vivacious, Georgeann had been an honor student, a cheerleader, and Daffodil Princess in high school, and now she was in the middle of finals week, trying to maintain her straight A record. That evening, several people saw Georgeann walk to within about forty feet of the door of her sorority house. She never arrived. Somewhere in that last forty feet, she met a tall, handsome young man on crutches, his leg in a cast, struggling with a briefcase. The young man asked Georgeann if she could help him get to his car, which was parked nearby. She consented. Then, a housemother sleeping by an open window in a nearby fraternity house was awakened by a high-pitched, terrified scream that suddenly stopped. That was the last anyone ever heard or saw of Georgeann Hawkins. Her bashed skull and broken body were dumped on a hillside many miles away, along with the bodies of several other young female victims who had also been lured to their deaths by the good-looking, clean-cut, courteous, intelligent, and charming Ted Bundy.

By the time Ted Bundy was caught in Utah with his bashing bar and other homemade tools of torture, he had bludgeoned and strangled to death at least thirty-two young women, raping and savaging many of them in the process. His "hunting" trips had extended into at least five Western states, including Washington, Oregon, Idaho, Utah, and Colorado.

Bundy was ultimately convicted of the attempted kidnapping of Carol DeRonche and imprisoned. For this charge he probably would have been paroled within eighteen months. However, before parole could be approved, Bundy was transferred to a jail in Colorado to stand trial for the murder of Caryn Campbell. With Bundy in jail, no

www.mhhe.com/**crusius**

For additional information an
writing analysis essays, go to

Writing >
Writing Tutors >
Interpretive Analysis and
Writing about Litature

one else died. Young women could go about their lives normally, "safe" and separated from Ted Bundy by prison walls. Yet any number of things could have occurred to set him free—an acquittal, some sympathetic judge or parole board, a psychiatrist pronouncing him rehabilitated and safe, a state legislature passing shorter sentencing or earlier parole laws, inadequate prison space, a federal court ruling abolishing life in prison without any possibility for parole, or an escape.

In Bundy's case, it was escape—twice—from Colorado jails. The first time, he was immediately caught and brought back. The second time, Bundy made it to Florida, where fifteen days after his escape he bludgeoned and strangled Margaret Bowman, Lisa Levy, Karen Chandler, and Kathy Kleiner in their Tallahassee sorority house, tearing chunks out of Lisa Levy's breast and buttock with his teeth. Ann Rule, a noted crime writer who became Bundy's confidant while writing her book The Stranger Beside Me, described Bundy's attack on Lisa Levy as like that of a rabid animal. On the same night at a different location, Bundy sneaked through an open window and so savagely attacked Cheryl Thomas in her bed that a woman in the apartment next door described the clubbing as seeming to reverberate through the whole house. Then, three weeks later, less than forty days after his escape from the Colorado jail, Bundy went hunting again. He missed his chance at one quarry, junior high school student Leslie Ann Parmenter, when her brother showed up and thwarted her abduction. But Bundy succeeded the next day in Lake City, where he abducted and killed twelve-year-old Kimberly Diane Leach and dumped her strangled, broken body in an abandoned pig barn.

The criminal justice system did not keep Margaret Bowman,   5
Lisa Levy, Karen Chandler, Kathy Kleiner, Cheryl Thomas, Leslie Ann Parmenter, or little Kimberly Leach safe from Ted Bundy. The state of Florida, however, with its death penalty, has made every other young woman safe from Ted Bundy forever. Capital punishment is society's means of self-defense. Just as a person is justified in using deadly force in defending herself against a killer, so society also has a right to execute those who kill whenever the opportunity and the urge arise.

However, while everyone wants a safe society, some people would say that capital punishment is too strong a means of ensuring it. Contemporary social critic Hendrick Hertzberg attacks the death penalty, using arguments that are familiar, but not compelling, to those who do not share his absolute value-of-life position. For example, in one article he paints a graphic picture of how horrible and painful even lethal injection is to the prisoner ("Premeditated"). Elsewhere he dismisses the deterrence argument as "specious," since "[n]o one has ever been able to show that capital punishment lowers the murder rate" ("Burning" 4). But the Florida death penalty has, in fact, made certain that Ted Bundy will never kill again. A needle prick in the arm is hardly cruel and unusual. Thousands of good people with cancer and other diseases or injuries endure much greater pain every day.

Of course, the possibility of executing an innocent person is a serious concern. However, our entire criminal justice system is tilted heavily toward the accused, who is protected from the start to the end of the criminal justice procedure by strong individual-rights guarantees in the Fourth, Fifth, Sixth, and Seventh Amendments of the U.S. Constitution. The burden of proof in a criminal case is on the government, and guilt must be proved beyond a reasonable doubt. The chances of a guilty person going free in our system are many times greater than those of an innocent person being convicted.

If, however, a mistake occurs despite all the safeguards, such an innocent death would be tragic, just as each of the nearly 50,000 deaths of innocent people each year on our highways is tragic. As much as we value human life, we inevitably weigh that value against social costs and benefits, whether we like to admit it or not. If the possibility that an innocent person might be executed is bad enough to require abolition of capital punishment, then why don't we also demand the abolition of automobiles as well? We don't because we accept the thousands of automobile deaths per year to keep our cars. It is interesting to note that opponents of capital punishment like Hertzberg do not demand abolition of the automobile. So preservation of life must not be the highest value in all cases.

Just as society has decided that the need for automobiles outweighs their threat to innocent life, so capital punishment is necessary for the safety and well-being of the general populace. The strongest reason for capital punishment is not retribution or deterrence, but simply self-defense. We have a right to demand that government remove forever first-degree murderers, like Bundy, who hunt and kill their victims with premeditation and malice.

There are only two alternatives—life in prison or death. We base our approval or disapproval of capital punishment on fundamental values relating to life itself, rather than on statistics or factual evidence. Few in our society go so far as to believe that we must preserve life above all else. Our founding fathers wrote in the Declaration of Independence that all men are endowed by their Creator with unalienable rights, including "life, liberty, and the pursuit of happiness." However, there is no indication that life was more sacred to them than liberty. In fact, Patrick Henry, who would later be instrumental in the adoption of the Bill of Rights to the U.S. Constitution, is most famous for his defiant American Revolutionary declaration, "I know not what course others may take, but as for me, give me liberty or give me death!"

The sentiment that some things are worse than death remains. Millions of soldiers have put themselves in harm's way and lost their lives to preserve and defend freedom. Many people will admit

10

to their willingness to use deadly force to protect themselves or their families from a murderer. The preservation of life, any life, regardless of everything else, is not an absolute value for most people.

In fact, many prisoners would prefer to die than to languish in prison. Bundy himself, in his letters from prison to Ann Rule, declared, "My world is a cage," as he tried to describe "the cruel metamorphosis that occurs in captivity" (qtd. in Rule 148). After his sentencing in Utah, Bundy described his attempts to prepare mentally for the "living hell of prison" (qtd. in Rule 191). Thus, some condemned prisoners, including Gary Gilmore, the first person to be executed after the U.S. Supreme Court found that Utah's death penalty law met Constitutional requirements, refused to participate in the appeals attempting to convert his death sentence to life in prison because he preferred death. In our society, founded on the principle that liberty is more important than life, the argument that it is somehow less cruel and more civilized to deprive someone of liberty for the rest of his or her life than to end the life sounds hollow. The Fifth Amendment of the U.S. Constitution prohibits the taking of either life or liberty without due process of law, but it does not place one at a higher value than the other.

The overriding concerns of the Constitution, however, are safety and self-defense. The chance of a future court ruling, a release on parole, a pardon, a commutation of sentence, or an escape—any of which could turn the murderer loose to prey again on society—creates a risk that society should not have to bear. Lisa Levy, Margaret Bowman, Karen Chandler, Kathy Kleiner, Cheryl Thomas, and Kimberly Leach were not protected from Bundy by the courts and jails in Utah and Colorado, but other young women who were potential victims are now safe from Bundy thanks to the Florida death penalty.

Capital punishment carries with it the risk that an innocent person will be executed; however, it is more important to protect innocent, would-be victims of convicted murderers. On balance, society was not demeaned by the execution of Bundy in Florida, as Hertzberg claimed ("Burning" 49). On the contrary, society is better off with Ted Bundy and others like him gone.

Works Cited

Hertzberg, Hendrick. "Burning Question." The New Republic 20 Feb. 1989: 4+.

---. "Premeditated Execution." Time 18 May 1992: 49.

Rule, Ann. The Stranger Beside Me. New York: Penguin, 1989.

A FINAL NOTE ABOUT LOGICAL ANALYSIS

No method for analyzing arguments is perfect, and no method can guarantee that everyone using it will assess an argument the same way. Uniform results are not especially desirable anyway. What would be left to talk about? The point of argumentative analysis is to step back and examine an argument carefully, to detect how it is structured, to assess the cogency and power of its logic. The Toulmin method helps us move beyond a hit-or-miss approach to logical analysis, but it cannot yield a conclusion as compelling as mathematical proof.

Convincing and persuading always involve more than logic, and, therefore, logical analysis alone is never enough to assess the strength of an argument. For example, William May's argument attempts to discredit those like Dr. Jack Kevorkian who assist patients wishing to take their own lives. May depicts Kevorkian as offering assistance without sufficient consultation with the patient. Is his depiction accurate? Clearly, we can answer this question only by finding out more about how Kevorkian and others like him work. Because such questions are not a part of logical analysis, they have not been of concern to us in this chapter. But any adequate and thorough analysis of an argument must also address questions of fact and the interpretation of data.

CHAPTER 4

Reading and Writing about Visual Arguments

We live in a world awash in pictures. We turn on the TV and see not just performers, advertisers, and talking heads but also dramatic footage of events from around the world, commercials as visually creative as works of art, and video images to accompany popular music. We boot up our computers and surf the Net; many of the waves we ride are visual swells, enticing images created or enhanced by the very machines that take us out to sea. We drive our cars through a gallery of street art—on billboards and buildings and on the sides of buses and trucks. We go to malls and window-shop, entertained by the images of fantasy fulfillment each retailer offers. Print media are full of images; in our newspapers, for instance, photos, drawings, and computer graphics vie with print for space. Even college textbooks, once mostly blocks of uninterrupted prose with an occasional black-and-white drawing or photo, now often have colorful graphics and elaborate transparency overlays.

Like language, visual images are rhetorical. They persuade us in obvious and not-so-obvious ways. And so we need some perspective on visual rhetoric; we need to understand its power and how to use it effectively and responsibly.

UNDERSTANDING VISUAL ARGUMENTS

Visual rhetoric is *the use of images, sometimes coupled with sound or appeals to the other senses, to make an argument or persuade us to act as the image-maker would have us act.* Probably the clearest examples are advertisements and political cartoons, a few of which we will examine shortly. But visual rhetoric is everywhere. We do not ordinarily think, say, of a car's body style as "rhetoric," but clearly it is, because people are persuaded to pay tens of thousands of dollars for the sleekest new body style when they could spend a few thousand for an older car that would get them from home to work or school just as well.

Consider also the billions of dollars we spend on clothes, hairstyles, cosmetics, diets, and exercise programs—all part of the rhetoric of making the right "visual statement" in a world that too often judges us solely by how we look. We spend so much because our self-images depend in part on others' responses to our cars, bodies, offices, homes—to whatever represents "us." No doubt we all want to be appreciated for our true selves, but distinguishing this "inside" from the "outside" we show the world has never been easy. Because we tend to become the image we cultivate, the claim that "image is everything" may not be as superficial as it sounds.

"READING" IMAGES

Rhetorical analysis of visual rhetoric involves examining images to see how they attempt to convince or persuade an audience. Pictures are symbols that must be read, just as language is read. To read an argument made through images, a critic must be able to recognize allusions to popular culture. For example, Americans knew that the white mustaches on the celebrities in the milk commercials referred to the way children drink milk; more recently, the milk mustache symbolizes the ad campaign itself, now part of our culture.

As with inquiry into any argument, we ought to begin with questions about rhetorical context: When was the visual argument created and by whom? To what audience was it originally aimed and with what purpose? Then we can ask what claim a visual argument makes and what reasons it offers in support of that claim. Then, as with verbal texts that make a case, we can examine visual arguments for evidence, assumptions, and bias, and we can ask what values they favor and what the implications of accepting their argument are.

However, many visuals do not even attempt reasoning; they rely instead on emotional appeals. Such appeals are most obvious in advertising, where the aim is to move a target audience to buy a service or product. In many advertisements, especially for products like beer, cigarettes, and perfume, where the differences are subjective, emotional appeal is all there is. Most emotional appeals work by promising to reward our desires for love, status, peace of mind, or escape from everyday responsibilities.

Advertisements also use ethical appeals, associating their claim with values the audience approves of and wants to identify with—such as images that show nature being preserved, races living in harmony, families staying in touch, and people attaining the American dream of upward mobility.

In evaluating the ethics of visual rhetoric, we need to consider whether the argument is at least reasonable: Does the image demonstrate reasoning, or does it oversimplify and mislead? We will want to look at the emotional and ethical appeals to decide if they pander to audience weaknesses and prejudices or manipulate fantasies and fears.

ANALYSIS: FIVE COMMON TYPES OF VISUAL ARGUMENT

In this section, we analyze some visual arguments in various genres: advertisements, editorial cartoons, public sculpture, news photographs, and graphics. We show how "reading" visual texts requires interpretive skills and how interpretive skills, in turn, depend on cultural knowledge.

Advertisements

We begin with a classic ad for Charlie perfume from 1988 that created quite a stir when it first appeared (see Figure C-1 in the color section). As James B. Twitchell noted in his *Twenty Ads That Shook the World*, the shot of a woman giving a man an encouraging fanny pat "subverted sexism, turned it on its head, [and] used it against itself." At first the editors at the *New York Times* "refused to run the ad, saying it was in 'poor taste.'" But the ad proved irresistibly appealing when it appeared in women's magazines. Why did it work so well?

Twitchell argues that "Charlie is not just in charge, she is clearly enjoying dominance."

> She is taller than her partner. . . . Not only does he have part of his anatomy removed from the picture so that the Charlie bottle can be foregrounded, and not only does she have the jaunty scarf and the cascading hair of a free spirit, but she is delivering that most masculine of signifiers, the booty pat. . . . In football especially, the pat signifies comradeship . . . and is applied dominant to submissive. . . . The coach delivers it to a hulking [player] returning to the field of battle. . . . When Charlie bestows it on her gentleman friend . . . , she is harvesting a rich crop of meaning. The tide has turned, and now men are getting their butts slapped, by of all people, women. (170)

It's possible, of course, to read the pat in other ways—for example, as the kind of thing a dominant man might do to a subordinate woman at the office, inappropriate behavior now widely understood as sexual harassment. But no matter how you read it, there's no doubt that the ad tapped into the woman's movement at a time when women routinely endured sexism at work. No wonder that the ad was hugely popular.

The other ads in our color section work in different ways. Try your hand at analyzing their persuasive power.

⊙⊙ FOLLOWING THROUGH

1. Figure C-2 may look like a poster but it is actually a "semi-postal" stamp, so called because a percentage of its cost goes to the cause it advocates. This stamp has raised over $22 million for breast cancer research since it was issued in 1998. What are the sources of its appeal?

2. Figure C-3, from the Southampton Anti-Bias Task Force, depends for full impact on remembering a crayon labeled *flesh* that was the color of the center crayon in the photo. People in their forties and fifties or older remember that crayon. What, then, is the ad's appeal for them? What does it say about skin color to younger people who don't remember the crayon?

3. Figure C-4 is a striking example of the power of photography and probably digital and other ways of enhancing photographs. How might women respond to it? How might men?

4. If Figure C-4 features the art of photography in selling glamour, C-5 is deliberately unglamorous, playing with the stereotype of the computer nerd. How does it work to promote the services of the Geek Squad?

5. Figure C-6, the Adidas ad, ingeniously exploits how the eye can be fooled by what it *expects* to see rather than what is actually there. Did you see the shadow at first simply as the runner's shadow? What made you reevaluate what you were seeing? What's the impact of playing with perception in this case?

6. As a class project, find ads for the same product in magazines that appeal to different market segments, as defined by age, income, sex, ethnicity, and so on. Compare and contrast the ads to see how they are designed to appeal to their target audiences.   •

Editorial Cartoons

Editorial cartoons comment on events and issues in the news. They are funny but offer concise arguments too. Most political cartoons rely on captions and dialogue to make their argument, combining the visual and verbal. Consider the one by Mike Keefe (Figure 4.1, page 65) that comments on the impact of computers.

The cartoon illustrates well how "reading" a visual argument depends on shared cultural knowledge. The image of a thirsty man crawling on hands and knees through a desert stands for anything important that humans lack. The cartoon depicts our common metaphor for the Internet, the "information superhighway," literally. The man has too much information and not enough

Figure C-1

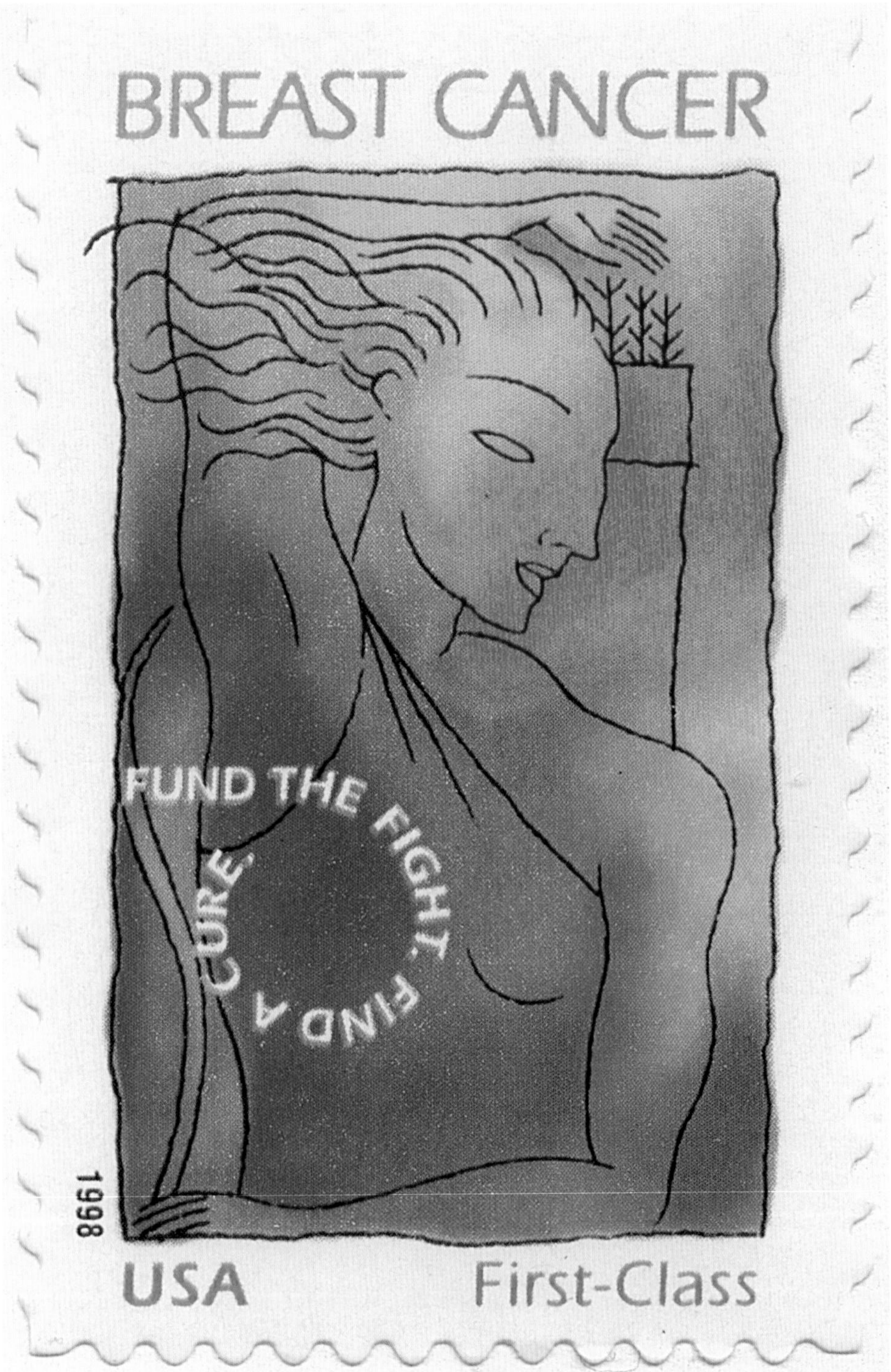

Figure C-2

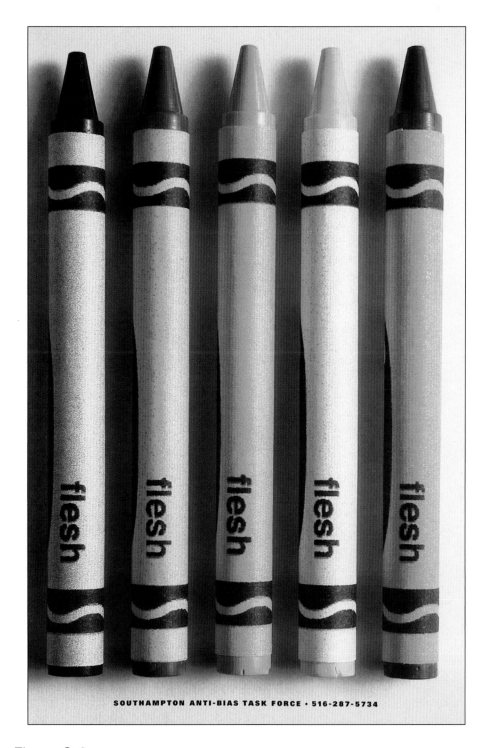

Figure C-3

LOUIS VUITTON

Figure C-4

Figure C-5

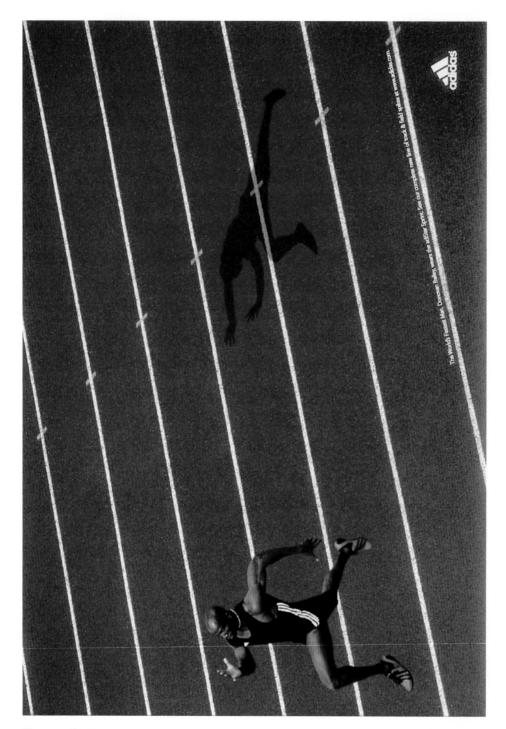

Figure C-6

Figure C-7

Figure C-8

Figure 4.1

Mike Keefe, dePIXion Studios. Reprinted with permission.

wisdom. To read the argument of the cartoon and appreciate its humor, the viewer has to know about the overwhelming glut of information on the Internet, suggested by the size of the letters on the road. The cartoon "argues" that relying on the Internet will deprive a civilization of the wisdom to sustain a good life.

⊙◎ FOLLOWING THROUGH

1. Cartoons probably are most persuasive when they satirize a familiar problem, as in the information superhighway example in Figure 4.1. A similar cartoon is Stuart Carlson's in Figure 4.3 (page 67). However, although most Americans struggle with the Net's information glut, fewer, but still a large percentage, drive gas-guzzling vehicles. If you don't, how do you react to Carlson's cartoon? Why do you react the way you do? If you drive a gas guzzler or would like to, is the cartoon still amusing? Why or why not?

2. Some cartoons are "factional," created by one side in a controversy to ridicule the position of the other side. Contrasting examples appear in Figure 4.2 (page 66). Clearly, neither cartoon will persuade anyone whose position is held up to ridicule. Yet, factional cartoons are common. They must serve some purpose. How do you think they work?

3. Find a recent editorial cartoon on an issue prominent in the news. Bring it to class and be prepared to explain its persuasive tactics. Consider also the fairness of the cartoon. Does the cartoon minimize the complexity of the issue it addresses?

Jim McCloskey, *The News Leader*, Staunton, Virginia. Reprinted by permission.

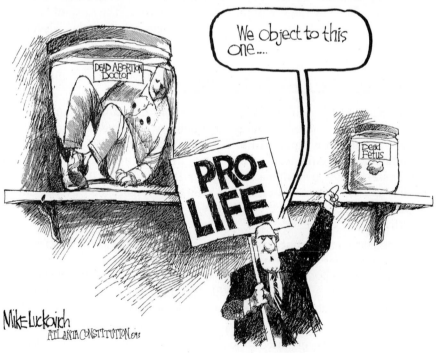

By permission of Mike Luckovich and Creators Syndicate, Inc.

Figure 4.2

CARLSON © 2006 Milwaukee Sentinel. Reprinted with permission of Universal Press Syndicate. All rights reserved.

Figure 4.3

Public Sculpture

Public sculptures, such as war memorials, aim to teach an audience about a nation's past and to honor its values. An example that can be read as an argument is the Marine Corps Memorial, erected in 1954 on the Mall in Washington, D.C. (see Figure 4.4, page 68). It honors all Marines who have given their lives by depicting one specific act of bravery, the planting of the American flag on Iwo Jima, a Pacific island captured from the Japanese in 1945. The claim the sculpture makes is clear: Honor your country. The image of the soldiers straining every muscle gives the reason: These men made extreme sacrifices to preserve the values symbolized by this flag. The sculpture also communicates through details like the wind-whipped flag.

The Iwo Jima sculpture is traditional, glorifying victory on enemy soil. Compare it with the Vietnam War Memorial, dedicated in Washington, D.C., in November 1982. Maya Lin designed what we now call "the Wall" while an undergraduate student at Yale. Her design was controversial because it was so unconventional (see Figures 4.5 and 4.6, page 69). and anti-war. Its black granite slates are etched with the names of war dead; it honors individuals who died in a war that tore the nation apart.

Figure 4.4

◎◎ FOLLOWING THROUGH

1. Because it does not portray a realistic scene as the Iwo Jima Memorial does, the Wall invites interpretation and analysis. If you have visited it, try to recall your reaction. What details led to your interpretation? Could you characterize the Wall as having logical, ethical, and emotional appeals?

2. Find public sculpture or monuments to visit and analyze. Alone or with some classmates, take notes and photographs. Then develop your interpretation of the sculpture's argument, specifying how visual details contribute to the case, and present your analysis to the class. Compare your interpretation with those of your classmates.   •

News Photographs

While some news photographs may seem merely to record an event, the camera is not objective. The photographer makes many decisions—whether to snap a picture, when to snap it, what to include and exclude from the image—and decisions about light, depth of field, and so on. Figure 4.7 (page 70), a photograph that appeared in the *New York Times*, shows a scene photographer Bruce Young encountered covering a snowstorm that hit Washington, D.C., in January 1994. The storm was severe enough to shut down the city and most government offices. Without the caption supplied by the

Figure 4.5

Figure 4.6

Figure 4.7

New York Times, readers might not recognize the objects in the foreground as human beings, homeless people huddled on benches, covered by undisturbed snow.

The picture depicts homelessness in America as a national disgrace. The White House in the background is our nation's "home," a grand and lavishly decorated residence symbolic of national wealth. In the foreground, the homeless people look like bags of garbage, marring the picture of the snow-covered landscape. No blame attaches to the homeless for their condition; they are too pathetic under their blankets of snow. The picture shows the homeless as a fact of life in our cities, challenging the idealized image of our nation.

FOLLOWING THROUGH

1. Figure C-7 in the color section depicts the family of Sgt. Jose M. Velez watching over his casket. Sgt. Velez was killed in Iraq. Any thoughtful response to such a photo has to be complex. How would you describe your response? To what extent is your view of the war in Iraq relevant?

2. Figure C-8 is a shot of the Tour de France, the annual bicycling race that Lance Armstrong made almost as big an event in the United States as it is in Europe. What impression does the photo convey? What details in the photo convey the impression?

3. The two news photos in Figure 4.8 (page 72) were both included in a collection of shots *Time* magazine published on the Net as "The Best Photos of the Year 2006." The top one had the title "Sweet Home, New Orleans" and depicts people in a lounge during Mardi Gras, a sign that normal life was returning to the city after Hurricane Katrina's devastation. The bottom one captures refugees in Chad, fleeing from Arab militias, one of several murderous conflicts going on in Africa and not getting much attention in the United States. What details make the photos so effective? Why are such photos almost indispensable to news stories? Put together, as they are in Figure 4.8, what thoughts and feelings do these photographs stimulate in you?

4. In a recent newspaper or news magazine, look for photos you think are effective when combined with a story about a controversial issue. What perspective or point of view do the pictures represent? How do you read their composition, including camera angle, light conditions, foreground and background, and so on?

 www.mhhe.com/**crusius** To find more photographs to analyze, check out:
Writing > Visual Rhetoric Tutorial > Catalyst Image Bank

Graphics

Visual supplements to a longer text such as an essay, article, or manual are known as **graphics.** Most graphics fall into one of the following categories:

 www.mhhe.com/**crusius**

If you want information on using PowerPoint to create graphics, go to

Writing > PowerPoint Tutorial

> Tables and charts (typically an arrangement of data in columns and rows that summarizes the results of research)
>
> Graphs (including bar, line, and pie graphs)
>
> Photographs
>
> Drawings (including maps and cartoons)

Although charts and tables are not images, they present data in visual form. Tables display information economically in one place so that readers can assess it as they read and find it easily afterward if they want to refer to it again. Consider Figure 4.9 (page 73), which combines a table with bar graphs. It comes from a study of poverty in the United States. Note how much information is packed into this single visual and how easy it is to read, moving top to bottom and left to right through the categories. Consider how many long and boring paragraphs it would take to say the same thing in prose.

Graphs are usually no more than tables transformed into visuals we can interpret more easily. Bar graphs are best at showing comparisons at some single point in time. In contrast, line graphs reveal trends—for example, the performance of the stock market. Pie graphs highlight relative proportions well. When newspapers want to show us how the federal budget is spent,

Figure 4.8

for example, they typically use pie graphs with the pieces labeled in some way to represent categories such as national defense, welfare, and entitlement programs. What gets the biggest pieces of the pie becomes *instantly clear* and *easy to remember*—the two major purposes of all graphs. Graphs don't make arguments, but they deliver evidence powerfully.

Figure 4.9

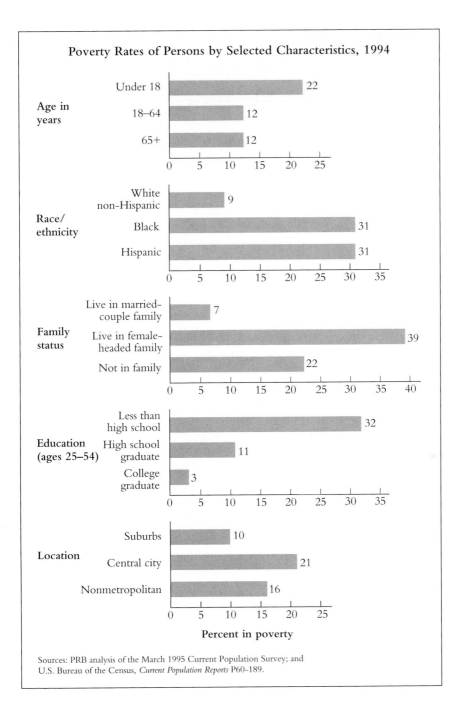

Poverty Rates of Persons by Selected Characteristics, 1994

Percent in poverty

Sources: PRB analysis of the March 1995 Current Population Survey; and U.S. Bureau of the Census, *Current Population Reports* P60-189.

www.mhhe.com/**crusius**   For more help with visual design, go to:

Writing > Visual Rhetoric Tutorial > Visualizing Data

and

Writing > Visual Rhetoric Tutorial > Designing Documents

As graphics, photographs represent people, objects, and scenes realistically. For instance, owner's manuals for cars often have a shot of the engine compartment that shows where fluid reservoirs are located. Clearly, such photos serve highly practical purposes, such as helping us locate the dipstick. But they're also used, for example, in biographies; we get a better sense of, say, Abraham Lincoln's life and times when pictures of him, his family, his home, and so on are included. But photographs can do much more than inform. They can be highly dramatic and powerfully emotional in ways that only the best writers can manage with prose. Photos are often potent persuaders.

Photographs, however, are not analytical—by their nature, they give us the surface, only what the camera can "see." A different type of graphic, the drawing, is preferable when we want to depict how something is put together or structured. For instance, instructions for assembling and installing a ceiling fan or a light fixture usually have many diagrams—a large one showing how all the parts fit together and smaller ones that depict steps in the process in more detail. Corporate publications often include diagrams of the company's organizational hierarchy. Scientific articles and textbooks are full of drawings or illustrations created with computer graphics; science writers want us to understand structures, particularly internal structures, impossible to capture on film. For example, our sense of DNA's double-helical structure comes entirely from diagrams.

The following article illustrates how a variety of graphics can contribute to the effectiveness of a written text.

The Rise of Renewable Energy

DANIEL M. KAMMEN

This article appeared in the September 2006 issue of *Scientific American*. Daniel Kammen is Distinguished Professor of Energy at the University of California, Berkeley, where he founded and directs the Renewable and Appropriate Energy Laboratory.

   Renewable energy refers to any source of power that does not depend on the limited supply of fossil fuels, such as oil or coal, and produces relatively little or none of the greenhouse gases that contribute significantly to global warming. There are many renewable energy sources. Kammen discusses the potential of solar power, wind power, and biofuels such as ethanol.

No plan to substantially reduce greenhouse gas emissions can succeed through increases in energy efficiency alone. Because economic growth continues to boost the demand for energy—more coal for powering new factories, more oil for fueling new cars, more natural gas for heating new cars, more natural gas for heating new homes—carbon emissions will keep climbing despite the introduction of more energy-efficient vehicles, buildings and appliances. To counter the alarming trend of global warming, the U.S. and other countries must make a major commitment to developing renewable energy sources that generate little or no carbon.

Renewable energy technologies were suddenly and briefly fashionable three decades ago in response to the oil embargoes of the 1970s, but the interest and support were not sustained. In recent years, however, dramatic improvements in the performance and affordability of solar cells, wind turbines and biofuels—ethanol and other fuels derived from plants—have paved the way for mass commercialization. In addition to their environmental benefits, renewable sources promise to enhance America's energy security by reducing the country's reliance on fossil fuels from other nations. What is more, high and wildly fluctuating prices for oil and natural gas have made renewable alternatives more appealing.

We are now in an era where the opportunities for renewable energy are unprecedented, making this the ideal time to advance clean power for decades to come. But the endeavor will require a long-term investment of scientific, economic and political resources. Policymakers and ordinary citizens must demand action and challenge one another to hasten the transition.

LET THE SUN SHINE

Solar cells, also known as photovoltaics, use semiconductor materials to convert sunlight into electric current. They now provide just a tiny slice of the world's electricity: their global generating capacity of 5,000 megawatts (MW) is only 0.15 percent of the total generating capacity from all sources. Yet sunlight could potentially supply 5,000 times as much energy as the world currently consumes. And thanks to technology improvements, cost declines and favorable policies in many states and nations, the annual production of photovoltaics has increased by more than 25 percent a year for the past decade and by a remarkable 45 percent in 2005. The cells manufactured last year added 1,727 MW to worldwide generating capacity, with 833 MW made in Japan, 353 MW in Germany and 153 MW in the U.S.

Solar cells can now be made from a range of materials, from the traditional 5 multicrystalline silicon wafers that still dominate the market to thin-film silicon cells and devices composed of plastic or organic semiconductors. Thin-film photovoltaics are cheaper to produce than crystalline silicon cells but are also less efficient at turning light into power. In laboratory tests, crystalline cells have achieved efficiencies of 30 percent or more; current commercial cells of this type range from 15 to 20 percent. Both laboratory and commercial efficiencies for all kinds of solar cells have risen steadily in recent years, indicating that an expansion of research efforts would further enhance the performance of solar cells on the market.

Solar photovoltaics are particularly easy to use because they can be installed in so many places—on the roofs or walls of homes and office buildings, in vast

A world of clean energy could rely on wind turbines and solar cells to generate its electricity and biofuels derived from switchgrass and other plants to power its vehicles.

KENN BROWN

arrays in the desert, even sewn into clothing to power portable electronic devices. The state of California has joined Japan and Germany in leading a global push for solar installations; the "Million Solar Roof" commitment is intended to create 3,000 MW of new generating capacity in the state by 2018. Studies done by my research group, the Renewable and Appropriate Energy Laboratory at the University of California, Berkeley, show that annual production of solar photovoltaics in the U.S. alone could grow to 10,000 MW in just 20 years if current trends continue.

The biggest challenge will be lowering the price of the photovoltaics, which are now relatively expensive to manufacture. Electricity produced by crystalline cells has a total cost of 20 to 25 cents per kilowatt-hour, compared with four to six cents for coal-fired electricity, five to seven cents for power produced by burning natural gas, and six to nine cents for biomass power plants. (The cost of nuclear power is harder to pin down because experts disagree on which expenses to include in the analysis; the estimated range is two to 12 cents per kilowatt-hour.) Fortunately, the prices of solar cells have fallen consistently over the past decade, largely because of improve-

ments in manufacturing processes. In Japan, where 290 MW of solar generating capacity were added in 2005 and an even larger amount was exported, the cost of photovoltaics has declined 8 percent a year; in California, where 50 MW of solar power were installed in 2005, costs have dropped 5 percent annually.

Surprisingly, Kenya is the global leader in the number of solar power systems installed per capita (but not the number of watts added). More than 30,000 very small solar panels, each producing only 12 to 30 watts, are sold in that country annually. For an investment of as little as $100 for the panel and wiring, the system can be used to charge a car battery, which can then provide enough power to run a fluorescent lamp or a small black-and-white television for a few hours a day. More Kenyans adopt solar power every year than make connections to the country's electric grid. The panels typically use solar cells made of amorphous silicon; although these photovoltaics are only half as efficient as crystalline cells, their cost is so much lower (by a factor of at least four) that they are more affordable and useful for the two billion people worldwide who currently have no access to electricity. Sales of

GROWING FAST, BUT STILL A SLIVER

Solar cells, wind power and biofuels are rapidly gaining traction in the energy markets, but they remain marginal providers compared with fossil-fuel sources such as coal, natural gas and oil.

THE RENEWABLE BOOM

Since 2000 the commercialization of renewable energy sources has accelerated dramatically. The annual global production of solar cells, also known as photovoltaics, jumped 45 percent in 2005. The construction of new wind farms, particularly in Europe, has boosted the worldwide generating capacity of wind power 10-fold over the past decade. And the production of ethanol, the most common biofuel, soared to 36.5 billion liters last year, with the lion's share distilled from American-grown corn.

Photovoltaic Production

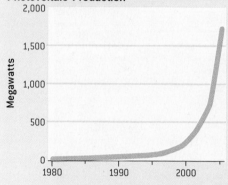

Wind Energy Generating Capacity

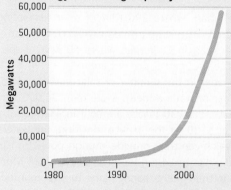

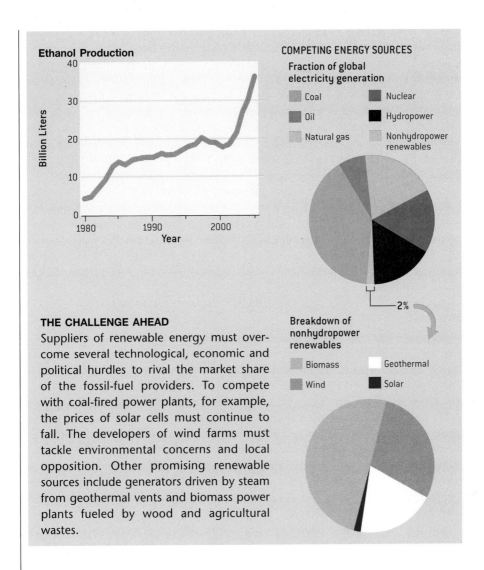

Ethanol Production

Billion Liters

COMPETING ENERGY SOURCES

Fraction of global
electricity generation

- Coal
- Oil
- Natural gas
- Nuclear
- Hydropower
- Nonhydropower renewables

2%

THE CHALLENGE AHEAD

Suppliers of renewable energy must over-come several technological, economic and political hurdles to rival the market share of the fossil-fuel providers. To compete with coal-fired power plants, for example, the prices of solar cells must continue to fall. The developers of wind farms must tackle environmental concerns and local opposition. Other promising renewable sources include generators driven by steam from geothermal vents and biomass power plants fueled by wood and agricultural wastes.

Breakdown of
nonhydropower
renewables

- Biomass
- Wind
- Geothermal
- Solar

small solar power systems are booming in other African nations as well, and advances in low-cost photovoltaic manufacturing could accelerate this trend.

Furthermore, photovoltaics are not the only fast-growing form of solar power. Solar-thermal systems, which collect sunlight to generate heat, are also undergoing a resurgence. These systems have long been used to provide hot water for homes or factories, but they can also produce electricity without the need for expensive solar cells. In one design, for example, mirrors focus light on a Stirling engine, a high-efficiency device containing a working fluid that circulates between hot and cold chambers. The fluid expands as the sunlight heats it, pushing a piston that, in turn, drives a turbine.

In the fall of 2005 a Phoenix company called Stirling Energy Systems announced 10 that it was planning to build two large solar-thermal power plants in southern California. The company signed a 20-year power purchase agreement with Southern California Edison, which will buy the electricity from a 500-MW solar plant to be constructed in the Mojave Desert. Stretching across 4,500 acres, the facility will include 20,000 curved dish mirrors, each concentrating light on a Stirling engine about the size of an oil barrel. The plant is expected to begin operating in 2009 and could later be expanded to 850 MW. Stirling Energy Systems also signed a 20-year contract with San Diego Gas & Electric to build a 300-MW, 12,000-dish plant in the Imperial Valley. This facility could eventually be upgraded to 900 MW.

The financial details of the two California projects have not been made public, but electricity produced by present solar-thermal technologies costs between five and 13 cents per kilowatt-hour, with dish-mirror systems at the upper end of that range. Because the projects involve highly reliable technologies and mass production, however, the generation expenses are expected to ultimately drop closer to four to six cents per kilowatt-hour—that is, competitive with the current price of coal-fired power.

BLOWING IN THE WIND

Wind power has been growing at a pace rivaling that of the solar industry. The worldwide generating capacity of wind turbines has increased more than 25 percent a year, on average, for the past decade, reaching nearly 60,000 MW in 2005. The growth has been nothing short of explosive in Europe—between 1994 and 2005, the installed wind power capacity in European Union nations jumped from 1,700 to 40,000 MW. Germany alone has more than 18,000 MW of capacity thanks to an aggressive construction program. The northern German state of Schleswig-Holstein currently meets one quarter of its annual electricity demand with more than 2,400 wind turbines, and in certain months wind power provides more than half the state's electricity. In addition, Spain has 10,000 MW of wind capacity, Denmark has 3,000 MW, and Great Britain, the Netherlands, Italy and Portugal each have more than 1,000 MW.

In the U.S. the wind power industry has accelerated dramatically in the past five years, with total generating capacity leaping 36 percent to 9,100 MW in 2005. Although wind turbines now produce only 0.5 percent of the nation's electricity, the potential for expansion is enormous, especially in the windy Great Plains states. (North Dakota, for example, has greater wind energy resources than Germany, but only 98 MW of generating capacity is installed there.) If the U.S. constructed enough wind farms to fully tap these resources, the turbines could generate as much as 11 trillion kilowatt-hours of electricity, or nearly three times the total amount produced from all energy sources in the nation last year. The wind industry has developed increasingly large and efficient turbines, each capable of yielding 4 to 6 MW. And in many locations, wind power is the cheapest form of new electricity, with costs ranging from four to seven cents per kilowatt-hour.

The growth of new wind farms in the U.S. has been spurred by a production tax credit that provides a modest subsidy equivalent to 1.9 cents per kilowatt-hour, enabling wind turbines to compete with coal-fired plants. Unfortunately, Congress has repeatedly threatened to eliminate the tax credit. Instead of instituting a long-term subsidy for wind power, the lawmakers have extended the tax credit on a year-to-year basis, and the continual uncertainty has slowed investment in wind farms. Congress is also threatening to derail a proposed 130-turbine farm off the coast of Massachusetts that would provide 468 MW of generating capacity, enough to power most of Cape Cod, Martha's Vineyard and Nantucket.

The reservations about wind power come partly from utility companies that 15 are reluctant to embrace the new technology and partly from so-called NIMBY-ism. ("NIMBY" is an acronym for Not in My Backyard.) Although local concerns over how wind turbines will affect landscape views may have some merit, they must be balanced against the social costs of the alternatives. Because society's energy needs are growing relentlessly, rejecting wind farms often means requiring the construction or expansion of fossil fuel–burning power plants that will have far more devastating environmental effects.

GREEN FUELS

Researchers are also pressing ahead with the development of biofuels that could replace at least a portion of the oil currently consumed by motor vehicles. The most common biofuel by far in the U.S. is ethanol, which is typically made from corn and blended with gasoline. The manufacturers of ethanol benefit from a substantial tax credit: with the help of the $2-billion annual subsidy, they sold more than 16 billion liters of ethanol in 2005 (almost 3 percent of all automobile fuel by volume), and production is expected to rise 50 percent by 2007. Some policymakers have questioned the wisdom of the subsidy, pointing to studies showing that it takes more energy to harvest the corn and refine the ethanol than the fuel can deliver to combustion engines. In a recent analysis, though, my colleagues and I discovered that some of these studies did not properly account for the energy content of the by-products manufactured along with the ethanol. When all the inputs and outputs were correctly factored in, we found that ethanol has a positive net energy of almost five megajoules per liter.

We also found, however, that ethanol's impact on greenhouse gas emissions is more ambiguous. Our best estimates indicate that substituting corn-based ethanol for gasoline reduces greenhouse gas emissions by 18 percent, but the analysis is hampered by large uncertainties regarding certain agricultural practices, particularly the environmental costs of fertilizers. If we use different assumptions about these practices, the results of switching to ethanol range from a 36 percent drop in emissions to a 29 percent increase. Although corn-based ethanol may help the U.S. reduce its reliance on foreign oil, it will probably not do much to slow global warming unless the production of the biofuel becomes cleaner.

But the calculations change substantially when the ethanol is made from cellulosic sources: woody plants such as switch-grass or poplar. Whereas most makers of corn-based ethanol burn fossil fuels to provide the heat for fermentation, the producers of cellulosic ethanol burn lignin—an unfermentable part of the organic material—to heat the plant sugars. Burning lignin does not add any greenhouse

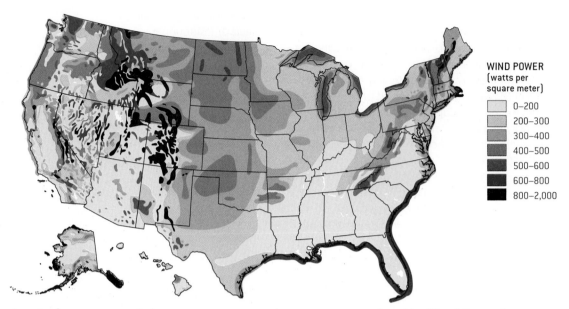

WIND POWER
(watts per
square meter)

	0–200
	200–300
	300–400
	400–500
	500–600
	600–800
	800–2,000

America has enormous wind energy resources, enough to generate as much as 11 trillion kilowatt-hours of electricity each year. Some of the best locations for wind turbines are the Great Plains states, the Great Lakes and the mountain ridges of the Rockies and the Appalachians.

gases to the atmosphere, because the emissions are offset by the carbon dioxide absorbed during the growth of the plants used to make the ethanol. As a result, substituting cellulosic ethanol for gasoline can slash greenhouse gas emissions by 90 percent or more.

Another promising biofuel is so-called green diesel. Researchers have produced this fuel by first gasifying biomass—heating organic materials enough that they release hydrogen and carbon monoxide—and then converting these compounds into long-chain hydrocarbons using the Fischer-Tropsch process. (During World War II, German engineers employed these chemical reactions to make synthetic motor fuels out of coal.) The result would be an economically competitive liquid fuel for motor vehicles that would add virtually no greenhouse gases to the atmosphere. Oil giant Royal Dutch/Shell is currently investigating the technology.

THE NEED FOR R&D

Each of these renewable sources is now at or near a tipping point, the crucial stage 20 when investment and innovation, as well as market access, could enable these attractive but generally marginal providers to become major contributors to regional and global energy supplies. At the same time, aggressive policies designed to open markets for renewables are taking hold at city, state and federal levels around the world. Governments have adopted these policies for a wide variety of reasons: to promote market diversity or energy security, to bolster industries and jobs, and to protect the environment on both the local and global scales. In the U.S. more than

20 states have adopted standards setting a minimum for the fraction of electricity that must be supplied with renewable sources. Germany plans to generate 20 percent of its electricity from renewables by 2020, and Sweden intends to give up fossil fuels entirely.

Even President George W. Bush said, in his now famous State of the Union address this past January, that the U.S. is "addicted to oil." And although Bush did not make the link to global warming, nearly all scientists agree that humanity's addiction to fossil fuels is disrupting the earth's climate. The time for action is now, and at last the tools exist to alter energy production and consumption in ways that simultaneously benefit the economy and the environment. Over the past 25 years, however, the public and private funding of research and development in the energy sector has withered. Between 1980 and 2005 the fraction of all U.S. R&D spending devoted to energy declined from 10 to 2 percent. Annual public R&D funding for energy sank from $8 billion to $3 billion (in 2002 dollars); private R&D plummeted from $4 billion to $1 billion (see box, "R&D Is key").

To put these declines in perspective, consider that in the early 1980s energy companies were investing more in R&D than were drug companies, whereas today investment by energy firms is an order of magnitude lower. Total private R&D funding for the entire energy sector is less than that of a single large biotech company. (Amgen, for example, had R&D expenses of $2.3 billion in 2005.) And as R&D spending dwindles, so does innovation. For instance, as R&D funding for photovoltaics and wind power has slipped over the past quarter of a century, the number of successful patent applications in these fields has fallen accordingly. The lack of attention to long-term research and planning has significantly weakened our nation's ability to respond to the challenges of climate change and disruptions in energy supplies.

Calls for major new commitments to energy R&D have become common. A 1997 study by the President's Committee of Advisors on Science and Technology and a 2004 report by the bipartisan National Commission on Energy Policy both recommended that the federal government double its R&D spending on energy. But would such an expansion be enough? Probably not. Based on assessments of the cost to stabilize the amount of carbon dioxide in the atmosphere and other studies that estimate the success of energy R&D programs and the resulting savings from the technologies that would emerge, my research group has calculated that public funding of $15 billion to $30 billion a year would be required—a fivefold to 10-fold increase over current levels.

Greg F. Nemet, a doctoral student in my laboratory, and I found that an increase of this magnitude would be roughly comparable to those that occurred during previous federal R&D initiatives such as the Manhattan Project and the Apollo program, each of which produced demonstrable economic benefits in addition to meeting its objectives. American energy companies could also boost their R&D spending by a factor of 10, and it would still be below the average for U.S. industry overall. Although government funding is essential to supporting early-stage technologies, private-sector R&D is the key to winnowing the best ideas and reducing the barriers to commercialization.

R&D IS KEY

Spending on research and development in the U.S. energy sector has fallen steadily since its peak in 1980. Studies of patent activity suggest that the drop in funding has slowed the development of renewable energy technologies. For example, the number of successful patent applications in photovoltaics and wind power has plummeted as R&D spending in these fields has declined.

U.S. R&D SPENDING IN THE ENERGY SECTOR

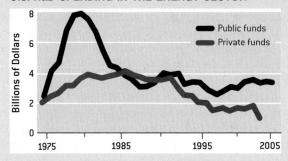

LAGGING INNOVATION IN PHOTOVOLTAICS . . .

. . . AND IN WIND POWER

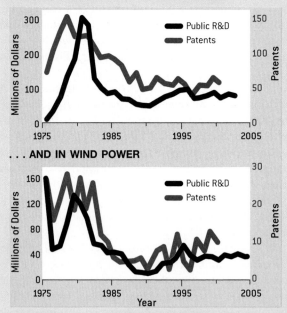

Spending amounts are expressed in 2002 dollars to adjust for inflation.

Raising R&D spending, though, is not the only way to make clean energy a 25 national priority. Educators at all grade levels, from kindergarten to college, can stimulate public interest and activism by teaching how energy use and production affect the social and natural environment. Nonprofit organizations can establish a series of contests that would reward the first company or private group to achieve a challenging and worthwhile energy goal, such as constructing a building or appliance that can generate its own power or developing a commercial vehicle that can go 200 miles on a single gallon of fuel. The contests could be modeled after the Ashoka awards for pioneers in public policy and the Ansari X Prize for the developers of space vehicles. Scientists and entrepreneurs should also focus on finding clean, affordable ways to meet the energy needs of people in the developing world. My colleagues and I, for instance, recently detailed the environmental benefits of improving cooking stoves in Africa.

But perhaps the most important step toward creating a sustainable energy economy is to institute market-based schemes to make the prices of carbon fuels reflect their social cost. The use of coal, oil and natural gas imposes a huge collective toll on society, in the form of health care expenditures for ailments caused by air pollution, military spending to secure oil supplies, environmental damage from mining operations, and the potentially devastating economic impacts of global warming. A fee on carbon emissions would provide a simple, logical and transparent method to reward renewable, clean energy sources over those that harm the economy and the environment. The tax revenues could pay for some of the social costs of carbon emissions, and a portion could be designated to compensate low-income families who spend a larger share of their income on energy. Furthermore, the carbon fee could be combined with a cap-and-trade program that would set limits on carbon emissions but also allow the cleanest energy suppliers to sell permits to their dirtier competitors. The federal government has used such programs with great success to curb other pollutants, and several northeastern states are already experimenting with greenhouse gas emissions trading.

Best of all, these steps would give energy companies an enormous financial incentive to advance the development and commercialization of renewable energy sources. In essence, the U.S. has the opportunity to foster an entirely new industry. The threat of climate change can be a rallying cry for a clean-technology revolution that would strengthen the country's manufacturing base, create thousands of jobs and alleviate our international trade deficits—instead of importing foreign oil, we can export high-efficiency vehicles, appliances, wind turbines and photovoltaics. This transformation can turn the nation's energy sector into something that was once deemed impossible: a vibrant, environmentally sustainable engine of growth.

Understanding Kammen's Graphics

The article certainly informs, and the graphics present information economically, clearly, and memorably. However, Kammen's central purpose is to convince us that renewable energy has enormous potential and needs significantly more public attention, research investment, and commercial development than it is currently getting. "Let's commit ourselves to renewable energy" is its central message, and so this apparently informative article is actually an argument. The graphics, therefore, function mainly as evidence to back up Kammen's main contentions. Let's examine the first two and reserve the others for your own analysis.

The opening drawing, an example of what's called an "artist's conception," depicts a green world, powered entirely by renewables, where agriculture and city exist side by side. The combine in the field runs on electricity generated by huge solar panels, perhaps using biofuels on days without sun, while wind (note the turbines in the background) and sun (note the solar panels on the roof of the houses in the right foreground) work together to provide all the power needed by the city. In the original color drawing, the sky is deep blue merging into purple, suggesting lack of pollution, and the fields are various shades of green and gold, with obvious implications.

"Why an artist's conception?" you might ask. The obvious answer, of course, is no such communities exist today to photograph. The article needs a way to stimulate our imagination, to help us envision a world that could be, where energy is cheap, abundant, inexhaustible, and, most of all, clean. Caught as we are in a world that burns oil, natural gas, and coal to supply nearly all energy, we have trouble conceiving a world powered by renewables. Anything we can't conceive, we can't aspire to—hence the importance of establishing this vision of the future.

The drawing, then, is persuasive: "Just imagine the possibilities" is the message. The box titled "Growing Fast . . ." (pages 78–79), in contrast, gives us the facts. Solar, wind, and ethanol production are all sharply up worldwide, as the three line graphs show, but the top pie graph puts the upswing in perspective—only a tiny sliver, 2%, of the world's power comes currently from renewables. The pie graph on the bottom depicts the relative proportions of green energy in use, showing us, among other things, that the enormous potential of wind and solar power has yet to be aggressively exploited. Finally, the prose combined with the visuals summarizes knowledge that the graphs and photos couldn't supply, making the box a fine example of combining visuals with words.

The "Growing Fast . . ." box packs a lot of information into an attractive space; it would take many pages to describe it in prose, boring pages of data that would not have half the impact of the graphics. That's part of why it's persuasive—we can see the big picture without trudging through many pages of text. But to appreciate its full persuasive power, the implications of the box and the opening drawing must be combined. The drawing seems almost futuristic, as if we will wait a long time to see anything like it, while the box shows us that it's all tantalizingly within reach. We just have to do more with what we've got. And so, in sum, the message is simple and upbeat: "We can do it."

◎◎ FOLLOWING THROUGH

1. Graphics, we must always remember, *supplement* texts. Reread the section "Blowing in the Wind," an allusion to a famous song by Bob Dylan, and then examine the map of the United States (page 82), which depicts the 11 trillion kilowatt-hours of wind energy that could be generated in the United States each year. What does text and graphic working together "say"?

2. We see what could happen in the map—wind power harnessed to full potential. And so we ask, Why not? The box "R&D Is Key" (page 84) tells us what the main problem is—not nearly enough R&D. The problem is not putting enough money in research and scientific innovation. We're not going to get there if we don't. Work backwards from this box: How do all the graphics link to one another to answer closely related questions? How much of Kammen's case for renewables is made in the graphics? If we had only the text without the graphics, how much persuasive power would be lost?

3. To see the potential for adding graphics in your own writing, bring a recent paper you wrote to class. If you didn't use graphics, consider whether the paper can be improved with graphic support. If so, given your audience and purposes, what graphic types would you use and why? If you did use graphics, be prepared to discuss them—what you did and why, and how you went about securing or creating the visuals. If you now see ways to improve them, discuss what you would do as well.   •

WRITING ASSIGNMENTS

Assignment 1: Analyzing an Advertisement or Editorial Cartoon

Choose an ad or cartoon from a current magazine or newspaper. First, inquire into its rhetorical context: What situation prompted its creation? What purpose does it aim to achieve? Where did it originally appear? Who is its intended audience? What would they know or believe about the product or issue? Then inquire into the argument being made. To do this, you should consult the questions for inquiry on pages 181–182 to the extent that they apply to visual rhetoric. You should also consider the following points: What visual metaphors or allusions appear? What prior cultural knowledge and experiences would the audience need to "read" the image? Consider how the visual argument might limit the scope of the issue or how it might play to the audience's biases, stereotypes, or fears. After thorough inquiry, reach some conclusion about the effectiveness and ethics of your ad or cartoon. Write your conclusion as a thesis or claim. Use your analysis to convince, supporting it with evidence gathered during inquiry.

Analysis of Visual Rhetoric

The following student essay is an example of Assignment 1. Before you begin your own essay, read it and discuss the conclusions reached about an advertisement for Eagle Brand condensed milk. We were unable to obtain permission to reprint the advertisement under discussion, but the descriptions of it should make the analysis easy to follow.

A Mother's Treat

Kelly Williams

Advertisements are effective only if they connect with their audiences. Advertisers study the group of people they hope to reach and know what the group values and what images they have of themselves. Often these images come from social expectations that tell businessmen, mothers, fathers, teens that they should look or act a certain way. Most people adhere to the norms because they give social status. Advertisers tend to look to these norms as a way to sell their products. For example, an ad depicts a man in an expensive suit driving a luxury car, and readers assume he is a lawyer, physician, or business executive. Such people will buy this car because they associate it with the status they want to project. Likewise, some advertisements manipulate women with children by associating a product with the ideal maternal image.

An advertisement for Eagle Brand condensed milk typifies this effort. The advertisement appeared in magazines aimed at homemakers and in *People* magazine's "Best and Worst Dressed" issue of September 1998. The readers are predominantly young women; those with children may be second-income producers or single mothers. They are struggling to raise a family and have many demands on their time. They feel enormous pressure to fulfill ideal work and domestic roles.

The advertisement creates a strong connection with a maternal audience. The black-and-white photograph depicts a young girl about kindergarten age. The little girl's facial expression connotes hesitation and sadness. In the background is a school yard. Other children are walking toward the school, their heads facing down, creating a feeling of gloom. All readers will recognize the situation. The little girl is about to attend her first day of school. One could easily guess that she is looking back at her mother with a sense of abandonment, pleading for support.

The wording of the text adds some comic relief. The ad is not intended to make the readers sad. The words seem to come from the mind of the child's mother. "For not insisting on bunny slippers for shoes, for leaving Blankie behind, for actually getting out of the car. . . ." These words show that the mother is a good mother, very empathetic. Even the print type is part of the marketing strategy. It mimics a "proper" mother's handwriting. There are no sharp edges, implying softness and gentleness.

The intent is to persuade mothers that if they buy Eagle   5
Brand milk and make the chocolate bar treat, they will be good mothers like the speaker in the ad. It tells women that cooking such treats helps alleviate stressful situations in everyday family life. The little girl reminds mothers of their duty to comfort their kids. She evokes the "feminine" qualities of compassion, empathy, and protectiveness.

The ad also suggests that good mothers reward good behavior. As the ad says, "It's time for a treat." But good mothers would also know that "Welcome Home Chocolate Bars" are rich, so this mother has to say, "I'll risk spoiling your dinner." The invisible mother in the ad is ideal because she does care about her child's nutrition, but more about the emotional state of her child.

In many ways this ad is unethical. While the ad looks harmless and cute, it actually reinforces social pressures on women to be "perfect" mothers. If you don't bake a treat to welcome your child back home after school, you are failing as a mother. The recipe includes preparation time, showing that the treat can be made with minimal effort. It gives mothers no excuse for not making it. Moreover, the advertisement obviously exploits children to sell their product.

Desserts do not have much nutritional value. It would be hard to make a logical case for Welcome Home Bars, so Eagle Brand appeals to emotion. There's nothing wrong with a treat once in a while, but it is wrong to use guilt and social pressure to persuade mothers to buy a product.

Assignment 2: Analyzing and Creating Posters or Flyers

As a class project, collect copies of posters or flyers you find around your campus. It's true that information in our culture is plentiful and cheap but attention is at a premium. Creators of posters and flyers must compete not only with each other but with all other visual sources of information to catch and keep our attention. How well do the posters and flyers your class found work? Why do some catch and hold attention better than others?

Create a poster or flyer to publicize an event, an organization, a student government election, or anything else relevant to your campus life. Use the best posters and flyers you found as a model, but don't be reluctant to use color, type sizes, images, and so on in your own way.

Assignment 3: Using Visual Rhetoric to Promote Your School

Colleges and universities compete fiercely for students and are therefore as concerned about their image as any corporation or politician. As a class project, collect images your school uses to promote itself, including brochures for prospective students, catalogs, class lists, and Web home pages. Choose three or four of the best ones, and in class discussions analyze them. Then, working in groups of three or four students or individually, do one or all of the following:

1. Find an aspect of your college or university overlooked in the publications that you believe is a strong selling point. Employing photographs, drawings, paintings, or some other visual medium, create an image appropriate for one of the school publications. Compose an appealing text to go with it. Then, in a page or two, explain why you think your promotional image would work well.

2. If someone in the class has the computer knowledge, create an alternative to your school's home page, or make changes that would make it more appealing to prospective students and their parents.

3. Imagine that for purposes of parody or protest you wanted to call attention to aspects of your school that the official images deliberately omit. Proceed as in item 1. In a short statement, explain why you chose the image you did and what purpose(s) you want it to serve.

4. Select a school organization (a fraternity or sorority, a club, etc.) whose image you think could be improved. Create a promotional image for it either for the Web or for some other existing publication.

5. As in item 3, create a visual parody of the official image of a school organization, perhaps as an inside joke intended for other members of the organization.

Assignment 4: Analyzing Your Own Visual Rhetoric

Study all the images your class created as argument and/or persuasion in the previous assignment. Select an image to analyze in depth. Write an essay that addresses these questions:

What audience does the image intend to reach?
What goal did the creator of the image seek to accomplish?

If something is being argued, ask:

What thesis is advanced by the image or accompanying text?
Do aspects of the image or text function as reasons for holding the thesis?

If an image persuades more than it argues, attempt to discover and understand its major source of appeal. Persuasion appeals to the whole person in an effort to create **identification,** a strong linking of the reader's interests and values with the image that represents something desired. Hence, we can ask

> How do the images your class created appeal to the audience's interests and values?
>
> Do the images embody emotional appeals? If so, how?

Assignment 5: Writing to Convince

Newspapers have been criticized for printing pictures that used to be considered too gruesome for publication. Highly respected newspapers like the *New York Times* have offered defenses of graphic photos. Look into what publishers, readers, and critics have to say on this topic. What issues and questions come up in these debates? Draw a conclusion of your own, and write an essay supporting it.

Assignment 6: Using Graphics to Supplement Your Own Writing or Other Texts

Select an essay that could be improved either by adding graphics or by revising the graphics used. Working alone or collaboratively with a writing group, revise it. For help with using graphics effectively in your writing, see the Best Practices box "Guidelines for Using Visuals." You have many revision options: Besides adding visuals, you can cut unneeded ones, redesign existing ones, change media (for example, from a photo to a drawing), change image types (for example, from a table to a graph), and so on. Revising graphics always means reworking the text as well. Expect changes in one to require changes in the other.

Assignment 7: Presenting Information Using PowerPoint

Revise and present the written text in Assignment 6 as an oral presentation using PowerPoint. If you don't know how to use PowerPoint, have another student who does show you how, or use the tutorial that comes with the program.

PowerPoint is a powerful tool for presenting visuals in a talk. *But it is more often used poorly, as a crutch for nervous speakers, than it is used well, to supplement a talk.* Inexperienced speakers want the audience's eyes on anything else but them, so they pack everything they have to say into the PowerPoint slides and have the audience looking at the projections all through the speech. Don't do this. Use PowerPoint to present your graphics to the audience and to summarize major points. Otherwise, keep the audience looking at and listening to you, not staring at a projection screen. Show them a graphic, for instance, and then discuss it, but don't leave it on screen to

www.mhhe.com/**crusius**

For further help on using Power-Point, visit the online tutorial at:

Writing > PowerPoint Tutorial

Guidelines for Using Visuals

Graphics come in a variety of useful forms: as tables to display numerical data economically, as graphs to depict data in a way that permits easy comparison of proportions or trends, as photographs to convey realism and drama, and as drawings to depict structures. Whatever graphics you use, be sure to do the following:

- Make sure every graphic has a definite function. Graphics are not decorative and should never be "thrown" into an essay.
- Choose the kind or form of visual best suited to convey the point you are trying to make.
- Design graphics so that they are easy to interpret. That is, keep them simple, make them large enough to be read without strain, and use clear labeling.
- Place graphics as close as possible to the text they explain or illustrate. Remember, graphics should be easier to understand than the text they supplement.
- Refer to all your graphics in the text. Readers usually need both the graphic and a text discussion for full understanding.
- Acknowledge the creator or source of each graphic next to the graphic itself. As long as you acknowledge the source or creator, you can borrow freely, just as you can with quotations from texts. Of course, if you wish to publish an essay that includes borrowed graphics, you must obtain written permission.

distract attention from you. Don't read from your text or memorize it, but talk from a few notes to remind yourself of what you need to say. Remember: PowerPoint complements a speech in much the same way graphics complement a written text. Don't let it take over or allow anxiety to cause you to lean on it too hard.

CHAPTER 5

Writing Research-Based Arguments

Most arguments are researched writing. You need to read sources to inform yourself about your topic, and then you need to cite sources in order to convince your readers that you have a good case. An argument with no research behind it is generally weak. Many published arguments may not appear to have research behind them. In journalism, sources may not be documented, but the authors have had to dig to learn the facts, and when they use someone else's views, they introduce that person as an authority because naming authorities' credentials strengthens a case.

Nevertheless, a researched argument must be your own case, with your own angle on the topic, not a case borrowed from your sources. The trick to writing well with sources is to keep them from taking over. You must be in charge, using your sources as supporting characters in what must remain your own show. This chapter will cover finding sources, evaluating them, using them in your own writing, and citing them correctly. To help you stay in charge through this whole process, we will emphasize the role of writing "behind the scenes" *before* you begin drafting your paper. The more you use writing to interact with your sources, to know them well, and to see what supporting parts they might play, the more you will be ready to write

www.mhhe.com/**crusius**

For a wealth of research resources, go to:

Research

as the author—the authority—of an argument of your own: an argument with your own claim, your own voice, your own design.

Using your sources with this kind of confidence helps reduce the possibility of misusing a source. Misuse of a source includes

- Taking material out of context and misrepresenting the viewpoint of the author. Most texts include "multiple voices"—that is, writers may describe opposing views, or they may speak ironically, so a casual reader may misunderstand their viewpoint. Applying the critical reading skills described in Chapter 2 will keep you from misusing a source.

- Using material without giving credit to the source. If you use someone else's words, you must put quotation marks around them. If you use someone else's ideas, even in your own words, you must give that other person credit. Failure to do so is plagiarism. Because plagiarism is a growing problem, partly owing to the ease with which material can be cut and pasted from online sources, we have devoted the next chapter, Chapter 6, to ethical writing and plagiarism. Because some plagiarism is not intentional—students may not understand what constitutes fair use of a source or may not realize how to paraphrase adequately and accurately—we recommend that you read this brief chapter before you start working with the sources you find.

www.mhhe.com/**crusius**

For more information on plagiarism, go to:

Research > Plagiarism

Research takes time and patience; it takes initiative; it takes genuine curiosity. You have to recognize what you do not know and be willing to accept good evidence even if it contradicts what you previously believed. The first step in research is finding an issue that is appropriate.

FINDING AN ISSUE

Let's say you have been assigned to write an argument on an issue of current public concern. If you have no idea what to write about, what should you do?

Understand the Difference between a Topic and an Issue

People argue about issues, not about topics. For example, global warming is a topic. It is the warming of the earth's atmosphere, a scientific observation. However, people argue about many issues related to the topic of global warming, such as whether human activity has contributed to the temperature increase. This was the argument made by the film *An Inconvenient Truth*. The conversation on that issue is subsiding because even the oil companies have come to accept the evidence about the effects of manmade greenhouse gases. But other issues remain, such as what sources of energy are the best alternatives to the fuels that produce greenhouse gases and how individuals might change their lifestyles to make less of an impact on global climate. The point here: To write a good argument, you must explore genuine questions at issue, not just topics. Furthermore, you should explore a question that really interests you. You will need to care about your issue because research takes time, patience, and—most of all—initiative.

Find Issues in the News

Pay attention to the news and to the opinions of newsmakers, leaders, and commentators. College students are busy, but there are some easy ways to keep abreast of issues in the news. Here are hints for various news sources.

The Internet

- Set one of the major news organizations or newspapers as your home page so that when you turn on your computer, the news will be the first thing you see. Some options are

  Cable News Network   <http://www.cnn.com>
  Microsoft NBC News   <http://www.msnbc.com>
  National Public Radio News   <http://www.npr.org/>
  The *New York Times*   <http://www.nytimes.com>
  The *Wall Street Journal*   <http://www.wsj.com>

  If you moved away to go to college, choose the online version of your hometown paper as a way of keeping in touch with events back home as well as around the world.

- Visit the index of mainstream and alternative online news sources listed on the Web site of FAIR (Fairness and Accuracy in Reporting) at <http://www.fair.org/index.php?page=134>. This Web site also provides links to media criticism and other resources for doing research into the news media.

- Visit CQ Researcher Online. This division of *Congressional Quarterly* allows you to search for issues and browse for in-depth reports and pro and con statements from public figures. This resource is located at <http://library.cqpress.com/cqresearcher/>.

Magazines and Newspapers

Browse your campus bookstore or library for magazines devoted to news and current affairs. In the library, ask for directions to the "recent periodicals" area. In addition to the obvious choices such as *Time* and *Newsweek*, look for the more opinionated magazines such as *Utne Reader, New Republic*, and *National Review*. For more coverage of issues, look for *Atlantic Monthly, Harper's, Science*, and *National Geographic*.

Lectures, Panel Discussions, Class Discussions, Conversations

Hearing in person what others have to say on an issue will help expose the important points and raise questions for research. Seek out discussion of issues you are considering for research.

Personal Observations

The best way to find an engaging issue is to look around you. Your instructor may not give you total freedom to choose an issue, but many current events and social concerns touch our daily lives. For example, the student whose paper we use as an example of researched writing found her issue when she realized the connection between something close to home that had been bothering her and the general topic area her instructor had specified for the class: global warming.

Finding an Issue on the Topic of Global Warming: A Student Example

Student Julie Ross was in a class that had been assigned the topic of global warming. To find an issue, Julie attended an on-campus screening of *An Inconvenient Truth,* followed by a panel discussion featuring representatives of government agencies, environmentalists, and professors of earth science. Julie asked the panelists what individual citizens could do to reduce their contributions to greenhouse gases. One panelist suggested that consuming "less stuff" would make a difference, since the production of consumer goods contributes to carbon dioxide and other greenhouse gases. Because Julie was already fuming about old houses on her street being torn down and replaced with super-sized McMansions, she decided to research the question of how destructive this kind of development is, not just to the immediate neighborhood, but also to the planet. She began wondering about its contribution to global warming and how much more energy it demands, because the new houses use much more energy than the ones they replace. She decided to write her paper to an audience of home buyers. If she could discourage them from buying these huge new houses, the developers would have to stop building them. To make a convincing case, Julie needed to find good arguments for preserving the older homes and evidence about how much more energy the large new homes use than the older, smaller ones. Julie's paper appears at the end of this chapter.

 www.mhhe.com/**crusius** You'll find more tools to help you find an issue at:
Learning > Links Across the Curriculum > Refdesk.com

FINDING SOURCES

The prospect of doing research can be overwhelming, given the many possible avenues to explore: the Internet, newspapers, magazines and journals, and all kinds of books. You need a strategy to guide you most efficiently to the best sources on your topic. The quality of your paper depends on its ingredients; you want to find not just *any* sources but the most credible, appropriate, and—if you are writing about current events—the most recent.

As you begin your research, two tips will make the journey much more efficient and orderly—and less stressful.

1. Keep a research log. Students often complain that they found a reference to an article but didn't save it or print it out, and then they could not find their way back to it. They waste precious time because they didn't take the time to write down the title and author, the journal it appeared in, and the index which led them to it. So our first advice on research strategy is to use your notebook to mark your trail

to anything that looks interesting. Better yet, if you think you might use a source, print it out right then or photocopy it.

2. Make complete photocopies and printouts. When you make printouts and photocopies, get *all* the information you will need later to cite these sources even if you are not sure you will use them. It's easier to take the time when you have the source at hand than to retrace your steps later. If you use a book that you cannot check out of the library, take the time to photocopy the title page and the copyright page with the date of publication. Also, photocopy the page (usually near the front or back if there is one) that gives information about the author. Be sure to place the book carefully on the copy machine to make sure you get the entire page copied, with no text cut off, including the page number.

Field Research

Consider beginning your research with what you can observe. That means going out into the "field," as researchers call it, and recording what you see, either in written notes or with photographs or drawings. Field research can also include recording what you hear, in audiotapes and in notes of interviews and conversations. An interview can also take place online, through e-mails or a chat, if you can preserve it. Following are some suggestions for field research.

Observations

Do not discount the value of your own personal experiences as evidence in making a case. You will notice that many writers of arguments offer as evidence what they themselves have seen, heard, and done.

Alternatively, you may seek out a specific personal experience as you inquire into your topic. For example, one student writing about homelessness in Dallas decided to visit a shelter. She called ahead to get permission and schedule the visit. Her paper was memorable because she was able to include the stories and physical descriptions of several homeless women, with details of their conversations.

Julie Ross began her research by walking the streets of her neighborhood, photographing the stark contrasts of size and style between the older homes and the new ones built on the sites of torn-down houses. Her photographs provided evidence for her case against super-sized homes in historic communities.

Questionnaires and Surveys

You may be able to get information on some topics, especially if they are campus related, by doing surveys or questionnaires. This can be done very efficiently in electronic versions (Web-based or e-mail). Be forewarned, however, that it is very difficult to conduct a reliable survey.

First, there is the problem of designing a clear and unbiased survey instrument. If you have ever filled out an evaluation form for an instructor or a course, you will know what we mean about the problem of clarity. For example, one evaluation might ask whether an instructor returns papers "in a reasonable length of time"; what is "reasonable" to some students may be too long for others. As for bias, consider the question "Have you ever had trouble getting assistance from the library's reference desk?" To get a fair response, this questionnaire had better also ask how many requests for help were handled promptly and well. If you do decide to draft a questionnaire, we suggest you do it as a class project so that students on all sides of the issue can contribute and troubleshoot for ambiguity.

Second, there is the problem of getting a representative response. For the same reasons we doubt the results of certain magazine-sponsored surveys of people's sex lives, we should be skeptical about the statistical accuracy of surveys targeting a group that may not be representative of the whole. For example, it would be impossible to generalize about all first-year college students in the United States based on a survey of only your English class—or even the entire first-year class at your college.

Surveys can be useful, but design, administer, and interpret them carefully.

Interviews

You can get a great deal of current information by talking to experts. As with any kind of research, the first step in conducting an interview is to decide exactly what you want to find out. Write down your questions.

The next step is to find the right person to interview. As you read about an issue, note the names (and possible biases) of any organizations mentioned; these may have local offices, the telephone numbers of which you could easily find. In addition, institutions such as hospitals, universities, and large corporations have public relations offices whose staffs provide information. Also, do not overlook the expertise available from faculty members at your own school.

Once you have determined possible sources for interviews, you must begin a patient and courteous round of telephone calls, continuing until you connect with the right person; this can take many calls. If you have a subject's e-mail address, you might write to introduce yourself and request an appointment for a telephone interview.

Whether your interview is face to face or over the telephone, begin by acknowledging that the interviewee's time is valuable. Tell the person something about the project you are working on, but withhold your own position on any controversial matters. Sound neutral and be specific about what you want to know. Take notes, and include the title and background of the person being interviewed and the date of the interview, which you will need to cite this source. If you want to tape the interview, ask permission first. Finally, if you have the individual's mailing address, send a thank-you note after the interview.

If everyone in your class is researching the same topic and more than one person wants to contact the same expert, avoid flooding that person with requests. One or two students could do the interview and report to the class, or the expert could visit the class.

Library and Internet Research

Since 80% of what is now published in print is also available online, the distinction between library and Internet research has blurred. You will be able to find many magazines, scholarly journals, and newspapers through the Internet, and many Internet sites through your library's online directories. Because so many documents are now electronic—even if they appeared first in print—librarians have coined the term "born digital" to distinguish purely cyberspace documents from documents that were born in print but have been made available online.

With the daily additions to information, articles, images, and even books available online, the resources for searching it are constantly being upgraded. The advice in this chapter should get you started, but it's always a good idea to consult your library's reference librarians for help with finding sources on your topic. They know what is in your school's library, what is online, and what the latest tools are for finding any kind of source. You will find these librarians at the reference desk; every library has one.

 www.mhhe.com/**crusius**   To find online guidance for using the library, check out:
Research > Using the Library

Kinds of Sources

The various kinds of sources available in print and online include books and periodicals as well as electronic media.

Books   Nonfiction books generally fall into three categories:

Monographs: Monographs are sustained arguments on a single topic. To use them responsibly, you should know the complete argument; that means reading the entire book, which time may not allow. Possibly, reading the introduction to a book will acquaint you with the author's argument well enough that you can selectively read sections of the book. Decide if you have time to use a book responsibly. Sometimes you can find a magazine or journal article by the author that covers some of the same ground as the book but in a condensed way.

Anthologies: These are collections of essays and articles, usually by many different writers, selected by an editor, who writes an introductory essay. Anthologies are good sources for short papers because they offer multiple voices, and each argument can be read in one sitting. Pay attention to whether a book is an anthology because you will cite these anthology selections differently from a regular book. Look near the back of the book for information about the author of any selection you choose to use.

Reference books: These are good for gathering background information and specific facts on your topic. You can find these online and in the library shelves; they cannot be checked out. Reference books include specialized encyclopedias on almost any subject, such as *The Encyclopedia of Serial Killers,* a 391-page book. We will tell you below how to search for encyclopedias and other reference books. Many reference books are now available electronically.

A note of caution about Wikipedia*: Wikipedia* is not a scholarly publication. In fact, it encourages a democratic notion of knowledge in which anyone can contribute, add to, alter, or delete material that has been posted on a topic. Although the editors scan it regularly for misinformation, errors, and deliberate lies, there is no guarantee that what you find there is credible. We suggest you use it for background information and for links to other, more authoritative sources whose authors' credentials you can confirm. Check any facts you plan to use in your papers against other, more scholarly sources.

A note of caution about general encyclopedias: Multi-volume online and print encyclopedias such as *Britannica* and *Microsoft Encarta* are good for background knowledge as you begin research on a topic or for fact-checking while you are writing. However, college students should not use general encyclopedias as primary sources. The entries do not cover topics in depth and are not usually products of original research. It is better to use specialized encyclopedias and reference works or books and articles by specialists in your topic.

Periodicals Periodicals are published periodically—daily, weekly, monthly, quarterly. They include the following types:

Articles in scholarly journals: These journals are usually published by university presses and aimed at readers in a particular scholarly discipline: Both the authors and intended readers are professors and graduate students. Scholarly articles are contributions to ongoing debates within a discipline. Therefore, they are credible sources, but scan them for accessibility. If you are not familiar with the debate they are joining, you may not find them accessible enough to use responsibly. Seek your instructor's help if you find a source hard to comprehend. Scholarly journals are usually born in print and put online, but some are born digital.

Articles in magazines: Magazines—print, online, and the born digital "e-zines"—are all good sources for short papers. Magazine articles vary greatly, depending on their intended readership. Some magazines, such as *Atlantic Monthly, Harper's, National Review, New Republic,* the *New Yorker,* and even *Rolling Stone,* offer articles by scholars and serious journalists. They give arguments on current public issues by the same people who write for scholarly journals, but the articles are aimed at an educated public readership, not other scholars. These are perfect for familiarizing yourself with viewpoints on an issue. You can find even more accessible articles and arguments in weekly newsmagazines, including columns by nationally syndicated writers. Trade magazines are good for business-related topics; Julie Ross found several online magazines published for the building industry. Many advocacy groups also publish magazines in print and online. Julie found ecological advocacy groups' magazines, such as *E: The Environmental Magazine,* helpful in her research.

Newspapers: Newspapers are ideal sources for arguments and information on current as well as historical issues. Feature articles, which are long and in-depth, usually present the reporter's angle on the topic; opinion columns are arguments and therefore good for getting perspectives on your topic. Major national newspapers such as the *Washington Post, Wall Street Journal,* and *New York Times* should be available online through your library's catalogue, as will the local newspaper for your college's city or town. Below, we tell more about how to search for newspaper articles, including those from student-run college papers and small-town and regional papers.

Audiovisual Materials Visuals so often supplement verbal arguments that you should be aware of the many resources for finding visuals to use in your papers and also to view as sources of information. Your library's book catalogue includes films available on campus; search engines like Google help you find visuals on the Internet.

Web Sites Web sites include nearly every kind of source described above and more. You have to evaluate everything you find in the wild and open world of cyberspace, but nearly all research institutes and centers associated with universities, advocacy groups, government bureaus, and political organizations are excellent sources for your arguments. Also, nearly all writers these days have their own page on the Web, where you can go to find more about their lives, views, and other writing, so the Web is a great resource for learning more about your sources. The only problem is searching the Web efficiently, and we offer advice later in this chapter on how to zero in on the best sites for your topic.

Blogs, Listservs, Usenet Groups, Message Boards The Web has become an exciting place for dialogue, where scholars within an area of interest can argue with each other and ask each other for help with their research. Although a first-year student may not feel ready to enter these discussions, "lurking"—reading a discussion without contributing to it—is a great way to learn about the debates firsthand. And an intelligent question will find people ready to share their knowledge and opinions. We'll tell you later in this chapter about directories that will take you to the most relevant resources for your topic.

Choose the Best Search Terms

The success of your search depends on what terms you use. Before beginning, write down, in your notebook or research log, possible terms that you might use in searching for sources on your topic. Do this by examining your research question to find its key terms. As you begin doing your research, you will discover which of these terms are most productive and which you can cross out. Adapt your search terms as you discover which ones are most productive.

We'll use Julie's search to illustrate how to find the best search terms. Julie's research question was, What are the negative effects of tearing down older homes and replacing them with bigger new ones? Julie wanted to know more about the environmental effects of large homes, both on climate change globally and on the local neighborhoods.

Use Phrase Searching Whether you are in a Google search, a directory or index search, or an online catalogue, put *quotation marks* around phrases to tell your search engine to search for the combined words, not the individual words. Put the words in the order you want them to appear and put quotation marks around the phrase; for example,

   "neighborhood preservation"

Start with General Words What are the most obvious words for your topic? Julie's topic about the big new houses replacing old ones fits into the larger category of *residential construction* or *home building.*

Think of Synonyms When Julie could not find any books in her library's catalogue on home building, she thought, What is a synonym for *home?* Answer: *house.* She looked again for books under the subject *house building.*

Use Unique or Specific Words and Phrases What words most specifically describe your topic? You may be able to think of these words, or they may show up as you search. Julie quickly discovered that the sources she found used the term *teardowns.* When she began using this as a search term, she found many relevant sources. As she began reading about the effects of residential construction on the environment, Julie also encountered the term *green building* to describe the more sustainable kinds of home construction materials and designs.

Use Boolean Searching Boolean searching (named after nineteenth-century English logician George Boole) allows you to narrow or broaden your search by joining words with AND OR NOT

   AND: "home size" AND "energy consumption"

Using AND narrowed Julie's search. However, she found nothing by combining "home size" AND "global warming." She needed to think more specifically about the connection between home size and global warming: Energy consumption is the link. (Note: Google and most other search engines automatically put AND in when you type words in succession.)

OR: "green houses" OR "sustainable homes"

Using OR broadened the search, yielding more hits. Using OR is helpful if you know your subject has many synonyms, such as *youth, teenagers, students.*

NOT: "green house" NOT agriculture

Using NOT limited the search by eliminating references to hothouses in agriculture.

Searching Your Library

Because much of the research material on the Internet is available for free through your school's library, it makes sense to start with your library's resources. Why pay for something that you already have free access to through your college or university? Also, unlike much of what you find on the Internet, the materials available through your library have been selected by scholars, editors, and librarians, so you can be more confident about the credibility of what you find.

Don't assume that searching the library means using bound books and periodicals only, or even going there in person. Libraries are going electronic, giving you online access to more high quality, full-text sources than you will find on the Web. Libraries subscribe to online indexes and journals that cannot be found through search engines, such as Google and Yahoo. These resources are on what is called the "Deep Web" or the "Invisible Web." Your enrollment at school gives you access to these resources, which are described later in this chapter. Your library's online home page is the gateway to all the library's resources. Figure 5.1 is an example of a library home page.

Your Library's Online Catalogue

Your library's online catalogue is the gateway to a wealth of sources: books, both printed and online in the form of e-books that you can "check out" and download; full-text online newspapers, including the complete archives of these papers; indexes to individual articles in magazines, newspapers, and scholarly journals, including links to the full text of most of them online; audiovisual materials; maps; and reference books of all kinds. Visit the home page of your library's online catalogue and explore the places it will take you. In the library catalogue, you can search for books by title, author, subject, and key word, as well as their Library of Congress call numbers. Here are some tips:

> *In a title search:* If you know a title you are looking for, do a title search with as much of the title needed to distinguish it from other titles. Omit initial articles (*a, the, an*).

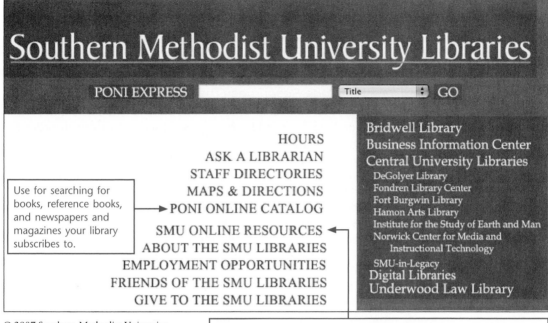

Southern Methodist University Libraries

PONI EXPRESS [   ] [Title ▸] GO

HOURS
ASK A LIBRARIAN
STAFF DIRECTORIES
MAPS & DIRECTIONS
▶ PONI ONLINE CATALOG
SMU ONLINE RESOURCES ◀
ABOUT THE SMU LIBRARIES
EMPLOYMENT OPPORTUNITIES
FRIENDS OF THE SMU LIBRARIES
GIVE TO THE SMU LIBRARIES

Bridwell Library
Business Information Center
Central University Libraries
  DeGolyer Library
  Fondren Library Center
  Fort Burgwin Library
  Hamon Arts Library
  Institute for the Study of Earth and Man
  Norwick Center for Media and
    Instructional Technology
SMU-in-Legacy
Digital Libraries
Underwood Law Library

Use for searching for books, reference books, and newspapers and magazines your library subscribes to.

© 2007 Southern Methodist University. Reprinted with permission.

Use for finding articles in magazines, scholarly journals, newspapers. Also for online resources in discipline-specific areas.

In a subject search: You will need to know what "subject heading" the Library of Congress has given your topic. Julie, for example, found no books in her library catalogue when she typed in "home construction" but found twenty-five books when she typed in "house construction." If you cannot find books with your term, you can try other synonyms or go to <http://authorities.loc.gov/> and put your search term in the "Search Authorities" box. It will tell you the right term to use according to the Library of Congress cataloging system. Or just try a key word search, described below.

In a key word search: This kind of search is more forgiving than a subject search and can be helpful if you don't know the exact right word. Put quotation marks around phrases: "global warming." You can use AND or OR to combine terms: "teardowns" AND "neighborhood preservation."

Figure 5.1
An example library home page

The library's online catalogue will also tell you if your library subscribes to a particular newspaper or magazine. The catalogue will not tell you about individual articles or stories in these periodicals, but you can find them by searching the publication's own online index or the online databases in your library, described below. Most university libraries now subscribe to major U.S. newspapers and have full-text archives online. Do a title search to find if your library has a particular newspaper.

To locate reference books, combine your key word search with words like *encyclopedia, dictionary,* or *almanac,* and you will find both online and on-the-shelf reference books. For an example of such a search and an example of a result, see Figures 5.2 and 5.3.

Your Library's Online Resources (The Deep Web)

Your school library's purchased online resources are available only to students, faculty, and staff. Your library has to subscribe to them in order for you to see them. They are known as the "Deep Web" or the "Invisible Web" because outsiders do not have access to them. Students can access them on campus or off campus by using computers connected to the campus server or by using a password. The main Web page of most university libraries offers a link to a page listing the online resources available to you. These usually include reference resources: dictionaries such as the Oxford English Dictionary; electronic encyclopedias, journals, and magazines; and most important, licensed databases to help you search for a wide variety of sources on any topic, both on and off the Web.

These databases are indexes to articles in periodicals: magazines, scholarly journals, and newspapers. You search them by typing in a subject, key word, author, or title. In most cases the search will produce a list of articles, an abstract of the article, and often, a link to full text of the article, which you can then save or print out.

If the full text is not available online, the database will tell you if the periodical is in your library's holdings. You may be able to access it electronically through the online catalogue. This is why it is good to know which magazines, journals, and newspapers are catalogued along with the books in your library's online catalogue.

Never use the abstract of an article as a source. Abstracts may not be written by the source's author; they may not be accurate. Most important, you cannot get the in-depth understanding of a source that would allow you to use it accurately.

The following are some common licensed databases you can link to from your library's online resources page:

- EBSCO Host Research Databases: If your library subscribes to EBSCO Host, you may have access to as many as fifty databases at a click of your mouse. Choose EBSCO Host and then the tab that says "Choose Databases." The list should include Academic Search Premier. This is the most useful, all-around database for multidiscipline searches, providing access to full-text documents in over 4,500 journals. While in Academic Search Premier, use the "Other Databases" tab to find a pull-down menu to other EBSCO databases. Some EBSCO databases are

Business Source Complete
Communication and Mass Media Complete
Film and Television Literature Index

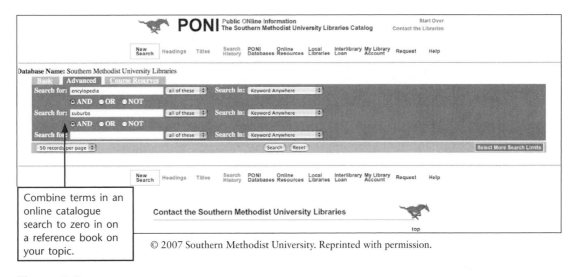

Combine terms in an online catalogue search to zero in on a reference book on your topic.

© 2007 Southern Methodist University. Reprinted with permission.

Figure 5.2

A search in online catalogue for specialized encyclopedias about suburbs

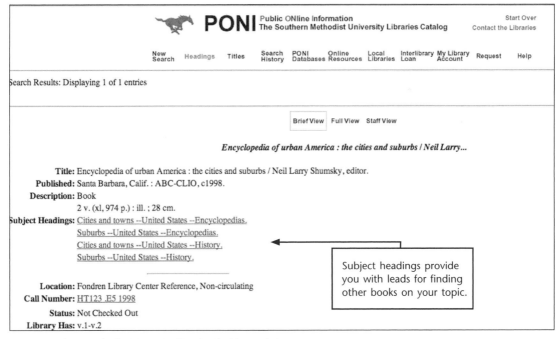

Subject headings provide you with leads for finding other books on your topic.

© 2007 Southern Methodist University. Reprinted with permission.

Figure 5.3

The result of an online search for encyclopedias about suburbs

Religion and Philosophy Collection

TOPICsearch (good for social, political, and other topics popular in classroom discussions)

- *InfoTrac* (for articles in magazines, journals, and major newspapers)
- *InfoTrac* Newspaper (good for finding articles in local newspapers; browse the titles to find if yours is here)
- UMI ProQuest Direct (similar to Infotrac)
- Lexis-Nexis (good for newspaper articles, including articles and editorials in many college campus papers; find the "university wire" index under the tab for "university news")

In addition to these common databases, most schools' online resources page will also give you access to more specialized databases. You can find them grouped according to subject, such as anthropology, economics, or psychology. For example, a search within the subject "communications" brought up this list of over twenty indexes:

Academic OneFile
All movie guide
American Film Institute catalog
American memory
Arts & humanities citation index
Arts and humanities search
Communication & mass media complete
Film & television literature index
Film literature Index
FITA
International Children's Digital Library
Journalist's toolbox
JSTOR
Mintel reports
MLA international bibliography
MRI+
NewPages.com
PollingReport.com
Population Reference Bureau
Poynter online
Project Muse
Redbooks
Social sciences citation index
SocioSite
Trademark Electronic Search System (TESS)

Of these, the JSTOR index (which stands for *Journal Storage*) is itself an index to over seven hundred scholarly journals in approximately forty disciplines. Clearly, the library's licensed databases are an expansive chain of resources for research.

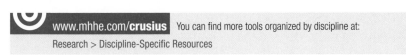

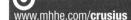

An advanced search in databases like *InfoTrac* and EBSCO Academic Premier (illustrated in Figure 5.4) allows you to combine terms to narrow your search. Julie Ross eliminated all hits not related to housing by including "houses" as a second term in her search. Note that EBSCO and *InfoTrac* allow you to select from academic journals, popular magazines, newspapers, or all three. The search in Figure 5.4 targeted newspapers only.

Internet Research

Because the Internet is so large—estimated to contain over 50 billion documents—we want to caution you about the potential for wasting time if you start browsing with one of the common search engines such as Yahoo or Google. However, there are some ways to use search engine features to narrow your search. One of those ways is to limit your search to certain domains.

For further advice on using the Internet to conduct research, go to:

Research > Using the Internet

Domains

Every Internet address or URL (Uniform Resource Locator) has certain components; it helps to know a little about them. What is known as the "top level domain name" tells you something about who put the site on the Web.

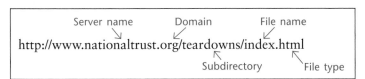

For Web sites from the United States, the following are the four most common top level domain names. Web sites from other nations typically have instead an abbreviation of the country's name.

Commercial (.com) "Dot com" sites include businesses and their publications—such as the real estate newsletter at <http://www.teardowns.com>—other commercial publications, such as magazines; and personal Web pages and blogs, such as those created on Blogger.com. The example, teardowns.com, is a site assisting builders who want to construct on the sites of torn-down houses. Although you will find magazine and newspaper articles through search engines like Yahoo and Google, a better way to ensure that you get them in full text for free is to find them through your library's licensed databases, as described on page 106. Because so much of the Web is commercial

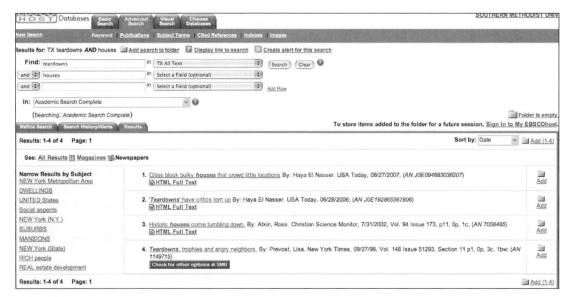

Figure 5.4

Results of a search for articles in a database

sites, you will probably want to use the advanced search options explained in the next section to filter "dot com" sites from your search.

Nonprofit Organizations (.org)   "Dot org" sites include organizations and advocacy groups, such as the National Trust for Historic Preservation at <http://www.nationaltrust.org/teardowns/>. Their purpose is to raise awareness of, participation in, and donations to their causes.

Educational Institutions (.edu)   "Dot edu" sites contain research and course materials of public and private schools, colleges, and universities. The URL <http://sciencepolicy.colorado.edu/> is a site for a center at University of Colorado at Boulder doing research on science, technology, and public policy. Although mostly what you find at these sites is the work of professors, some of the material may be by graduate and undergraduate students, so as always, check out the author's credentials.

Government Agencies (.gov)   "Dot gov" sites are useful for getting the latest information about any aspect of American government or about government agencies and policies. The URL <http://www.census.gov/Press-Release/www/releases/archives/housing/007127.html> leads to an article published by the U.S. Census Bureau on the size of houses in 2006.

Advanced Features for Searching the Web

Search engines provide a variety of ways to focus your search, and Google has some that are especially useful for students.

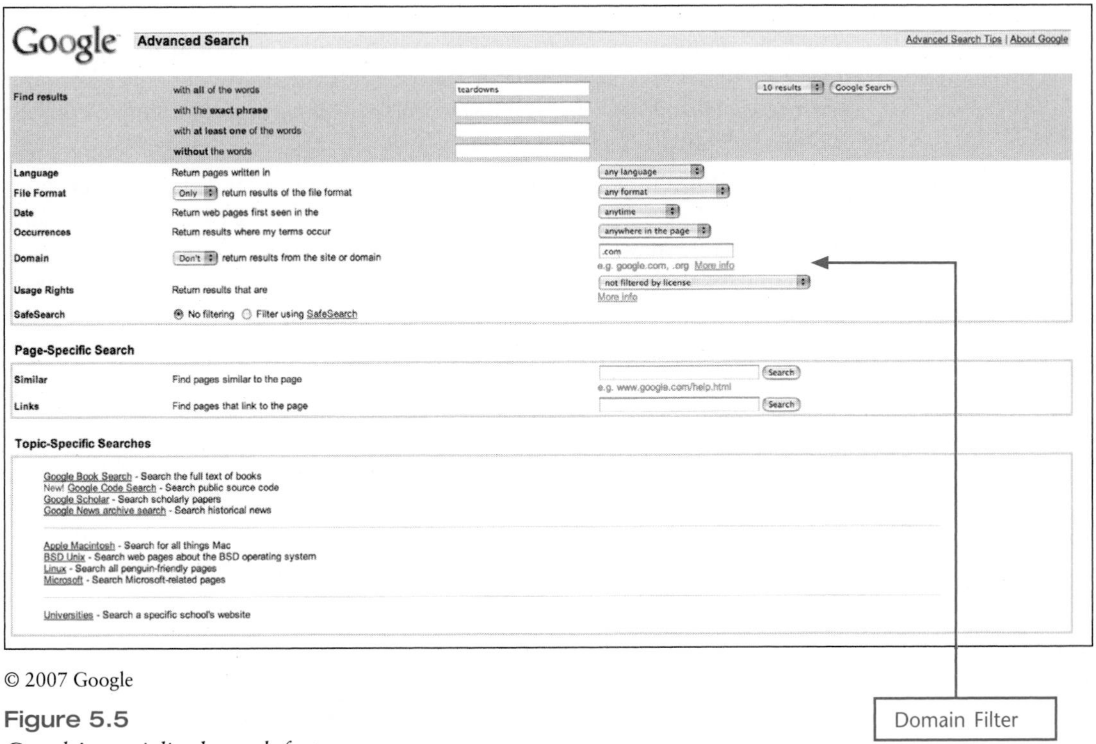

© 2007 Google

Figure 5.5
Google's specialized search features

Advanced Searches Search engines will let you customize your search, allowing you to limit your search to just one or two of the domains listed above, or to exclude one. Filtering out the "dot com" sites is like turning on a spam blocker, so you will get fewer hits by writers with no academic or professional credentials. (See Figure 5.5.)

Google Specialized Searches Google offers an ever-increasing number of specific kinds of searches, such as News Archives, Books, Images, and Earth. Many link you to materials that you will have to pay for. However, you can probably find many of these for free through your school library, which subscribes to the archives of many magazines and newspapers. See the earlier section, "Your Library's Online Catalogue."

Google Book Google Book Search can find your key word as it appears on a specific page in a book, even if the title may not indicate that the book contains information on that topic. So, for example, when Julie typed in "teardowns" in Google Book, she was taken to a list of books where that term appeared. By choosing one, she could see the actual page where the term was used. This feature is both helpful and dangerous, however. Google Book shows you one page only, not the whole book, although it gives you information about the whole book. You should not use Google Book as a source. Using material taken so far out of context, knowing very little about the whole argument of the book is not a solid way of doing research, even if you cite the book correctly. On the other hand, knowing that the book contains something you are interested in, you can then look for a copy of the book in your library or a bookstore.

Google Scholar   Google Scholar is where your library and the Internet intersect. Google Scholar is an index to scholarly articles and book reviews, many of them available at your university library. If you open Google Scholar from a computer on campus or if your home computer connects to your school's network (or if you have a password that will grant you off-campus access to your school's network), you will be able to access full texts of materials available from your school's library.

Subject Directories to the Web

You can narrow your search for Web sites by going first to a subject directory that organizes Web sites by topic. Some examples are

Google Directory

Yahoo Directory

Figure 5.6
An example Web directory page

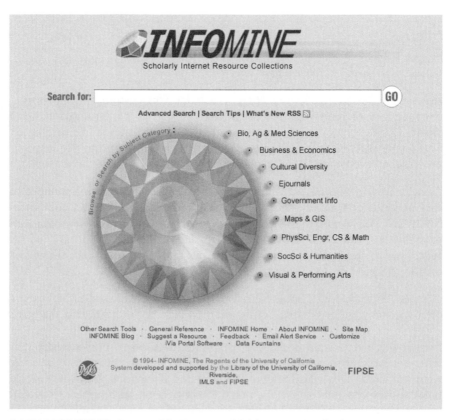

© 1994 INFOMINE, The Regents of the University of California. Reprinted wth permission.

Infomine (assembled by librarians, not machines)

About.com

Other Web Resources: Blogs, Listservs,
Message Boards, and Chat Groups

Don't overlook the potential of interactive sites on the Internet. Many authors of your sources have blogs and personal Web pages where they try out new ideas and get feedback from others interested in their topics. As a student, you may not feel ready to join these conversations, but you can learn a lot by lurking—that is, just reading them. You can find them by using "blogs," "listservs," "message board," or "chat room" as a search term in your browser. By searching for "academic blogs," we found this good portal to professors' blogs: <http://www.academicblogs.net/wiki/index.php/Main_Page>.

 www.mhhe.com/**crusius** For more online research resources, go to:

Research > Additional Links on Research

EVALUATING SOURCES

Before beginning to read and evaluate your sources, you may need to reevaluate your issue. If you have been unable to find many sources that address the question you are raising, consider changing the focus of your argument.

For example, one student, Michelle, had the choice of any issue under the broad category of the relationship between humans and other animals. Michelle decided to focus on the mistreatment of circus animals, based on claims made in leaflets handed out at the circus by animal-rights protestors. Even with a librarian's help, however, Michelle could find no subject headings that led to even one source in her university's library. She then called and visited animal-rights activists in her city, who provided her with more materials written and published by the animal-rights movement. She realized, however, that researching the truth of their claims was more than she could undertake, so she had to acknowledge that her entire argument was based on heavily biased sources.

Once you have reevaluated your topic, use the following method to record and evaluate sources.

Eliminate Inappropriate Sources

You may find that some books and articles are intended for audiences with more specialized knowledge than you have. If you have trouble using a source, put it aside, at least temporarily.

 www.mhhe.com/**crusius**

For a tutorial on evaluating sources, go to:

Research > Source Evaluation Tutor: CARS

Also, carefully review any electronic sources you are using. While search engines make it easy to find material on the Web, online documents often have met no professional standards for scholarship. Material can be "published" electronically without review by experts, scholars, and editors that must occur in traditional publishing. Nevertheless, you will find legitimate scholarship on the Internet—news reports, encyclopedias, government documents, and even scholarly journals appear online. While the freedom of electronic publishing creates an exciting and democratic arena, it also puts a much heavier burden on students and researchers to ensure that the sources they use are worthy of readers' respect.

Carefully Record Complete Bibliographic Information

For every source you consider using, be sure to record full bibliographic information. Take this information from the source itself, not from an index, which may be incomplete or inaccurate. If you make a record of this information immediately, you will not have to go back later to fill in omissions. We recommend that you use a separate index card for each source, but whatever you use, record the following:

1. For a book:

   Author's full name (or names)
   Title of book
   City where published
   Name of publisher
   Year published

   For an article or essay in a book, record all of the information for the book, including the name(s) of the book's author or editor and the title and the author(s) of the article; also record the inclusive page numbers of the article or chapter (for example, "pp. 100–150").

2. For a periodical:

   Author's full name (or names)
   Title of the article
   Title of the periodical
   Date of the issue
   Volume number, if given
   Inclusive page numbers

3. For a document found on the World Wide Web:

   Author's full name (or names)
   Title of the work
   Original print publication data, if applicable
   Title of the database or Web site
   Full URL
   Date you accessed the document

4. For material found through listservs and Usenet newsgroups:

Author's full name (or names)
Author's e-mail address
Subject line from the posting
Date of the posting
Address of the listserv or newsgroup
Date you accessed the document

Read the Source Critically

As discussed in Chapter 2, critical reading depends on having some prior knowledge of the subject and the ability to see a text in context. As you research a topic, your knowledge naturally becomes deeper with each article you read. But your sources are not simply windows, giving you a clear view; whether argumentative or informative, they have bias. Before looking through them, you must look *at* your sources. Therefore, devote conscious attention to the rhetorical context of each source. Keep these questions in mind.

Who Is the Writer, and What Is His or Her Bias?

Is there a note that tells about the writer's professional title or institutional affiliation? If not, search the Internet for the writer's personal home page or university Web site. Or look in the *Dictionary of American Biographies,* or the *Biography and Genealogy Master Index,* which will send you to numerous specialized biographical sketches.

How Reliable Is the Source?

Again, checking for credibility is particularly important when you are working with electronic sources. For example, one student found two sites on the Web, both through a key word search on "euthanasia." One, entitled "Stop the Epidemic of Assisted Suicide," was posted by a person identified only by name, the letters MD, and the affiliation "Association for Control of Assisted Suicide." There was no biographical information, and the "snail mail" address was a post office box. The other Web site, "Ethics Update: Euthanasia," was posted by a professor of philosophy at the University of San Diego whose home page included a complete professional biography detailing his education, titles, and the publishers of his many books and articles. The author gave his address at USD in the Department of Philosophy. The student decided that, although the first source had some interesting information—including examples of individual patients who were living with pain rather than choosing suicide—it was not a source that skeptical readers would find credible. Search engines often land you deep within a Web site, and you have to visit the site's home page to get any background information about the source and its author. Be suspicious

Additional Guidelines for Evaluating Internet Sources

1. Look at the last segment of the domain name, which will tell you who developed the site. The most reliable ones are developed by colleges and universities (.edu) or by the government (.gov). Of course, commercial sites (.com, .biz) are profit-minded.

2. Check whether the name of the creator of the Web page or its Webmaster appears, complete with an e-mail address and the date of the last update, near either the top or the bottom of the page.

3. Check whether the source includes a bibliography, a sign of scholarly work.

4. Ask yourself if the links are credible.

5. A tilde (~) indicates a personal page; these pages must be evaluated with special care.

of sites that do not contain adequate source information; they probably aren't reliable.

When Was This Source Written?

If you are researching a current issue, decide what sources are too old. Arguments on current issues often benefit from earlier perspectives.

Where Did This Source Appear?

If you are using an article from a periodical, be aware of the periodical's readership and editorial bias. For example, *National Review* is conservative, *The Nation* liberal. An article in the *Journal of the American Medical Association* will usually defend the medical profession. Looking at the table of contents and scanning editorial statements will give you a feel for the periodical's politics. Also look at the page that lists the publisher and editorial board. You will find, for example, that *New American* is published by the ultra-right-wing John Birch Society. If you need help determining bias, ask a librarian. A reference book that lists periodicals by subject matter and explains their bias is *Magazines for Libraries*.

Why Was the Book or Article Written?

Although some articles are occasioned by news events, most books and arguments are written as part of an ongoing conversation among scholars or journalists. Being aware of the issues and the participants in this conversation is essential, as you will be joining it with your own researched argument. You can check *Book Review Index* to find where a book has been reviewed, and then consult some reviews to see how the book was received.

*"I just feel fortunate to live in a world with so
much disinformation at my fingertips."*

What Is the Author's Aim?

First, determine whether the source informs or argues. Both are useful and both will have some bias. When your source is an argument, note whether it aims primarily to inquire, to convince, to persuade, or to mediate.

How Is the Source Organized?

If the writer doesn't use subheadings or chapter titles, break the text into parts yourself and note what function each part plays in the whole.

Special Help with Evaluating Web Sites

The Internet is a dangerous place for researchers in a hurry. If you are not careful to look closely at what you find on the Web, you could embarrass yourself badly. For example, why would a college student want to cite a paper written for a high school class? Many high school teachers put their best student papers on class sites—good papers, but nevertheless, not exactly the kind of authority a college student should be citing. So before choosing to use something from the Web, go through the following checklist:

1. **Know the site's domain.** See pages 109–110 for how to read a Web address and what the various domain suffixes tell you about the site.

Note if the site is commercial, educational, governmental, or some kind of advocacy group, usually indicated by *.org* in the domain name. Commercial sites may be advertising something—they are not disinterested sources.

2. **Find the home page.** A search engine or online directory may take you to a page deep within the site; always look for links back to the home page because that is where you can find out more about the bias of the site and the credentials of the people behind it.

3. **Read about the bias and mission of the site.** At the home page, you should see a link to more information about the site—often the link is called "About Us" or "Mission Statement." Follow it and learn about the ideology of the site and how it compares with your own bias and that of other sources you are using.

4. **Read about the credentials of the site's creators.** The creators' degrees and professional affiliations should be easy to find. Regard any site as bogus if the only link to finding more about the authors is an e-mail address. Also, note whether the credentials of its board of directors or trustees are in the fields of specialization for your topic. For example, many writers for some Web sites on global warming dispute scientific findings, but are not scientists. They may be economists or historians.

5. **Note if the site reports on its funding and donors.** The rule of "follow the money" becomes important when you are using sources outside of the academic world. Think tanks and advocacy groups receive money from large corporations. Consider how the funding might influence their research and reported findings. There should be a link to material about funding, corporate sponsors, and the group's annual tax reports.

6. **Note how current the site is.** Near the beginning or the end of any Web site or part of a Web site, you should be able to find a note about when the site was last updated. You will need this information in order to cite the site—a site that has not been updated in years is not a good choice.

The Web site for the National Trust for Historic Preservation, where Julie found a speech about the effects of teardowns on neighborhoods, checks out as a credible site. From the home page, Julie was able to link to a page titled "About the National Trust," where she learned that it is a private, nonprofit organization founded in 1949 and dedicated to saving historical places. It advocates for legislation to protect communities and places of cultural heritage. The home page also provides a link titled "Funding," with information about donations, corporate sponsors, and tax returns. A link to the organization's "Management" gave the credentials of its trustees and its executive staff, including Richard Moe, the author of the speech. Julie learned that

Figure 5.7
The home page of the Web site of the National Trust for Historic Preservation

© 2007 National Trust for Aistoric Preservation. Reprinted with permission.

Moe graduated from Williams College in 1959 and from the University of Minnesota Law School in 1966. He has been president of the National Trust since 1993. He is an honorary member of The American Institute of Architects and co-author of a book titled *Changing Places: Rebuilding Community in the Age of Sprawl,* published in 1997. Clearly, this source from a Web site passed the test.

USING SOURCES

The first way to use your sources is to familiarize yourself with viewpoints on your topic. Your thesis will grow out of your research; you do not do research to find information to support a position you have not investigated. In high school, you may have grabbed quotations or facts from a source; in college you must know the source itself, including something about the author and the author's argument, unless your source is an encyclopedia or almanac or other reference work. For more on getting to know sources, read Chapter 2, "Reading an Argument," and the preceding section in this chapter, "Evaluating Sources," pages. 113–119.

When you have gathered and evaluated some sources, you should next spend some time with each one, reading it, marking it up, and writing about it in your notebook or on a notepad. This essential step will help you use your sources confidently and accurately in a paper with your own angle and voice. One teacher calls this step "writing in the middle" since it bridges the gap between the sources you have found and the paper you will turn in. If you skip this step, you risk misrepresenting your source, taking material out of context, plagiarizing (see Chapter 6, "Ethical Writing and Plagiarism"), or, more commonly, letting your sources take over with too much of their voice and wording, resulting in a paper that sounds patched together.

Because you should not use a source that you have not read in its entirety, we reproduce below one of Julie Ross's sources for her argument on neighborhood preservation. We will demonstrate various kinds of "writing in the middle" about this source.

Note that we have annotated this reading, an important "writing in the middle" step you should perform for every source you plan to use.

Battling Teardowns, Saving Neighborhoods

Note author's credentials

RICHARD MOE, president of the National Trust for Historic Preservation

Speech given to the Commonwealth Club, San Francisco, CA; June 28, 2006

A growing disaster is tearing apart many of America's older neighborhoods. They're being devoured, one house at a time, here in the Bay Area, across California, and in scores of communities from coast to coast.

Quotable passage here

I'm talking about teardowns—the practice of purchasing and demolishing an existing house to make way for a new, much bigger house on the same site. Teardowns wreck neighborhoods. They spread through a community like a cancer, destroying the character and livability that are a neighborhood's lifeblood. I believe teardowns represent the biggest threat to America's older neighborhoods since the heyday of urban renewal and interstate highway construction during the 1950s and 60s.

Claim

Here's how it works: Developers and home-buyers look through desirable neighborhoods for a building lot that can lawfully accommodate a much bigger house than that which currently stands on it. The property is acquired, the existing house is torn down and a bigger house is constructed in its place. There are variations: Sometimes a large estate is leveled and subdivided to accommodate several new houses; in others, several smaller houses are cleared to make way for a single, massive new one.

Extent of the problem

It's a simple process, but it can totally transform the streetscape of a neighborhood and destroy its character. It's especially destructive in older and historic communities.

Teardowns are occurring all over America—from fashionable resorts such 5 as Palm Beach and Palm Springs to the inner-ring suburbs around Washington and Chicago and the Richmond District here in San Francisco. The trend has become so alarming that the National Trust included "Teardowns in Historic Neighborhoods" on our list of America's 11 Most Endangered Historic Places in 2002. Back then, we identified 100 communities in 20 states that were having major problems with teardowns. That statistic was troubling in 2002—but four years later, the news is much worse: Today we can document the impact of teardowns in more than 300 communities in 33 states. The National Association of Home Builders says that 75,000 houses are razed and replaced with larger homes each year. . . .

Background information

This disaster goes by many names. In New Jersey, the practice is often called "bash-and-build." In Colorado, teardowns are known as "scrape-offs." In Oregon, the new houses are sometimes called "snout houses" because of the big, protruding garages that dominate their facades. In other places they're known simply—and aptly—as "bigfoots" or "monster homes."

Extent of the problem

Whatever you call it, one teardown usually sparks others. A New Jersey builder says, "It's a trend that keeps on rolling. Builders used to be afraid to be the first person in a neighborhood to tear a house down. Now they're looking around and saying they don't mind taking the risk."

Why is this happening?

Three factors are at work in the spread of teardowns.

The first is the rise in real-estate prices. In some areas, home values have 10 doubled or tripled over the past decade, and this leads developers to look for "undervalued" properties—many of which exist in older neighborhoods.

More background

The second factor is the trend toward bigger houses. In 1950, the average American home incorporated less than 1,000 sq. ft. By 2005, the average new home had more than doubled in size, to 2,412 sq. ft. According to the National Association of Home Builders, almost 40% of new homes have four or more bedrooms; that's more than twice as many as in the early 1970s—despite the fact that the average family size decreased during that same period. Subdivisions of luxury homes of 5,000 sq. ft. and more are becoming commonplace. Clearly, burgers and french fries aren't the only things in America being "super-sized."

Reasons for teardowns

The final factor is that many people are looking for an alternative to long commutes or are simply fed up with the soulless character of sprawling new subdivisions. For these people, older in-town neighborhoods and inner-ring suburbs are enormously appealing because of their attractive architecture, mature landscaping, pedestrian orientation, easy access to public transportation and amenities such as local shopping districts, libraries and schools.

Other reasons for teardowns

The problem is that too many people try to impose their preference for suburban-style mini-mansions on smaller-scale neighborhoods where they just don't fit. And since most of these older areas offer few vacant lots for new construction, the pressure to demolish existing houses can be intense. A modest cottage gets torn down and hauled off to the landfill, and what goes up in its place is "Tara" on a quarter-acre lot.

Reason against tearing down: effect on neighborhood

Neighborhood livability is diminished as trees are removed, backyards are eliminated, and sunlight is blocked by bulky new structures built right up to the property lines. Economic and social diversity are reduced as costly new "faux chateaux" replace more affordable houses—including the modest "starter homes" that our parents knew and that first-time homebuyers still search for today. . . .

While the destruction of historic houses is wasteful, environmentally unsound 15 and unnecessary, it's often just the beginning of the problems caused by teardowns.

It's not uncommon for a demolished older home to be replaced with a new one that is three times as big as any other house on the block. These structures loom over their neighbors and break the established building patterns of the area. Front yards are often given over to driveways, and three- or four-car garages are the dominant elements in the façade. Floor plans are often oriented to private interior spaces, making the new houses look like fortresses that stand totally aloof from their surroundings. . . .

Another reason against teardowns

Apart from their visual impact, teardowns can profoundly alter a neighborhood's economic and social environment. A rash of teardowns can cause property taxes to rise—and while this may be a good thing for communities in search of revenue, it can drive out moderate-income or fixed-income residents. Those who remain start to feel they've lost control of their neighborhood to developers and speculators. A house that once might have been praised as "charming and historic" now gets marketed as "older home on expansive lot"—which is realtor language for "teardown." Once that happens—once the value of an older house is perceived to be less than that of the land it's built on—the house's days are probably numbered. And sadly, the neighborhood's days as a viable historic enclave may be numbered too.

It doesn't have to be this way. There are alternatives to teardowns.

Alternatives to tearing down

First of all, prospective builders should realize that most older, established neighborhoods simply can't accommodate the kind of sprawling new mini-mansion that is appropriate on a suburban cul-de-sac. People who want to move into the city can often find development opportunities in underused historic buildings and vacant land in older areas. Even in areas where vacant land is scarce, existing older houses can be enlarged in sensitive ways: A new zoning ordinance in Coronado, California, for example, gives homebuilders "bonus" square footage if they incorporate design elements that maintain the historic character of the community.

Qualification of his argument

No one is saying that homebuyers shouldn't be able to alter or expand their 20 home to meet their needs, just as no one is saying that older neighborhoods should be frozen in time like museum exhibits. A neighborhood is a living thing, and change is both inevitable and desirable. The challenge is to manage change so that it respects the character and distinctiveness that made these neighborhoods so appealing in the first place.

Let me mention a few things that people and communities can do.

Solutions to the problem

First and most important, communities must realize that they aren't helpless in the face of teardowns. They have choices: They can simply take the kind of community they get, or they can go to work to get the kind of community they want. They have to decide what they like about the community and don't want to lose. They must develop a vision for the future of their community, including where and how to accommodate growth and change. Then they must put in place mechanisms to ensure that their vision is not compromised.

Ideally, this consensus-building should take place as part of a comprehensive planning process—but that can take time, and sometimes the pressure of teardowns calls for immediate action. In those situations, some communities have provided a "cooling-off" period by imposing a temporary moratorium on demolition. This moratorium prevents the loss of significant structures while allowing time for residents and city officials to develop effective means of preserving neighborhood character.

One of those means is local historic district designation. Notice that I said "local historic district." Many people believe that listing a property in the National Register of Historic Places is enough to protect it, but that isn't true. The only real protection comes through the enactment of a local ordinance that regulates demolition, new construction and alteration in a designated historic area. More than 2,500 communities across the country have enacted these ordinances. Most of them require that an owner get permission before demolishing or altering a historic building; many also offer design guidelines to ensure that new buildings will harmonize with their older neighbors.

More solutions

If historic district designation isn't feasible or appropriate, other forms of regu- 25 lation may work. Conservation districts or design-review districts can address issues such as demolition and new construction with less administrative burden than historic districts. Floor-area ratios or lot-coverage formulas can remove the economic incentive for teardowns by limiting the size of new buildings. In the same way, setback requirements, height limits and open-space standards can help maintain traditional neighborhood building patterns. At least two communities in San Mateo County have recently adopted regulations of this sort to limit the height and floor area of newly built homes.

Not all approaches require government involvement. Local preservation organizations or neighborhood groups can offer programs to educate realtors and new residents about the history of older neighborhoods and provide guidance in rehabbing or expanding older houses. They can acquire easements to ensure that the architectural character of historic buildings is permanently protected. They can provide low-interest loans to help encourage sensitive rehabilitation. Incentives such as these are particularly effective when combined with technical assistance and some form of tax abatement from state or local government.

Some people go so far as to claim that teardowns actually support smart growth by directing new-home construction to already-developed areas, thereby increasing density and offering an alternative to suburban sprawl. Again, I disagree.

Opposing view and rebuttal

Tearing down a smaller house to build a bigger one simply adds square footage, not population density. In addition, teardowns affect neighborhood livability, reduce affordability, consume energy, and send thousands of tons of demolition debris to landfills. That doesn't sound like smart growth to me.

Equally important, teardowns exact too high a price in the wasteful destruction of our nation's heritage. Of course we need to encourage investment in existing communities as an alternative to sprawl—but not at the expense of the historic character that makes older neighborhoods unique, attractive and livable. Some say that change is simply the price of progress—but this kind of change isn't progress at all; it's chaos.

The National Trust is committed to helping local residents put the brakes on 30 teardowns. It will be a huge job—but it's eminently worthy of our best efforts.

America's older neighborhoods are important chapters in the story of who we are as a nation and a people. Working together, we can keep that story alive. Working together, we can keep America's older and historic communities intact so that generations to come can live in them, learn from them, be sheltered and inspired by them—just as we are today.

Ways of "Writing-in-the-Middle" to Gain Mastery over Your Sources

We borrow the term "writing-in-the-middle" from Bruce Ballenger, whose excellent book *The Curious Researcher* contains many suggestions for bridging the chasm between the writing that you read and the writing that you produce as a result of reading. The more you engage your sources with "talk-back" such as annotations, notebook responses to the ideas in the sources, notebook entries that make connections between and among ideas in sources, and paraphrases and summaries that make you really think about the key points and passages, the easier it will be for you to assume the voice of authority when it is time to start drafting your paper. Here are some suggestions for writing in the middle zone between researching and drafting.

1. Annotate the Source

Use the advice in Chapter 2, "Reading an Argument," which suggests things to look for in sources that are arguments. If a source is not an argument, note the author's angle, bias, and main points.

2. Respond to the Source in Your Notebook

After annotating, write more in your notebook about how you might use the source. If you have roughed out a case, note which reason or reasons of your own case this source could help you develop. If you find a new reason for your case, note it and think how you could develop it with your own observations and other sources you have found.

If you think the source will be mainly useful for facts, make a note about what kind of facts it has and the page numbers, so that when you start drafting, you can find them quickly.

If the author is an expert or authority, note the credentials or at least where you can go to find these as you start drafting—perhaps the author's Web page or a biographical note at the end of the book or article.

If this will be a major source for your paper, you should be sure you grasp the most important concepts in it. Look for the passages that pose a challenge; to use the source with authority, you need to own, not borrow, these ideas. That means instead of just dropping them in as quotations, you will have to work them in, explaining them in your own words. Try out *paraphrases* (see more on paraphrases in item 3 in this list) to make these points completely clear to you and then respond to the major ideas with what you think about them: If it's a good idea, why do you think so? What in your own experiences (field research) confirms it? What can you add of your own as you discuss this idea in your paper?

Look for memorable passages that are worth *direct quotations* (see more on direct quotations in this chapter's section on incorporating source material). The best quotes are strongly worded opinions and writing that cannot be paraphrased without losing its punch.

Think about how additional research might help you develop an idea given to you by this source.

Here are some notes Julie put in her notebook after deciding to use the National Trust source.

Notes on Moe, Richard. "Battling Teardowns."

- *Perfect source for my paper. I need to mention the National Trust for Historic Preservation. This source supports my "preserve the neighborhood character" reason. Good description of the garages—"snout houses." Also mention the way these new houses block the sunlight. Good on the economic impact on the older people in my neighborhood. Many can't afford to stay. This source helps explain why.*

- *I also hadn't thought about how these homebuyers are destroying the very thing that makes them want to live here. Old charm won't last if everybody does what they are doing. This could appeal to their interest—restore, not tear down.*

- *I like the part about allowing for change. I'll use this quote: "A neighborhood is a living thing. Change is both inevitable and desirable." What kinds of changes would I consider OK? Could a new house of different architectural style actually add character to the neighborhood? Maybe look for a source that describes some kind of acceptable change.*

- *He mentions the other part of my case, the environment, but not enough to use this source for that part.*

---

3. Paraphrase Important Ideas from the Source

Although you will use paraphrases as you incorporate material from your sources into your essay, consider paraphrase as a study skill that helps you understand key ideas by putting them into your own words. It helps you to "own" the key ideas rather than simply borrowing the author's words to insert into your paper. Here are some suggestions for paraphrasing:

- Read the entire source or section in which the passage appears. You cannot write a good paraphrase of a passage you have taken out of context.

Surrounding sentences will provide information essential for understanding the material you are paraphrasing, and to make the idea clear to yourself, you may need to add some of that information to your paraphrase. Later, if you use the paraphrase in your paper, you will need to provide enough context so that your readers will understand the idea as well.

- Read the passage several times through, including surrounding text, until you think you understand it. Annotate it. Look up any words that are even slightly unfamiliar to you.

- Put the text away so that you will not be tempted to look at it. Then think of the main ideas and try to put each one into your own words and your own wording. A paraphrase must not be an echo of the original's sentence patterns with synonyms plugged in. That is really a form of plagiarism, since it involves "stealing" the author's sentence pattern. You may want to break up complex sentences into shorter, more simple ones that make the idea easier to comprehend.

- Do not feel that you must find a substitute word for every ordinary word in the passage. For example, if a passage has the word *children,* don't feel you have to say *kids.*

- Go back and check your paraphrase against the original to see if you have accurately represented the full content of the original passage. Make adjustments as needed.

Examples of Adequate and Inadequate Paraphrasing
Original Passage:

Some people go so far as to claim that teardowns actually support smart growth by directing new-home construction to already-developed areas, thereby increasing density and offering an alternative to suburban sprawl. Again, I disagree. Tearing down a smaller house to build a bigger one simply adds square footage, not population density.

Inadequate Paraphrase: This example borrows too much of the wording and sentence patterns (underlined) from the original text by Moe.

Some people even claim that tearing down old houses supports smart growth by increasing new-home construction and density in already developed areas. Therefore, teardowns are an alternative to suburban sprawl. Moe disagrees because tearing down small houses and building bigger ones only adds more square footage, not more people.

Inadequate Paraphrase: The paraphrase below doesn't do justice to the idea: It does not include the concept of smart growth; it does not mention the problem of new development in suburban areas versus rebuilding in existing neighborhoods; and it does not give Moe credit for the opinion.

It's not smart to tear down old houses and replace them with bigger ones because you don't get more population density.

Good Paraphrase: This explains "smart growth," gives Moe credit, and represents all the points in original sentence patterns. It even offers an interpretation at the end.

> Smart growth is an attempt to develop cities while minimizing suburban sprawl. According to Moe, tearing down older, small homes in close-in neighborhoods and replacing them with bigger ones is not really "smart growth" because bigger houses do not necessarily increase population density; they just offer more square footage for the same size household. So they are really a kind of urban sprawl.

4. Write Summaries of Portions of a Source

As a way to help get your own handle on important sections of a source, write a summary of it in your notebook. That means putting just the most important parts of the text into your own words (paraphrase) and joining them into a smooth paragraph. To write a summary, follow these steps.

1. Read and reread the portion of a text you want to summarize, looking up unfamiliar words.

2. Choose the main points.

3. Paraphrase them, using the advice on paraphrasing above.

4. Combine sentences to make the new version as concise as possible.

Here is an example of a portion of Richard Moe's speech that Julie used in her paper by shortening it and presenting it in her own words. The underlined sections are the ones she deemed important enough to go into the summary.

Original Passage:

Three factors are at work in the spread of teardowns.

The first is the rise in real-estate prices. In some areas, home values have doubled or tripled over the past decade, and this leads developers to look for "undervalued" properties—many of which exist in older neighborhoods. The second factor is the trend toward bigger houses. In 1950, the average American home incorporated less than 1,000 sq. ft. By 2005, the average new home had more than doubled in size, to 2,412 sq. ft. According to the National Association of Home Builders, almost 40% of new homes have four or more bedrooms; that's more than twice as many as in the early 1970s—despite the fact that the average family size decreased during that same period. Subdivisions of luxury homes of 5,000 sq. ft. and more are becoming commonplace. Clearly, burgers and french fries aren't the only things in America being "super-sized." The final factor is that many people are looking for an alternative to long commutes or are simply fed up with the soulless character of sprawling new subdivisions. For these people, older in-town neighborhoods and inner-ring suburbs are enormously appealing because of their attractive architecture, mature landscaping, pedestrian orientation, easy access to public transportation and amenities such as local shopping districts, libraries and schools.

Guidelines for Summarizing

1. Read and reread the original text until you have identified the claim and the main supporting points. You ought to be able to write an outline of the case, using your own words. Depending on your purpose for summarizing and the amount of space you can devote to the summary, decide how much, if any, of the evidence to include.

2. Make it clear at the start whose ideas you are summarizing.

3. If you are summarizing a long passage, break it down into subsections and work on summarizing one at a time.

4. As with paraphrasing, work from memory. Go back to the text to check your version for accuracy.

5. Maintain the original order of points, with this exception: If the author delayed presenting the thesis, refer to it earlier in your summary.

6. Use your own words.

7. Avoid quoting entire sentences. If you want to quote key words and phrases, incorporate them into sentences of your own, using quotation marks around the borrowed words.

Julie's Summary:

> Moe sees three reasons for the increase in teardowns:
>
> - In the past decade, the value of houses has doubled or tripled, except in some older neighborhoods. Developers look for these "'undervalued' properties" to build on.
>
> - Homebuyers want more space, with the average home size going from 1,000 square feet in 1950 to 2,412 square feet in 2005.
>
> - Some homebuyers desire to move from the "soulless . . . sprawling subdivisions" to close-in neighborhoods that have more character and more amenities, such as public transportation and local shopping.

5. Write Capsule Summaries of Entire Sources

Writers frequently have to summarize the content of an entire source in just a brief paragraph. Such summaries appear in the introduction to a volume of collected essays, in an opening section of scholarly articles in which the author reviews previously published literature on the topic, and at the end of books or articles in annotated bibliographies or works cited lists. The purpose of these is to let other scholars know about sources they might also want to consult.

If your class is working on a common topic, your instructor may ask the class to assemble a working bibliography of sources all of you have found, including a brief summary of each one to let other students know what the source contains. This is called an "annotated bibliography." Following is some advice on creating capsule summaries and annotated bibliographies.

Sample Entry in an Annotated Bibliography

Here is an annotated bibliography entry for Julie's National Trust source.

> Moe, Richard. "Battling Teardowns, Saving Neighborhoods." The National Trust for Historic Preservation. June 28, 2006. <http://www.national-trust.org/news/2006/20060628_speech_sf.html> Jan. 21, 2007.
>
> In this transcript of a speech given to a San Francisco civic organization, Moe, who is president of the National Trust for Historic Preservation, argues that builders should respect the integrity of older neighborhoods and that local residents should join the Trust's efforts to block the teardown trend, which is fueled by rising real estate values, homebuyers' desire for bigger houses, and fatigue with life in the distant suburbs. Teardowns "wreck neighborhoods" by removing trees and backyards, blocking the sun, ruining historic character, raising taxes so that poorer residents are forced out, and generating environmental waste. Communities can organize to fight teardowns by applying for historical designation or other kinds of government regulations on building as well as offering incentives for realtors and new buyers to respect neighborhood quality.

1. As explained in Chapter 2, "Reading an Argument," read and annotate the entire source, noting claims, reasons, the subdivisions into which the text breaks down, and definitions of words you looked up.

2. Working with one subdivision at a time, write paraphrases of the main ideas in each. Decide how much specific evidence would be appropriate to include, depending on the purpose of your summary. As with any paraphrase, work from memory and recheck the original later for accuracy.

3. You may include brief direct quotations, but avoid quoting whole sentences. That is not efficient.

4. Join your paraphrases into a coherent and smooth paragraph.

5. Edit your summary to reduce repetitions and to combine points into single sentences where possible.

Note that a good capsule summary restates the main points; it doesn't just describe them.

> *Not:* Moe gives three reasons for the rise of the teardown trend.

> *But:* Moe argues that the teardown trend is fueled by rising real estate values, homebuyers' desire for bigger houses, and fatigue with life in the distant suburbs.

Guidelines for Writing with Sources

Avoid plagiarism by *distinguishing sharply* between quoting and paraphrasing. Anytime you take exact words from a source, even if it is only a phrase or a significant word, you are quoting. You must use quotation marks and documentation. If you make any change at all in the wording of a quotation, you must indicate the change with square brackets. If you remove any words from a direct quotation, use ellipses (three spaced dots) to indicate the deletion. If you use your own words to summarize or paraphrase portions of a source, name that source in your text and document it. Be careful to use your own words when paraphrasing and summarizing.

1. Use an attributive tag such as "According to . . ." to introduce quotations both direct and indirect. Don't just drop them in.

2. Name the person whose words or idea you are using. Provide the full name on first mention.

3. Identify the author(s) of your source by profession or affiliation so that readers will understand the significance of what he or she has to say. Omit this if the speaker is someone readers are familiar with.

4. Use transitions into quotations to link the ideas they express to whatever point you are making.

5. If your lead-in to a quotation is a phrase, follow it with a comma. But if your lead-in can stand alone as a sentence, follow it with a colon.

6. Place the period at the end of a quotation or paraphrase, after the parenthetical citation, except with block quotations. (See page 134 for treatment of block quotations.)

6. Dialogue about Sources

Inside or outside of class, any conversations you can have about your research with others researching the same topic will help you get an angle and an understanding of your sources. This is the reason many scholars keep blogs— a blog is a place to converse about ideas. Your instructor may set up an electronic bulletin board for students to chat about their research, or you might make your own blog with friends and start chatting.

INCORPORATING AND DOCUMENTING SOURCE MATERIAL

We turn now to the more technical matter of how to incorporate source material in your own writing and how to document it. You incorporate material through direct quotation or through summary or paraphrase; you document material by naming the writer and providing full publication details of the source—a two-step process. In academic writing, documenting sources is essential, with one exception: You do not need to document sources of factual information that can easily be found in common references, such as an encyclopedia or atlas, or of common knowledge. See page 155 in Chapter 6, "Ethical Writing and Plagiarism," for more explanation of common knowledge.

Different Styles of Documentation

Different disciplines have specific conventions for documentation. In the humanities, the most common style is the Modern Language Association (MLA). In the physical, natural, and social sciences, the American Psychological Association (APA) style is most often used. We will illustrate both in the examples that follow. Both MLA and APA use parenthetical citations in the text and simple, alphabetical bibliographies at the end, making revision and typing much easier. (For a detailed explanation of these two styles, visit the Web sites for the MLA at <http://www.mla.org> and the APA at <http://apa.org>.)

In both MLA and APA formats, you provide some information in the body of your paper and the rest of the information under the heading "Works Cited" (MLA) or "References" (APA) at the end of your paper. The following summarizes the essentials of both systems.

Instructions for Using MLA and APA Styles

MLA Style

In parentheses at the end of both direct and indirect quotations, supply the last name of the author of the source and the exact page number(s) where the quoted or paraphrased words appear. If the name of the author appears in your sentence that leads into the quotation, omit it in the parentheses.

Direct quotation with source identified in the lead-in:

> According to Jessie Sackett, a member of the U.S. Green Building Council, home ownership is "the cornerstone of the American dream. Recently, however, we've realized that keeping that dream alive for future generations means making some changes to how we live today" (36).

Indirect quotation with source cited in parenthetical citation:

> A spokesperson for the U.S. Green Building Council reminds us that home ownership is fundamental to the American dream; however, in order to preserve that dream for the generations to come, we need to develop more energy efficient houses and lifestyles today (Sackett 36).

APA Style

In parentheses at the end of direct or indirect quotations, place the author's last name, the date published, and the page number(s) where the cited material appears. If the author's name appears in the sentence, the date of publication should follow it in parentheses; the page number still comes at the end of the sentence. Unlike MLA, the APA style uses commas between the parts of the citation and "p." or "pp." before the page numbers.

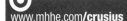

www.mhhe.com/**crusius**

For Web sites with information on documentation styles, go to:

Research > Annotated Links to Documentation Sites

www.mhhe.com/**crusius**

You can find more documentation information at:

Research > Links to Documentation Sites

www.mhhe.com/**crusius**

For a student sample of a paper in MLA format, go to:

Research > Sample Paper in MLA Style

www.mhhe.com/**crusius**

For a student sample of a paper in APA format, go to:

Research > Sample Paper in APA Style

Direct quotation with source cited in the lead-in:

> Jessie Sackett (2006), a member of the U.S. Green Building Council, writes, "Owning a home is the cornerstone of the American dream. Recently, however, we've realized that keeping that dream alive for future generations means making some changes to how we live today" (p. 36).

Indirect quotation with source cited in parenthetical citation:

> A spokesperson for the U.S. Green Building Council reminds us that home ownership is fundamental to the American dream; however, in order to preserve that dream for the generations to come, we need to develop more energy efficient houses and lifestyles today (Sackett, 2006, p. 36).

Direct Quotations

Direct quotations are exact words taken from a source. The simplest direct quotations are whole sentences worked into your text, as illustrated in the following excerpt.

MLA Style

> Richard Moe of the National Trust for Historic Preservation explains, "The problem is that too many people try to impose their preference for suburban-style mini-mansions on smaller scale neighborhoods where they just don't fit."

This source will be listed in the MLA Works Cited list as follows:

> Moe, Richard. "Battling Teardowns, Saving Neighborhoods." The National Trust for Historic Preservation. 28 June 2006. 15 Jan. 2007 <http://www.nationaltrust.org/news/2006/20060628_speech_sf.html>.

APA Style

> Richard Moe (2006) of the National Trust for Historic Preservation explains, "The problem is that too many people try to impose their preference for suburban-style mini-mansions on smaller scale neighborhoods where they just don't fit."

This source will be listed in the APA reference list as follows:

> Moe, R. (2006, June 28). Battling teardowns, saving neighborhoods. Retrieved Jan. 15, 2007, from *The National Trust for Historic Preservation* web site: http://www.nationaltrust.org/news/2006/20060628_speech_sf.html

Note that for both MLA and APA format, a page number is usually required with any citation. Because the source does not use page numbers, in this instance they are not included.

Altering Direct Quotations with Ellipses and Square Brackets

Although there is nothing wrong with quoting whole sentences, it is often more economical to quote some words or parts of sentences from the original in your own sentences. When you do this, use *ellipses* (three evenly spaced periods) to signify the omission of words from the original; use square *brackets* to substitute words, to add words for purposes of clarification, and to change the wording of a quotation so that it fits gracefully into your own sentence. (If ellipses already appear in the material you are quoting and you are omitting additional material, place your ellipses in square brackets to distinguish them.)

The following passage illustrates quoted words integrated into the sentence, using ellipses and square brackets. The citation is in MLA style.

Square Brackets   Use square brackets to indicate any substitutions or alterations to a direct quotation.

Original passage:

> Teardowns wreck neighborhoods. They spread through a community like a cancer, destroying the character and livability that are a neighborhood's lifeblood.

Passage worked into the paper: Part of the quotation has been turned into paraphrase.

> Moe compares the teardown trend to a cancer on the community: "Teardowns wreck neighborhoods. They [destroy] the character and livability that are a neighborhood's lifeblood."

Ellipses   Use three spaced periods to indicate where words have been removed from a direct quotation.

Original passage:

> Almost every one of these new, large homes is made out of wood—roughly three-quarters of an acre of forest. Much of the destructive logging around the world is fueled by our demand for housing. But home-building doesn't have to translate into forest destruction. By using smart design and forest-friendly products, builders can create new homes that save trees and money.
>
> Many houses today are still built using outdated, inefficient construction methods. About one-sixth of the wood delivered to a construction site is never used, but simply hauled away as waste.

Passage worked into the paper: Two entire sentences have been removed, replaced with ellipses, because they were not relevant to the point Julie was making. There are no quotation marks because this will be a blocked quotation in the paper.

Almost every one of these new, large homes is made out of wood—roughly three-quarters of an acre of forest. Much of the destructive logging around the world is fueled by our demand for housing. . . . Many houses today are still built using outdated, inefficient construction methods. About one-sixth of the wood delivered to a construction site is never used, but simply hauled away as waste.

Using Block Quotations

If a quoted passage runs to four or more lines of text in your essay, indent it one inch (ten spaces of type) from the left margin, double-space it as with the rest of your text, and omit quotation marks. In block quotations, a period is placed at the end of the final sentence, followed by one space and the parenthetical citation.

In a consumer society, when people see their neighbors driving a new car, they think they need to buy a new one too. This is called "keeping up with the Joneses." Gregg Easterbrook has coined a new phrase, "call and raise the Joneses." He explains his new term this way:

> In call-and-raise-the-Joneses, Americans feel compelled not just to match the material possessions of others, but to stay ahead. Bloated houses, for one, arise from a desire to call-and-raise-the-Joneses— surely not from a belief that a seven-thousand-square-foot house that comes right up against the property setback line would be an ideal place in which to dwell. (140)

Indirect Quotations

Indirect quotations are paraphrases or summaries of a source. Here is how this quotation might be incorporated in a paper as an indirect quotation.

MLA Style

A spokesperson for the U.S. Green Building Council reminds us that home ownership is fundamental to the American dream; however, in order to preserve that dream for the generations to come, we need to develop more energy efficient houses and lifestyles today (Sackett 36).

The entry in the Works Cited list would appear as follows:

Sackett, Jessie. "The Green American Dream: LEED for Homes Is Currently Being Piloted." The LEED Guide: Environmental Design & Construction. 9.6 (2006): 36+. InfoTrac Thomson Gale. Southern Methodist U, Fondren Lib., Dallas, TX. 18 Oct. 2006 <http://find.galegroup.com>.

APA Style

A spokesperson for the U.S. Green Building Council reminds us that home ownership is fundamental to the American dream; however, in order to

Leading into Direct Quotations

Direct quotations need to be set up, not dropped into your paper. Setting up a quotation means leading into it with words of your own. A lead-in may be a short introductory tag such as "According to Smith," if you have already introduced Smith, but lead-ins usually need more thought. You need to connect the quotation to the ideas surrounding it in the original source.

Provide enough of the original context to fit the quotation coherently into your paragraph. You may need to paraphrase some of the surrounding sentences from the original source from which the quotation was taken. If you have not done so already, you may need to introduce the speaker of the words, along with his or her credentials if the speaker is an important writer or authority.

Here is an example of a quotation that does not fit coherently into the student's paper.

Quotation dropped in:

> Affluent Americans are buying new super-sized homes in older, urban residential areas. These lots were once occupied by historic and humble homes. "Teardowns wreck neighborhoods. They [destroy] the character and livability that are a neighborhood's lifeblood" (Moe).

Here is how Julie Ross led into the same quotation so that her readers would know more about the speaker and his point.

Quotation worked in:

> Affluent Americans are buying new super-sized homes in older, urban residential areas. These lots were once occupied by historic and humble houses. The older houses are now known as "teardowns." In their place, towering "McMansions" dominate the street. Richard Moe, President of the National Trust for Historic Preservation, reports that teardowns affect over 300 U.S. cities, with a total of 75,000 older houses razed each year. Moe compares the teardown trend to a cancer on the community: "Teardowns wreck neighborhoods. They [destroy] the character and livability that are a neighborhood's lifeblood" (Q00).

Introduces the speaker.

Provides context for the quotation.

Parenthetical citation of author's name not needed because author is cited in text.

> preserve that dream for the generations to come, we need to develop more energy efficient houses and lifestyles today (Sackett, 2006, p. 36).

The entry in the References list would appear as follows:

> Sackett, J. (2006). The green American dream: LEED for homes is currently being piloted. *The LEED Guide: Environmental Design & Construction.* 9.6 (2006): 36+. Retrieved 18 Oct. 2006, from InfoTrac Thomson Gale.

In-Text References to Electronic Sources

The conventions just described apply to print sources. Adapt the examples to Internet and other electronic sources. Because you must include the electronic sources in your works-cited or reference list, your in-text citations should connect the material quoted or paraphrased in your text to the matching work or posting on the list. Therefore, your in-text citation should begin with the author's name or, lacking that, the title of the work or posting. The APA format requires that you also include the posting date.

CREATING WORKS-CITED AND REFERENCE LISTS

www.mhhe.com/**crusius**

For an electronic tool that helps create properly formatted works-cited pages, go to:

Research > Bibliomaker

At the end of your paper, include a bibliography of all sources that you quoted, paraphrased, or summarized. If you are using MLA style, your heading for this list will be *Works Cited*; if you are using APA style, it will be *References*. In either case, the list is in alphabetical order based on either the author's (or editor's) last name or—in the case of unidentified authors—the first word of the title, not counting the articles *a, an, the*. The entire list is double-spaced both within and between entries. See the works-cited page of the sample student paper at the end of this chapter for the correct indentation and spacing. Note that MLA format requires that the first line of each entry be typed flush with the left margin; subsequent lines of each entry are indented half an inch (five spaces on a typewriter). The APA recommends the same indentation.

The following examples illustrate the correct MLA and APA style for the types of sources you will most commonly use.

Books

Book by One Author

MLA: Crusius, Timothy W. Discourse: A Critique & Synthesis of Major Theories. New York: MLA, 1989.

APA: Crusius, T. W. (1989). *Discourse: A critique & synthesis of major theories*. New York: Modern Language Association.

(Note that APA uses initials rather than the author's first name and capitalizes only the first word and proper nouns in titles and subtitles.)

Two or More Works by the Same Author

MLA: Crusius, Timothy W. Discourse: A Critique & Synthesis of Major Theories. New York: MLA, 1989.

  --- A Teacher's Introduction to Philosophical Hermeneutics. Urbana: NCTE, 1991.

(Note that MLA arranges works alphabetically by title and uses three hyphens to show that the name is the same as the one directly above.)

APA: Crusius, T. W. (1989). *Discourse: A critique & synthesis of major theories*. New York: Modern Language Association.

  Crusius, T. W. (1991). *A teacher's introduction to philosophical hermeneutics*. Urbana, IL: National Council of Teachers of English.

(Note that APA repeats the author's name and arranges works in chrono-
logical order.)

Book by Two or Three Authors

MLA: Deleuze, Gilles, and Felix Guattari. <u>Anti-Oedipus: Capitalism and Schizo-
phrenia.</u> New York: Viking, 1977.

APA: Deleuze, G., & Guattari, F. (1977). *Anti-Oedipus: Capitalism and schizo-
phrenia.* New York: Viking.

(Note that MLA style inverts only the first author's name. APA style, however, inverts both authors' names and uses an ampersand [&] between authors
instead of the word "and.")

Book by Four or More Authors

MLA: Bellah, Robert N., et al. <u>Habits of the Heart: Individualism and Commitment in American Life</u>. New York: Harper, 1985.

(Note that the Latin abbreviation *et al.*, meaning "and others," stands in for
all subsequent authors' names. MLA style also accepts spelling out all authors'
names instead of using *et al.*)

APA: Bellah, R., Madsen, R., Sullivan, W., Swidler, A., & Tipton, S. (1985).
*Habits of the heart: Individualism and commitment in American
life.* New York: Harper & Row.

(Note that APA uses *et al.* only for more than six authors.)

Book Prepared by an Editor or Editors

MLA: Connors, Robert J., ed. <u>Selected Essays of Edward P. J. Corbett</u>. Dallas:
Southern Methodist UP, 1989.

APA: Connors, R. J. (Ed.). (1989). *Selected essays of Edward P. J. Corbett.*
Dallas: Southern Methodist University Press.

Work in an Edited Collection

MLA: Jackson, Jesse. "Common Ground: Speech to the Democratic National Convention." <u>The American Reader</u>. Ed. Diane Ravitch. New York:
Harper, 1991. 367–71.

APA: Jackson, J. (1991). Common ground: Speech to the Democratic National
Convention. In D. Ravitch (Ed.), *The American reader* (pp. 367–371).
New York: HarperCollins.

Translated Book

MLA: Vattimo, Gianni. <u>The End of Modernity: Nihilism and Hermeneutics in
Postmodern Culture</u>. Trans. Jon R. Snyder. Baltimore: Johns
Hopkins UP, 1988.

APA: Vattimo, G. (1988). The end of modernity: *Nihilism and hermeneutics in postmodern culture.* (J. R. Snyder, Trans.). Baltimore: Johns Hopkins University Press.

Periodicals

Article in a Journal with Continuous Pagination

MLA: Herron, Jerry. "Writing for My Father." College English 54 (1992): 928–37.

APA: Herron, J. (1992). Writing for my father. *College English, 54,* 928–937.

(Note that in APA style the article title is not fully capitalized, but the journal title is. Note also that the volume number is italicized in APA style.)

Article in a Journal Paginated by Issue

MLA: McConnell, Margaret Liu. "Living with Roe v. Wade." Commentary 90.5 (1990): 34–38.

APA: McConnell, M. L. (1990). Living with *Roe v. Wade. Commentary,* 90(5), 34–38.

(In both examples, "90" is the volume number and "5" is the number of the issue.)

Article in a Magazine

MLA: D'Souza, Dinesh. "Illiberal Education." Atlantic Mar. 1990: 51+.

(Note that the plus sign indicates that the article runs on nonconsecutive pages.)

APA: D'Souza, D. (1990, March). Illiberal education. *Atlantic,* pp. 51–58, 62–65, 67, 70–74, 76, 78–79.

(Note that APA requires all page numbers to be listed.)

Anonymous Article in a Newspaper

MLA: "Clinton Warns of Sacrifice." Dallas Morning News 7 Feb. 1993: A4.

APA: Clinton warns of sacrifice. (1993, February 7). *The Dallas Morning News,* p. A4.

(In both examples, the "A" refers to the newspaper section in which the article appeared.)

Editorial in a Newspaper

MLA: Lewis, Flora. "Civil Society, the Police and Abortion." Editorial. New York Times 12 Sept. 1992, late ed.: A14.

APA: Lewis, F. (1992, September 12). Civil society, the police and abortion [Editorial]. *The New York Times,* p. A14.

(Note that in MLA style the edition of the newspaper must be specified.)

Nonprint Sources

Interview

MLA: May, William. Personal interview. 24 Apr. 1990.

(Note that APA style documents personal interviews only parenthetically within the text: "According to W. May [personal interview, April 24, 1990], . . ." Personal interviews are not included on the reference list.)

Sound Recording

MLA: Glass, Philip. Glassworks. CBS Sony, MK 37265, 1982.

APA: Glass, P. (1982). *Glassworks* [CD Recording No. MK 37265]. Tokyo: CBS Sony.

Film

MLA: Scott, Ridley, dir. Thelma and Louise. Perf. Susan Sarandon, Geena Davis, and Harvey Keitel. 1991. Videocassette. MGM/UA Home Video, 1996.

APA: Scott, R. (Director). (1991). *Thelma and Louise* [Motion picture]. Culver City, CA: MGM/UA Home Video.

(Note that with nonprint media, you identify the medium—CD, DVD, videocassette, film, and so forth. MLA includes the principal actors, but APA does not. APA specifies the place of production, but MLA does not.)

Electronic Sources

Although the documentation requirements for MLA and APA citations of electronic sources contain much of the same information, there are also differences. Use the following lists as general guides when you cite Internet sources.

MLA Style: Citing Internet Sources

1. Author's or editor's name, followed by a period
2. Title of the article or short work (such as a short story or poem) followed by a period and enclosed by quotation marks
3. Name of the book, journal, or other longer work underlined
4. Publication information, followed by a period:
   City, publisher, and date for books
   Volume and year for journals
   Date for magazines
   Date for and description of government documents
5. Date on which you accessed the information (no period)
6. URL, placed inside angle brackets, followed by a period

APA Style: Citing Internet Sources

1. Author's or editor's last name, followed by a comma and the initials
2. Year of publication, followed by a comma, with the month and day for magazine and newspaper articles, within parentheses and followed by a period
3. Title of the article, book, or journal (follow APA conventions for titles of works)
4. Volume number
5. Page numbers
6. The words "Retrieved from," followed by the date of access, followed by the source (such as the World Wide Web) and a colon
7. URL, without a period

Online Book

MLA: Strunk, William. <u>The Elements of Style</u>. 1st ed. Geneva: Humphrey, 1918. May 1995. Columbia U Academic Information Systems, Bartleby Lib. 12 Apr. 1999 <http://www.Columbia.edu/acis/bartleby/strunk/strunk100.html>.

APA: Strunk, W. (1918). *The elements of style* (1st ed.). [Online]. Retrieved April 12, 1999, from http://www.Columbia.edu/acis/bartleby/strunk/strunk100.html

(Note that MLA requires that the original publication data be included if it is available for works that originally appeared in print. The APA, however, requires only an online availability statement.)

World Wide Web Site

MLA: <u>Victorian Women Writers Project</u>. Ed. Perry Willett. Apr. 1999. Indiana U. 12 Apr. 1999 <http://www.indiana.edu/~letrs/vwwp>.

APA: Willett, P. (1999, April). *Victorian women writers project* [Web page]. Retrieved April 12, 1999, from http://www.indiana.edu/~letrs/vwwp

Document on a Web Site

MLA: Moe, Richard. "Battling Teardowns, Saving Neighborhoods." <u>The National Trust for Historic Preservation</u>. 28 June 2006. 15 Jan. 2007 <http://www.nationaltrust.org/news/2006/20060628_speech_sf.html>.

APA: Moe, R. (2006, June 28). Battling teardowns, saving neighborhoods. Retrieved Jan. 15, 2007, from *The National Trust for Historic Preservation* Web site: http://www.nationaltrust.org/news/2006/20060628_speech_sf.html

Article in an Electronic Journal

MLA: Harnack, Andrew, and Gene Kleppinger. "Beyond the *MLA Handbook:* Documenting Sources on the Internet." <u>Kairos</u> 1.2 (Summer 1996). 7 Jan. 1997 <http://english.ttu.edu/Kairos/1.2/index.html>.

APA: Harnack, A., & Kleppinger, G. (1996). Beyond the *MLA Handbook:* Documenting sources on the Internet. *Kairos* [Online], *1*(2). Retrieved January 7, 1997, from http://english.ttu.edu/Kairos/1.2/index. html

Encyclopedia Article on CD-ROM

MLA: Duckworth, George. "Rhetoric." <u>Microsoft Encarta</u> '95. CD-ROM. Redmond: Microsoft, 1995.

APA: Duckworth. G. (1995). Rhetoric. In *Microsoft encarta '95* [CD-ROM]. Redmond, WA: Microsoft.

Encyclopedia Article Online

MLA: "Toni Morrison." <u>Encyclopaedia Britannica Online</u>. 1994–1999. Encyclopaedia Britannica. 4 Mar. 1999 <http://members.eb.com/bol/topic?eu=55183&sctn=#s_top>.

APA: (1994–1999). Toni Morrison. In *Encyclopaedia Britannica Online* [Online]. Retrieved March 4, 1999, from http://members.eb.com/bol/topic?eu=55183&sctn=#s_top

E-Mail, Listserv, and Newsgroup Citations

For MLA, give in this order the author's name, the title of the document (in quotation marks), followed by the description *Online posting,* the date when the material was posted, the name of the forum (if known), the date of access, and in angle brackets the online address of the list's Internet site or, if unknown, the e-mail address of the list's moderator.

MLA: Stockwell, Stephen. "Rhetoric and Democracy." Online posting. 13 Jan. 1997. 22 Jan. 1997 <H-Rhetor@msu.edu>.

For APA, the custom is not to include e-mail, listservs, and newsgroups in a reference list but rather to give a detailed in-text citation as follows: (S. Stockwell, posting to H-Rhetor@msu.edu, January 13, 1997).

However, if the content of the message is scholarly, many researchers do include messages in the references:

APA: Stockwell, S. (1997, January 13). Rhetoric and democracy. Retrieved January 22, 1997, from e-mail: H-Rhetor@msu.edu

STUDENT SAMPLE: A RESEARCH PAPER (MLA STYLE)

Ross 1

Standard heading

Julie Ross
ENGL 1301, Section 009
April 20, 2007
Professor Channell

Title centered

Why Residential Construction Needs to Get a Conscience

www.mhhe.com/**crusius**

For another model essay in MLA format, go to:

Research > Sample Paper in MLA Style

Entire essay is double-spaced

Introduction announces topic

Home ownership is a significant part of the American dream. Americans take great pride in putting down roots and raising a family in a good neighborhood. And, if a recent boom in residential construction is any indication, more Americans are realizing that dream. In addition to the number of new homes being built, the average home size has also grown significantly, almost twice as large as in the 1960s ("How to Build"). The question is: what is the impact of super-sized houses on our neighborhoods and our environment?

Poses issue the argument will address

No word breaks at end of lines

In big cities like Dallas, huge new houses are springing up in the outer-ring suburbs like Frisco and Flower Mound. The National Association of Homebuilders reports that the average size of a single-family home has grown from 983 square feet in 1950 to 2,434 square feet in 2005, "even as the average household shrunk from 3.4 to 2.6 people" (Brown 23). This desire for more living space keeps cities sprawling outward as developers look for open land. However, urban residential areas are also now impacted by new building. Affluent Americans are buying new super-sized homes in older, urban residential areas. These lots were once occupied by historic and humble houses. The older houses are now known as "teardowns." In their place, towering "McMansions" dominate the street. Richard Moe, President of the National Trust for Historic Preservation, reports that

Author's last name and page number in MLA style

Full name and credentials of authors who have expertise

Ross 2

teardowns affect over 300 U.S. cities, with a total of 75,000 older houses razed each year.

Moe compares the teardown trend to a cancer on the community: "Teardowns wreck neighborhoods. They [destroy] the character and livability that are a neighborhood's life-blood." He sees three reasons for the rise in teardowns:

- In the past decade, the value of houses has doubled or tripled, except in some older neighborhoods. Developers look for these "'undervalued' properties" to build on.

- Homebuyers demand more space.

- Some homebuyers want to move from the "soulless . . . sprawling subdivisions" to close-in neighborhoods that have more character and more amenities, such as public transportation and local shopping.

Moe explains, "The problem is that too many people try to impose their preference for suburban-style mini-mansions on smaller scale neighborhoods where they just don't fit."

My neighborhood in Dallas, known as Lakewood Heights, has been plagued by more than its share of tearing down and building up. Once famous for its 1920s Craftsman and Tudor architecture, my quiet residential street is now marred by rows of McMansions, bustling traffic, and noisy, new construction. These colossal residences vary little in outward appearance from one to the next. "Starter mansions" as they are often called, have no particular architectural style and only remotely resemble Tudor or Craftsman styles. No matter where you look, these giants tower over their single-story neighbors, blocking the sunlight and peering into once-private backyards from their tall, garish peaks.

Paraphrases for information from source, quotations for opinions

Colon after full-sentence as introductory tag

Reasons against teardowns begin

Personal observation as support for this reason

Another reason against tearing down

Ross 3

A super-sized new home towers over its older next-door neighbor.

The builders and buyers of these giant homes are callous to community and environmental concerns. Preserving an old Dallas neighborhood's rich architectural history and green landscape is of little importance to them. For example, most McMansions occupy an extremely large footprint, leaving little or no yard space. Original homes in my neighborhood occupied about a third of their rectangular lot. This design permitted a sizable back yard with room for a small one-car garage as well as an inviting front lawn where children could play. By contrast, mega homebuilders show no appreciation for conventional site planning. They employ bulldozers to flatten the lot and uproot native trees. Their goal is to make room for as much house as possible, raking in more profit with each square foot. Furthermore, each tall fortress has a wide cold, concrete driveway leading to the grandiose two-Tahoe garage, equivalent to nearly half the size of my one-story house.

Ross 4

What was once a grassy lawn is now paved with concrete.

Only ten years ago pecan trees, the official state tree of
Texas, and flowering magnolias graced every lawn on my
block. These beautiful native trees, some over a century old,
shaded our homes from the harsh Texas sun and our
sidewalks from the triple-digit, summer heat. There is no
way the new home owners' landscaping can replace what is
lost. The charm of the neighborhood is being destroyed.

Aside from changing the face of my neighborhood, these
monster houses, many selling for half a million or more,
have skyrocketed property taxes and pushed out many older,
lower-income, long-time residents. As a result, several senior
citizens and other long-time residents of Lakewood have been
forced to sell their homes and move to apartments. Many
custom homeowners argue that more expensive, larger homes
positively contribute to a neighborhood by increasing the
resale value of smaller, older homes. This may be true to a
certain extent. However, from a wider perspective, short-term

Transition into
another reason

Ross 5

gains in resale prices are no compensation for the irreversible harm done to our neighborhoods.

But the destruction of a neighborhood is only half the story. These over-sized homes, and others like them everywhere, are irresponsible from a larger environmental perspective. According to Peter Davey, editor of the <u>Architectural Review</u>, "Buildings [residential and commercial combined] take up rather more than half of all our energy use: they add more to the pollution of the atmosphere than transport and manufacture combined." Not only is pollution a consequence of this surge in residential structure size, but also the building of larger homes drains our natural resources, such as lumber. The National Resource Defense Council notes that forested areas, necessary for absorbing greenhouse gas emissions, are being depleted by the super-sizing trend in residential building:

> Almost every one of these new, large homes is made out of wood—roughly three-quarters of an acre of forest. Much of the destructive logging around the world is fueled by our demand for housing. . . . Many houses today are still built using outdated, inefficient construction methods. About one-sixth of the wood delivered to a construction site is never used, but simply hauled away as waste. And much of the wood that goes into the frame of a house is simply unnecessary. ("How to Build")

Obviously, residential construction must "go green" in an effort to save valuable resources and conserve energy. But what does it mean to "go green"? As Earth Advantage, a green building certification organization, explains: "Green building entails energy efficiency, indoor air quality, durability and minimal site impact" (Kaleda). However, whether a home can be designated as "green" depends on more than just

Double-space blocked quotations; use no quotation marks

Period ends sentence. Ellipses of three dots indicates material omitted

With block form, period goes before parenthetical citation

Ross 6

energy-efficient construction methods and materials. According to Martin John Brown, an ecologist and independent consultant, green homebuilding is being used to describe a wide range of residential construction, and not all homes should qualify. Essentially, while some homebuilders are selling "environmentally-friendly" design, the epic scale of these new homes outweighs any ecological benefits provided through materials and construction methods. So, size does matter. A recent article in the <u>Journal of Industrial Energy</u>, published by M.I.T. Press, reports that a 1,500 square foot house with "mediocre energy-performance standards" will consume far less energy than a 3,000 square foot house with all the latest energy-saving materials and details (Wilson 284). In Boston, a house rated "poor" in terms of energy standards used 66% less energy than one rated "good" but twice the size (Wilson 282).

For articles by reporters or staff writers, rather than experts and authorities, their names can be cited parenthetically only

Brown argues that practically minded, ecologically conscious homebuilding should be part of our overall effort to decrease our consumption of limited resources and energy. Evidence from the Department of Energy supports his claim: "From 1985 to 2002, total residential energy consumption per capita climbed eight percent, and residential consumption for the nation—the figure most relevant to global effects like carbon dioxide (CO_2) emissions—climbed 32 percent" (Brown 23).

Unfortunately, many Americans who can afford it won't stop buying environmentally irresponsible, un-humble abodes. Their motives may stem from the competitive nature of consumer society. When people see their neighbors driving a new car, they think they need to buy a new one too. This is called "keeping up with the Joneses." Discussing the supersized house, best-selling author Gregg Easterbrook has coined a new phrase, "call and raise the Joneses." As he explains it,

Ross 7

In call-and-raise-the-Joneses, Americans feel compelled
not just to match the material possessions of others,
but to stay ahead. Bloated houses . . . arise from a
desire to call-and-raise-the-Joneses—surely not from a
belief that a seven-thousand-square-foot house that
comes right up against the property setback line
would be an ideal place in which to dwell. (140)

Daniel Chiras, the author of <u>The Natural House: A Complete
Guide to Healthy, Energy-Efficient, Environmental Homes,</u> warns:
"People tell themselves that if they can afford a 10,000-
square-foot house, then that's what they should have . . .
but I wonder if the earth can afford it" (qtd. in Iovine).

Fortunately, other Americans are starting to recognize
the folly of buying more space than they need. A survey by
Lowe's and Harris Interactive found that "46% of homeowners
admit to wasting up to half of their home" ("Are McMansions
Giving Way"). Felicia Oliver of <u>Professional Builder</u> magazine
suggests that the marriage of conservation and construction
is the next natural step in the evolution of residential building.
One example of a builder taking this step is the Cottage
Company in Seattle, which specializes in "finely detailed and
certified-green" houses of between 1,000 and 2,000 square
feet. Company co-owner Linda Pruitt says Cottage Company
houses "'live as big' as McMansions because they're better
designed, with features like vaulted ceilings and abundant
built-ins. 'It's kind of like the design of a yacht,' she says.
The theme is quality of space, not quantity" (qtd. in Brown
24).

Even Richard Moe of the National Trust for Historic
Preservation admits that responsible new construction has a
place in older neighborhoods:

Cite author of article, not speaker. Use "qtd." to indicate quotation appeared in the source

If no author, use shortened form of title
Shows possible solution to problem

Ross 8

Trees tower over this stretch of original modest-scale homes in
Lakewood Heights, reminding us of what is being lost.

No one is saying that homebuyers shouldn't be able to
alter or expand their home to meet their needs, just
as no one is saying that older neighborhoods should be
frozen in time like museum exhibits. A neighborhood
is a living thing, and change is both inevitable and
desirable. The challenge is to manage change so that it
respects the character and distinctiveness that made
these neighborhoods so appealing in the first place.
This is the challenge that must be met in my own neighborhood.
If new construction and additions are as architecturally
interesting as the older homes and comparable with them in
size and footprint, preserving lawns and trees, the neighborhood
can retain its unique character.

Jessie Sackett, a member of the U.S. Green Building Council,
writes: "Owning a home is the cornerstone of the American
dream. Recently, however, we've realized that keeping that

Conclusion returns
to idea used in
introduction

Ross 9

dream alive for future generations means making some changes to how we live today" (36). We must ensure that the American Dream doesn't translate into a horrific nightmare for our planet or future generations. Therefore, I ask would-be homebuyers to consider only the more conscientious construction in both urban and suburban areas. When we demand more modest and responsible homebuilding, we send a clear message: younger generations will know that we value our planet and our future more than we value excessive personal living space.

Works Cited

Use alphabetical order according to author's last name or if no author, according to first word in title, ignoring articles (a, an, the)

Double-space in and between entries

"Are 'McMansions' Giving Way to Smaller, Cozy Homes?" <u>Coatings World</u>. Aug. 2004: 12. <u>InfoTrac</u> Thomson Gale. Southern Methodist U, Fondren Library, Dallas, TX. 12 Jan. 2007. <http://find.galegroup.com>.

Brown, Martin John. "Hummers on the Homefront: At 4,600 square feet, Is It an Eco-House?" <u>E, The Environmental Magazine</u>. Sept–Oct 2006: 23–24. <u>InfoTrac</u> Thomson Gale. Southern Methodist U, Fondren Lib., Dallas, TX. 6 Oct. 2006. <http://find.galegroup.com>.

Davey, Peter. "Decency and Forethought: It Is Foolish to Behave As If We as a Race Can Go on Treating the Planet As We Have Been Doing Since the Industrial Revolution." <u>The Architectural Review</u> 213.1281 (2003): 36–37. <u>InfoTrac</u> Thomson Gale. Southern Methodist U, Fondren Lib., Dallas, TX. 18 Oct. 2006 <http://find.galegroup.com>.

Easterbrook, Gregg. <u>The Progress Paradox: How Life Gets Better While People Feel Worse</u>. New York: Random House, 2003.

"How to Build a Better Home: A New Approach to Homebuilding Saves Trees and Energy—and Makes for Economical,

Ross 10

Comfortable Homes." <u>National Resources Defense Council</u>. 22 July 2004. 22 Oct. 2006. <http://www.nrdc.org/cities/ building/fwoodus.asp>.

Iovine, Julie V. "Muscle Houses Trying to Live Lean; Solar Panels on the Roof, Five Cars in the Garage." <u>The New York Times</u>. 30 Aug. 2001. B9. <u>InfoTrac</u> Thomson Gale. Southern Methodist U, Fondren Lib., Dallas, TX. 18 Oct. 2006 <http://find.galegroup.com>.

Kaleda, Colleen. "Keeping It 'Green' With Panels and More." <u>The New York Times</u>. 15 Oct. 2006: 11. <u>InfoTrac</u> Thomson Gale. Southern Methodist U, Fondren Lib., Dallas, TX. 22 Oct. 2006 <http://find.galegroup.com>.

Moe, Richard. "Battling Teardowns, Saving Neighborhoods." <u>The National Trust for Historic Preservation</u>. 28 June 2006. 23 Jan. 2007 <http://www.nationaltrust.org/ news/2006/20060628_speech_sf.html>.

Oliver, Felicia. "The Case for Going Green." <u>Professional Builder (1993)</u>. 2.5. (2006): 38. <u>InfoTrac</u> Thomson Gale. Southern Methodist U, Fondren Lib., Dallas, TX. 6 Oct. 2006 <http://find.galegroup.com>.

Sackett, Jessie. "The Green American Dream: LEED for Homes Is Currently Being Piloted." <u>The LEED Guide: Environmental Design & Construction</u>. 9.6 (2006): 36+. <u>InfoTrac</u> Thomson Gale. Southern Methodist U, Fondren Lib., Dallas, TX. 18 Oct. 2006 <http://find.galegroup.com>.

Wilson, Alex and Jessica Boehland. "Small Is Beautiful: U.S. House Size, Resource Use, and the Environment." <u>Journal of Industrial Energy</u>. 9.1 (Winter/Spring 2005) 277–287. EBSCO Academic Host. Southern Methodist U, Fondren Lib., Dallas, TX. 17 Feb. 2007 <http://ebscohost.com>.

CHAPTER 6

Ethical Writing and Plagiarism

WHY ETHICS MATTER

To write well, you need to be informed about your topic, which means doing research into what others have already said about it. You will want to put some of these ideas into your papers, but it is unethical to do so in a way that does not give credit to the source.

For more information on plagiarism, go to:

Research > Plagiarism

By citing your sources, you earn your reader's respect as well. Readers are more likely to accept your views if you project good character, what the ancient rhetoricians called *ethos*. Honesty is part of good character. Part of writing honestly is distinguishing your ideas from the ideas of others.

The news has been filled in recent years with stories about unethical writers, people who have been caught using other writers' words and ideas without citing the source. This is *plagiarism,* which we will define shortly. Although painters and poets often borrow freely from each other's ideas, in the academic world, such borrowing is a serious breach of ethics, with serious consequences. One university president who borrowed too freely in a convocation speech without mentioning his source was forced to resign. Recently, some history professors' books were found to contain long passages taken verbatim from sources, the result—they claimed—of careless

note-taking. Whether deliberate or accidental, such mistakes can destroy a person's career.

Plagiarism by students has also become an increasing problem, partly as a result of the Internet. Students may plagiarize by accident, not realizing that material that is so easy to copy and paste from the Web must be treated as a quotation and cited as a source. The Internet has also become part of the solution to this problem: Professors using programs like Turnitin.com can check submitted work for originality. At schools using this software, plagiarized work dropped by 82%.*

For students, the consequences of plagiarizing are severe, ranging from failure on the writing project to failure in the course and even to suspension or expulsion from the university. Many universities will indicate on a student's transcript if there has been an honor violation, something that potential employers will see.

The purpose of this chapter is to help you avoid plagiarizing, even by accident. Also, we will show that failure to cite sources is not the only kind of unethical writing. Students can get too much help through misuse of tutoring, study groups, and other sources in the process of writing a paper.

---

*"Largest Study of Cheating in the World Reveals 82% Drop in Plagiarism After Using Turnitin.com for Five or More Years." *PR Newswire*. Oct. 4, 2006.

Plagiarism: The Presentation or Submission of Another's Work as Your Own

This includes summarizing, paraphrasing, copying, or translating words, ideas, artworks, audio, video, computer programs, statistical data, or any other creative work, without proper attribution.

Plagiarism can be deliberate or accidental. It can be partial or complete. No matter which, the penalties are often similar. Understanding what constitutes plagiarism is your first step to avoiding it.

SOME ACTS OF PLAGIARISM:

- Copying and pasting from the Internet without attribution
- Buying, stealing, or ghostwriting a paper
- Using ideas or quotations from a source without citation
- Paraphrasing an author too lightly

—"What Constitutes Plagiarism?" by Ramona Islam, Senior Reference Librarian and Instruction Coordinator at Fairfield University. Reprinted with permission.

WHAT PLAGIARISM IS

We like the definition of plagiarism on Fairfield University's online honor tutorial because it includes the various kinds of media that count as sources and must be acknowledged when you draw from them in academic writing. See Concept Close-Up, above, to read this definition.

As we explain in Chapter 5, "Writing Research-Based Arguments," you must document the sources of all direct quotations, all paraphrased ideas taken from sources, and even information paraphrased from sources, unless it is "common knowledge."

A good definition of *common knowledge* comes from Bruce Ballenger's excellent book *The Curious Researcher:* "Basically, common knowledge means facts that are widely known and about which there is no controversy."* If you already knew something that shows up in your research, that's a good indication that it is common knowledge, but you also have to consider whether your *readers* would already know it. If your readers know less about your topic than you do, it is good to cite the source, especially if the information might surprise them. Consider, too, that "common knowledge" shifts with time. When Ballenger wrote his book in the early 1990s, he gave as an example of common knowledge the fact that

---

*Bruce Ballenger, *The Curious Researcher: A Guide to Writing Research Papers*, 3rd ed. Boston: Allyn and Bacon, 2001, p. 236.

Understanding the Ethics of Plagiarism

A student who plagiarizes faces severe penalties: a failing grade on a paper, perhaps failure in a course, even expulsion from the university and an ethics violation recorded on his or her permanent record. Outside of academe, in the professional world, someone who plagiarizes may face public humiliation, loss of a degree, rank, or job, perhaps even a lawsuit. Why is plagiarism such a serious offense?

Plagiarism is theft. If someone takes our money or our car, we rightly think that person should be punished. Stealing ideas or the words used to express them is no less an act of theft. That's why we have laws that protect *intellectual property* such as books and essays.

Plagiarism is a breach of ethics. In our writing, we are *morally obligated* to distinguish between our ideas, information, and language and somebody else's ideas, information, and language. If we don't, it's like taking someone else's identity, pretending to be what we're not. Human society cannot function without trust and integrity—hence the strong condemnation of plagiarism.

Plagiarism amounts to taking an unearned and unfair advantage. You worked hard to get that "B" on the big paper in your political science class. How would you feel if you knew that another student had simply purchased an "A" paper, thereby avoiding the same effort? At the very least, you'd resent it. We hope you'd report the plagiarism. Plagiarism is not just a moral failure with potentially devastating consequences for an individual. *Plagiarism, like any form of dishonesty intended to gain an unfair advantage, damages human society and hurts everyone.*

Ronald Reagan made a movie with a chimpanzee. You may have known that, but do you think most college students today know it? The decision about when to cite information depends on to whom it is "common knowledge." Remember, if you use direct quotation to present any information, you must cite the source.

THE ETHICS OF USING SOURCES

There are five major kinds of violations of ethics in using sources.

Purchasing a Paper

A simple Internet browser search for most topics will turn up services that offer pre-written essays for sale. These services claim that the essays are merely "examples" of what could be written on the topic, but we all know better. In almost every arena of life, people are ruthlessly trying to make a buck off the gullible or the desperate. These services are counting on college students to take the bait. It's a bad idea for all these reasons:

- You learn nothing about writing, so you are cheating yourself.
- You can be charged with an honor violation.
- College professors can find the same essays by searching the Internet and by using more sophisticated search engines designed by textbook publishers to help them find plagiarism.
- The paper will be a poor fit with the prompt your teacher has given you, and the style of the writing will not match previous examples of your own voice and style—red flags professors are able to see from miles away.
- Some of these papers are poorly written and produced at sweatshop pace, so they are often filled with generalizations, bad thinking, and errors of grammar and punctuation. The example below is taken from the opening of one essay available for purchase online. We've underlined some of the grammar, punctuation, and spelling errors.

> All the choices we make reveal something about our personality, <u>surrounding and our upbringing influences</u> these choices. The <u>way we speak, dress, the food we eat, the music</u> we listen to tells <u>allot</u> about us and how we came to be. Everywhere we look in <u>America we</u> can see different cultural signs. It's really amazing how we can tell the difference between an American <u>person, and</u> a <u>non American</u> just by looking at <u>them; and between people</u> from different parts of our own country.

Using a Paper Found Online

Many college professors and high school teachers have class Web sites where they post the best work of their students. These papers will often turn up in online searches. Don't be tempted to use these papers or parts of them without citing them, and that includes giving the qualifications of the author. Many of the other reasons for not buying a paper apply here:

- The paper may be inferior in writing quality and use of sources, so you may be borrowing someone else's mistakes or even someone else's plagiarism.
- You learn nothing about how to write.
- You can be charged with an honor violation.
- Professors can find these papers online even more easily than you can.

Using Passages from Online Sources without Citing the Source

It is easy to cut and paste material from the Internet, and much of it is not protected by copyright. Nevertheless, to take passages, sentences, or even phrases or single significant words from another text is plagiarism. Significant words express strong judgment or original style, such as metaphors.

Compare the source text below with the uses of it. It comes from an interview with Al Gore about his film *An Inconvenient Truth*. The interview appeared in *Sierra Magazine*, found on the Sierra Club Web site.*

Sierra: In your movie, you cite U.S. determination in World War II as an example of the kind of resolve we need to confront global warming. But it took the attack on Pearl Harbor to galvanize the country. Are we going to have a similar moment in this crisis?

Gore: Obviously, we all hope it doesn't come to that, but for hundreds of thousands of people in New Orleans, that moment has already been reached. And for millions of people in Africa's Sahel, that moment has already been reached with the disappearance of Lake Chad. For an untold number of species, it has been reached. The challenge for the rest of us is to connect the dots and see the picture clearly. H. G. Wells wrote that "history is a race between education and catastrophe." And this is potentially the worst catastrophe in the history of civilization. The challenge now is to seize our potential for solving this crisis without going through a cataclysmic tragedy that would be the climate equivalent of wartime attack. And it's particularly important because, by the nature of this crisis, when the worst consequences begin to manifest themselves, it will already be too late.

Unethical use of source:

> It will take an environmental crisis to galvanize the country into confronting the problem of global warming, and for hundreds of thousands of people in New Orleans, that moment has already been reached. The challenge for the rest of us is to connect the dots and see the picture clearly. H. G. Wells wrote that "history is a race between education and catastrophe." And this is potentially the worst catastrophe in the history of civilization, so we must step up our efforts to learn about global warming and the means to keep it in check.

In this example, the writer has made no reference to the source of the words or ideas. This is wholesale theft of another's words and ideas. This kind of borrowing from sources is every bit as unethical as buying a paper online and turning it in as your own writing.

Ethical use of source:

> There are two routes to discovering the need to confront the problem of global warming, as Al Gore explained to *Sierra* magazine. We can wait for catastrophes like Hurricane Katrina, or we can learn from other environmental crises that are occurring around the globe and take action now. Quoting H. G. Wells, who said that "history is a race between education and catastrophe," Gore argues that we need to get educated because global

---

*Pat Joseph, "Start by Arming Yourself with Knowledge: Al Gore Breaks Through with His Global-Warming Message." *Sierra*. Sept.-Oct. 2006. Oct. 21, 2006 <http://www.sierraclub.org/sierra/200609/interview.asp>.

warming is "potentially the worst catastrophe in the history of civilization. . . ." (Joseph).

The ethical way to use a source is

- to integrate paraphrase and direct quotation into a paragraph of your own, and
- to cite the source.

Notice that good paraphrasing does not borrow either the language or the sentence pattern of the original text. The source is cited and the style of the sentences is the student's own.

Inadequate Paraphrasing

Paraphrasing is tricky because paraphrases must be *entirely* your own words, not a mixture of your words and the words of the source. Even if you cite the source, it is plagiarism to borrow words and phrases from another author. Therefore, you must put quotation marks around sentences, parts of sentences, and even significant words taken directly from another text.

Here is a source text, and opposite is the picture, to which the examples of paraphrase that follow refer:

Subversive masculine modes in the second half of this century began with the tee-shirts and blue jeans of rural laborers, later adopted by rebellious urban youth.

—Anne Hollander, *Sex and Suits* (New York: A. A. Knopf, 1994)

Unethical use of source:

Marlon Brando symbolizes the subversive masculine mode of the second half of the twentieth century with the tee-shirts and blue jeans of rural laborers (Hollander 186).

Even though the student cited his source, this is plagiarism because his sentence contains words from the source without quotation marks. This example illustrates the most common kind of unintentional plagiarism. This passage also fails to identify Hollander as the interpreter of the image.

To avoid this accidental plagiarism:

- When taking notes, highlight in color any wording that you copy directly from a source.
- When paraphrasing, study the original passage but then put it aside when you write your paraphrase, so that you will not be tempted to use the wording of the source. Then go back and check your paraphrase for accuracy and for originality of expression. As the ethical version below shows, any quoted parts must be treated as quotations.

Ethical use of source:

According to art historian Anne Hollander, Marlon Brando's tee-shirt and blue jeans illustrate a rebellious kind of late-twentieth-century masculinity, a look originally associated with "rural laborers" (186).

Marlon Brando in A Streetcar Named Desire, *1951.*

This version has reworded the sentence into an adequate paraphrase and used quotation marks around a phrase taken word for word from Hollander. It also identifies Hollander as an art historian, which establishes her credibility. When you tell your readers something about your source, you increase the credibility of your own writing.

Paraphrasing Ideas or Information without Naming the Source

Although it is not necessary to cite sources of commonly available information, such as the percentage of high school graduates who go to college, you must give credit when a source presents someone's idea, interpretation, or opinion, or when the information would be difficult for your readers to verify on their own. If in doubt, it is always better to cite. The source text below comes from a book about the college experience:

> Many [college] seniors single out interdisciplinary classes as the courses that meant the most to them. As a corollary, they cite faculty members who, while expert in their own fields, are able to put the fields in proper perspective. Students find this important. They believe that the real world, and the way people think about the world, does not divide neatly into categories called history, chemistry, literature, psychology, and politics.
>
> —Richard J. Light, *Making the Most of College: Students Speak Their Minds* (Cambridge: Harvard UP, 2001)

Unethical use of source:

> Studies have shown that college students find interdisciplinary courses the most meaningful. They also prefer professors who can think outside the box of their own areas of academic specialization.

Richard Light's research led him to this information; he deserves credit for his work.

Ethical use of source:

> In interviews with seniors at Harvard, where he teaches, Richard Light found that college students say that interdisciplinary courses are the most meaningful. They also prefer professors who can think outside the box of their own areas of academic specialization (126).

By citing Light as the source of this information, the writer has also added credibility to his or her own essay.

When Opinions Coincide

Students often ask what to do when they have an idea, opinion, or interpretation and then encounter that same idea, opinion, or interpretation as they are doing research. For example, after looking into the problem of global warming, a student could easily come to the conclusion that rising temperatures and ocean levels could become a threat to civilization. Reading the *Sierra* interview with Al Gore, that student sees that she and Gore share the opinion that global warming "is potentially the worst catastrophe in the history of civilization." If the student doesn't use Gore's exact words, is it plagiarism to use the opinion without citing him? A classic book on the subject of research, *The Craft of Research*, advises the cautious approach: "In the world of research, priority counts not for everything, but for a lot. If you do not cite that prior source, you risk having people think that you plagiarized it, even though you did not."* You don't have to check to see that all of your own ideas are not already out there; however, if you encounter one of your own in a source, you should acknowledge that source.

THE ETHICS OF GIVING AND RECEIVING HELP WITH WRITING

Writing is not a solitary act. Most professional writers seek feedback from colleagues, editors, family, and friends, and they thank those who have contributed in the acknowledgments section of the book. Students benefit from help with their projects—in conferences with their instructors, peer exchanges with other students in class, and visits to their campus's tutorial services. Whether you are giving help or receiving it, you need to realize that inappropriate help is also plagiarism because it involves using someone else's ideas and language. If someone tells you what to write, rewrites your work for you, or even proofreads or "edits" your work, that is plagiarism, because you are using someone else's work as if it were your own. Likewise, it is unethical for you to provide such help to anyone else, a practice known as "facilitating plagiarism" and equally punishable at most schools.

The following list describes three unethical ways of giving and receiving help.

1. **Having someone "ghostwrite" your paper.** College campuses attract unscrupulous people who offer to "help" students with their writing. It is dangerous to use an off-campus tutor because his or her primary interest is income, not education. If someone offers to write a paper for you or to write parts of it, do not agree to work with that person. Likewise, parents may not understand the line between constructive advice and doing the writing for you. Instructors can detect writing that does not sound like the voice of an undergraduate or that is not consistent with your in-class work and other papers.

2. **Having someone edit your paper for style.** It is plagiarism to have someone else change your wording and word choices for you. Your instructor will teach you about elements of style and illustrate principles of editing. This textbook covers such material in Appendix A.

   After you have used this advice to edit your own paper, it is okay to ask someone else to point out passages that need more attention and even to explain why those passages are wordy or unclear. But it is up to you to improve the expression. Reworking awkward passages is problem solving. The one who does it gets the benefit of the experience and deserves the credit. That should be you.

3. **Having someone proofread your paper for grammar and punctuation.** As with editing for style, proofreading is your responsibility. You plagiarize if you hand your paper to someone else to "clean it up," whether

---

*Wayne C. Booth, Gregory Colomb, and Joseph M. Williams, *The Craft of Research*. Chicago: U of Chicago P, 2003, p. 203.

"My parents didn't write it—they just tweaked it."

as a favor or for money. Many students need help with proofreading, and your instructor or on-campus tutorial service can offer instruction that will help you catch errors in the future. Instead of making "corrections" line by line, a good tutor will look over your draft for patterns of error. Then he or she can explain the "rule" or convention, show you how to detect and correct the problem, give you some examples for practice, and finally, watch as you go through your draft to find the places that need correction.

ETHICAL WRITING AND GOOD STUDY HABITS

Good study habits are central to ethical writing.

- **Do not procrastinate.** Students who procrastinate are more likely to make the kind of careless errors that lead to accidental plagiarism. They are also more likely to use intentional plagiarism as the only way to meet a deadline.
- **Take careful notes.** Use your notebook or notecards to write about your sources, being sure to distinguish your own ideas from the material

you copy directly or paraphrase. Use quotation marks around any words you take directly from a source. You may even want to highlight these to mark them as material that you will have to cite if it goes into your paper.

- **Ask your instructor about proper sources of help with your writing.** Avoid using untrained family members and friends as tutors. Avoid off-campus tutors who work for profit. If your school has a writing center, take advantage of the tutors there.

- **Work on improving your reading skills.** Good reading skills will empower you to use sources more confidently. Read Chapter 2, "Reading an Argument," for advice on how to improve your comprehension and analysis of texts.

The Aims
of Argument

THE AIMS OF ARGUMENT

CHAPTER 7

Looking for Some Truth: Arguing to Inquire

To inquire is to look into something. Inquiry can be a police investigation or a doctor's effort to diagnose a patient's illness, a scientist's experiment or an artist's attempt to see the world differently. According to singer and songwriter Lucinda Williams, one of the joys of life in this "sweet old world" is "looking for some truth."

It is satisfying to be able to say, "This is true." If we are religious, we find truth in the doctrines of our faith. But in our daily lives, we often must discern for ourselves what is true. We look for truth in messages from family and friends and lovers, in nature, and in art, music, and literature. Often we have to work to decide what to believe, for newspapers and textbooks offer differing versions of fact. The search for truth, then, is closely allied to the question "What is knowledge?" The pursuit of both is inquiry.

INQUIRY AND INTERPRETATION IN ACADEMIC WRITING

Inquiry is an important part of college learning because college is where we learn that one "true" body of knowledge or facts about the world does not exist. Take, for example, something usually considered fact:

Columbus discovered America in 1492.

If this statement were on a true/false test, would your answer be "true," "false," or "that depends"? With hardly any inquiry at all, we see that this "fact" depends on

- the calendar you use to mark time on this Earth
- your definition of the word "discover"
- your definition of "America"
- whether your ancestors were here before Columbus
- whether you know anything about Vikings and other early explorers

So what we accept as fact, as truth, is *an interpretation*. Most significant claims to truth are *efforts to understand and explain;* as such, they are interpretations that need defending. Later in this chapter, you will read several arguments, each claiming to know the truth about whether violence on television causes children to act out violently. All offer data to prove their claims, but data are meaningless without interpretation. And interpretations are open to inquiry.

The current state of knowledge on any given topic depends on who is doing the interpreting and whether the data are of interest to people in a particular culture. Some facts remain unknown for centuries because no one thought they mattered. What one considers knowledge or truth, then, depends on the perspective of the interpreters, which in turn depends on the interpreters' social class, politics, religion, and a host of other factors that make up who they are and how they see the world.

Like the high school research paper, college writing requires research. Unlike the high school paper, which typically requires only that you obtain information, organize it, and restate it in your own words, most college assignments will require *inquiry* into sources.

It's important to gather information and viewpoints. But research itself is not the goal of inquiry. The most important part of inquiry is the thinking you do before and after gathering sources. The quality of your paper will depend on your initial thinking as well as on your sources and your understanding of them. Nothing is more vital to writing well than learning how to inquire well.

As we begin to inquire, it is important not to try to "prove" anything. Argument as inquiry is not confrontational; rather, it is conversational. It is conversation with friends, family, and colleagues. We can have these kinds of conversations with ourselves, too, asking and answering questions about the arguments we read.

To inquire well, we must question our initial viewpoints instead of holding on to them. We need to ask hard questions, even if the answers threaten our preconceptions and beliefs. Before Copernicus, "common sense" held that the Earth was stationary and religious beliefs reinforced this "truth." To question our truths makes us uncomfortable. But inquiry requires holding a question open. The scientist whose theory wins respect from other scientists must test its truth rather than protect it from further inquiry. Likewise, a college student needs to test received wisdom from his or her past to grow intellectually. After inquiry, you may still hold the same belief, but because you have tested it, your belief will be a claim to truth that you have earned, not just been told.

This chapter offers guidelines for inquiring and shows how writing plays a part in it. The writing project is the exploratory essay, through which the following pages will guide you.

THE WRITING PROJECT: PART 1

The exploratory essay is an account of inquiry. Your goal is to share the experience of questioning your opinions and the arguments of others on your chosen topic. The paper will be a journey with a starting point, a tour of viewpoints on the issue, and a destination, a claim you can defend. The essay has three parts, one written before inquiry, the other two written after. In this informal paper, you will refer to yourself and your own thoughts and experiences. Write in first person.

Here is an overview of the paper:

In Part 1, you will tell what question or issue interests you most about a given topic and express your initial opinion.

Part 2 will be the exploration itself. The point is to open the question and keep it open, testing your opinions and exploring the issue through conversations and research that connect you to a range of expert opinions. You are not trying to support your initial opinion but to test it. You'll write about readings that confirm and contradict your thinking and evaluate these arguments fairly.

Part 3, the conclusion, will be a statement of your thinking after inquiry, an explanation of the truth as you now see it. Think of exploration as the process of *arriving* at a claim.

Your instructor may follow this paper with Chapter 8, "Making Your Case: Arguing to Convince," and an assignment to convince others to assent to your claim. But in this paper you'll explore, not make a case.

We illustrate inquiry and the steps of writing the exploratory essay by exploring violence in the media and its relation to violence in society. We show some students' initial thinking about this issue and take you through their exploration of it.

Step 1: Choosing a Topic for Inquiry

If your instructor has not assigned a topic, begin by looking at newspapers. Current events offer good topics that need interpretation. If you are familiar with a news topic, you probably already have an opinion, and that is a good place to begin inquiry. We came upon our violence in the media topic by noticing an op-ed column in the *New York Times,* but yours could come from a front-page story or an item on television news.

www.mhhe.com/**crusius**

For more sources of a potential topic, go to:

Research > Discipline-Specific Resources in the Library and on the Internet

Once you have selected a topic, consider what you already know about it and consider narrowing the focus. Violence in the media is a huge subject. There's staged or *pretend violence*—the quarrels, muggings, rapes, and so on of television and movie dramas. There's *virtual violence* in computer games. And there's *actual violence,* the staple of broadcast news. "If it bleeds, it leads": Local TV news programs often start with an account of a brutal murder or a big traffic accident.

The more you narrow your topic, the easier it will be to find issues to argue about and sources that converse with each other. For example, narrowing media violence to video games or music lyrics is a good strategy.

Step 2: Finding an Issue

An issue is a controversial question. With the example topic, such questions include: Why do people find violence so engrossing, so entertaining? Why do we like to see it in sports like football, hockey, and auto racing? Why do we go to movies that feature violence? Is it our nature or our culture? How is it related to gender?

All are worthwhile questions, but we need to identify a central or primary issue. In this instance, that issue is whether pretend violence can be connected to aggressive acts. It's central because most articles about the topic address it and because our answer determines what the other issues are.

Inquiry looks for order or hierarchy among issues; that is, our answer to one question leads to the next. *If* there is a link between fantasy violence and actual violence, *then* the next question is, How significant is the connection? We can't ask the second question until we answer the first. *If* we decide that pretend violence is a major contributor to actual aggression, *then* we must decide what action should be taken—and this leads to issues of censorship. For media violence, then, we can list this hierarchy of issues:

- Is there a link between fantasy violence and real-world violence? If so, what is it exactly?

- How strong is the link? Does media violence make people more aggressive and less sensitive to the suffering of others? Does it contribute to murders and assaults?

- If the contribution is significant, should we consider censorship, or does the Constitution prohibit taking this kind of action?

- If we can't censor, what other action(s) can we suggest to reduce the negative effect?

Locating the issues is usually not difficult. Often we can supply them from general knowledge and experience. We need only ask, What have we heard people arguing about when this topic came up? What have we ourselves argued about it? If we can't identify the issues before research, sources will reveal them. Once you begin reading what others have said about your topic, you may discover an issue more interesting than ones you thought of beforehand.

◎◎ FOLLOWING THROUGH

In preparation for writing your exploratory paper, select a topic of current interest. What do you see as the main issue that people debate? With answers to that question, draw up a chain of questions that follow one another. Which interests you most? •

◎◎ FOLLOWING THROUGH

Read an argument on the topic you intend to explore. What issue does this argument primarily address? What is the author's answer to this question—in other words, what is the author's claim? Restate it in your own words. What other issues are raised in the argument? What *other* issues do you know about? •

Step 3: Stating Your Initial Opinions

In this step, you will write Part 1 of your exploratory essay, where you state your initial ideas before inquiry. Write this part of your paper before doing any serious research. Begin by introducing your topic and the issue or issues you intend to consider. State your opinions on those issues now and explain your reasoning. Include some explanation of what, in your own experiences or observations, has contributed to your opinions.

Below is an example on the media violence topic.

STUDENT SAMPLE Exploratory Essay, Part 1—Lauren's Initial Opinions

I have to admit that I am somewhat biased when it comes to the topic of the relation between entertainment and violence in children. I have been involved in several life-altering experiences before this assignment that made me feel very strongly that virtual violence and aggressive behavior in children are causally related. When I was in high school, a group of kids I grew up with got mixed up in the whole "gangster" scene. They listened to rap music about murder and drugs. Ultimately, these boys took the life of a fellow student at the McDonald's down the street from my school. They used a shotgun to murder him in a drug deal gone bad. Because I knew these kids when they were younger, I can say that when they were in the seventh grade they were incapable of committing such a crime. Did the rap music influence them? They had to get the idea from somewhere, and I cannot think of another reasonable explanation.

Even though music may not plant evil in a child's mind, it can lead to problems. Throughout my senior year, I did volunteer work at the Salvation Army recreation center. It's located in the so-called ghetto of Lincoln, Nebraska, and intended for children to walk to after school when their parents are still working. Working here opened my eyes to how the future of America is growing up.

My first encounter was with a six-year-old boy who called me profane names. Not only was I verbally abused, but also pushed, shoved, and kicked. Later, after discussing the situation with the boy in time-out, I found out that he had heard these names in an Eminem song that bashes women.

Because of these experiences, my negative opinion about media violence is strong.

◎◎ FOLLOWING THROUGH

Draft Part 1 of your paper. In the opening paragraph or two, state what your opinions were before you researched the topic. Describe and explain experiences that influenced your outlook. Refer to specific films or music or news broadcasts. If you've read or heard about the topic before or discussed it in school or elsewhere, recall both context and content and share them with your readers. Edit for clarity and correctness.   •

Step 4: Exploring an Issue

Once you have written Part 1, concentrate on exploring—reading and talking about your topic. Because you will eventually write about these experiences in Part 2, use your writer's notebook and make good annotations in the margins of what you read, to record your thoughts. These notes are the raw material from which you will eventually write the account of your exploration.

CONVERSATION AND DIALOGUE IN INQUIRY

A good way to begin inquiry is to talk through your position in serious conversation with a friend, family member, classmate, or teacher. Inquiry often takes the form of discussion or conversation. And conversation is a big part of higher education. Many college classes are devoted to discussion rather than lecture; even lecturers encourage classes to discuss controversial questions. Out of class, students can talk with professors and each other.

As you know from watching talk shows, conversation is not always a search for truth. There's an art to productive conversation. In Chapter 2, we noted that critical reading depends on developing certain practices and habits. Conversation aimed at finding some truth also depends on good practices and habits. Participants need to move beyond ordinary conversation, often just an exchange of opinions, to *dialogue*, a *questioning* of opinions.

Let's begin by looking at a conversation about violence in entertainment.

An Example Conversation

The conversation that follows took place shortly after the Columbine High School killings. It was recorded and transcribed, and an excerpt of it appeared in the May 17, 1999, issue of *Newsweek*. The conversation is neither especially good nor especially bad but rather typical, the sort of thing we encounter routinely in media-arranged talk. Read it carefully. Comments follow explaining what we can learn from it.

Moving beyond the Blame Game

JONATHAN ALTER, MODERATOR

A month after the Littleton tragedy, the conversation continues—in schools, in homes and at this week's White House conference on youth violence. The theories of why Eric Harris and Dylan Klebold went on their rampage have given way to a broader discussion of the deeper sources of the problem and where to go from here. Obviously, there are no quick fixes; everything from more values [in] education to better supervision of antidepressant medication has been introduced into the debate. But Americans have singled out a few issues for special attention. According to the new *Newsweek* Poll, about half of all Americans want to see the movie industry, the TV industry, computer-game makers, Internet services and gun manufacturers and the NRA make major policy changes to help reduce teen violence. Slightly fewer want the music industry to change fundamentally. Younger Americans are less concerned about media violence than their elders are. On guns, there's a racial gap, with 72 percent of nonwhites and 41 percent of whites seeking major changes.

To further the conversation, *Newsweek* assembled a panel last week to explore the complexities. One after another, the people who actually make heavily violent movies, records and games declined to participate, just as they did when the White House called. This could be a sign that they are feeling the heat—or perhaps just avoiding it. Those who did take part in the *Newsweek* forum include Wayne LaPierre, executive director of the NRA; Jack Valenti, president of the Motion Picture Association of America; Hillary Rosen, president of the Recording Industry Association of America; Doug Lowenstein, president of the Interactive Digital Software Association; Marshall Herskovitz, TV and movie producer and director; and Jonah Green, a 15-year-old New York high-school student. *Newsweek's* Jonathan Alter moderated the discussion.

Excerpts:

Alter: Youth shall be served, so I want to start with Jonah. You seem to think that there's [a] lot of scapegoating going on.

Green: Well, I have to say that America is very confused and scared. There's no one simple answer to teen violence. It's understandable because we're seeking answers, but right now people are focusing too much on putting the blame somewhere. We should be focusing on solutions.

Alter: OK, Wayne, wouldn't making guns less easily accessible be at least a partial solution?   5

LaPierre: You can't talk about easy access to guns by people we all don't want to have guns without talking about the shameful secret that really hasn't been reported. Which is the complete collapse of enforcement of the existing firearm laws on the books by the Department of Justice [in] the last six years. The proof is in the statistics. Six thousand kids illegally brought guns to school the last two years. We've only had 13 [federal] prosecutions. And only 11 prosecutions for illegally transferring guns to juveniles.

Alter: Do you think that if an 11-year-old brings his father's gun to school, the child should be prosecuted?

LaPierre: Yes, I do. They did not prosecute Kip Kinkel out in Oregon after he was blowing up cats, threatening people. He walks into school with a gun. They do nothing to him except send him home. And he comes back to the school two days later with a gun and shoots those kids. I mean, the fact is we're either serious about this situation or we're not.

Alter: How about Clinton's gun-limit proposal? Why does anyone need to buy more than one gun a month?

LaPierre: That's just a sound bite.   10

Alter: Doug, some of your industry's games are a long way from Pac-Man, right?

Lowenstein: Oh, absolutely. There are some very violent videogames, although they represent only a small fraction of the market. There's a critical parental role here: It costs over $1,000 to own a computer. A hundred dollars plus to own a videogame machine. There's a very conscious choice involved in bringing this kind of entertainment into your home. And the parent needs the tools to make an informed choice.

Alter: You don't think it desensitizes kids to violence to play games over and over?

Green: Personally, I think some kids use videogames, especially the violent ones, just as some violent movies, as a vent. You know, they like to live vicariously and vent their anger through that. And Doug was right that we can't really map out everything a kid has and how they use it and what makes them able to kill somebody.

Alter: Hillary, MTV is doing a stop-the-violence campaign, but then they   15
air—and you supported—something like Eminem's song about stuffing a
woman into the trunk of a car. Don't you see a contradiction here?

Rosen: Young people are so much smarter than anybody—the media or politicians or most adults, in fact—may give them credit for being. They understand the difference between fantasy and reality, and that's why giving them
concrete steps to take when they face personal conflict or when they face a
gang conflict or school bullying, or those sorts of things, are much more
productive means for giving them tools to be nonviolent in their lives than
taking away their culture.

Alter: Do you think that a music-rating system just makes it forbidden fruit
and makes kids want to play or see it more?

Rosen: We've done surveys that show it doesn't encourage young people
to buy artists. People buy music that they connect with, that they like, that
has a good beat, that sounds good. The label is there for parents and for
retailers.

Green: I actually think artists like Eminem are very sarcastic. It is more play-
ful than hard core. I find rap being a little more human than it used to be.
Gangsta rap isn't as big anymore, and now sampling is.

Rosen: It's true.   20

Green: Edgar Allan Poe talked about death—he was dark, but he was a celebrated poet. It's about having an edge, a hook. That can be violence.

Alter: You don't have any problem with Marilyn Manson naming himself
after a serial killer?

Green: I think it's in bad taste. It was just stupid and controversial.

Alter: Hillary, how about you?

Rosen: Well, I agree with Jonah that it's bad taste, but that's the point.   25
Marilyn Manson is an act. It's an act that's sort of designed to create a persona of empowering the geek. Unfortunately, Charles Manson was a real
person. People don't have to make up horrible tragedies in this world.

Green: Entertainment and the media were never really for getting across
good, moral messages like "I love my school and my mother." People rarely
feel they need to express bland feelings like that.

Rosen: But it is on some level, because Britney Spears sells more records
than Marilyn Manson. You know there's been a resurgence of young pop
music. B*Witched and the Dixie Chicks and Britney Spears and 'N Sync.
I mean, these artists are selling a hell of a lot more records than Marilyn
Manson.

Alter: Do you think that kids have kind of gotten that message and are less
interested in gratuitously violent lyrics than they used to be? Because they've
seen so much death, either in their own neighborhoods or on TV?

Rosen: Well, there's no question that what used to be known as gangsta rap is definitely played out. Rap is much more light-hearted. It's about getting money and getting women. The music has evolved.

Alter: Why is that?   30

Rosen: Well, this might be controversial, but I'm actually one of those people who believes that young people are a lot more positive about the world today than most of the media is giving them credit for in the last couple of weeks. Surveys have shown that young people are more optimistic about their future, they're more positive, they're more connected to their parents than they have been in generations. And these all speak to really good, positive things.

Alter: Marshall, what do you think are some of Hollywood's responsibilities in this area?

Herskovitz: I think we now have virtual reality available to people that is nihilistic, anarchic and violent. And it is possible for a person to so completely live in that virtual reality that they come to confuse it for the real world around them.

Alter: But you know from firsthand experience that violence sells.

Herskovitz: "Legends of the Fall" was a very violent movie. I think violence   35
has a potentially strong part in any artistic venture. It's not something I would ever want to talk about legislatively. I would like to talk about it in terms of individual responsibility, yes.

Alter: So where should the thoughtful consumer of all of this draw the line between gratuitous violence and necessary violence for dramatic purposes?

Herskovitz: Oh, I think that's the point. The thoughtful consumers feel it in their gut. I think the problem in this culture is that thoughtful consumers are not particularly influencing their children.

Alter: But isn't it a little too easy to just say it's all the parent's responsibility?

Valenti: Well, I don't think the movie industry can stand in *loco parentis*. Over 30 years ago I put in place a movie-rating system, voluntary, which gives advanced cautionary warnings to parents so that parents can make their own judgments about what movies they want their children to see.

Alter: I think what a lot of parents wonder is, why is it that NC-17 is not   40
applied to gratuitously violent movies?

Valenti: Well, it's because the definition of "gratuitous" is shrouded in subjectivity. There is no way to write down rules. I think Marshall can tell you that creative people can shoot a violent scene a hundred different ways. Sex and language are different, because there are few ways that you can couple on the screen that—there's only a few. And language is language. It's there or it isn't. But violence is far more difficult to pin down. It's like picking up mercury with a fork.

Alter: A movie director told me recently that he went to see "The Matrix," and there was a 5-year-old at the film with his mother. Isn't that a form of child abuse?

Valenti: If a parent says he wants his 5-year-old to be with him, who is to tell this parent he can't do it? Who is to tell him?

Alter: But if it was NC-17, that 5-year-old wouldn't be allowed to go, right?

Valenti: Well, that's right.   45

Alter: So why allow them in when it's R?

Valenti: Because the way our system is defined, we think there's a dividing line.

Alter: When parents aren't doing their job properly, where does the responsibility of everybody else begin?

LaPierre: I was talking with John Douglas, the FBI's criminal profiler. And he said, "Wayne, never underestimate the fact that there are some people that are just evil." And that includes young people. We go searching for solutions, and yet some people are just plain bad apples. You look around the country—the cities that are making progress across the board are really combining prevention and working with young people when you get the first warning signs. And making sure they find mentors. Making sure they're put into programs. And they're combining that with very, very tough enforcement of things like the gun laws.

Herskovitz: I have a fear that modern society, and in particular television,   50
may be beyond the ability of parents to really control. I think movies are different, because the kid has to go out of the house and go there. TV is a particular problem because it's in the house.

Alter: But Marshall, maybe that's because the values that are being propagated by the media, broadly speaking, are so much more powerful that parents can't compete as easily as they used to.

Herskovitz: I don't believe that. I accept a lot of responsibility for the picture the media create of the world. But I don't think there's a conflict between that and the responsibility of parents to simply sit down and talk with their children. Most violent crime is committed by males. Young men are not being educated in the values of masculinity by their fathers.

Alter: So why then let all of these boys see scenes of gratuitous violence that don't convey human values to them?

Valenti: There are only three places where a child learns what Marshall was talking about, values. You learn them in the church. You learn them in school. And you learn them at home. And if you don't have these moral shields built in you by the time you're 10 or 12 years old, forget it.

Alter: I'm not sure that people in Hollywood are thinking, "Is what we do   55
part of the solution on this values question, or does it just contribute to the problem?"

Herskovitz: The answer is the people who aren't contributing to the problem are thinking about it a lot, and the people who are contributing to the problem are not thinking about it.

Valenti: Well, how does *Newsweek* then condone its putting on the cover of your magazine Monica Lewinsky? What kind of a value system does that convey?

Alter: Well, that's a separate discussion.

Valenti: Oh, I don't think it is.

Alter: Well, let me say this. We very explicitly did not put Dylan Klebold   60
and Eric Harris on our cover the first week. We're wrong in these judgments sometimes, but we do at least try to think about the consequences of what we put out there, instead of just saying it's up to the parents. That seems to me a cop-out.

Lowenstein: What you're looking for is an elimination of any problematic content.

Alter: No, I'm not. I'm looking for a sense of shame and a sense of responsibility. I'm wondering where it is in all of the industries that we have represented here today.

Herskovitz: Most people, especially in electronic journalism, don't think at all about this, and their role is incredibly destructive, just like most people in the movie and television business don't think at all about this. And their role is destructive. I think there's a great need for shame. Most people I know and speak to are very ashamed, but unfortunately they're not the people who make violent movies.

Analysis of "Moving beyond the Blame Game"

It's obvious that the *Newsweek* excerpts are not part of a natural, spontaneous conversation, the sort of thing we might have with friends around a campfire or at a bar after work. It's been *arranged*. The participants didn't just happen to come together some place and start talking; they were invited. Furthermore, they knew why they were invited—each represents a group or industry implicated in teen violence. Even Jonah Green, the fifteen-year-old, is cast (that's the right word) as "youth," as if one young person could stand for all young people. Each participant knew his or her role in advance, then, and what was at stake. Except perhaps for Jonah Green, each had an agenda and an interest in protecting their reputations and the public image of their businesses and organizations. Therefore, unlike the conversations in which we ask you to engage, theirs from the start was something less than an open-minded search for truth. In a genuine dialogue, people do not attack each other or become defensive.

In addition to its adversarial tone, this discussion falls short of good inquiry because it lacks depth. It is an extreme example of what tends to go wrong with *all* discussions, including class discussions. In the classroom, the teacher plays Alter's role, trying to get students to talk. When a question is greeted by silence from the class, sometimes teachers do what Alter does: solicit opinions by addressing questions to individuals, who then have no choice but to answer. Often the instructor is happy to get any opinion just to get things going. Once the ice is broken, students usually join in. It can be stimulating just to hear what everybody else is thinking. Before long, we're caught up in the discussion and don't perceive what it is: a superficial exchange of opinions, like the *Newsweek* example. Much is said, but almost nothing is *examined, pursued, genuinely explored.*

Exactly what do we mean? Look at the first few exchanges in the *Newsweek* example. Alter addresses Jonah Green, the fifteen-year-old high school student, who had apparently talked enough previously to reveal an opinion. Alter summarizes that opinion: "There's a lot of scapegoating going on." Green himself immediately offers two more intelligent observations, better than anything we get from the adult participants: "There's no one simple answer to teen violence" and "we should be focusing on solutions" rather than on blame.

These statements merit attention. But what happens? Alter must get the others into the discussion, so he turns to LaPierre and asks if better gun control might be part of the solution. *The secret of a good discussion is not to allow intelligent comments to go unquestioned.* Imagine, for example, what the following line of questioning might lead to. ("Q" stands for "questioner," who could be anyone involved in the discussion.)

Green: There's a lot of scapegoating going on.

Q: What do you mean by "scapegoating"?

Green: A scapegoat is someone who gets blamed or punished for doing something everyone is guilty of or responsible for.

Q: So you're saying that youth violence is a collective problem that everyone contributes to in one way or another. Is that right?

Green: Yes.

Now that we know what Green's assertion actually means, we can really discuss it, look for whatever truth it may convey. Are we *all* really implicated in youth violence? How exactly? If we are, what can each of us do?

We handle Green's comment about looking for solutions the same way. All we need to ask is, What might be part of the solution? It would be interesting to hear Jonathan's ideas. Maybe he has an idea how high schools could build more community or how parents could get involved. But no—the conversation moves in a new direction.

Our intent is not to put down conversation. Exchanging opinions is one of the great pleasures of social life. For inquiry, however, we need genuine dialogue.

To help your conversations become dialogue, we offer "Questions for Inquiry" on pages 181–182. These same questions will help you inquire into written texts, such as the sources encountered in research. Most of the questions on this list can be traced to the origins of dialogue in ancient Greece

Understanding the Art of Dialogue

To be useful for inquiry, conversations must become dialogues. They become dialogues when someone questions, in a nonhostile way, what someone else has said. Only then are we really discussing something, not just stating our opinion and talking for talking's sake.

---

and have demonstrated their value for about 2,500 years. Commit the list to memory, and practice asking these questions until they become second nature.

FOLLOWING THROUGH

Mark up the *Newsweek* dialogue. Use the "Questions for Inquiry" to probe the participants' comments. For example, one question suggests that you inquire about analogies and comparisons. You might ask Jonah if Edgar Allen Poe's "darkness" is truly comparable to the creations of Marilyn Manson. Aren't there some significant differences in the context in which these art forms present violence? Be ready to point out places where the discussants failed to answer questions directly or where you would have posed a good question if you had been there. Note places where the discussion moved toward dialogue and where it moved toward mere venting of opinion. Does Alter do a good job as moderator, or is he mainly concerned with going broader rather than deeper? Be ready to discuss your annotations in class. •

Step 5: Engaging in a Dialogue about Your Initial Opinions

Earlier, you wrote Part 1 of your exploratory essay, a statement of your initial opinions. A good way to begin exploration is with what you said in Part 1. Exchanging these initial statements with a classmate and then asking each other questions will get you thinking more deeply about what you already believe.

Read the examples on page 182, which show one student's first thoughts and the dialogue that he and another student had. These students used a software program that allowed them to record their conversation, and what follows is a transcript of a real-time chat. They had printouts of each other's initial opinions in front of them as they took turns being each other's friendly questioner. First, read Matt's initial thoughts and then the dialogue he had with Lauren, whose own first thoughts we reproduced earlier. Note where the dialogue seems to be a conversation and where Lauren attempts to make it an inquiry. Where does it succeed as inquiry, and where does it not?

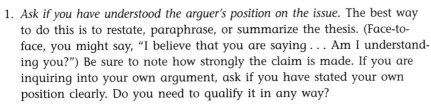

Questions for Inquiry

1. *Ask if you have understood the arguer's position on the issue.* The best way to do this is to restate, paraphrase, or summarize the thesis. (Face-to-face, you might say, "I believe that you are saying . . . Am I understanding you?") Be sure to note how strongly the claim is made. If you are inquiring into your own argument, ask if you have stated your own position clearly. Do you need to qualify it in any way?

2. *Ask about the meaning of any words central to the argument.* You can do this at any point in a conversation and as often as it seems necessary. When dealing with a written text, try to discern the meaning from the context. For instance, if an author's case depends on the fairness of a proposed solution, you'll need to ask what "fair" means, because the word has a range of possible applications. You might ask, "Fair to whom?"

3. *Ask what reasons support the thesis.* Paraphrasing reasons is a good way to open up a conversation to further questions about assumptions, values, and definitions.

4. *Ask about the assumptions on which the thesis and reasons are based.* Most arguments are based on one or more unstated assumptions. For example, if a college recruiter argues that the school he or she represents is superior to most others (thesis) because its ratio of students to teachers is low (reason), the unstated assumptions are (1) that students there will get more attention and (2) that more attention results in a better education. As you inquire into an argument, note the assumptions, and ask if they are reasonable.

5. *Ask about the values expressed or implied by the argument.* For example, if you argue that closing a forest to logging operations is essential even at the cost of dozens of jobs, you are valuing environmental preservation over the livelihoods of the workers who must search for other jobs.

6. *Ask how well the reasons are supported.* Are they offered as opinions only, or are they supported with evidence? Is the evidence recent? sufficient? What kind of testimony is offered? Who are the authorities cited? What are their credentials and biases?

7. *Consider analogies and comparisons.* If the author makes an argument by analogy, does the comparison hold up? For example, advocates of animal rights draw an analogy with civil rights when they claim that just as we have come to recognize the immorality of exploiting human beings, so we should recognize the immorality of exploiting other species. But is this analogy sound?

8. *Ask about the arguer's biases and background.* What past experiences might have led the arguer to take this position? What does the holder of this position stand to gain? What might someone gain by challenging it?

(continued)

BEST PRACTICES

9. *Ask about implications.* Where would the argument ultimately lead if we accept what the speaker advocates? For example, if someone contends that abortion is murder, asking about implications would lead to the question "Are you willing to put women who get abortions on trial for murder and, if they are convicted, to punish them as murderers are usually punished?"

10. *Ask whether the argument takes opposing views into account.* If it does, are they presented fairly and clearly or with mockery and distortion? Does the author take them seriously or dismiss them? Are they effectively refuted?

STUDENT SAMPLE Example Dialogue for Analysis—Matt's Initial Opinions

I think the issue of violence in the media is overdone. I believe that violence is a conscious act by people who are evil, not people motivated by what they have seen or heard in the media. Some people are violent, and they cannot be stopped from committing their crimes simply by censoring media violence. Violence is natural, an instinct all humans have, yet most restrain themselves from acting on their impulse. Though I have seen and heard my share of violence in the media, I am not a violent person. Sure, sometimes after watching a violent movie, I think about what it would be like to do some of that stuff, but I am not stupid enough to act out my curiosity.

STUDENT SAMPLE Example Dialogue between Matt and Lauren

Lauren: You don't think there is any relation between violence and the entertainment industry?

Matt: Not really. I don't see how music could influence someone to the point of violence.

Lauren: I kind of agree with you, but I don't know. I think that sometimes it gives a person the mentality to do that kind of stuff when their friends are—when people are impressionable like that, they will do a lot of stupid things. When I was in high school, a group of kids I grew up with started getting into the whole "gangster" scene. They listened to rap talking about murder, drugs, and destruction. They murdered a fellow student at the McDonalds down the street from the school. Did the music make them do this? We'll never know, but they had to get the idea from somewhere.

Matt: What happened to the guys that killed that person?

Lauren: They are all in jail now. Only one has gone to trial.   5

Matt: That's crazy. I listened to all kinds of music, and I am not violent.

Lauren: You can't assume everyone is like you. How do you explain kids doing the kind of stuff they are doing?

Matt: There are just some violent, evil people. They just aren't right, if you know what I mean.

Lauren: Do you mean they are crazy?

Matt: Yes, they're crazy.   10

Lauren: I think you said violence is an act of nature. Does that mean we are born violent? Is it normal to be violent?

Matt: I think everyone has a violent side, but they act on it in different ways. I go play sports or work out to get rid of the aggression.

Lauren: But is violence the same thing as evil? Or aggression? Those kids at my school were evil, not natural. I think you need to think more about what you mean by violent when you say it's natural. Maybe it's natural for animals to have aggression and to attack and kill to stay alive, but is that evil? When you say people are "just not right," do you mean that they are natural or not natural?

Matt: Okay, I think we are born violent, but some of us are also born evil.

Lauren: So, are you saying that nothing good could change these   15
people for the better, like having a good family or going to church? Are they just how they were born?

Matt: I'd have to think about that. They could maybe be taught.

Lauren: Well, I'm just saying, if they can be influenced for the better, why not for the worse—that the media could influence them to be worse?

Matt: I don't know.

Lauren: What about real life? When the media pays too much attention to one issue, like the school shooting in Columbine, do you think it makes other people want to do the same thing?

Matt: I don't know. A good friend of mine got kicked out of school   20
for calling in a bomb threat. He probably wouldn't have done that if all that hadn't been on the news.

◎◎ FOLLOWING THROUGH

Look at Matt's initial opinion statement on page 182. Use the "Questions for Inquiry" (pages 181–182) to suggest questions you would have asked him if you had been his partner.   •

◎◎ FOLLOWING THROUGH

Writing should be a rhythm between "drawing in"—the solo act of composing—and "reaching out" through dialogues during every phase of the composing process.

Exchange initial opinion statements with a classmate. Take turns asking each other questions based on the "Questions for Inquiry" on pages 181–182. Explore one person's thinking at a time. After twenty minutes, trade roles. If you do not have a software program that allows you to make a transcript of the discussion, tape it, or simply take notes after each questioning session. Be ready to report on how the dialogue clarified or modified your thinking. What did the dialogue make you realize you need to think and read about more?

We should never think of dialogue as something unrelated to writing. Dialogue can help us write better. The notes and written records of dialogues will provide material for your paper, so save them as we turn to the next step, reading about the topic.   •

Step 6: Engaging in Dialogue with a Reading

Inquiry into a text begins with a critical reading of it, including attention to its rhetorical context, as discussed in Chapter 2 (pages 22–23). Sample the text quickly to see if it is worth your attention. If it is, read it thoroughly and mark it up, noting its subdivisions and case structure—that is, mark claims and note evidence.

What we have just discussed about turning conversation into dialogue also applies to reading, but obviously conversations and written arguments can't be approached the same way.

In conversations, we mostly encounter simple statements of opinion. People say what they think without much explanation or support unless someone asks for it. In contrast, writers *argue* their opinions. That is, a written piece typically contains a *thesis* or *claim*. That claim is *explained* and justified or defended with reasons backed up by evidence. A text must stand on its own—a writer cannot respond to a reader's questions. Instead, *the writer must anticipate the questions an alert, critical reader will have and answer them in advance.*

Consequently, whereas in conversation we can question simple state-ments of opinion as they occur, with written arguments we question *entire cases*. We need to use "Questions for Inquiry" (pages 181–182), which lead us to question all parts of a case. We should also note whether opposing views appear in the argument and how the author handles them.

Example Dialogue with a Reading

As an example of how to engage in dialogue with a written text, let's work with "Hollow Claims about Fantasy Violence," by Richard Rhodes, which appeared September 17, 2000, in the *New York Times*. Rhodes has won awards for his books on the making of the atomic and hydrogen bombs. This essay appeared after the publication of *Why They Kill*, based on inter-views with convicted murderers.

Hollow Claims about Fantasy Violence

RICHARD RHODES

The moral entrepreneurs are at it again, pounding the entertainment industry for advertising its Grand Guignolesque confections to children. If exposure to this mock violence contributes to the development of violent behavior, then our political leadership is justified in its indignation at what the Federal Trade Commission has reported about the marketing of violent fare to children. Senators John McCain and Joseph Lieberman have been especially quick to fasten on the F.T.C. report as they make an issue of violent offerings to children.

But is there really a link between entertainment and violent behavior?

The American Medical Association, the American Psychological Association, the American Academy of Pediatrics and the National Institute of Mental Health all say yes. They base their claims on social science research that has been sharply criticized and disputed within the social science profession, especially outside the United States. In fact, no direct, causal link between exposure to mock violence in the media and subsequent violent behavior has ever been demonstrated, and the few claims of modest correlation have been contradicted by other findings, sometimes in the same studies.

History alone should call such a link into question. Private violence has been declining in the West since the media-barren late Middle Ages, when homicide rates are estimated to have been 10 times what they are in Western nations today. Historians attribute the decline to improving social controls over violence—police forces and common access to courts of law—and to a shift away from brutal physical punishment in child-rearing (a practice that still appears as a common factor in the background of violent criminals today).

The American Medical Association has based its endorsement of the media 5 violence theory in major part on the studies of Brandon Centerwall, a psychiatrist in Seattle. Dr. Centerwall compared the murder rates for whites in three countries from 1945 to 1974 with numbers for television set ownership. Until 1975, television broadcasting was banned in South Africa, and "white homicide rates remained stable" there, Dr. Centerwall found, while corresponding rates in Canada and the United States doubled after television was introduced.

A spectacular finding, but it is meaningless. As Franklin E. Zimring and Gordon Hawkins of the University of California at Berkeley subsequently pointed out, homicide rates in France, Germany, Italy and Japan either failed to change with increasing television ownership in the same period or actually declined, and American homicide rates have more recently been sharply declining despite a proliferation of popular media outlets—not only movies and television, but also video games and the Internet.

Other social science that supposedly undergirds the theory, too, is marginal and problematic. Laboratory studies that expose children to selected incidents of televised mock violence and then assess changes in the children's behavior have sometimes found more "aggressive" behavior after the exposure—usually verbal, occasionally physical.

But sometimes the control group, shown incidents judged not to be violent, behaves more aggressively afterward than the test group; sometimes comedy produces the more aggressive behavior; and sometimes there's no change. The only obvious conclusion is that sitting and watching television stimulates subsequent physical activity. Any kid could tell you that.

As for those who claim that entertainment promotes violent behavior by desensitizing people to violence, the British scholar Martin Barker offers this critique: "Their claim is that the materials they judge to be harmful can only influence us by trying to make us be the same as them. So horrible things will make us horrible—not horrified. Terrifying things will make us terrifying—not terrified. To see something aggressive makes us feel aggressive—not aggressed against. This idea is so odd, it is hard to know where to begin in challenging it."

Even more influential on national policy has been a 22-year study by two 10 University of Michigan psychologists, Leonard D. Eron and L. Rowell Huesmann, of boys exposed to so-called violent media. The Telecommunications Act of 1996, which mandated the television V-chip, allowing parents to screen out unwanted programming, invoked these findings, asserting, "Studies have shown that children exposed to violent video programming at a young age have a higher tendency for violent and aggressive behavior later in life than children not so exposed."

Well, not exactly. Following 875 children in upstate New York from third grade through high school, the psychologists found a correlation between a preference for violent television at age 8 and aggressiveness at age 18. The correlation—0.31— would mean television accounted for about 10 percent of the influences that led to this behavior. But the correlation only turned up in one of three measures of aggression: the assessment of students by their peers. It didn't show up in students' reports about themselves or in psychological testing. And for girls, there was no correlation at all.

Despite the lack of evidence, politicians can't resist blaming the media for violence. They can stake out the moral high ground confident that the First Amendment will protect them from having to actually write legislation that would be likely to alienate the entertainment industry. Some use the issue as a smokescreen to avoid having to confront gun control.

But violence isn't learned from mock violence. There is good evidence—causal evidence, not correlational—that it's learned in personal violent encounters, beginning with the brutalization of children by their parents or their peers.

The money spent on all the social science research I've described was diverted from the National Institute of Mental Health budget by reducing support for the construction of community mental health centers. To this day there is no standardized reporting system for emergency-room findings of physical child abuse. Violence is on the decline in America, but if we want to reduce it even further, protecting children from real violence in their real lives—not the pale shadow of mock violence—is the place to begin.

Inquiring into sources presents a special challenge: to overcome the authority the source projects. When ideas are in print, we tend to accept them uncritically, especially when they support our own opinion. If the argument appears in a leading newspaper like the *New York Times,* the piece can seem to have such authority that people just quote it and don't bother to assess it critically, especially when the author is as respected as Rhodes. We think, Who am I to question what he says? After all, I've gone to him to find out about fantasy violence. Shouldn't I just accept what he says, at least until I read other sources that oppose his view?

Our earlier chapters on reading and analyzing an argument show how we can overcome this natural tendency to be passive when we encounter an authoritative text. It's true that we are only inquirers, not experts, and so we cannot question Rhodes as another expert might. But we are hardly powerless. We can put into practice the critical-reading habits and skills discussed in Chapter 2. And we can use the "Questions for Inquiry" on pages 181–182 to open an argument to scrutiny.

A Dialogue with Rhodes

Looking at the "Questions for Inquiry," note that some seem perfect entry points into Rhodes's argument. We have no problems understanding his claim, but we might ask about the second item on our list, "the meaning of any words central to the argument." How does Rhodes define "violence"? In the fourth, fifth, and sixth paragraphs, he refers to declining homicide rates despite proliferating media violence. But when we think of violence today, we think not only of homicide but also of date rape, domestic violence, bullying, and even road rage.

——⦿⦿ **FOLLOWING THROUGH**

After sampling Rhodes's essay and reading it through, mark it up. What are the introduction and the conclusion? Are there any other subsections besides the presentation of the reasoning? Do you see the claim, reasons, and evidence? (See Chapter 3, "Analyzing Arguments," pages 45–59.) Mark and annotate them. How does Rhodes handle opposing views? Finally, use the "Questions for Inquiry" on pages 181–182. Make marginal annotations in response to Rhodes, and compare them with our discussion of the argument's strengths and weaknesses, pages 187–189.   •

——⦿⦿ **FOLLOWING THROUGH**

If you are working on a different topic, find an argument that addresses one of the topic's central issues. Do it as we have done it with Rhodes.   •

We could also question the thinking of one of Rhodes's sources, Martin Barker, who says it is "odd" to assume that watching "horrible things will make us horrible—not horrified." There are many depictions of violent acts shown in the media, and some glorify violence or make it seem funny. Barker's language oversimplifies the problem.

We might also ask the sixth question for inquiry, about evidence. In the third paragraph, Rhodes acknowledges that the American Medical Association, the American Psychological Association, the American Academy of Pediatrics, and the National Institute of Mental Health all affirm "a link between entertainment and violent behavior." Much of the rest of the article is an effort to undermine the science that claims to establish such a link. Is it likely that the AMA, APA, and the other institutions mentioned are *all* wrong? Is it likely that the AMA based its opinion "in major part" on only *one* study of fantasy violence, as Rhodes claims in paragraph 5? Neither seems very likely. We should be suspicious enough to visit one of the Web sites for these organizations to find out more about the basis of their opinion.

And we might question an assumption Rhodes makes, using question 4 as our inspiration. When he says that the rates of television ownership rose in France, Germany, Italy, and Japan while homicide rates did not change, is he assuming that the same shows were broadcast in these countries as in the United States and Canada, where homicide rates doubled? He seems to assume that the technology rather than the programs is an appropriate basis for comparison.

Finally, we might question Rhodes's assumption that if one thing is not necessary for another thing to happen, it therefore cannot be a factor at all. For example, cell phone use is not necessary for a car wreck to occur. However, cell phone use does *contribute* to automobile accidents. Rhodes claims that "violence isn't learned from mock violence. There is good evidence—causal evidence, not correlational—that it's learned in personal violent encounters, beginning with the brutalization of children by their parents or their peers." Does anyone doubt that real violence in children's lives contributes more than fantasy violence to aggressive behavior? Of course not. But that doesn't mean that fantasy violence contributes *nothing*. We can't dismiss something altogether just because something else contributes more.

FOLLOWING THROUGH

If you are inquiring into a topic of your own, use the "Questions for Inquiry" to open it up, as we have with Rhodes's essay. Do not try to pose all possible questions; find those that point to areas of weakness in the argument.   •

Another Example of Dialogue with a Reading

Let's also examine a book on violent entertainment, Sissela Bok's *Mayhem* (1998). Following is a chapter in which Bok assesses various ways to resist the effects of media violence. The chapter is especially interesting because it focuses on what children can do "to think for themselves and to become discriminating viewers."

Formerly professor of philosophy at Brandeis University, Sissela Bok is now a senior visiting fellow at the Harvard Center for Population and Development Studies.

Media Literacy

SISSELA BOK

How can children learn to take a more active and self-protective part in evaluating what they see? For an example of such learning, consider a class of second-graders in Oregon that Peter Jennings introduced on ABC's evening news in March 1995. With the help of their teacher, these children had arranged to study the role that television violence played in their lives: now they were presenting their "Declaration of Independence from Violence" to the rest of the student body. Their assignment had been to watch half an hour of television at home for several days running and to count the incidents of violence in each one—kicking, shooting, bombarding, killing. To their amazement, they had found nearly one such incident a minute in the programs they watched. The media mayhem they had taken for granted as part of their daily lives was suddenly put in question. One girl acknowledged that "before, I didn't even know what violence was."

The children then discussed the role of media violence in their own lives and concluded that what they saw on TV did affect them. Together, they considered different types of responses, often also discussing these choices in their homes. In their "Declaration of Independence from Violence," they addressed not only their school but the county board of education and community service organizations. Some pledged to limit their intake of violent programming and to refuse to watch certain shows; others wrote letters to television stations; a few organized a boycott of the products advertised on the programs they considered most violent.

These children were learning the rudiments of critical judgment and experiencing the pleasure of thinking for themselves about the messages beamed at them by advertisers and programmers. They were beginning to draw distinctions with respect to types of violence and their effects and to consider what might lie in their power to do in response. Throughout, they were learning to make active use of the media, including having their own initiative beamed to millions via the Jennings broadcast.

In so doing, the second-graders were participating in what has come to be called "media literacy education."[1] The media literacy movement, begun in Australia in the 1980s, views all media as offering scope for participants to learn not to submit passively to whatever comes along, but instead to examine offerings critically while recognizing the financial stakes of programmers and sponsors, to make informed personal and group choices, and to balance their own TV intake with participation in other activities. The hope is that children who become able to take such an approach will be more self-reliant, more informed, and correspondingly less fearful and passive, when it comes to their use of modern media. And since few adults have acquired critical viewing skills, such education is important at all ages.

Maturing, learning how to understand and deal with violence, coping better 5 with its presence on the screen as in the world, knowing its effects, and countering them to the extent possible involves exploring distinctions such as the following:

- between physical violence and psychological and other forms of violence
- between actual and threatened violence
- between direct and indirect violence
- between active violence and violence made possible by neglect or inaction
- between unwanted violence and, say, surgery, performed with consent
- between violence done to oneself and that done to others
- between seeing real violence and witnessing it on the screen
- between portrayals of "real" and fictional violence
- between violence conveyed as information and as entertainment
- between levels of violence in the media and in real life
- between oneself as viewer and as advertising or programming target
- between gratuitous portrayals of violence and others
- between violence glamorized or not

Learning to deal with violence involves sorting out such distinctions and categories and seeking to perceive when they overlap and interact and shade into one another. It is as inaccurate to view all these distinctions as utterly blurred as to imagine each category in a watertight compartment. Exploring these distinctions and their interactions is facilitated by talking them over with others and by seeing them illuminated, first in the simplest stories and pictures, later in literature and works of art.

Because the approach must be gradual and attuned to children's developmental stage, a film such as Steven Spielberg's *Schindler's List,* which offers searing insight into most of the distinctions listed above, is inappropriate for small children, who have not learned to make the necessary distinctions.[2] If they are exposed to such a film before they have learned to draw even rudimentary distinctions with respect to violence, they can respond with terror, numbing, sometimes even misplaced glee. As far as they are concerned, it is beside the point whether the horrors the film conveys are gratuitous or not, real or fictional, or meant as entertainment or not. They cannot tell the difference and should not be exposed to such material before they can do so. The film can be misunderstood, too, by those who would ordinarily be old enough to perceive such distinctions but whose capacity to respond to them has been thwarted or numbed, through personal experience, perhaps from violence in the home, or through overexposure to entertainment violence. The half-embarrassed, half-riotous laughter with which some high school audiences greeted the film troubled many: it was as if these students had lost their ability to make even the most basic distinctions.

A number of these distinctions are hard even for the most experienced media critics to pin down. Take the concept of "gratuitous" violence, violence not needed for purposes of the story being told but added for its shock or entertainment value. Some regard it as a characterization primarily in the eye of the beholder, while others insist that it can be clearly identified in particular films and television programs. Whatever the answer, there are borderline cases of violence where it is hard for anyone to be sure whether it is gratuitous or not. Works such as Spielberg's *Schindler's List* show instances of extreme cruelty that are necessary to convey the horror and inhumanity of the work's subject, and are thus not gratuitous in their own right; yet that film also explores how gratuitous violence is inflicted, even enjoyed, by its perpetrators. The film is about gratuitous violence, then, without in any sense exploiting it or representing an instance of it; and it is emphatically not meant as entertainment violence. Perhaps this is part of what Spielberg meant in saying that he made the film "thinking that if it did entertain, then I would have failed. It was important to me not to set out to please. Because I always had."[3]

Long before callous or uncomprehending ways of responding become ingrained, children can learn, much as the second-graders in the Jennings program were learning, to play a greater part in sorting out the distinctions regarding violence and media violence and to consider how they wish to respond. They can learn to think for themselves and to become discriminating viewers and active participants, rather than passive consumers of the entertainment violence beamed at them daily. Such learning helps, in turn, with the larger goal of achieving resilience—the ability to bounce back, to resist and overcome adversity.

Just as "buyer beware" is an indispensable motto in today's media environment 10 but far from sufficient, so is a fuller understanding of the role of violence in public entertainment. Individuals, families, and schools can do a great deal; but unless they can join in broader endeavors devoted to enhancing collective resilience, the many admirable personal efforts now under way will not begin to suffice. When neither families nor schools, churches, and neighborhoods can cope alone, what is the larger social responsibility?

NOTES

1. See Neil Anderson, *Media Works* (Oxford: Oxford University Press, 1989); and Madeline Levine, *Viewing Violence* (New York: Doubleday, 1996).
2. When *Schindler's List* was about to be broadcast on television, Spielberg was quoted as saying that the film was not, in his opinion, one that should be shown to the very young. His own children, of elementary school age, had not seen it in 1997; but he would want them to once they were of high school age. See Caryn James, "Bringing Home the Horror of the Holocaust," *New York Times,* February 23, 1997, p. 36 H.
3. Steven Spielberg, quoted by Stephen Schiff in "Seriously Spielberg," *New Yorker,* March 21, 1994, p. 101.

Possibilities for Dialogue with "Media Literacy"

There's no one right way to have a dialogue, just as there's no magic question that will always unlock the text in front of us. But it's a good idea to begin with the question *What exactly is the arguer's position?* It's clear that Bok favors "media literacy education." She advocates it, but as only part of the solution to children's exposure to media violence. Her last paragraph implies that we will need other measures as well. And so we might ask, "Why is media education not the only solution?" or "Why isn't media education enough?" Can we tell what she thinks the limitations are?

Having begun with the position question, where we go from there *depends on the nature of the text.* In this case, we need to ask question 2, *What do certain key terms mean?* Paragraph 5 is about the kind of distinctions necessary to a mature understanding of violence. But are we sure about the distinctions? What is "psychological violence"? Bok doesn't say. How would we answer? If there are both physical and psychological forms of violence, what other forms are there? Again, Bok provides no explanation or examples. Can we? It's far from clear what she means. We must figure this out ourselves or work through these distinctions in class discussion.

We should also ask about assumptions and implications. Bok admits that "[a] number of these distinctions are hard even for the most experienced media critics to pin down" (paragraph 8). As adults and college students, we're certainly having our troubles with them; how can we assume that the second-graders referred to in the first paragraph can make them? Do they really understand whatever distinctions their teacher is helping them to make?

Once we question what the argument assumes—that young children (about seven or eight years old) can make meaningful distinctions and understand them—we begin to wonder about implications as well. For instance, the students present what they call a "Declaration of Independence from Violence" to "the rest of the student body." Does the declaration imply that violence is *not* part of the human condition? Are we ignoring reality or learning how to cope with it? More broadly, Bok's discussion implies that media education must continue as students grow up. Is this practical? realistic? Is it something our schools can or should undertake?

◎◎ FOLLOWING THROUGH

In class discussion, continue the dialogue with "Media Literacy." What other questions are relevant from our list of "Questions for Inquiry"? What questions can we ask that do not appear on the list? Be sure to consider the rather unusual case of *Schindler's List.* Why might high school students laugh at it? Is the *only* explanation the one that Bok offers, that the students didn't understand the horror of Nazi violence? Does a movie like *Schindler's List,* when audiences understand and react appropriately to it, help us in "achieving resilience—the ability to bounce back, to resist and overcome adversity"?
                                                                                          •

◎◎ FOLLOWING THROUGH

As prewriting for Part 2 of your exploratory essay, read one substantial argument on the topic. Write a brief summary of the argument, noting its claim and reasons. Then write a few paragraphs of response to it, as we have done with Rhodes's essay and Bok's chapter, showing how the "Questions for Inquiry" opened up that argument to closer inspection. How did the argument compare with your own initial opinions? Was your thinking changed in any way? Why or why not?
                                                                                          •

INQUIRY AGAIN: DIGGING DEEPER

Inquiry can always lead to more inquiry. For example, if, after reading Bok, we doubt that media literacy can work, we can find out more about it, including what went on in Australia in the 1980s. If we question what second-graders can understand about media violence, we can research the cognitive development of young children. If we aren't sure about the impact of *Schindler's List,* we can watch it ourselves or read about Spielberg's making of the film and the popular and critical reception of it. There's nothing important in "Media Literacy" that can't be researched and explored further. Digging deeper means getting more information. But mere quantity is not the goal. Moving deeper also means moving closer to genuine expertise. For example, Richard Rhodes is a journalist, not a social scientist. He consulted social scientists to write his argument. To evaluate Rhodes's claims we need to do the same. Digging deeper should take us closer to people who ought to know the most.

Digging deeper also means sharpening the focus of inquiry. As we said earlier, the narrow but deep inquiry will produce a better argument than a broad survey. Look for arguments and informative sources that address the same aspect of a topic. You may find two or more arguments that debate each other.

To find good sources, read the sections on finding and evaluating sources, pages 97–119. There are always resources for digging deeper into a question. Reference librarians can help. They are experts at finding the experts.

When should you stop digging deeper? You can tell when you're near the end of inquiry. You'll be reading but not finding much you haven't seen already. That's the time to stop—or find another avenue for further research.

Most important, *seek out some sources with points of view that differ from your own.* The whole point of inquiry is to seek the new and challenging. *Remember: We are not defending what we think but putting it to the test.*

FOLLOWING THROUGH

Read pages 97–119 on finding and evaluating sources. Using the library and electronic indexes available, find at least five good articles and arguments about your chosen issue. Be sure to find sources that contain a variety of opinions but that address the same issues. Read each carefully, and write notes and annotations based on the "Questions for Inquiry."   •

When the Experts Disagree

A professor once advised his classes, "If you want to think you know something about a subject, read one book, because reading a second will just confuse you." Some confusion is unavoidable in inquiry. Digging deeply will reveal sources that conflict. Instead of avoiding conflicting sources (the professor was mocking those who do), seek out conflict and analyze it. Decide which sources to accept, which to reject. We illustrate some strategies for dealing with conflict in the following exploration of two articles that assess the research linking fantasy violence to actual violence.

An Example of Experts Disagreeing

When we left Richard Rhodes, we still wondered, Does violent entertainment contribute to violence in our society? He made a good case against such a link, but we can't ignore all the experts he mentions who do take it seriously. Nor can we put aside the results of our own inquiry into the article, which gave us good reason to doubt his position. So we went to the social scientists themselves to see how they interpret the research. We located the following exchange from the *Harvard Mental Health Letter* (1996). Jonathan L. Freedman, a professor of psychology at the University of Toronto, argues much as Rhodes did—that there's no proof linking fantasy violence to actual violence. L. Rowell Huesmann, a professor of psychology at the University of Michigan, and his graduate assistant, Jessica Moise, defend the link, based in part on their own research.

Now we have conflicting arguments. Read the following articles and assess them on your own. Ask yourself, Who makes the better case?

Children watching violence on TV.

Violence in the Mass Media and Violence in Society: The Link Is Unproven[1]

JONATHAN L. FREEDMAN

Imagine that the Food and Drug Administration (FDA) is presented with a series of studies testing the effectiveness of a new drug. There are some laboratory tests that produce fairly consistent positive effects, but the drug does not always work as expected and no attempt has been made to discover why. Most of the clinical tests are negative; there are also a few weak positive results and a few results suggesting that the drug is less effective than a placebo. Obviously the FDA would reject this application, yet the widely accepted evidence that watching television violence causes aggression is no more adequate.

In laboratory tests of this thesis, some children are shown violent programs, others are shown nonviolent programs, and their aggressiveness is measured immediately afterward. The results, although far from consistent, generally show some increase in aggression after a child watches a violent program. Like most laboratory studies of real-world conditions, however, these findings have limited value. In the first place, most of the studies have used dubious measures of aggression. In one experiment, for example, children were asked, "If I had a balloon, would you want me to prick it?" Other measures have been more plausible, but none is unimpeachable. Second, there is the problem of distinguishing effects of violence from effects of interest and excitement. In general, the violent films in these experiments are more arousing than the neutral films. Anyone who is aroused will display more of

[1]Jonathan L. Freedman, "Violence in the Mass Media and Violence in Society: The Link Is Unproven." Excerpted from the *Harvard Mental Health Letter,* May 1996. © 1996, President and Fellows of Harvard College. For more information, visit www.health.harvard.edu/mental. Harvard Health Publications does not endorse any products or medical procedures.

almost any behavior; there is nothing special about aggression in this respect. Finally and most important, these experiments are seriously contaminated by what psychologists call demand characteristics of the situation: the familiar fact that people try to do what the experimenter wants. Since the children know the experimenter has chosen the violent film, they may assume that they are being given permission to be aggressive.

PUTTING IT TO THE TEST

The simplest way to conduct a real-world study is to find out whether children who watch more violent television are also more aggressive. They are, but the correlations are small, accounting for only 1% to 10% of individual differences in children's aggressiveness. In any case, correlations do not prove causality. Boys watch more TV football than girls, and they play more football than girls, but no one, so far as I know, believes that television is what makes boys more interested in football. Probably personality characteristics that make children more aggressive also make them prefer violent television programs.

To control for the child's initial aggressiveness, some studies have measured children's TV viewing and their aggression at intervals of several years, using statistical techniques to judge the effect of early television viewing on later aggression. One such study found evidence of an effect, but most have found none.

For practical reasons, there have been only a few truly controlled experiments 5 in which some children in a real-world environment are assigned to watch violent programs for a certain period of time and others are assigned to watch nonviolent programs. Two or three of these experiments indicated slight, short-lived effects of TV violence on aggression; one found a strong effect in the opposite of the expected direction, and most found no effect. All the positive results were obtained by a single research group, which conducted studies with very small numbers of children and used inappropriate statistics.

SCRUTINIZING THE EVIDENCE

An account of two studies will give some idea of how weak the research results are and how seriously they have been misinterpreted.

A study published by Lynette Friedrichs and Aletha Stein is often described (for example, in reports by the National Institute of Mental Health and the American Psychological Association) as having found that children who watched violent programs became more aggressive. What the study actually showed was quite different. In a first analysis the authors found that TV violence had no effect on physical aggression, verbal aggression, aggressive fantasy, or object aggression (competition for a toy or other object). Next they computed indexes statistically combining various kinds of aggression, a technique that greatly increases the likelihood of connections appearing purely by chance. Still they found nothing.

They then divided the children into two groups—those who were already aggressive and those who were not. They found that children originally lower in aggression seemed to become more aggressive and children originally higher in aggression seemed to become less aggressive no matter which type of program they watched. This is a well-known statistical artifact called regression toward the mean, and it has no substantive significance. Furthermore, the less aggressive children actually became more aggressive after watching the neutral program than after watching the violent program. The only comfort for the experimenters was that the level of aggression in highly aggressive children fell more when they watched a neutral program than when they watched a violent program. Somehow that was sufficient for the study to be widely cited as strong evidence that TV violence causes aggression.

An ambitious cross-national study was conducted by a team led by Rowell Huesmann and Leonard Eron and reported in 1986. In this widely cited research the effect of watching violent television on aggressiveness at a later age was observed in seven groups of boys and seven groups of girls in six countries. After controlling for initial aggressiveness, the researchers found no statistically signifi-cant effect for either sex in Australia, Finland, the Netherlands, Poland, or kibbutz children in Israel. The effect sought by the investigators was found only in the United States and among urban Israeli children, and the latter effect was so large, so far beyond the normal range for this kind of research and so incongruous with the results in other countries, that it must be regarded with suspicion. Neverthe-less, the senior authors concluded that the pattern of results supported their posi-tion. The Netherlands researchers disagreed; they acknowledged that they had not been able to link TV violence to aggression, and they criticized the methods used by some of the other groups. The senior authors refused to include their chapter in the book that came out of the study, and they had to publish a separate report.

A SECOND LOOK

If the evidence is so inadequate, why have so many committees evaluating it con- [10] cluded that the link exists? In the first place, these committees have been composed largely of people chosen with the expectation of reaching that conclusion. Further-more, committee members who were not already familiar with the research could not possibly have read it all themselves, and must have relied on what they were told by experts who were often biased. The reports of these committees are often seriously inadequate. The National Institute of Mental Health, for example, con-ducted a huge study but solicited only one review of the literature, from a strong advocate of the view that television violence causes aggression. The review was sketchy—it left out many important studies—and deeply flawed.

The belief that TV violence causes aggression has seemed plausible because it is intuitively obvious that this powerful medium has effects on children. After all, children imitate and learn from what they see. The question, however, is what they see on television and what they learn. We know that children tend to imitate actions that are rewarded and avoid actions that are punished. In most violent television programs villains start the fight and are punished. The programs also show heroes using violence to fight violence, but the heroes almost always have special legal or moral authority; they are police, other government agents, or protectors of society like Batman and the Power Rangers. If children are learning anything from these programs, it is that the forces of good will overcome evil assailants who are the first to use violence. That may be overoptimistic, but it hardly encourages the children themselves to initiate aggression.

TELLING THE DIFFERENCE

Furthermore, these programs are fiction, and children know it as early as the age of five. Children watching Power Rangers do not think they can beam up to the command center, and children watching "Aladdin" do not believe in flying carpets. Similarly, children watching the retaliatory violence of the heroes in these programs do not come to believe they themselves could successfully act in the same way. (Researchers concerned about mass media violence should be more interested in the fights that occur during hockey and football games, which are real and therefore may be imitated by children who play those sports.)

Recently I testified before a Senate committee, and one Senator told me he knew TV made children aggressive because his own son had met him at the door with a karate kick after watching the Power Rangers. The Senator was confusing aggression with rough play, and imitation of specific actions with learning to be aggressive. Children do imitate what they see on television; this has strong effects on the way they play, and it may also influence the forms their real-life aggression takes. Children who watch the Ninja Turtles or Power Rangers may practice martial arts, just as years ago they might have been wielding toy guns, and long before that, wrestling or dueling with wooden swords. If there had been no television, the Senator's son might have butted him in the stomach or poked him in the ribs with a gun. The question is not whether the boy learned his karate kick from TV, but whether TV has made him more aggressive than he would have been otherwise.

Television is an easy target for the concern about violence in our society but a misleading one. We should no longer waste time worrying about this subject. Instead let us turn our attention to the obvious major causes of violence, which include poverty, racial conflict, drug abuse, and poor parenting.

Media Violence: A Demonstrated Public Health Threat to Children[2]

L. ROWELL HUESMANN AND JESSICA MOISE

Imagine that the Surgeon General is presented with a series of studies on a widely distributed product. For 30 years well-controlled experiments have been showing that use of the product causes symptoms of a particular affliction. Many field surveys have shown that this affliction is always more common among people who use the product regularly. A smaller number of studies have examined the long-term effects of the product in different environments, and most have shown at least some evidence of harm, although it is difficult to disentangle effects of the product itself from the effects of factors that lead people to use it. Over all, the studies suggest that if a person with a 50% risk for the affliction uses the product, the risk rises to 60% or 70%. Furthermore, we have a fairly good understanding of how use of the product contributes to the affliction, which is persistent, difficult to cure, and sometimes lethal.

[2]L. Rowell Huesmann and Jessica Moise, "Media Violence: A Demonstrated Public Health Threat to Children." Excerpted from *Harvard Mental Health Letter,* June 1996. © 1996, President and Fellows of Harvard College. For more information, visit www.health.harvard.edu/mental. Harvard Health Publications does not endorse any products or medical procedures.

The product is economically important, and its manufacturers spend large sums trying to disparage the scientific research. A few scientists who have never done any empirical work in the field regularly point out supposed flaws in the research and belittle its conclusions. The incidence of the affliction has increased dramatically since the product was first introduced. What should the Surgeon General do?

This description applies to the relationship between lung cancer and cigarettes. It also applies to the relationship between aggression and children's viewing of mass media violence. The Surgeon General has rightly come to the same conclusion in both cases and has issued similar warnings.

CAUSE AND EFFECT

Dr. Freedman's highly selective reading of the research minimizes overwhelming evidence. First, there are the carefully controlled laboratory studies in which children are exposed to violent film clips and short-term changes in their behavior are observed. More than 100 such studies over the last 40 years have shown that at least some children exposed to visual depictions of dramatic violence behave more aggressively afterward both toward inanimate objects and toward other children. These results have been found in many countries among boys and girls of all social classes, races, ages, and levels of intelligence.

Freedman claims that these studies use "dubious measures of aggression." He cites only one example: asking children whether they would want the researcher to prick a balloon. But this measure is not at all representative. Most studies have used such evidence as physical attacks on other children and dolls. In one typical study Kaj Bjorkqvist exposed five- and six-year-old Finnish children to either violent or non-violent films. Observers who did not know which kind of film each child had seen then watched them play together. Children who had just seen a violent film were more likely to hit other children, scream at them, threaten them, and intentionally destroy their toys.

Freedman claims that these experiments confuse the effects of arousal with the 5 effects of violence. He argues that "anyone who is aroused will display more of almost any behavior." But most studies have shown that prosocial behavior decreases after children view an aggressive film. Finally, Freedman says the experiments are contaminated by demand characteristics. In other words, the children are only doing what they think the researchers want them to do. That conclusion is extremely implausible, considering the wide variety of experiments conducted in different countries by researchers with different points of view.

LARGE BODY OF EVIDENCE

More than 50 field studies over the last 20 years have also shown that children who habitually watch more media violence behave more aggressively and accept aggression more readily as a way to solve problems. The relationship usually persists when researchers control for age, sex, social class, and previous level of aggression. Disbelievers often suggest that the correlation is statistically small. According to Freedman, it accounts for "only 1% to 10% of individual differences in children's aggressiveness." But an increase of that size (a more accurate figure would be 2%

to 16%) has real social significance. No single factor has been found to explain more than 16% of individual differences in aggression.

Of course, correlations do not prove causality. That is the purpose of laboratory experiments. The two approaches are complementary. Experiments establish causal relationship, and field studies show that the relationship holds in a wide variety of real-world situations. The causal relationship is further confirmed by the finding that children who view TV violence at an early age are more likely to commit aggressive acts at a later age. In 1982 Eron and Huesmann found that boys who spent the most time viewing violent television shows at age eight were most likely to have criminal convictions at age 30. Most other long-term studies have come to similar conclusions, even after controlling for children's initial aggressiveness, social class, and education. A few studies have found no effect on some measures of violence, but almost all have found a significant effect on some measures.

Freedman singles out for criticism a study by Huesmann and his colleagues that was concluded in the late 1970s. He says we found "no statistically significant effect for either sex in Australia, Finland, the Netherlands, Poland, or kibbutz children in Israel." That is not true. We found that the television viewing habits of children [as] young as six or seven predicted subsequent increases in childhood aggression among boys in Finland and among both sexes in the United States, in Poland, and in Israeli cities. In Australia and on Israeli kibbutzim, television viewing habits were correlated with simultaneous aggression. Freedman also suggests that another study conducted in the Netherlands came to conclusions so different from ours that we banned it from a book we were writing. In fact, the results of that study were remarkably similar to our own, and we did not refuse to publish it. The Dutch researchers themselves chose to publish separately in a different format.

CULTURAL DIFFERENCES

Freedman argues that the strongest results reported in the study, such as those for Israeli city children, are so incongruous that they arouse suspicion. He is wrong. Given the influence of culture and social learning on aggressive behavior, different results in different cultures are to be expected. In fact, the similarity of the findings in different countries is remarkable here. One reason we found no connection between television violence viewing and aggression among children on [kib]butzim is the strong cultural prohibition against intra-group aggression in those communities. Another reason is that kibbutz children usually watched television in a group and discussed the shows with an adult caretaker afterward.

Two recently published meta-analyses summarize the findings of many studies 10 conducted over the past 30 years. In an analysis of 217 experiments and field studies, Paik and Comstock concluded that the association between exposure to television violence and aggressive behavior is extremely strong, especially in the data accumulated over the last 15 years. In the other meta-analysis, Wood, Wong, and Chachere came to the same conclusion after combined analysis of 23 studies of unstructured social interaction.

We now have well-validated theoretical explanations of these results. Exposure to media violence leads to aggression in at least five ways. The first is imitation, or observational learning. Children imitate the actions of their parents, other children, and

media heroes, especially when the action is rewarded and the child admires and identifies with the model. When generalized, this process creates what are sometimes called
cognitive scripts for complex social problem-solving: internalized programs that guide
everyday social behavior in an automatic way and are highly resistant to change.

TURNING OFF

Second, media violence stimulates aggression by desensitizing children to the
effects of violence. The more televised violence a child watches, the more acceptable aggressive behavior becomes for that child. Furthermore, children who watch
violent television become suspicious and expect others to act violently—an attribu-
tional bias that promotes aggressive behavior.

Justification is a third process by which media violence stimulates aggression. A
child who has behaved aggressively watches violent television shows to relieve guilt
and justify the aggression. The child then feels less inhibited about aggressing again.

A fourth process is cognitive priming or cueing—the activation of existing aggressive thoughts, feelings, and behavior. This explains why children observe one kind of
aggression on television and commit another kind of aggressive act afterward. Even
an innocuous object that has been associated with aggression may later stimulate
violence. Josephson demonstrated this . . . in a study of schoolboy hockey players.
She subjected the boys to frustration and then showed them either a violent or a
non-violent television program. The aggressor in the violent program carried a walkie-
talkie. Later, when the referee in a hockey game carried a similar walkie-talkie, the boys
who had seen the violent film were more likely to start fights during the game.

A NUMBING EFFECT

The fifth process by which media violence induces aggression is physiological 15
arousal and desensitization. Boys who are heavy television watchers show lower
than average physiological arousal in response to new scenes of violence. Similar
short-term effects are found in laboratory studies. The arousal stimulated by viewing violence is unpleasant at first, but children who constantly watch violent television become habituated, and their emotional and physiological responses decline.
Meanwhile the propensity to aggression is heightened by any pleasurable arousal,
such as sexual feeling, that is associated with media violence.

Freedman argues that in violent TV shows, villains start the fight and are punished
and the heroes "almost always have special legal or moral authority." Therefore, he
concludes, children are learning from these programs that "the forces of good will
overcome evil assailants." On the contrary, it is precisely because media heroes are
admired and have special authority that children are likely to imitate their behavior
and learn that aggression is an acceptable solution to conflict. Freedman also claims
that media violence has little effect because children can distinguish real life from fiction. But children under 11 do not make this distinction very well. Studies have shown
that many of them think cartoons and other fantasy shows depict life as it really is.

The studies are conclusive. The evidence leaves no room for doubt that exposure to media violence stimulates aggression. It is time to move on and consider
how best to inoculate our children against this insidious threat.

Commentary on the Experts' Disagreement

When experts disagree, the rest of us can respond in only a few ways. We can throw up our hands and say, "Who knows?" But this response doesn't work because expert disagreement is so common. We'd have to give up on most issues. Another response is to take seriously only those experts who endorse the opinion we favor and ignore the rest, a common tactic in debate, legal pleadings, business, and politics whenever truth gives way to self-interest. We can also "go with our gut," opting for the opinion that "feels right." But gut feelings amount to little more than our prejudices talking. And so we are left with the only response appropriate to inquiry: *rational assessment of the competing arguments*. We should take as true the better or best case.

How can we decide which of two or several arguments is better or best?

In this instance, let's recognize that Huesmann and Moise have an advantage simply because they wrote second, after Freedman, who has no opportunity to respond to what they've said. Huesmann and Moise can *both* refute Freedman *and* make their own case without the possibility of rebuttal. Granting this it's still hard to find Freedman's case more convincing. Why?

We'll offer only a few reasons for assenting to the Huesmann–Moise argument. You and your class can take the analysis further—it's a good opportunity to practice critical reading and thinking.

Both articles begin with an analogy. Freedman compares the research on violent TV programs with the research required to approve a drug. Huesmann and Moise compare the research linking cigarettes to lung cancer with the research linking violent TV to aggressive behavior in children. The second comparison is better because the two instances of research compared are more nearly alike. Furthermore, the fact that the Surgeon General has issued warnings both for cigarettes and for violent entertainment's effect on children shows how seriously research on the latter is taken by qualified authorities. In fact, one of the more convincing aspects of the Huesmann–Moise case is the amount of support they claim for their position. They are specific about the numbers: "50 field studies over the last 20 years" (paragraph 6); "an analysis of 217 experiments and field studies" (paragraph 10)—all confirm their conclusion. If Freedman has evidence to rival this, he does not cite it. We must assume he doesn't because he doesn't have it.

Another strength of the Huesmann–Moise article is that they go beyond linking TV violence to aggression by offering five *explanations* for the negative impact of fantasy violence (paragraphs 11–15). We come away not only convinced that the link exists but also understanding why it exists. Freedman has no well-developed explanation to support his position. What he offers, such as the assertion that children know the difference between pretend and real violence, is refuted by Huesmann and Moise.

If you are thinking that the better or best case isn't always so easy to discern, you're right. Comparative assessment will not always yield a clearly superior case. We will sometimes argue with ourselves and others over whose case merits our support. Nonetheless, when we encounter opposing positions, we should set aside our prejudices and study the arguments made. We should resolve the conflict by taking the better or best case as the closest thing we have to the truth.

In most cases, the better or best argument will emerge as you think your way through the arguments, comparing their strengths and weaknesses. What's hard is to let go of a position we're attracted to when another one has the better case. *The real challenge of inquiry is to change or revise our own opinions as we encounter arguments stronger than our own.*

FOLLOWING THROUGH

Even if they do not speak directly to each other, as our examples here do, find two sources that present conflicting data or information or conflicting interpretations of the same information. Write an evaluation of these arguments, telling which one has the better case. Explain why you think so. Did you find that comparing these arguments influenced your own thinking? If so, how? •

THE WRITING PROJECT: PART 2

By now you have many notes that you can use as raw material for writing Part 2 of your essay. You have had a serious dialogue with at least one other person about your ideas. You should have notes about this dialogue and maybe a recording or transcript of it. Look over this material, and make more notes about how this conversation modified your ideas—by clarifying them, by presenting you with a new idea, or by solidifying a belief you already held.

You have also read several printed arguments. You have written evaluations of these arguments and marked them up. Now note places where they touch upon the same points. Use highlighters to color-code passages that connect across the readings. Draft paragraphs about what different experts have to say on the same question, including an estimate of how sound their points are and how they increased your own knowledge. Which viewpoints seemed most persuasive, and why?

You are ready to draft the body of your paper. It should contain at least four well-developed paragraphs that describe your inquiry. Discuss the conversations you had and the materials you read, and show how these lines of inquiry influenced your thinking. Assess the arguments you read, consider their rhetorical context, include the names of the authors and the biases they might have. Talk about why an author's argument was sound or not sound, why it influenced your initial opinion or why it did not.

Part 2 could be organized around a discussion of initial opinions strengthened by your research versus those reconsidered because of it. Did a source offer new information that caused you to reconsider what you thought? Tell what the information was, and explain why it's changed your outlook. Did you encounter a well-developed argument defending a position different from your own? How did you react? What aspects of the argument do you take seriously enough to modify or change your own opinion? Explain why. If you found sources who disagreed, which side did you find more convincing, and why?

Some paragraphs could be devoted to a single source. Others could compare an idea across two or more sources; you could point out ways in which they agree or disagree, showing how each contributed to changing your opinion.

No matter how you organize your paper, *be specific about what you have read.* You will need to quote and paraphrase; when you refer to sources, do so very specifically. See our advice about using sources on pages 119–130.

Don't merely summarize your sources or use them to support and illustrate your own argument. *You are evaluating the thinking expressed in the sources,* not making your own case.

Rhetorical context is vital and it should be part of your consideration of each source. *Be selective.* Your readers don't want to get bogged down in needless detail; they want the information that altered your understanding of the topic and the arguments that opened up new considerations. *The point is to show how your research-inquiry refined, modified, or changed your initial opinions and to explain why.* Anything that doesn't do this should be cut from the final draft of your paper.

THE WRITING PROJECT: PART 3

In preparation for writing the conclusion of your essay, reread Part 1, the overview of your exploration. Have you arrived at a claim you could defend in an essay to convince or persuade an audience? If so, what is it? Perhaps you're still unsure—what then? One option is to conclude your paper by explaining what you are unsure of and why, and what you'd like to learn from further research. An inconclusive but honest ending is better than a forced one making a claim you don't really believe.

Draft a conclusion in which you honestly discuss the results of your exploration, whatever they were. This section is about *where you stand now,* but it needn't be final or conclusive. If you have doubts, state them and indicate how you might resolve them through further research and inquiry.

AFTER DRAFTING YOUR ESSAY

Revise your draft to make sure each paragraph is unified around one point and to remove any unnecessary summarizing. Check your work against the guidelines for incorporating source material in your own writing (pages 130–135).

Edit your paper for wordiness, repetition, and excessive passive voice. See the suggestions for editing in Appendix A.

Proofread your paper. Read it aloud to catch omissions and errors of grammar and punctuation.

STUDENT SAMPLE An Exploratory Essay

Exploratory Essay
Sydney Owens

Part 1

I think that the relationship between violence and the media is hard to define. There is definitely some relation between them, but to what extent it is hard to say. Media itself is only one word, but it includes television, radio, CDs, video games, papers, books, the Internet, and more. It's hard to say what each contributes. Also, you have to look at what kind of violence you are talking about. Do media influence extreme aggressive behavior, such as killing? Lastly, a child's environment, personality, and parents also have to be considered. It is difficult to say why people do anything, including acts of violence.

Each human is unique so that it's hard to say that media violence makes people more violent. One person could watch gruesome violence every day and remain caring and loving, whereas another individual might see minimal violent media and go out and kill. How do you explain the difference? You have to define a norm. But that norm only defines "normal" people's reactions to media violence. A person outside of the norm may still commit acts of violence.

When I see or hear violence in the media, I know that I am not inclined to do anything more violent than if I had not. Granted, a high-action movie thriller has given me that feeling of kick-ass satisfaction and exposure to rap has caused me to use strong language. But feelings and slang are not acts of violence. These examples do show that there is a connection between the media and people's behavior.

Part 2

When I read "Violence in the Mass Media and Violence in Society: The Link Is Unproven," I began to think that there really is not much evidence indicating that media violence leads to violent behavior. The author, Jonathan Freedman, argued that you could not prove the link because the "studies . . . used dubious measures of aggression," they could not "distinguish effects of violence from effects of interest and excitement," and the studies were "seriously contaminated by . . . demand characteristics of the situation." All of this made sense to me. I especially agreed with the contamination of the demand characteristics because I had just learned about this in my psychology class. I was taught that experimenters have to take into

www.mhhe.com/**crusius**

For more examples of student writing, go to:

Writing

account that subjects alter their own behavior to meet what they think the experimenter wants.

Freedman also gave an example that stuck in my mind as proof   5 that there is not a strong enough link to prove anything. He said to imagine that the FDA was testing the effectiveness of a new drug. The results came out negative, even less effective than a placebo. He said that obviously the FDA would reject this drug and that, similarly, media should be rejected as having a significant effect on violence. This made perfect sense until I compared it to "Media Violence: A Demonstrated Public Health Threat to Children," an article by L. Rowell Huesmann and Jessica Moise that counters Freedman's position. The FDA analogy that had sounded so good now looked faulty compared with Huesmann's Surgeon General analogy. In Huesmann's analogy, he points out that if something has shown even the slightest negative effect, it can't be dismissed. Freedman was right to say that we cannot prove for certain that media violence leads to violent behavior, but what he failed to acknowledge is that we should still warn about negative effects. After contrasting these two articles, I had changed my mind and decided that media violence does play a role in violent behavior.

With this new state of mind, I read several other articles that reinforced the claim that media violence promotes violent behavior. In the article "We Are Training Our Kids to Kill," Dave Grossman claims that "the desensitizing techniques used for training soldiers are being replicated in contemporary mass media movies, television, and video games, giving rise to the alarming rate of homicide and violence in our schools and communities." Not only was this article interesting, but it also made sense. Grossman, who travels the world training medical, law enforcement, and U.S. military personnel about the realities of warfare, supported his claim by showing how classical and operant conditioning used in the military parallel the effects of violent media on young children. Grossman's article was simple and straightforward. I followed his argument and agreed that the desensitizing effects of media train our kids to kill.

To be sure that his argument was true, I tried looking for some evidence that would prove that desensitizing did not have an effect. The only text I could find was the article by Richard Rhodes, "Hollow Claims about Fantasy Violence." In this article, there is one short and very confusing paragraph (paragraph 9) in which Rhodes offers "a British scholar's" critique of the desensitization argument:

> [T]heir claim is that the materials they judge to be harmful can only influence us by trying to make us be the same as them. So horrible things will make us horrible—not horrified. . . . This idea is so odd, it is hard to know where to begin in challenging it.

After reading this, I felt like saying the same thing to Rhodes. His paragraph was so confusing I had a hard time knowing where to begin in challenging it. In reality, it is not really an argument at all because Rhodes offers only a quote without explanation. The quote lumps all forms of violence together and ignores the different ways violence is depicted. I stuck with my new view that desensitization does promote violent behavior.

Part 3

After reading all of these articles and deciding that I do think that media contributes to violent behavior, I began thinking about my own personal experiences again. I thought about that "kick-ass feeling" I get when I watch certain action movies, and I began feeling somewhat ashamed. As film producers Edward Zwick and Marshall Herskovitz pointed out in their New York Times column "When the Bodies Are Real," written after 9/11, "perhaps what this event has revealed, with its real bodies blown to bits and real explosions bringing down buildings, is the true darkness behind so much of the product coming out of Hollywood today."

Annotated Bibliography

Freedman, Jonathan L. "Violence in the Mass Media and Violence in Society: The Link Is Unproven." Harvard Mental Health Letter May 1996: 4–6.

This article claims that there is not solid proof that mass media leads to violence. The author, Jonathan Freedman, proves his claim by showing that the studies have used dubious measures of aggression, by showing that it is hard to distinguish effects of violence from effects of excitement, and to separate either from the effects of demand characteristics. This would be a good article to use to prove that media does not influence aggressive behavior; however, I used the article's weak points to prove that media does lead to aggressive behavior.

Grossman, Dave. "We Are Training Our Kids to Kill." Saturday Evening Post July/Aug. 1999: 64–70.

This article explains the killings committed by America's youth as a result of media violence. First the author discusses how killing is unnatural. He then goes on to show how several military techniques for training soldiers resemble the ways the media interact with children. This article gives logical support to the claim that media influences violent behavior.

Herskovitz, Marshall, and Edward Zwick. "When the Bodies Are Real." Editorial. New York Times 23 Sept. 2001.

This is a short article written in response to the horrible tragedy of 9/11. It is written for the general public but focuses specifically on how the media community will respond to this tragedy. The authors, Marshall Herskovitz and Edward Zwick, are producers, directors, and writers. They point out how 9/11 has caused Hollywood, and all of us, to reexamine violence.

Huesmann, L. Rowell, and Jessica Moise. "Media Violence: A Demonstrated Public Health Threat to Children." Harvard Mental Health Letter June 1996: 5–7.

This article responds to Jonathan Freedman's article, "Violence in the Mass Media and Violence in Society: The Link Is Unproven." The authors refute most of Freedman's article with research. The article offers good support for the link between media and real violence.

Rhodes, Richard. "Hollow Claims about Fantasy Violence." Editorial. New York Times 17 Sept. 2000.

This essay attempts to prove that there is not enough evidence to claim that media violence leads to real violence. The author says that people (in particular, politicians) use media as a scapegoat for not looking at the real problems behind violence.

Note: For a discussion of how to create an annotated bibliography, see Chapter 5, pages 128–129.

INQUIRY: SUMMING UP THE AIM

In this chapter, we've introduced you to college-level inquiry. Here are the key points:

- In college, we don't just ransack sources for information and quotes. *We interact with them.* "Interact" means be critical of sources and allow them to influence, even change, our point of view.

- Informal conversation is a valuable medium of inquiry. But it becomes more valuable when we turn conversation into dialogue. *Assert opinions less, and question opinions more.* When a good question elicits a good response, pursue it with more questions.

- The best and most stimulating sources need dialogue. *Think of texts as something to "talk with."* Such dialogues will uncover more research possibilities. Pursue these, and you'll approach the depth of inquiry valued in college work and beyond, in graduate school and the workplace.

Inquiry is learning. Inquiry is finding what we really think and have to say. It's the most creative part of the writing process. Invest in it. It will repay your best efforts.

CHAPTER 8

Making Your Case: Arguing to Convince

The last chapter ended where inquiry ends—with the attempt to formulate a position, an opinion that we can assert with some confidence. Once our aim shifts from inquiring to convincing, everything changes.

The most significant change is in audience. In inquiry, our audience consists of our fellow inquirers—friends, classmates, and teachers we can talk with face to face. We seek assurance that our position is at least plausible and defensible, a claim to truth that can be respected whether or not the audience agrees with it. In convincing, however, our audience consists of readers whose positions differ from our own or who have no position at all. The audience changes from a small, inside group that helps us develop our argument to a larger, public audience who will either accept or reject it.

As the audience changes, so does the situation or need for argument. Inquiry is a cooperative use of argument; it cannot take place unless people are willing to work together. Conversely, convincing is competitive. We pit our case against the case(s) of others to win the assent of readers who will compare the various arguments and ask, Who makes the best case? With whom should I agree? Our arguments now compete for "best or better" status, just as do the disagreeing arguments of experts.

From Inquiry to Convincing

Inquiry ⟶	Convincing
Intimate audience	Public readership
Cooperative	Competitive
Earns a conviction	Argues a thesis
Seeks a case convincing *to us*	Makes a case convincing *to them*, the readers

We take the position we discovered through inquiry and turn it into a thesis supported by a case designed to gain the assent of a specific group of readers.

Because of the change in audience and situation, our thinking also changes, becomes more strategic and calculated to influence readers. In inquiry, we make a case we can believe in; in convincing, we make a case readers can believe in. What we find compelling in inquiry will sometimes also convince our readers, but *in convincing we must adapt our reasoning to appeal to their beliefs, values, and self-interest.* We will also likely offer reasons that did not occur to us at all in inquiry but come as we attempt to imagine the people we hope to convince. Convincing, however, does not mean abandoning the work of inquiry. Our version of the truth, our convictions, gained through inquiry, are what we argue for.

In this chapter, we look first at the structure and strategy of complete essays that aim to convince. Then we provide a step-by-step analysis of the kind of thinking necessary to produce such an essay.

THE NATURE OF CONVINCING: STRUCTURE AND STRATEGY

An argument is an assertion supported by a reason. To convince an audience, writers need to expand on this structure. They usually must offer more than one reason and support all reasons with evidence. We use **case structure** to describe a flexible plan for making *any argument to any audience* who expects sound reasoning. We use **case strategy** to describe the reader-centered moves writers make *to shape a particular argument*—selecting reasons, ordering them, developing evidence, and linking the sections of the argument together for maximum impact.

Case Structure

All cases have at least three levels of assertion. The first level is the thesis, or central claim, which everything else in the case supports. The second level is the reason or reasons the arguer advances for holding the thesis. The third

Key Questions for Case-Making

1. Who is your **target audience**?
2. What **preconceptions** and **biases** might they hold about your topic?
3. What **claim** do you want your readers to accept?
4. What **reasons** are likely to appeal to this audience?
5. How should you **arrange** these reasons for **maximum impact** on your target audience?
6. How might you **introduce** your case?
7. How might you **conclude** it?
8. How can you gain the **trust** and **respect** of your audience?

Convincing is audience centered. Every choice we make must be made with the target audience in mind.

level is the evidence offered to support each reason, typically drawn from some authoritative source.

In the abstract, then, cases look like this:

Figure 8.1

Our diagram shows three reasons, but good cases can be built with only one reason or with more than three.

Case Strategy

In Chapter 2, we explain that you can read an argument with greater comprehension if you have a sense of the rhetorical context in which the writer worked. Likewise, in preparing to write an argument, consider your own context by using the Concept Close-Up "Key Questions for Case-Making."

By working out answers to these questions in your writer's notebook, you'll create a **rhetorical prospectus** that will help you envision a context within which to write and a tentative plan to follow.

To demonstrate case strategy, we'll look at "Arrested Development: The Conservative Case against Racial Profiling" (pp. 214–217). The author, James

Forman, Jr., is an educator and fellow at the New American Foundation in Washington, D.C. His article was published in *The New Republic,* September 10, 2001.

Thinking about Audience

To make an effective case for his position, Forman envisions an audience who favors racial profiling, and his strategy is to use reasons and evidence to convince readers who will resist his thesis. Therefore, he had to consider their likely responses. He posed questions like these:

- Who will my readers be?
- How will they be predisposed to view racial profiling?
- What will they have on their minds as soon as they see that my argument is against it?

Based on these questions, Forman assumes something like the following about the intended audience:

> My conservative audience supports the police and approves of or at least tolerates racial profiling as a tactic for apprehending criminals. I want to show them not only that profiling doesn't work but also, more importantly, that it violates fundamental conservative principles.

Strategy, then, must begin with thoughts about the audience, its values and preconceptions. Next, we examine how Forman shapes the elements of case structure—thesis, reasons, and evidence—to appeal to his readers.

Formulating the Thesis

Your thesis may not be explicitly stated but it must be *strongly implied,* clear to you and your reader. It must be clear to you because you must build a case around it. It must be clear to your readers so that they know what you're claiming and what to expect from your case. Forman's thesis is implied and can be stated as follows: *Political conservatives, most of whom now support racial profiling, ought to oppose it.*

Choosing Reasons

Forman constructs his case around four reasons, all designed to appeal to his audience and undercut their support of racial profiling.

Thesis: Political conservatives, most of whom now support racial profiling, ought to oppose it.

> *Reason 1:* Racial profiling is ineffective—it doesn't reliably identify criminals. (Strategy: Forman wants to take away the major justification for profiling, that it helps the police catch lawbreakers.)
>
> *Reason 2:* Racial profiling harasses law-abiding blacks just because they are black. (Strategy: Forman wants his readers, most of whom

have not been stopped and frisked by the police, to appreciate how discriminatory profiling is and the damage it does to people's respect for authority.)

Reason 3: Racial profiling violates the conservative principle that equates equal rights with equal responsibilities. (Strategy: Forman wants his readers to see that racial profiling contradicts his audience's values—in this instance, the relationship of individual achievement to full, equal participation in the community.)

Reason 4: Racial profiling violates the conservative ideal of a color-blind society. (Strategy: Forman wants his audience to see that their reasons for opposing affirmative action apply with equal force to racial profiling.)

As you read Forman's argument, note how he arranges his reasons; the order of presentation matters. Note also his strategies for developing reasons, especially his use of evidence.

Figure 8.2

Hulbert Waldroup, the artist who painted the controversial mural of Amadou Diallo in the Bronx near where Diallo was shot, signs his initials to his latest work, a painting on racial profiling, after unveiling it in New York's Times Square, Tuesday, July 24, 2001. Waldroup says his work portrays racial profiling "through the eyes of a cop—what he sees, what he thinks, the stereotypes we are all responsible for."

Arrested Development: The Conservative Case against Racial Profiling

JAMES FORMAN, JR.

The Maya Angelou Public Charter School in Washington, D.C., is the kind of institution conservatives love—a place that offers opportunity but demands responsibility. Students are in school ten and a half hours per day, all year long, mostly studying core subjects like reading, writing, math, and history. When not in class, they work in student-run businesses, where they earn money and learn job skills. Those who achieve academically are held in high esteem not only by their teachers but by their peers. Those who disrupt class or otherwise violate the rules are subject to punishment, including expulsion, as determined by a panel of students and teachers.

The results have been impressive. Most Maya Angelou students had academic difficulty at their previous schools. In fact, more than one-half had stopped even attending school on a regular basis before they came to Maya Angelou, while more than one-third had been in the juvenile court system. Yet more than 90 percent of its graduates go on to college, compared with a citywide rate of just 50 percent. This success stems in part from the school's small classes, innovative curriculum, and dedicated staff. But it is also due to its fundamentally conservative ethos: If you work hard and don't make excuses, society will give you a chance, no matter what your background is.

I can speak to this with some authority because I helped establish the school four years ago and still teach an elective there today. But, for all the school's accomplishments, we keep running up against one particularly debilitating problem. It's awfully hard to convince poor, African American kids that discrimination isn't an obstacle, that authority must be respected, and that individual identity matters more than racial identity when experiences beyond school walls repeatedly contradict it. And that's precisely what's happening today, thanks to a policy many conservatives condone: Racial profiling by the police.

The prevalence of racial profiling is no secret. Numerous statistical studies have shown that being black substantially raises the odds of a person being stopped and searched by the police—even though blacks who are stopped are no more likely than whites to be carrying drugs. As David Cole and John Lamberth recently pointed out in *The New York Times,* in Maryland "73 percent of those stopped and searched on a section of Interstate 95 were black, yet state police reported that equal percentages of the whites and blacks who were searched, statewide, had drugs or other contraband." Blacks were actually far less likely than whites to be found carrying drugs in New Jersey, a state whose police force has acknowledged the use of racial profiling. According to Cole and Lamberth, consensual searches "yielded contraband, mostly drugs, on 25 percent of whites, 13 percent of blacks and only 5 percent of Latinos."

Behind these statistics are hundreds if not thousands of well-chronicled anec- 5 dotes, some from America's most prominent black citizens. Erroll McDonald, vice president and executive editor of Pantheon publishing, was driving a rented Jaguar in New Orleans when he was stopped—simply "to show cause why I shouldn't be deemed a problematic Negro in a possibly stolen car.". . .

Even off-duty black police frequently tell of being harassed by their unsuspecting white colleagues. Consider the case of Robert Byrd, an eleven-year veteran of the D.C. police, who was off duty and out of uniform when he tried to stop a carjacking and robbery in Southeast Washington last March. After witnessing the crime, Byrd used his police radio to alert a police dispatcher, then followed the stolen van in his own. Byrd got out of his van as marked police vehicles arrived. According to Byrd, white officers then began beating him in the belief that he was the African American suspect. The real perpetrators were caught later that night.

None of these stories would surprise the students at Maya Angelou. Almost weekly this past spring, officers arrived at the corner of 9th and T Streets NW (in front of our school), threw our students against the wall, and searched them. As you might imagine, these are not polite encounters. They are an aggressive show of force in which children are required to "assume the position": legs spread, face against the wall or squad car, hands behind the head. Police officers then search them, feeling every area of their bodies. Last spring, a police officer chased one male student into the school, wrestled him to the ground, then drew his gun. Another time, when a student refused a police request to leave the corner in front of our school (where the student was taking a short break between classes, in complete compliance with school rules and D.C. law), the officer grabbed him, cuffed him, and started putting him into a police van, before a school official intervened. These students committed no crime other than standing outside a school in a high-drug-use neighborhood. Indeed, despite the numerous searches, no drugs have ever been discovered, and no student has ever been found in violation of the law.

Liberals generally decry such incidents; conservatives generally deny that they take place. "[T]he racial profiling we're all supposed to be outraged about doesn't actually happen very much," explained Jonah Goldberg in his *National Review Online* column last spring. And even those conservatives who admit the practice's frequency often still insist it does more good than harm. "The evidence suggests," William Tucker wrote in a recent issue of *The Weekly Standard,* "that racial profiling is an effective law enforcement tool, though it undeniably visits indignity on the innocent."

In other words, liberals—who are generally more concerned about individual rights and institutionalized racism—believe racial profiling contradicts their principles. Conservatives, on the other hand—who tolerate greater invasions of privacy in the name of law and order—consider racial profiling to be generally consistent with theirs. But conservatives are wrong—racial profiling profoundly violates core conservative principles.

It is conservatives, after all, who remind us that government policy doesn't 10 affect only resources; it affects values, which in turn affect people's behavior. This argument was at the heart of the conservative critique of welfare policy. For years, conservatives (along with some liberals) argued that welfare policies—like subsidizing unmarried, unemployed women with children—fostered a culture of dependency. Only by demanding that citizens take responsibility for their own fates, the argument went, could government effectively combat poverty.

But if sending out welfare checks with no strings attached sends the wrong message, so does racial profiling. For the conservative ethos about work and responsibility to resonate, black citizens must believe they are treated the same way as white citizens—that with equal responsibilities go equal rights. In *The Dream and the Nightmare,* which President Bush cites as one of the most influential books he has ever read, the conservative theorist Myron Magnet writes: "[W]hat underclass kids need most . . . is an authoritative link to traditional values of work, study, and self-improvement, and the assurance that these values can permit them to claim full membership in the larger community." Magnet quotes Eugene Lange, a businessman who promised scholarships to inner-city kids who graduated from high school: "It's important that [inner-city kids] grow up to recognize that they are not perpetuating a life of the pariah, but that the resources of the community are legitimately theirs to take advantage of and contribute to and be a part of."

Magnet is right. But random and degrading police searches radically undermine this message. They tell black kids that they are indeed pariahs—that, no matter how hard they study, they remain suspects. As one Maya Angelou first-year student explained to me: "We can be perfect, perfect, doing everything right, and they still treat us like dogs. No, worse than dogs, because criminals are treated worse than dogs." Or, as a junior asked me, noting the discrepancy between the message delivered by the school and the message delivered by the police: "How can you tell us we can be anything if they treat us like we're nothing?"

Indeed, people like myself—teachers, counselors, parents—try desperately to convince these often jaded kids that hard work really will pay off. In so doing, we are quite consciously pursuing an educational approach that conservatives have long advocated. We are addressing what conservative criminologist James Q. Wilson calls "intangible problems—problems of 'values,'" the problems that sometimes make "blacks less likely to take advantage of opportunities." But we are constantly fighting other people in the neighborhood who tell kids that bourgeois norms of work, family, and sexuality are irrelevant and impossible. Since the state will forever treat you as an outlaw, they say, you might as well act like one. Every time police single out a young black man for harassment, those other people sound more credible—and we sound like dupes.

Then there's that other vaunted conservative ideal: color-blindness. In recent years, conservatives have argued relentlessly for placing less emphasis on race. Since discrimination is on the wane, they suggest, government itself must stop making race an issue—i.e., no more affirmative action in admissions, no more set-asides in contracting, no more tailoring of government programs to favor particular racial or ethnic groups. In the words of affirmative action critics Abigail and Stephen Thernstrom, it's essential to fight the "politics of racial grievance" and counter the "suspicion that nothing fundamental [has] changed." Society, says Magnet, "needs to tell [blacks] that they can do it—not that, because of past victimization, they cannot."

But it's hard to tell young black men that they are not victims because of their 15 race when police routinely make them victims because of their race. Students at Maya Angelou are acutely aware that the police do not treat young people the same way at Sidwell Friends and St. Albans, schools for Washington's overwhelmingly white elite. As another Maya Angelou first-year told me, "You think they would try that stuff with white kids? Never." Such knowledge makes them highly suspicious of the conservative assertion that blacks should forego certain benefits—such as racial preferences in admissions—because of the moral value of color-blindness. Why, they wonder, aren't white people concerned about that principle when it hurts blacks as well as when it benefits them? And racial profiling makes them cynical about the conservative demand that blacks not see the world in racialized, group-identity terms. Why, they wonder, don't white people demand the same of the police?

Most conservatives who support racial profiling are not racist; they simply consider the practice an essential ingredient of effective law enforcement. But it isn't. Indeed, the great irony of conservative support for racial profiling is that conservative principles themselves explain why racial profiling actually makes law enforcement less effective.

. . . [D]iscriminatory police practices create unnecessary and unproductive hostility between police and the communities they serve. Imagine that you are 17, standing outside your school during a break from class, talking to friends, laughing, playing, and just relaxing. Imagine that squad cars pull up; officers jump out, shouting, guns drawn; and you are thrown against the wall, elbowed in the back, legs kicked apart, and violently searched. Your books are strewn on the ground. You ask what's going on, and you are told to "shut the fuck up" or you will be taken downtown. When it finally ends, the officers leave, giving no apology, no explanation, and you are left to fix your clothes, pick up your books, and gather your pride. Imagine that this is not the first time this has happened to you, that it has happened repeatedly, in one form or another, throughout your adolescence. Now imagine that, the day after the search, there is a crime in your neighborhood about which you hear a rumor. You know the police are looking for information, and you see one of the officers who searched you yesterday (or indeed any officer) asking questions about the crime. How likely are you to help? . . .

Arranging Reasons

Conservative support for racial profiling depends on belief in its effectiveness, especially in combating illegal drugs. Forman therefore challenges this belief first. If he can show that profiling doesn't produce the results claimed for it, his readers should then be more receptive to his other reasons, all of which establish its negative impact.

His second reason has force because no law-abiding citizen wants to be treated as if she or he were suspected of criminal activity. No matter who you are, however, and no matter what you are doing, you can be so treated if you fit the profile. Such harassment would not be tolerated by the conservative, mostly white audience Forman is trying to reach and so should not be condoned by that audience when directed toward other racial and ethnic groups. It's a matter of fairness.

Forman's first two reasons engage relatively concrete and easily grasped issues: Does racial profiling work? Are innocent people harassed when it's used? His third and fourth reasons are more abstract and depend on the reader's recognition of contradiction. If we oppose welfare because it encourages dependency and lack of personal responsibility, shouldn't we oppose racial profiling because it "tell[s] black kids that they are indeed pariahs—that, no matter how hard they study, they remain suspects"? Similarly, if we oppose affirmative action because it favors people because of race, shouldn't we also oppose profiling because it also singles out race? Rational people want to be consistent; Forman shows his readers that they haven't been—a powerful strategy after showing that profiling doesn't work and harasses innocent people.

Using Evidence

How well does Forman use the third level of case structure, the supporting evidence for each reason?

Note that he uses different *kinds* of evidence appropriately. To support his contention that racial profiling doesn't work, he cites *data*—in this case, statistics—showing that blacks are less likely than whites or Latinos to be caught with contraband (paragraph 4). Profiling blacks, therefore, makes no sense. Next, he uses *individual examples* to confirm that innocent people, including police officers, are treated as suspects simply because they're black. These individual examples may have more impact than statistics because they personalize the problem. Used together, individual examples and statistics complement each other.

Then, in paragraph 7, Forman draws on *personal experience* as evidence, what he himself has observed. He's seen police shake down students at the school where he teaches. He wants his readers to *feel* the sense of violation involved and so offers a graphic description. Clearly, personal experience can be a powerful source of evidence.

Finally, to back up his last two reasons, Forman cites *well-known authorities,* prominent conservatives such as Myron Magnet and Abigail and Stephen Thernstrom (paragraphs 11 and 14). He cites these sources, obviously, because his audience considers them representative of their own viewpoint and respects them. Forman combines these authorities with the voices of his own students, who gain additional credibility simply by being cited along with the experts.

Forman's essay merits close study for its use of evidence alone. He employs different kinds of evidence, combines different types well, and never forgets that evidence must appeal to his audience.

Introducing and Concluding the Argument

We have analyzed Forman's strategies for using the three levels of case structure—thesis, reasons, and evidence—to build a convincing argument. Arguing to convince also requires a writer to think about effective ways to open and close the case.

The Introduction   When you read Forman's essay the first time, you may have thought that somehow we had attached the wrong title to an essay about school reform. Not until the end of the third paragraph does the author announce his actual subject, racial profiling. Why this long introduction about the Maya Angelou Public Charter School?

The introduction accomplishes at least the following key purposes. Conservatives are strong supporters of alternatives to public schools. One of these is the charter school, and the author uses his story about a highly successful one to confirm conservative policy. Note how he emphasizes the seriousness of the curriculum and other school activities. He also points to the strict rules and discipline and how the Maya Angelou school has turned around standard public school failures, including kids headed for serious trouble with the law. All of this is likely to sound especially good to conservatives.

The story also establishes the author's authority as someone who makes conservative ideas work. Later on, when he cites his students' words to confirm his points, we do not doubt their authenticity. We can see, then, how crucial the introduction is to setting up the case.

Finally, the introduction anticipates the contradictions he'll address later, especially in reasons 3 and 4. The Maya Angelou school has succeeded in educating the kind of student that other schools often don't reach. Kids who could be a public danger now and adult criminals later are apparently becoming good citizens instead. But everything the school has accomplished can be undone by racial profiling. Thus, conservative educational reform clashes with conservative law enforcement policy. They don't fit together, and clearly the former is more important than the latter because the school is creating students who will stay on the right side of the law. Forman is already implying that racial profiling must go, which is the whole point of his essay.

The point for us is that introductions shouldn't be dashed off carelessly, thrown together just because we know we need one. Our introductions must prepare the way for our case.

The Conclusion   Paragraphs 16 and 17 conclude his argument. What do they achieve?

Paragraph 16 states that most conservatives are not racists, that they just have been misled into thinking profiling works. In effect, these assertions release conservatives from the common accusation that they don't care about blacks and support policies that discriminate against them. Forman also reminds his readers that he has used *conservative principles* to explain why racial profiling diminishes police effectiveness.

Paragraph 17 explains in a concrete and memorable way how police tactics like profiling can interfere with law enforcement. Forman wants his

Case Strategy

1. Your thesis can be stated or implied, but **you and your readers must have no doubt about what you're contending.**

2. **Begin with your most important reason.** (For example, if your audience supports racial profiling because they think it works, begin your case against profiling by showing them that it doesn't.)

3. In general, **provide the kind of evidence each reason requires.** (For example, if you contend that helmet laws will reduce head injuries in motorcycle accidents, such a reason requires *data* for support. In contrast, if you contend that helmet laws do not seriously intrude upon personal freedom, data won't help—you must show that helmet laws are no more restrictive than other laws we accept as justified, such as seat belt or maximum speed laws.)

4. Use the **full range** of evidence available (data, individual examples, personal experience, expert opinion, etc.). When possible and appropriate, **mix different kinds of evidence to support a single reason.**

5. **Devote serious effort to introductions and conclusions.** They should accomplish definite tasks, such as generating interest at the beginning and leaving your reader with something memorable at the end. Avoid "throwaway," high school introductions that begin with "In this essay, I will discuss . . ." or "In conclusion . . ." conclusions.

readers to remember the harshness of the procedures and that the experience makes minorities suspicious of and uncooperative with police. We see the damage profiling does from the inside, and we cannot help but appreciate its negative consequences. The implied message is: If you value law and order, be against racial profiling. In this way, Forman advances his major point from another conservative value—support for the police.

Like introductions, conclusions are not throwaways, not merely hasty summaries. Like introductions, they should do something, not just repeat what we've said already. *The conclusion must clinch our case by ending it forcefully and memorably.*

FOLLOWING THROUGH

A successful essay has smooth transitions between its opening and its first reason and between its last reason and its conclusion, as well as between each reason in the body of the essay. In your writer's notebook, describe how Forman (1) announces that he is moving from his introduction to the first reason, from the first reason to the second, and so on and (2) at the same time links each section to what has come before.

WRITING A CONVINCING ARGUMENT

Few people draft an essay sequentially, beginning with the first sentence of the first paragraph and ending with the last sentence of the last paragraph. But the final version of any essay must read as if it had been written sequentially, with the writer fully in control.

www.mhhe.com/**crusius**

For some electronic guidance on writing arguments, go to:

Writing > Writing Tutors > Argument

A well-written essay is like a series of moves in a chess game, in which each move is part of an overall plan. In the case of convincing, the purpose is to gain the agreement of the reader.

Although readers may not be fully aware of the "moves" that make up a convincing argument, the writer probably made most of them consciously. As we have seen in this chapter, we can learn much about how to convince by studying finished essays. However, it is one thing to understand how something works and quite another to make it work ourselves. Part of the difficulty is that we cannot see in the final product everything that went into making it work so well. Just as a movie audience typically cannot imagine all the rehearsals, the many takes, and the editing that make a scene powerful, so it is hard for us to imagine all the research and thinking, the many drafts, and the process of editing and proofreading that Forman must have gone through to make "Arrested Development" effective. Yet it's precisely this process you must understand and immerse yourself in to produce convincing arguments of your own.

The following discussion of the composing process assumes that the work of research (Chapter 5) and inquiry (Chapter 7) has already been done. It also assumes that you have worked out a rhetorical prospectus (see Chapter 1, pages 18–19) to guide you in combining structure with strategy.

Preparing a Brief

Before you begin to draft, it is a good idea to prepare a **brief,** which shows the thesis and reasons you plan to use and gives some indication of how you will support each reason with evidence. The brief ought to arrange the reasons in order, but the order may change as you draft and revise.

Working toward a Position

First, we need to distinguish a position from a thesis. A **position** (or a stance or opinion) amounts to an overall, summarizing attitude or judgment about some issue. "Universities often exploit student athletes" is an example of a position. A **thesis** is not only more specific and precise but also more strategic, designed to appeal to readers and be consistent with available evidence. For example, "Student athletes in revenue-generating sports ought to be paid for their services" is one possible thesis representing the preceding position, perhaps for an audience of college students. We cannot construct a case without a thesis. But without a position, we cannot experiment with various thesis formulations. Positions precede theses.

Finding a position can be a significant challenge in itself. What often happens is that we begin with a strong opinion, find it failing under scrutiny, discover other positions that do not fully satisfy us, and so emerge from inquiry uncertain about what we do think. Another common path is to start with no opinion at all, find ourselves attracted to parts of several conflicting positions, and so wind up unsure, confused, even vexed because we can't decide what to think.

In such situations, resolve to be patient with yourself. The best, most mature positions typically come only after a struggle. Second, take out your writer's notebook and start making lists. Look over your research materials, especially the notecards on which you have recorded positions and evidence from your sources. Make lists in response to these questions:

> What positions have you encountered in research and class discussion?

> What seems strongest and weakest in each position? What modifications might be made to eliminate or minimize the weak points? Are there other possible positions? What are their strong and weak points?

> What evidence impressed you? What does each piece of evidence imply or suggest? What connections can you draw among the pieces of evidence given in various sources? If there is conflict in the implications of the evidence, what is that conflict?

While all this list-making may seem only doodling, you'll begin to sort things out.

Bear in mind that, although emotional commitment to ideas and values is important, it can impede clear thought. Sometimes we find our stance by relinquishing a strongly held opinion—perhaps for lack of compelling reasons or evidence. The more emotional the issue—abortion or pornography, for instance—the more likely we are to cling to a position that is difficult to defend. When we sense deep conflict, when we want to argue a position even in the face of strong contradictory evidence, it's time to consider changing our minds.

Finally, if you find yourself holding out for the "perfect" position, all strength and no weakness, give up. Controversial issues are controversial precisely because no single stance convinces everyone, because there is always room for counterargument and for other positions that have their own power to convince.

STUDENT SAMPLE   Working toward a Position

Justin Spidel's class began by reading many arguments about homosexuality and discussing issues related to gay rights. Justin decided to investigate whether same-sex marriage should be legal. His initial position was that same-sex marriage ought to be legal because gays and lesbians should be treated like everyone else. Research revealed that a majority of Americans oppose same-sex marriage because they believe its legalization would change the definition of marriage and alter its sacred bond. Justin read articles opposing gay marriage by such well-known public figures as William Bennett, an advocate of conservative causes, but he also read many in favor. He found especially convincing the arguments by gays and lesbians who were in stable, loving, monogamous relationships but barred from marrying. Justin's initial round of research led him to the position "Gays and lesbians should be able to marry."

During the inquiry stage, Justin discussed his position with his classmates and instructor. Knowing that gays and lesbians do sometimes get married in churches, Justin's classmates asked him to clarify "able to marry." Justin explained that he meant *legal recognition* of same-sex marriages by all state governments. When asked if other countries recognize same-sex marriage, Justin said that some do. He thought that the United States should be among the leaders in valuing equality and individual rights. He was asked about the implications of his position: Would granting legal status to same-sex marriage devalue the institution? He said that the people fighting for legalization have the deepest respect for marriage and that marriage is about love and commitment, not sexual orientation.

◎◎ FOLLOWING THROUGH

Formulate a tentative position on a topic that you have researched and into which you have inquired. Write it up with a brief explanation of why you support this stand. Be prepared to defend your position in class or with a peer in a one-on-one exchange of position statements. •

Analyzing the Audience

Before you decide on a thesis, give some thought to the rhetorical context of your argument. Who needs to hear it? What are their values? What common ground might you share with them? How might you have to qualify your position to influence their opinions?

To provoke thought, people occasionally make cases for theses that they know have little chance of winning assent. One example is the argument for legalizing all drug use; although a reasonably good case can be made, most Americans find it too radical. If you want to convince rather than provoke, formulate a thesis that *both* represents your position *and* creates as little resistance in your readers as possible. Instead of arguing for legalizing all drug use, for example, you might argue that much of the staggering amount spent on the war on drugs should be diverted to rehabilitation and dealing with social problems connected with drug abuse. Because positions allow for many possible theses, you should analyze your audience before settling on one.

STUDENT SAMPLE Analyzing the Audience

Justin knew that many people would view same-sex marriage as radical. Some audiences, such as conservative Christians, would never assent to it. So Justin targeted an audience he had some chance of convincing—people who opposed same-sex marriage but were tolerant of homosexuals. Justin wrote the following audience profile:

> My audience would be heterosexual adults who accept that some people are homosexual or lesbian; they know people who are. They would be among the nearly 47 percent of Americans who do not object to same-sex relationships between consenting adults. They may be fairly well educated and could belong to any age group. They are not likely to have strong religious objections, so my argument will not focus on whether homosexuality is a sin. However, these readers oppose legalizing marriage between gays and lesbians because they think it would threaten the traditional role of marriage as the basis of family life. They think that marriage is troubled enough by divorce, and they want to preserve its meaning. Their practical position is that, if same-sex couples want to live together and act like they're married, there's nothing to stop them—so leave things as they are. They believe in the value of heterosexual marriage; I can appeal to that. They also hold basic American principles of equal rights and the right to the "pursuit of happiness." But mainly I want to show my readers that gays and lesbians are missing out on basic civil rights and that permitting marriage would benefit everyone.

◎◎ FOLLOWING THROUGH

Write a profile of the audience you hope to reach through an argument you want to make. Be as specific as possible; include any information—age, gender, economic status, and so forth—that may contribute to your audience's outlook and attitudes. What interests, beliefs, and values might they hold? How might you have to phrase your thesis to give your argument a chance of succeeding? What reasons might they be willing to consider? What would you have to rule out?   •

Developing a Thesis

A good thesis grows out of many factors: your position, your research, your exploration of reasons to support your position, and your understanding of the audience. During drafting, you may refine the thesis by phrasing it more precisely, but for now concentrate on stating a thesis that represents your position clearly and directly.

Your thesis should present only the claim. Save the reasons for the body of the paper.

STUDENT SAMPLE Developing a Thesis

Justin's original statement, "Gays and lesbians should be able to marry," expresses a position, but it could be more precise and better directed toward the readers Justin defined in his audience profile. He refined his position to the following:

> A couple's right to marry should not be restricted because of sexual orientation.

This version emphasized that marriage is a right everyone should enjoy, but it did not clarify why readers should recognize it as a right. Justin tried again:

> Every couple who wishes to commit to each other in marriage should have the right to do so, regardless of sexual preference.

Justin was fairly satisfied with this version because it appealed to a basic value—commitment.

He then started thinking about how committed relationships benefit society, an argument that would appeal to his readers. He wanted to portray the thesis not just as an issue of rights for homosexuals but also as a benefit for everyone, broadening its appeal. He tried one more time and settled on the following thesis:

> Everyone, gay and straight, will benefit from extending the basic human right of marriage to all couples, regardless of sexual preference.

◎◎ FOLLOWING THROUGH

1. Refine your thesis as Justin did for the essay on which you are currently working. Why did you settle on one way of stating it?

2. As we saw in analyzing William May's case against assisted suicide (Chapter 3), sometimes a thesis needs to be qualified and exceptions to the thesis stated and clarified. Now is a good time to think about qualifications and exceptions.

You can handle qualifications and exceptions in two ways. First, you can add a phrase to your thesis that limits it, as William May did in his argument on assisted suicide: "*On the whole,* our social policy . . . should not regularize killing for mercy." May admits that a few extreme cases of suffering justify helping someone die. The other method is to word the thesis in such a way that exceptions or qualifications are implied rather than spelled out. For example, "Life sentences with no parole are justifiable for all sane people found guilty of first-degree murder." Here the exceptions would be "those who are found insane" and "those tried on lesser charges."

Using your best thesis statement, decide whether qualifications and exceptions are needed. If so, decide how best to handle them.   •

Analyzing the Thesis

Once you have a thesis, *unpack* it to determine what you must argue. To do this, put yourself in the place of your readers. To be won over, what must they find in your argument? Answering that question requires looking very closely at both what the thesis says and what it implies. It also requires thinking about the position and attitudes of your readers as you described them earlier in your audience profile.

Many thesis sentences appear simple, but analysis shows they are complex. Let's consider a thesis on the topic of whether Mark Twain's *Huckleberry Finn* should be taught in public schools. Some people have argued that Twain's classic novel should be removed from reading lists because some readers, especially African-Americans, find its subject matter and language offensive. In some schools the novel is not assigned, whereas in others it's optional. In our example thesis, the writer supports teaching the novel: "Mark Twain's *Huckleberry Finn* should be required reading for all high school students in the United States."

Unpacking this thesis, we see that the writer must first argue for *Huckleberry Finn* as *required* reading—not merely a good book but an indispensable one. The writer must also argue that the book should be required at the high school level rather than in middle school or college. Finally, the author must defend the novel from charges of racism, even though the thesis does not explicitly state, "*Huckleberry Finn* is not a racist book." Otherwise, these charges stand by default; to ignore them is to ignore the context of the issue.

STUDENT SAMPLE   Analyzing the Thesis

By analyzing his thesis—"Everyone, gay and straight, will benefit from extending the basic human right of marriage to all couples, regardless of sexual preference"—Justin realized that his main task was to explain specific benefits that would follow from allowing gays to marry. He knew that his readers would agree that marriage is a "basic human right" for heterosexual adults, but could not assume that they would see it that way for homosexual couples. Therefore, he had to lead them to see that same-sex couples have the same needs as other couples. He also wanted his readers to understand that he was arguing only that *the law* should recognize such marriages. Churches would not have to sanctify them.

◎◎ FOLLOWING THROUGH

Unpack a thesis of your own or one that your instructor gives you to see what key words and phrases an argument based on that thesis must address. Also consider what an audience would expect you to argue given the current context of the dispute.   •

Finding Reasons

For the most part, no special effort goes into finding reasons to support a thesis. They come to us as we attempt to justify our opinions, as we listen to the arguments of our classmates, as we encounter written arguments in research, and as we think about how to reach the readers we hope to convince. Given good writing preparation, we seldom formulate a thesis without already having some idea of the reasons we will use to defend it. Our problem, rather, is usually selection—picking out the best reasons and shaping and stating them in a way that appeals to our readers. When we do find ourselves searching for reasons, however, it helps to be aware of their common sources.

The Audience's Belief System Ask yourself, What notions of the real, the good, and the possible will my readers entertain? Readers will find any reason unconvincing if it is not consistent with their understanding of reality. For example, based on their particular culture's notions about disease, people will accept or reject arguments about how to treat illness. Likewise, people have differing notions of what is good. Some people think it is good to exploit natural resources so that we can live with more conveniences; others see more good in preserving the environment. Finally, people disagree about what is possible. Those who believe that some aspects of human nature can't be changed will not accept arguments that certain types of criminals can be rehabilitated.

Special Rules or Principles Good reasons can also be found in a community's accepted rules and principles. For example, we believe that a person is innocent until proven guilty. We apply this principle in even nonlegal situations when someone is accused of misconduct.

The law is only one source of special rules or principles. We also find them in politics ("one person, one vote"), in business (the principle of seniority, which gives preference to employees who have been on the job longest), and even in the home, where each family formulates its own house rules. In other words, all human settings and activities have norms and we can draw on them.

Expert Opinion and Hard Evidence We rely on expert opinion when we lack direct experience with a particular subject. Most readers respect the opinion of trained professionals with advanced degrees and prestige in their fields. Especially when you can show that most experts agree, you have a good basis for a reason.

Hard evidence can also yield good reasons. Research shows, for example, that wearing a bicycle helmet significantly reduces the incidence of head injuries in accidents. Therefore, we can support the thesis "Laws should require bicycle riders to wear helmets" with the reason "because statistics show that fewer serious head injuries occurred in bicycle accidents when the riders were wearing helmets."

Tradition   We can sometimes strengthen a position by citing or alluding to well-known sources that are part of our audience's cultural tradition—for example, the Bible and the sayings or writings of people our readers recognize and respect. Although reasons drawn from tradition may lose force if audience members identify with different cultures or resist tradition itself, they will be effective when readers revere the source.

Comparison   A reason based on similarity argues that what is true in one instance should be true in another. For example, we could make a case for legalizing marijuana by showing that it is similar in effect to alcohol, which is legal—and also a drug. The argument might look like this:

> *Thesis:* Marijuana use should be decriminalized.
>
> *Reason:* Marijuana is no more harmful than alcohol.

Many comparison arguments attempt to show that present situations are similar to past ones. For example, many who argue for the civil rights of gays and lesbians say that discrimination based on sexual preference should not be tolerated today just as discrimination based on race, common thirty-five years ago, is no longer tolerated.

A special kind of argument based on similarity is *analogy*, which attempts to explain one thing, usually abstract, in terms of something else, usually more concrete. For example, in an argument opposing sharing the world's limited resources, philosopher Garrett Hardin reasons that requiring the wealthy nations of the world to feed the starving ones is like requiring the occupants of a lifeboat filled to capacity to take on those still in the water until the lifeboat sinks and everyone perishes.

Arguments of comparison can also assert difference, showing how two things are not the same. For example, some Americans supported participation in the 1991 Persian Gulf War by arguing that, unlike the disastrous conflict in Vietnam, this war was winnable. The argument went as follows:

> *Thesis:* America can defeat Iraq's military.
>
> *Reason:* Warfare in the deserts of Kuwait and Iraq is very different from warfare in the jungles of Vietnam.

The Probable or Likely   All reasoning about controversial issues relies on making a viewpoint seem probable or likely, but specific reasons drawn from the probable or likely come into play when we want to defend one account of events over another or when we want to attack or support a proposed policy. For example, in 1991 defenders of Supreme Court nominee Clarence Thomas attempted to discredit Anita Hill's accusations of sexual harassment in a number of ways, all related to probability: Is it likely, they asked, that she would remember so clearly and in such detail events that happened as long as ten years ago? Is it probable that a woman who had been harassed would follow Thomas from one job to another, as Hill did?

Cause and Effect People think that most circumstances result from causes and that most changes in circumstances result in new effects. Belief in cause-and-effect relationships can provide reasons for certain arguments. For example, environmentalists have successfully argued for reductions in the world's output of hydrofluorocarbons by showing that the chemicals damage the Earth's ozone layer.

Cause-and-effect arguments are difficult to prove; witness the fact that cigarette manufacturers argued for years that the connection between smoking and lung disease cannot be demonstrated. Responsible arguments from cause and effect depend on credible and adequate hard evidence and expert opinion. And they must always acknowledge the possible existence of hidden factors; smoking and lung disease, for example, may be influenced by genetic predisposition.

Definition Arguments often require definitions for clarification. However, a definition can also provide a reason in support of a thesis. If we define a term by placing it in a category, we are saying that whatever is true for the category is true for the term we are defining. For example, Elizabeth Cady Stanton's landmark 1892 argument for women's rights ("The Solitude of Self") was based on the definition "women are individuals":

> *Thesis:* Women must have suffrage, access to higher education, and sovereignty over their own minds and bodies.
>
> *Reason:* Women are individuals.

Stanton's audience, the American Congress, believed that all individuals are endowed with certain inalienable rights. Stanton's definition reminded them that women belong in the category "individual" as much as men and deserve the same rights.

Most good reasons come from one or a combination of these eight sources. However, simply knowing the sources will not automatically provide you with good reasons. Nothing can substitute for research and thoughtful inquiry.

Also, do not feel that quantity is crucial in finding good reasons. Be selective: focus on those reasons that appeal most to your audience and that you can develop thoroughly. A good argument is often based on one or two good reasons.

STUDENT SAMPLE Finding Reasons

Justin used five of the eight sources listed in this section to help find some of his reasons. Here are the possible reasons he found; note that each reason is stated as a complete sentence.

From the audience's belief system:

> Marriage is primarily about love and commitment, not sex.
> Marriage is a stabilizing influence in society.

From rules or principles the audience would hold:

> Everyone has an equal right to life, liberty, and the pursuit of happiness.

From expert opinion (in this case, a lawyer and some noted authors on gay rights):

> Denying gays and lesbians the right to marry is discrimination.
> Allowing gays and lesbians to marry will promote family values such as monogamy and the two-parent family.

From comparison or analogy:

> Just as many people once thought marriage between blacks and whites should be illegal, now a majority think same-sex marriage should be illegal.
> Gay and lesbian couples can love each other just as devotedly as heterosexual couples.

From cause and effect:

> Marriage is a way for people to take care of each other rather than being a burden on society should they become ill or unemployed.

Justin now had far more reasons for his case than he needed. He now had to evaluate his list.

◎◎ FOLLOWING THROUGH

Here is one way to brainstorm for reasons. First, list the eight sources for finding reasons discussed on pages 227–229 in your writer's notebook, perhaps on the inside front cover or on the first or last page—someplace where you can easily find them. Practice using these sources by writing your current thesis at the top of another page and going through the list, writing down reasons as they occur to you.

Selecting and Ordering Reasons

Selecting reasons depends on two considerations: your thesis and your readers. Any thesis demands a certain line of reasoning. For example, the writer contending that *Huckleberry Finn* should be required reading in high school must offer a compelling reason for accepting no substitute—not even another novel by Mark Twain. Such a reason might be "Because many critics and novelists see *Huckleberry Finn* as the inspiration for much subsequent American fiction, we cannot understand the American novel if we are not familiar with *Huckleberry Finn*." A reason of this kind should appeal to teachers or school administrators.

It is often difficult to see how to order reasons prior to drafting. Because we can easily reorder reasons as we rewrite, in developing our case we need only attempt an order that seems right. The writer advocating *Huckleberry Finn*, for example, might first defend the novel from the racism charge. Readers unaware of the controversy will want to know why the book needs defending, and well-informed readers will expect an immediate response to the book's critics who want to remove it from the classroom. Once racism has been disposed of, readers will be prepared to hear the reasons for keeping the book on required-reading lists.

Besides thinking about what your readers need and expect and how one reason may gain force by following another one, keep in mind a simple fact about memory: We recall best what we read last; next best, what we read first. A good rule of thumb, therefore, is to begin and end your defense of a thesis with your strongest reasons. A strong beginning also helps keep the reader reading; a strong conclusion avoids a sense of anticlimax.

STUDENT SAMPLE   Selecting and Ordering Reasons

Justin generated eight possible reasons to support his position on gay and lesbian marriage. To help decide which ones to use, he looked again at his audience profile. What had he said about the concerns of people who oppose same-sex marriage? Which of his potential reasons would best address these concerns?

Because his audience did not believe that the ban on same-sex marriage was a great loss to gays and lesbians, Justin decided to use the lawyer's point that the ban is discriminatory. The audience's other main concern was with the potential effect of gay marriage on the rest of society, particularly traditional marriage and family. Therefore, Justin decided to use the reasons about the benefits of same-sex marriage to society: that family values would be reinforced and that marriage keeps people from burdening society if they become unable to support themselves.

Justin noticed that some of his reasons overlapped. For example, the point that marriage is stabilizing was better expressed in combination with his more specific reasons about economic benefits and family values. And discrimination overlapped with his point about "life, liberty, and the pursuit of happiness." Overlap is common and requires some consolidation of reasons.

What is the best strategy for arranging the reasons? Initially, Justin wanted to begin with the point about discrimination, but then he decided to appeal to his audience's interests by listing the advantages of same-sex marriage first. Saving discrimination until the second half of his essay would let him end more strongly with an appeal to the readers' sense of fairness.

Then Justin rechecked his thesis to confirm that the reasons really supported it. He decided that his readers might not accept that marriage is a "basic human right" for those of the same sex, so he decided to add one more reason to support the similarities between heterosexuals and homosexuals.

Justin outlined his argument:

> Thesis: Everyone, gay and straight, will benefit from extending the basic human right of marriage to all couples, regardless of sexual preference.
>
> Reason: It would reinforce family values such as monogamy and the two-parent family.
>
> Reason: It would help keep people from burdening society.
>
> Reason: Denying people the right to marry is discrimination.
>
> Reason: The love homosexuals have for each other is no different from love between heterosexuals.

◎◎ FOLLOWING THROUGH

We call case structure flexible because as long as you maintain the three-level structure of thesis, reasons, and evidence, you can change everything else: throw out one thesis for another or alter its wording, add or take away reasons or evidence, or reorder both to achieve the desired impact. Order your reasons based on these questions:

What will my audience need or expect to read first?

Will one reason help set up another?

Which of my reasons are stronger? Can I begin and conclude my argument with the better reasons I have?

To a thesis you have already refined, now add the second level of your brief, the reason or reasons. Be ready to explain your decisions about selection and arrangement. Final decisions about ordering may come late in drafting—in a second or third writing. Spending a little time now thinking about orderings can save time later and make composing less difficult.   •

Using Evidence

The skillful use of evidence involves many judgments. Let's begin with some basic questions.

What Counts as Evidence?   Because science and technology rely on the hard data of quantified evidence—especially statistics—some people assume that hard data are the only really good form of evidence. Such a view, however, is far too narrow. Besides hard data, evidence includes

- Quotation from authorities: expert opinion and traditional authorities such as respected political leaders, philosophers, and well-known authors. Besides printed sources, you can gather quotations from interviews and electronic sources.

- Constitutions, statutes, court rulings, organizational bylaws, company policy statements, and the like

- Examples and case histories (that is, extended narratives about an individual's or an organization's experience)

- The results of questionnaires that you devise and administer

- Personal experience

In short, evidence includes anything that confirms a good reason or that might increase your readers' acceptance of a reason.

What Kind of Evidence Is Best?   It depends on the particular reason. To argue for bicycle helmet legislation, we need facts and figures—hard data—to back up our claim that wearing helmets reduces the number of serious head injuries. To defend *Huckleberry Finn* by saying that it indicts racism will require quoted passages from the novel itself, statements from respected interpreters, and so forth.

When you have many pieces of evidence to choose from, select based on the quality of the evidence itself and its likely impact on readers. In general the best evidence is the most recent. The more trusted and prestigious the source, the more authority it will have. Arguments about AIDS in the United States, for example, often use data from the Centers for Disease Control in Atlanta, a research facility that specializes in the study of epidemics.

Finally, always look for evidence that will give you an edge in winning reader assent. For example, given the charge that *Huckleberry Finn* is offensive to blacks, its defense by an African-American literary scholar would carry more weight than its defense by a white scholar.

How Much Evidence Is Needed?   The amount of evidence required depends on two judgments: (1) how crucial a reason is to your case and (2) how much resistance readers are likely to have. Most cases have a pivotal reason, one point on which the whole case is built and therefore either stands or falls. Forman's case against racial profiling turns on accepting its unreliability. Such a reason needs much evidence; about one-fourth of Forman's essay supports this reason alone.

Of course, the pivotal reason may also be one which readers will resist. For instance, many arguments supporting women's right to abortion depend on a fetus not being considered fully human until it reaches a certain stage of development. This reason is obviously both pivotal and likely to be resisted, so devoting much space to evidence would be justified.

STUDENT SAMPLE Using Evidence

Justin took the brief showing his case so far and on a table laid out all of his notecards and the material he had photocopied and marked up during research. He needed to select the expert opinions, quotations, statistics, dates, and other evidence to support his reasons. Doing this before drafting reveals where evidence is lacking or thin and what further research is necessary. To handle many sources, use different-colored markers to indicate which passages will work with which reasons. Justin then added evidence to his case structure, including noting the sources and page numbers.

Thesis: Everyone, gay and straight, will benefit from extending the basic human right of marriage to all couples, regardless of sexual preference.

Reason: It would reinforce family values such as monogamy and the two-parent family.

Evidence: Marriage stabilizes relationships. (Sources: Rauch 23; Dean 114)

Evidence: Children of gays and lesbians should not be denied having two parents. (Sources: Dean 114; Sullivan; Salholz)

Evidence: If gays can have and adopt children, they should be able to marry. (Source: Salholz)

Reason: It would provide a means of keeping people from burdening society.

Evidence: Spouses take care of each other. (Source: Rauch)

Reason: Denying gays and lesbians the right to marry is discriminatory.

Evidence: Marriage includes rights to legal benefits. (Source: Dean 112)

Evidence: Domestic partnerships fail to provide these rights. (Sources: Dean 112; Salholz)

Evidence: Barring these marriages violates many democratic principles. (Sources: "Declaration"; Dean 113; Salholz)

Reason: The love homosexuals have for each other is no different from love between heterosexuals.

Evidence: Many gays and lesbians are in monogamous relationships. (Source: Ayers 5)

Evidence: They have the same need to make a public, legal commitment. (Source: Sullivan)

◎◎ FOLLOWING THROUGH

Prepare a complete brief for an argument. Include both reasons and evidence and note sources. Remember that a brief is flexible, not engraved in stone. It can change as you draft and revise. •

The Brief

1. A position or general outlook on a topic is not a thesis. A thesis is a carefully worded **claim** that your entire essay backs up with reasons and evidence. **Experiment with various ways of stating your thesis** until it says *exactly* what you want it to say and creates the least resistance in your readers.

2. Be willing to give up or modify significantly a thesis you find you cannot support with good reasons and strong evidence that appeal *to your readers*. We **must argue a thesis that fits the available** evidence, which may differ a little or a lot from what we really believe.

3. Take the time to create a specific **audience profile**. What are the age, gender, and economic status of your target audience? What interests, beliefs, and values might they bring to your topic and thesis? Remember: There is no such thing as a "general audience." **We are always trying to convince some definite group of possible readers.**

4. **Unpack your thesis** to discover what you must argue. If you say, for instance, that *Huckleberry Finn* should be *required* reading in high school, you must show why *this particular novel* should be an experience shared by all American high school students. It won't be enough to argue that it's a good book.

5. Select your reasons based on what you must argue to defend your thesis combined with what you should say **given your audience's prior knowledge, preconceptions, prejudices, and interests.**

6. Be prepared to **try out different ways of ordering your reasons.** The order that seemed best in your brief might not work best as you draft and redraft your essay.

From Brief to Draft

Turning a brief into a paper is never easy. You will have to create parts of the essay that are not represented in the brief, such as an effective introduction and conclusion. You may also need paragraphs that provide background on your topic, clarify or define an important term, or present and rebut an opposing argument. Following are suggestions and examples that should help.

The Introduction

Introductions are among the hardest things to write well. *Remember that an introduction need not be one paragraph;* it is often two or even three short ones. A good introduction (1) meets the needs of the audience by setting up the topic with just enough background information and (2) goes right to the heart of the issue as it relates to the audience's concerns.

Should the introduction end with the thesis statement? Such placement can work well in offering a transition to the reasons. However, the thesis need not be the last sentence in the introduction; it need not appear until much later—or at all, provided that readers can tell what it is from the title or from reading the essay.

STUDENT SAMPLE The Introduction

Justin had to consider whether he should refer to the history of marriage and why people feel strongly about its value. Because his readers oppose same-sex marriage, presumably they were familiar with the traditions underpinning the institution. What would these readers need in the introduction? That the gay and lesbian rights movement calls for extending to same-sex couples the legal right to marry and that Justin's argument supports its position.

If Justin had opened with "The current intolerant attitudes toward homosexuality are excluding a whole class of citizens from exercising the right to marry," he would have been assuming that no valid reasons exist for denying same-sex marriage. Such a statement would offend his target audience members, who are not homophobic and would resent the implication that their view is based on prejudice. Justin's introduction attempts to establish some common ground with his readers:

> When two people fall deeply in love, they want to share every part of their lives with each other. For some, that could mean making a commitment, living together, and having children. But most people want more than that; they want to make their commitment public and legal through marriage, a tradition thousands of years old that has been part of almost every culture.
>
> But not everyone has the right to make that commitment. In this country and in most others, gays and lesbians are denied the right to marry. According to many Americans, allowing them to marry would destroy the institution and threaten traditional family values. Nevertheless, "advances in gay and lesbian civil rights [are] bringing awareness and newfound determination to many," and hundreds of same-sex couples are celebrating their commitment in religious ceremonies (Ayers 6). These couples would like to make their unions legal, and we should not prohibit them. Everyone, gay and straight, will benefit from extending the basic human right of marriage to all couples, regardless of sexual orientation.

Justin's first paragraph builds common ground by offering an overview of marriage that his readers are likely to share. In the second paragraph, he goes on to introduce the conflict, showing his awareness of the main objections to same-sex marriage. Note the tone: he's presenting himself as fair and responsible. Finally, Justin builds common ground by showing gays and lesbians positively, as people who love and commit to each other just as heterosexuals do.

A good introduction gains reader interest. To do this, writers use a number of techniques. They may open with the story of a person whose experience illustrates some aspect of the topic. Or they may begin with a surprising fact or opinion, as Jonathan Rauch, one of Justin's sources, did when he began his essay with this: "Whatever else marriage may or may not be, it is certainly falling apart." Usually, dictionary definitions are dull open-ers, but a *Newsweek* writer used one effectively to start her article on gay marriage: "Marry. 1 a) to join as husband and wife; unite in wedlock, b) to join (a man) to a woman as her husband, or (a woman) to a man as his wife." All of these are fairly dramatic techniques, but the best advice about openings is that *specifics work better than generalizations.* The *Newsweek* article just mentioned had this statement: "Say marriage and the mind turns to three-tiered cakes, bridal gowns, baby carriages."

How you open depends on your audience. Popular periodicals like *News-week* are more appropriate for dramatics than academic journals and college papers, but readers appreciate a memorable opening.

The Body: Presenting Reasons and Evidence

We now turn to drafting the body paragraphs. Although it's possible for one paragraph to develop a reason, *avoid thinking in terms of only one para-graph per reason.* Multiple paragraphs are the norm.

Paragraphs perform some function in presenting the case. You ought to be able to say what the function of a given paragraph is—and your readers ought to be able to sense it. Does it introduce a reason? Does it define a term? Does it support a reason by setting up an analogy? Does another paragraph support the same reason by offering examples or data or an illustrative case?

Not all paragraphs need topic sentences. Try instead to open each para-graph with hints that allow readers to see its function. For example, a tran-sitional word or phrase announces that you are turning from one reason to a new one. When you introduce a new reason, be sure that readers can see how it relates to the thesis.

STUDENT SAMPLE Presenting Reasons and Evidence

Let's look at how Justin developed his first reason. Recall that he decided to put the two reasons about benefits to society ahead of his reasons against discrimination. Of the two benefits he planned to cite, strengthening family values seemed the stronger one, so he led with it. Note how Justin's transi-tional phrase connects his first reason to the introduction, which had men-tioned opposing views. Observe how he *develops his reason over a number of paragraphs,* drawing upon multiple sources, using both paraphrase and direct quotation.

> In contrast to the critics, allowing gays and lesbians to marry promotes family values because it encourages monogamy and two-parent homes. As Jonathan Rauch, a gay writer, explains, marriage stabilizes relationships:
>
>> One of the main benefits of publicly recognized marriage is that it binds couples together not only in their own eyes but also in the eyes of society at large. Around the partners is woven a web of expecta-tions that they will spend nights together, go to parties together, take

out mortgages together, buy furniture . . . together, and so on—all of which helps tie them together and keep them off the streets and at home. (23)

Some people would say that gays and lesbians can have these things without marriage by living together, but if marriage is not necessary for gays, it's not necessary for heterosexuals either. If it's immoral to live together outside marriage, then gays and lesbians should marry too. Craig Dean, a Washington, D.C., lawyer and gay-marriage activist, says that it is "paradoxical that mainstream America stereotypes Gays and Lesbians as unable to maintain long-term relationships, while at the same time denying them the very institutions to stabilize such relationships" (114).

Furthermore, many homosexual couples have children from previous marriages or by adoption. According to a study by the American Bar Association, gay and lesbian families with children make up six percent of all families in the United States (Dean 114). A secure environment is important for raising children, and allowing same-sex couples to marry would help. It would also send children the positive message that marriage is the foundation for family life. As Andrew Sullivan, a senior editor of *The New Republic,* says, why should gays be denied the very same family values that many politicians are arguing everyone else should have? Why should their children be denied these values? *Newsweek* writer Eloise Salholz describes the problem: If "more and more homosexual pairs are becoming parents . . . but cannot marry, what kind of bastardized definition of family is society imposing on their offspring?"

At this point, Justin is ready to take up his next reason: Marriage provides a system by which people take care of each other, lessening the burden on society. Justin's entire essay appears on pages 243–246. Look it over carefully before you draft your essay. Note which paragraphs bring in the remaining reasons and which paragraphs present and rebut opposing views.

The Conclusion

Once you have presented your case, what else is there to say? Short papers don't need summaries. And the conclusion is not a place for new points.

Strategically, in your conclusion you want to imply, "Case made!" Here are some suggestions for doing so:

1. Look back at your introduction. Perhaps a question you posed there has an answer, a problem a solution.

2. Think about larger contexts for your argument. For example, the *Huckleberry Finn* case could end by pointing out that education becomes diluted and artificial when the curriculum avoids controversy.

3. If you end with a memorable quotation, comment on it as you would whenever you quote.

4. Be aware that many conclusions should be shorter. If you are dissatisfied with yours, lop off the last sentence or so. You may uncover the real ending.

5. Pay attention to style, especially in the last sentence. An awkwardly worded sentence will not have a sound of finality, but one with some rhythmic punch or consciously repeated sounds can wrap up an essay neatly.

STUDENT SAMPLE The Conclusion

Following is Justin's conclusion.

> It's only natural for people in love to want to commit to each other; this desire is the same for homosexuals and lesbians as it is for heterosexuals. One recent survey showed that "over half of all lesbians and almost 40% of gay men" live in committed relationships and share a home together (Ayers 5). As Sullivan, who is gay, explains, "At some point in our lives, some of us are lucky enough to meet the person we truly love. And we want to commit to that person in front of family and country for the rest of our lives. It's the most simple, the most natural, the most human instinct in the world. How could anyone seek to oppose that?" And what does anyone gain when that right is denied? That's a question that everyone needs to ask themselves.

FOLLOWING THROUGH

Using your brief as a guide, write a draft version of your argument to convince. In addition to the advice in this chapter, refer to Chapter 5, which covers paraphrasing, summarizing, quoting, incorporating, and documenting source material.   •

 **www.mhhe.com/crusius** For further writing coverage, including information on writing in the traditional modes, visit:

Writing > Writing Tutors

Revising the Draft

Too often, revising is confused with editing. Revising makes large changes in content and organization, not sentence-level corrections or stylistic changes, which are part of editing.

To get a sense of what is involved in revising, you should know that the brief of Justin Spidel's essay on page 234 is actually a revised version. Justin had originally written a draft with his reasons presented in a different order and without three of the sources that now appear in his paper. When

Justin exchanged drafts with another classmate who was writing on the same topic, he discovered that some of her sources would also help him. The following paragraph was the original third paragraph of Justin's draft, immediately following the thesis. Compare it to the revised essay, printed on pages 243–246. Justin improved this part of his argument by developing the point more thoroughly in two paragraphs and by placing them toward the end of the paper.

> Not to allow same-sex marriage is clearly discriminatory. The Human Rights Act of 1977 in the District of Columbia "prohibits discrimination based on sexual orientation. According to the Act, 'every individual shall have an equal opportunity to participate in the economic, cultural, and intellectual life of the District and have an *equal opportunity to participate in all aspects of life*'" (Dean 112). If politicians are going to make such laws, they need to recognize all their implications and follow them. Not allowing homosexuals to marry is denying the right to "participate" in an aspect of life that is important to every couple that has found love in each other. Also, the Constitution guarantees equality to every man and woman; that means nondiscrimination, something that is not happening for gays and lesbians in the present.

Reading Your Own Writing Critically

Chapter 2 discussed critical or analytical reading. Apply what you learned to reading your own writing.

Read for Structure   Remember, different parts of an argument perform different jobs. Read to see if you can divide your draft easily into its strategic parts and can identify the role each group of paragraphs plays in the paper. If you have trouble identifying the parts and how they fit together, you need to see where you repeat yourself or separate connected points. This may be the time for scissors and tape, or electronic cutting and pasting.

Read for Rhetorical Context   You may need to revise to make the rhetorical context clearer: Why are you writing and to whom? You establish this reader awareness in the introduction, and you need to think about your readers' values and beliefs that underlie their position on the issue. You may need to revise your introduction to engage your readers better. The more specific you can make your opening, the more likely you are to succeed.

Inquire into Your Own Writing   Have a dialogue with yourself about it. Some of the questions listed on pages 181–182 are relevant:

1. Ask what you mean by the words that are central to the argument. Have you provided definitions as needed?

Reader's Checklist for Revision

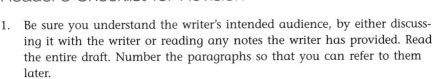
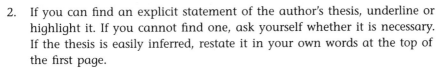

1. Be sure you understand the writer's intended audience, by either discussing it with the writer or reading any notes the writer has provided. Read the entire draft. Number the paragraphs so that you can refer to them later.

2. If you can find an explicit statement of the author's thesis, underline or highlight it. If you cannot find one, ask yourself whether it is necessary. If the thesis is easily inferred, restate it in your own words at the top of the first page.

3. Think about how the thesis could be improved. Is it offensive, vague, too general? Does it have a single focus? Is it clearly stated?

4. Circle the words most central to the thesis. Could there be disagreement about the meaning of any of them? If so, has the author clarified what he or she means?

5. Look for the argument's structure and strategy. Underline the sentences that present the reasons. If you can't identify the reasons, let the author know. Also think about the order of the reasons. Suggest improvements if you can.

6. Identify the author's best reason. How would it appeal to the audience? Has the author placed it in a good position for emphasizing it?

7. What reasons need more or better support? Indicate what factual information seems lacking, what sources don't seem solid or credible, what statements sound too general, or what reasoning—such as analogies— seems shaky.

8. Ask whether the author shows awareness of opposing arguments. If not, should this be added? What are the best challenges you can make to anything the author has said?

9. Evaluate the introduction and conclusion.

2. Find the reasons, and ask about their relation to the thesis. State the connection with the word "because."

3. Explore the assumptions behind your thesis and your reasons. Ask yourself, What's not said that someone has to believe? Be sure your audience will share the assumption. If not, state the assumption and argue for it.

4. Look at your comparisons and analogies. Are they plausible?

5. Look at your evidence. Have you offered facts, expert opinion, illustrations, and so on? Have you presented these in a way that would not raise doubts but eliminate them?

6. Consider your own bias. What do you stand to gain from advocating the position you take? Is your argument self-serving or truth-serving?

Getting Feedback from Other Readers

Because it's hard to be objective about our own work, getting feedback from a friend, classmate, or teacher is a good way to see where revision would help. Ask your readers to use a revision checklist, such as the one on page 241.

◎◎ FOLLOWING THROUGH

1. After you have written a draft of your own argument, revise it using the suggestions in the preceding section. Then exchange your revised draft for a classmate's, and use the "Reader's Checklist for Revision" on page 241 to guide you in making suggestions for each other's drafts.

2. Read the final version of Justin Spidel's argument, following. Then apply the questions for inquiry listed on pages 181–182 to assess his argument.

3. If you were assigned to suggest ways to improve Justin's argument, what would you advise? Reread his audience profile (page 224), and use the "Reader's Checklist for Revision" (page 241) to help you decide.   •

www.mhhe.com/**crusius**

For help editing your essay, go to:

Editing

Editing and Proofreading

The final steps of writing any argument are editing and proofreading, which we discuss in the Appendix A.

STUDENT SAMPLE An Essay Arguing to Convince

www.mhhe.com/**crusius**

For other student-written
arguments, go to:

Writing > Sample Argument
Papers

Who Should Have the Right to Marry?
Justin Spidel

When two people fall deeply in love, they want to share their lives. For some, that could mean making a commitment, living together, and maybe having children. But most people in love want more: they want to make their commitment public and legal through marriage, a tradition thousands of years old and part of almost every culture.

But not everyone has the opportunity to make that commitment. In this country and most others, gays and lesbians are denied the right to marry. According to many citizens and politicians, allowing them that right would destroy the institution and threaten traditional family values. Nevertheless, "advances in gay and lesbian civil rights [are] bringing awareness and newfound determination to many," and hundreds of same-sex couples are celebrating their commitment to each other in religious ceremonies (Ayers 6). These couples would like to make their unions legal, and we should not prohibit them. Everyone, gay and straight, will benefit from extending marriage to all couples, regardless of sexual orientation.

In contrast to the critics, allowing gays and lesbians to marry promotes family values because it encourages monogamy and two-parent homes. As Jonathan Rauch, a gay writer, explains, marriage stabilizes relationships:

> One of the main benefits of publicly recognized marriage is that it binds couples together not only in their own eyes but also in the eyes of society at large. Around the partners is woven a web of expectations that they will spend nights together, go to parties together, take out mortgages together, buy furniture . . . together, and so on—all of which helps tie them together and keep them off the streets and at home. (23)

Some people would say that gays and lesbians can have these things without marriage by living together, but if marriage is not necessary for gays, it's not necessary for heterosexuals either. If it's immoral to live together outside of marriage, then gays and lesbians should marry too. Craig Dean, a Washington, D.C., lawyer and gay-marriage activist, says that it is "paradoxical that mainstream America stereotypes Gays and Lesbians as unable to maintain long-term relationships, while at the same time denying them the very institutions to stabilize such relationships" (114).

Furthermore, many homosexual couples have children from previous marriages or by adoption. According to a study by the American Bar Association, gay and lesbian families with children make up six percent of all families in the United States (Dean 114). A secure environment is important for raising children, and allowing same-sex couples to marry would help. It would also send children the positive message that marriage is the foundation for family life. As Andrew Sullivan, a senior editor of The New Republic, asks, why should gays be denied the very same family values that many politicians are arguing everyone else should have? Why should their children be denied these values? Newsweek writer Eloise Salholz describes the problem: If "more and more homosexual pairs are becoming parents . . . but cannot marry, what kind of bastardized definition of family is society imposing on their offspring?"

Binding people together in marriage also benefits society because marriage encourages people to take care of each other. Marriage means that individuals are not a complete burden on society when they become sick, injured, old, or unemployed. Jonathan Rauch argues, "If marriage has any meaning at all, it is that when you collapse from a stroke, there will be at least one other person whose 'job' it is to drop everything and come to your aid" (22). This benefit of marriage may be even more important for homosexuals because their relationships with parents and other relatives may be strained. Same-sex couples already show such devotion to each other; recognition of legal marriage would strengthen that devotion.

In spite of the benefits, some say that same-sex marriage would upset our society's conventional idea of marriage. According to William Bennett, letting people of the same sex marry "would obscure marriage's enormously consequential function—procreation and childrearing." Procreation may be a consequence of marriage, but it is not the main reason people get married. Today "even for heterosexuals, marriage is becoming an emotional union and commitment rather than an arrangement to produce . . . children" ("Marriage" 770). And what about sterile heterosexual couples? No one would say they should not be allowed to marry. If the right to marry is based on the potential to have children, "then a post-menopausal woman who applies for a marriage license should be turned away at the courthouse door" (Rauch 22). No one expects couples who get married to prove that they can have children and intend to do so.

In the same way, to outlaw same-sex marriage is clearly discriminatory. According to Craig Dean, "Marriage is an important civil right because it gives societal recognition and legal protection to a relationship and confers numerous benefits to spouses" (112). Denying same-sex marriage means that gays and lesbians cannot enjoy such benefits as health insurance through a spouse's employer, life insurance benefits, tax preferences, leaves for bereavement, and

A marriage in San Francisco, February 13, 2004. At 79 and
83, these women had lived together fifty years before they
were allowed to marry.

inheritance. In some states, laws about domestic partnership give
same-sex couples some of these rights, but they are not as secure
as they would be if the couple were legally next of kin. Thomas
Stoddard, a lawyer, says that domestic partnership is the equivalent
of "second-class citizenship" (qtd. in Salholz).

Aside from these concrete forms of discrimination, denying
same-sex marriage keeps gay and lesbian citizens from enjoying
the basic human right to "life, liberty, and the pursuit of happiness." The Human Rights Act of 1977 in the District of Columbia
makes one of the strongest stands against discrimination based on
sexual orientation. According to the Act, "every individual shall
have an equal opportunity to participate in the economic, cultural,
and intellectual life of the District and have an equal opportunity
to participate in all aspects of life" (qtd. in Dean 113). Not allowing homosexuals to marry does deny them the right to participate
in an aspect of life important to almost every loving couple.

Of course, some churches will never agree to perform same-sex
marriages because they believe that homosexuality is a sin. The
separation of church and state allows all churches to follow their
own doctrines; many things that are legal in this country are
opposed by some churches. The government should not deny the
legal right to marry because some churches oppose it.

It's only natural for people in love to want to commit to each
other; this desire is the same for homosexuals and lesbians as it is
for heterosexuals. One recent survey showed that "over half of all
lesbians and almost 40% of gay men" live in committed relationships and share a house together (Ayers 5). As Sullivan explains,

"At some point in our lives, some of us are lucky enough to meet the person we truly love. And we want to commit to that person in front of family and country for the rest of our lives. It's the most simple, the most natural, the most human instinct in the world. How could anyone seek to oppose that?" And what does anyone gain when the right is denied? That's a question that everyone needs to ask themselves.

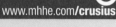

www.mhhe.com/**crusius**

For an electronic tool that helps create properly formatted works-cited pages, go to:

Research > Bibliomaker

Works Cited

Ayers, Tess, and Paul Brown. The Essential Guide to Lesbian and Gay Weddings. San Francisco: Harper, 1994.

Bennett, William, "Leave Marriage Alone." Newsweek 3 June 1996: 27.

Dean, Craig R. "Gay Marriage: A Civil Right." The Journal of Homosexuality 27.3–4 (1994): 111–15.

"Marriage." The Encyclopedia of Homosexuality. Ed. Wayne R. Dynes. New York: Garland, 1990.

Rauch, Jonathan. "For Better or Worse?" The New Republic 6 May 1996: 18–23.

Salholz, Eloise. "For Better or For Worse." Newsweek 24 May 1993: 69.

Sullivan, Andrew. "Let Gays Marry." Newsweek 3 June 1996: 26.

CHAPTER 9

Motivating Action: Arguing to Persuade

In Chapter 1, we defined persuasion as "convincing *plus*" because, in addition to reason, three other forms of appeal come into play: (1) appeal to the writer's character, (2) appeal to the emotions of the audience, and (3) appeal to style, the artful use of language itself. Building on what you learned about making cases in Chapter 8, this chapter's goal is to help you understand and control persuasion's wider range of appeals. (See Concept Close-Up, page 248.)

WHEN TO CONVINCE AND WHEN TO PERSUADE: A MATTER OF EMPHASIS

When should you aim to persuade rather than convince? Always notice what an assignment calls for because the full range of persuasive appeal is not always appropriate in college. In general, the more academic the audience or the more purely intellectual the issue, the less appropriate the full resources of persuasion are. Philosophy or science papers require you to convince, but seldom to persuade. Good reasons and evidence are all that matters.

When you are working with public issues, matters of policy or questions of right and wrong, persuasion's fuller range of appeal is usually appropriate. Arguments in these areas affect not just how we think but also how we act.

The Four Forms of Appeal

Form	Function	Presence in Text
Reason	Logical cogency	Your case; any supported contention
Character	Personal appeal	Indications of author's status and values
Emotion	Appeals to feelings	Concrete descriptions, moving images
Style	Appeals through language	Word choice, sentence structure, metaphor

Essentially, persuasion differs from convincing in seeking action, not just agreement; it integrates rational appeal with other ways to influence people.

Convincing requires control over case-making. In persuasion we must also (1) gain our readers' confidence and respect, (2) touch our readers' emotions, and (3) focus on language itself. We want an essay that integrates all appeals so that they work together.

ANALYZING YOUR READERS

Successful persuasion brings readers and writer together, creating a sense of connection between people previously separated by viewpoint. What can we do to overcome difference and create identity? First, we need to understand our readers' frame of mind.

Who Is the Audience, and How Do They View the Topic?

Good persuaders are able to empathize and sympathize with other people, building solidarity. To aid audience analysis, ask these questions:

- Who are my readers? How do I define them in terms of age, economic and social class, gender, education, and so forth?
- What typical attitudes or stances toward my topic do they have?
- What in their background or daily experiences helps explain their point of view?
- What are they likely to know about my topic?
- How might they be uninformed or misinformed about it?
- How would they like to see the problem, question, or issue resolved, answered, or handled? Why? That is, what *personal stake* do they have in the topic?
- In what larger framework—religious, ethical, political, economic—do they see my topic? That is, what general beliefs and values are involved?

What Are Our Differences?

Audience analysis isn't complete until you specify exactly what divides you from your readers. These questions can help:

- Is the difference a matter of assumptions? If so, how can I shake my readers' confidence in their assumptions and offer others favorable to my position?

- Is the difference a matter of principle, the application of general rules to specific cases? If so, should I dispute the principle itself and offer a competing one the audience also values? Or should I show why the principle does not apply to my subject?

- Is the difference a matter of a hierarchy of values—that is, do we value the same things but in a different order of priority? If so, how might I restructure my readers' values?

- Is the difference a matter of ends or of means? If ends, how can I show that my vision of what ought to be is better or that realizing my ends will also secure the ends of my readers? If a difference of means, how can I show that my methods are justified and effective, preferable to others?

- Is the difference a matter of interpretation? If so, how can I show that my interpretation is better, accounting more adequately for the facts?

- Is the difference a matter of implications or consequences? If so, how can I convince my readers that what they fear may happen will not happen, or that the outcome will not be as bad as they think, or that any negatives will be outweighed by positives?

What Do We Have in Common?

In seeking common ground with your readers, remember that, no matter how sharply you and your readers disagree, resources for identification always exist. Ask

- Do we have a shared local identity—as members of the same organization or as students at the same university?

- Do we share a more abstract, collective identity—citizens of the same region or nation, worshippers in the same religion, and so forth?

- Do we share a common cause—such as preventing child abuse or overcoming racial prejudice?

- Is there a shared experience or human activity—raising children, caring for aging parents, helping a friend in distress, struggling to make ends meet?

- Can we connect through a well-known event or cultural happening—a popular movie, a best-selling book, something in the news of interest to both you and your readers?

- Is there a historical event, person, or document we both respect?

READING A PERSUASIVE ESSAY

To illustrate the importance of audience analysis, we turn to a classic persuasive essay of the twentieth century, Martin Luther King's "Letter from Birmingham Jail." As we will see, King masterfully analyzed his audience and used the full range of appeals for his readership.

Background

To appreciate King's persuasive powers, we must first understand the events that led to the "Letter" and the actions King wanted his readers to take. In 1963, as president of the Southern Christian Leadership Conference, King had been organizing and participating in civil rights demonstrations in Birmingham, Alabama. He was arrested, and while he was in jail, eight white Alabama clergymen of various denominations issued a public statement critical of his activities. Published in a local newspaper, the statement deplored the demonstrations as "unwise and untimely":

> We the undersigned clergymen are among those who, in January, issued "An Appeal for Law and Order and Common Sense," in dealing with racial problems in Alabama. We expressed understanding that honest convictions in racial matters could properly be pursued in the courts, but urged that decisions of those courts should in the meantime be peacefully obeyed.
>
> Since that time there had been some evidence of increased forbearance and a willingness to face facts. Responsible citizens have undertaken to work on various problems which cause racial friction and unrest. In Birmingham, recent public events have given indication that we all have opportunity for a new constructive and realistic approach to racial problems.
>
> However, we are now confronted by a series of demonstrations by some of our Negro citizens, directed and led in part by outsiders. We recognize the natural impatience of people who feel that their hopes are slow in being realized. But we are convinced that these demonstrations are unwise and untimely.
>
> We agree rather with certain local Negro leadership which has called for honest and open negotiation of racial issues in our area. And we believe this kind of facing of issues can best be accomplished by citizens of our own metropolitan area, white and Negro, meeting with their knowledge and experience of the local situation. All of us need to face that responsibility and find proper channels for its accomplishment.
>
> Just as we formerly pointed out that "hatred and violence have no sanction in our religious and political traditions," we also point out that such actions as incite to hatred and violence, however technically peaceful those actions may be, have not contributed to the resolution of our local problems. We do not believe that these days of new hope are days when extreme measures are justified in Birmingham.
>
> We commend the community as a whole, and the local news media and law enforcement officials in particular, on the calm manner in which these

CONCEPT CLOSE-UP

Audience Analysis

CONCEPT

To understand any audience we hope to persuade, we must know *both* what separates us from them *and* what common ground we share.

We may **differ** from our audience in:

Kind of Difference	Example
Assumptions	Western writers assume that separation of church and state is normal; some Muslim audiences do not make the distinction.
Principles	Most conservative writers believe in the principle of the open market; labor audiences often believe in protecting American jobs from foreign competition.
Value rankings	Some writers value personal freedom over duty and obligation; some audiences place duty and obligation above personal freedom.
Ends and means	Writer and audience may agree about purpose (for example, making America safe from terrorism) but disagree about what policies will best accomplish this end.
Interpretation	Some writers understood the September 11, 2001, attacks as acts of war; some audiences saw them as criminal acts that demanded legal rather than military measures.
Consequences	Some writers think making divorce harder would keep more couples together; some audiences think it would only promote individual unhappiness.

We may **share** with our audience:

Kind of Identification	Example
Local identity	Students and teachers at the same university
Collective identity	Citizens of the same state or the same nation
Common cause	Improving the environment
Common experience	Pride in the success of American Olympic athletes
Common history	Respect for soldiers who have died defending the United States

Essentially, we must understand differences to discover how we need to argue; we must use the resources of identification to overcome differences separating us from our readers.

demonstrations have been handled. We urge the public to continue to show restraint should the demonstrations continue, and the law enforcement officials to remain calm and continue to protect our city from violence.

We further strongly urge our own Negro community to withdraw support from these demonstrations, and to unite locally in working peacefully for a better Birmingham. When rights are consistently denied, a cause should be pressed in the courts and in negotiations among local leaders,

Figure 9.1

Rosa Parks, whose refusal to move to the back of a bus touched off the Montgomery bus boycott and the beginning of the civil rights movement, is fingerprinted by Deputy Sheriff D. H. Lackey in Montgomery, Alabama, February 22, 1956. She was among some 100 people charged with violating segregation laws.

and not in the streets. We appeal to both our white and Negro citizenry to observe the principles of law and order and common sense.

Signed by:

C. C. J. Carpenter, D.D., LL.D., Bishop of Alabama

Joseph A. Durick, D.D., Auxiliary Bishop, Diocese of Mobile, Birmingham

Rabbi Milton L. Grafman, Temple Emanu-El, Birmingham, Alabama

Bishop Paul Hardin, Bishop of the Alabama-West Florida Conference of the Methodist Church

Bishop Nolan B. Harmon, Bishop of the North Alabama Conference of the Methodist Church

George M. Murray, D.D., LL.D., Bishop Coadjutor, Episcopal Diocese of Alabama

Edward V. Ramage, Moderator, Synod of the Alabama Presbyterian Church in the United States

Earl Stallings, Pastor, First Baptist Church, Birmingham, Alabama

Martin Luther King, Jr., with his son, about 1963.

In his cell, King began his letter on the margins of that newspaper page, addressing it specifically to the eight clergymen, hoping to move them from disapproval to support, to recognizing the need for demonstrations. King knew that his letter would reach a larger audience, including the demonstrators themselves, who were energized by its message when 50,000 copies were later distributed. King's letter has since reached a global audience with its argument for nonviolent protest in the service of moral law.

Letter from Birmingham Jail

MARTIN LUTHER KING, JR.

My Dear Fellow Clergymen: *April 16, 1963*

While confined here in the Birmingham city jail, I came across your recent statement calling my present activities "unwise and untimely." Seldom do I pause to answer criticism of my work and ideas. If I sought to answer all the criticisms that cross my desk, my secretaries would have little time for anything other than such correspondence in the course of the day, and I would have no time for constructive work. But since I feel that you are men of genuine good will and that your criticisms are sincerely set forth, I want to try to answer your statement in what I hope will be patient and reasonable terms.

I think I should indicate why I am here in Birmingham, since you have been influenced by the view which argues against "outsiders coming in." I have the honor of serving as president of the Southern Christian Leadership Conference, an organization operating in every southern state, with headquarters in Atlanta, Georgia. We have some eighty-five affiliated organizations across the South, and one of them is the Alabama Christian Movement for Human Rights. Frequently we share staff, educational, and financial resources with our affiliates. Several months ago the affiliate here in Birmingham asked us to be on call to engage in a nonviolent direct-action program if such were deemed necessary. We readily consented, and when the hour came we lived up to our promise. So I, along with several members of my staff, am here because I was invited here. I am here because I have organizational ties here.

But more basically, I am in Birmingham because injustice is here. Just as the prophets of the eighth century BC left their villages and carried their "thus saith the Lord" far beyond the boundaries of their home towns, and just as the Apostle Paul left his village of Tarsus and carried the gospel of Jesus Christ to the far corners of the Greco-Roman world, so am I compelled to carry the gospel of freedom beyond my own home town. Like Paul, I must constantly respond to the Macedonian call for aid.

Moreover, I am cognizant of the interrelatedness of all communities and states. I cannot sit idly by in Atlanta and not be concerned about what happens in Birmingham. Injustice anywhere is a threat to justice everywhere. We are caught in an inescapable network of mutuality, tied in a single garment of destiny. Whatever affects one directly, affects all indirectly. Never again can we afford to live with the narrow, provincial "outside agitator" idea. Anyone who lives inside the United States can never be considered an outsider anywhere within its bounds.

You deplore the demonstrations taking place in Birmingham. But your state- 5 ment, I am sorry to say, fails to express a similar concern for the conditions that brought about the demonstrations. I am sure that none of you would want to rest content with the superficial kind of social analysis that deals merely with effects and does not grapple with underlying causes. It is unfortunate that demonstrations are taking place in Birmingham, but it is even more unfortunate that the city's white power structure left the Negro community with no alternative.

In any nonviolent campaign there are four basic steps: collection of the facts to determine whether injustices exist; negotiation; self-purification; and direct action. We have gone through all these steps in Birmingham. There can be no gainsaying the fact that racial injustice engulfs this community. Birmingham is probably the most thoroughly segregated city in the United States. Its ugly record of brutality is widely known. Negroes have experienced grossly unjust treatment in the courts. There have been more unsolved bombings of Negro homes and churches in Birmingham than in any other city in the nation. These are the hard, brutal facts of the case. On the basis of these conditions, Negro leaders sought to negotiate with the city fathers. But the latter consistently refused to engage in good-faith negotiation.

Then, last September, came the opportunity to talk with leaders of Birmingham's economic community. In the course of the negotiations, certain promises were made by the merchants—for example, to remove the stores' humiliating racial signs. On the basis of these promises, the Reverend Fred Shuttlesworth and the leaders of the Alabama Christian Movement for Human Rights agreed to a moratorium on all demonstrations. As the weeks and months went by, we realized that we were the victims of a broken promise. A few signs, briefly removed, returned; the others remained.

As in so many past experiences, our hopes had been blasted, and the shadow of deep disappointment settled upon us. We had no alternative except to prepare for direct action, whereby we would present our very bodies as a means of laying our case before the conscience of the local and the national community. Mindful of the difficulties involved, we decided to undertake a process of self-purification. We began a series of workshops on nonviolence, and we repeatedly asked ourselves: "Are you able to accept blows without retaliating?" "Are you able to endure the ordeal of jail?" We decided to schedule our direct-action program for the Easter season, realizing that except for Christmas, this is the main shopping period of the year. Knowing that a strong economic-withdrawal program would be the by-product of direct action, we felt that this would be the best time to bring pressure to bear on the merchants for the needed change.

Then it occurred to us that Birmingham's mayoral election was coming up in March, and we speedily decided to postpone action until after election day. When we discovered that the Commissioner of Public Safety, Eugene "Bull" Connor, had piled up enough votes to be in the run-off, we decided again to postpone action until the day after the run-off so that the demonstrations could not be used to cloud the issues. Like many others, we waited to see Mr. Connor defeated, and to this end we endured postponement after postponement. Having aided in this community need, we felt that our direct-action program could be delayed no longer.

You may well ask: "Why direct action? Why sit-ins, marches and so forth? Isn't 10 negotiation a better path?" You are quite right in calling for negotiation. Indeed, this is the very purpose of direct action. Nonviolent direct action seeks to create such a crisis and foster such a tension that a community which has constantly refused to negotiate is forced to confront the issue. It seeks so to dramatize the issue that it can no longer be ignored. My citing the creation of tension as part of the work of the nonviolent-resister may sound rather shocking. But I must confess that I am not afraid of the word "tension." I have earnestly opposed violent tension, but there is a type of constructive, nonviolent tension which is necessary for growth. Just as Socrates felt that it was necessary to create a tension in the mind so that individuals could rise from the bondage of myths and half-truths to the unfettered realm of creative analysis and objective appraisal, so must we see the need for nonviolent gadflies to create the kind of tension in society that will help men rise from the dark depths of prejudice and racism to the majestic heights of understanding and brotherhood.

The purpose of our direct-action program is to create a situation so crisis-packed that it will inevitably open the door to negotiation. I therefore concur with you in your call for negotiation. Too long has our beloved Southland been bogged down in a tragic effort to live in monologue rather than dialogue.

One of the basic points in your statement is that the action that I and my associates have taken in Birmingham is untimely. Some have asked: "Why didn't you give the new city administration time to act?" The only answer that I can give to this query is that the new Birmingham administration must be prodded about as much as the outgoing one, before it will act. We are sadly mistaken if we feel that the election of Albert Boutwell as mayor will bring the millennium to Birmingham. While Mr. Boutwell is a much more gentle person than Mr. Connor, they are both segregationists, dedicated to maintenance of the status quo. I have hope that Mr. Boutwell will be reasonable enough to see the futility of massive resistance to desegregation. But he will not see this without pressure from devotees of civil rights. My friends, I must say to you that we have not made a single gain in civil rights without determined legal and nonviolent pressure. Lamentably, it is an historical fact that privileged groups seldom give up their privileges voluntarily. Individuals may see the moral light and voluntarily give up their unjust posture; but, as Reinhold Niebuhr has reminded us, groups tend to be more immoral than individuals.

We know through painful experience that freedom is never voluntarily given by the oppressor; it must be demanded by the oppressed. Frankly, I have yet to engage in a direct-action campaign that was "well timed" in the view of those who have not suffered unduly from the disease of segregation. For years now I have heard the word "Wait!" It rings in the ear of every Negro with piercing familiarity. This "Wait" has almost always meant "Never." We must come to see, with one of our distinguished jurists, that "justice too long delayed is justice denied."

We have waited for more than 340 years for our constitutional God-given rights. The nations of Asia and Africa are moving with jetlike speed toward gaining political independence, but we still creep at horse-and-buggy pace toward gaining a cup of coffee at a lunch counter. Perhaps it is easy for those who have never felt the stinging darts of segregation to say, "Wait." But when you have seen vicious mobs lynch your mothers and fathers at will and drown your sisters and brothers at whim; when you have seen hate-filled policemen curse, kick, and even kill your black brothers and sisters; when you see the vast majority of your twenty million Negro brothers smothering in an airtight cage of poverty in the midst of an affluent society; when you suddenly find your tongue twisted and your speech stammering as you seek to explain to your six-year-old daughter why she can't go to the public amusement park that has just been advertised on television, and see tears welling up in her eyes when she is told that Funtown is closed to colored children, and see ominous clouds of inferiority beginning to form in her little mental sky, and see her beginning to distort her personality by developing an unconscious bitterness toward white people; when you have to concoct an answer for a five-year-old son who is asking: "Daddy, why do white people treat colored people so mean?"; when you take a cross-country drive and find it necessary to sleep night after night in the uncomfortable corners of your automobile because no motel will accept you; when you are humiliated day in and day out by nagging signs reading "white" and "colored"; when your first name becomes "nigger," your middle name becomes "boy" (however old you are), and your last name becomes "John," and your wife and mother are never given the respected title "Mrs."; when you are harried by day and haunted by night by the fact that you are a Negro, living constantly at tiptoe stance, never quite knowing what to expect next, and are plagued with inner fears and outer resentments; when you are forever fighting a degenerating sense of "nobodiness"—then you will understand why we find it difficult to wait. There comes a time when the cup of endurance runs over, and men are no longer willing to be plunged into the abyss of despair. I hope, sirs, you can understand our legitimate and unavoidable impatience.

You express a great deal of anxiety over our willingness to break laws. This is 15 certainly a legitimate concern. Since we so diligently urge people to obey the Supreme Court's decision of 1954 outlawing segregation in the public schools, at first glance it may seem rather paradoxical for us consciously to break laws. One may well ask: "How can you advocate breaking some laws and obeying others?" The answer lies in the fact that there are two types of laws: just and unjust. I would be the first to advocate obeying just laws. One has not only a legal but a moral responsibility to obey just laws. Conversely, one has a moral responsibility to disobey unjust laws. I would agree with St. Augustine that "an unjust law is no law at all."

Now, what is the difference between the two? How does one determine whether a law is just or unjust? A just law is a man-made code that squares with the moral law or the law of God. An unjust law is a code that is out of harmony with the moral law. To put it in the terms of St. Thomas Aquinas: An unjust law is a human law that is not rooted in eternal law and natural law. Any law that uplifts human personality is just. Any law that degrades human personality is unjust. All segregation statutes are unjust because segregation distorts the soul and damages the personality. It gives the segregator a false sense of superiority and the segregated a false sense of inferiority. Segregation, to use the terminology of the Jewish philosopher Martin Buber, substitutes an "I–it" relationship for an "I–thou" relationship and ends up relegating persons to the status of things. Hence, segregation is not only politically, economically, and sociologically unsound, it is morally wrong and sinful. Paul Tillich has said that sin is separation. Is not segregation an existential expression of man's tragic separation, his awful estrangement, his terrible sinfulness? Thus it is that I can urge men to obey the 1954 decision of the Supreme Court, for it is morally right; and I can urge them to disobey segregation ordinances, for they are morally wrong.

Let us consider a more concrete example of just and unjust laws. An unjust law is a code that a numerical or power majority group compels a minority group to obey but does not make binding on itself. This is *difference* made legal. By the same token, a just law is a code that a majority compels a minority to follow and that it is willing to follow itself. This is *sameness* made legal.

Let me give another explanation. A law is unjust if it is inflicted on a minority that, as a result of being denied the right to vote, had no part in enacting or devising the law. Who can say that the legislature of Alabama which set up that state's segregation laws was democratically elected? Throughout Alabama all sorts of devious methods are used to prevent Negroes from becoming registered voters, and there are some counties in which, even though Negroes constitute a majority of the population, not a single Negro is registered. Can any law enacted under such circumstances be considered democratically structured?

Sometimes a law is just on its face and unjust in its application. For instance, I have been arrested on a charge of parading without a permit. Now, there is nothing wrong in having an ordinance which requires a permit for a parade. But such an ordinance becomes unjust when it is used to maintain segregation and to deny citizens the First-Amendment privilege of peaceful assembly and protest.

I hope you are able to see the distinction I am trying to point out. In no sense 20 do I advocate evading or defying the law, as would the rabid segregationist. That would lead to anarchy. One who breaks an unjust law must do so openly, lovingly, and with a willingness to accept the penalty. I submit that an individual who breaks a law that conscience tells him is unjust, and who willingly accepts the penalty of imprisonment in order to arouse the conscience of the community over its injustice, is in reality expressing the highest respect for law.

Of course, there is nothing new about this kind of civil disobedience. It was evidenced sublimely in the refusal of Shadrach, Meshach, and Abednego to obey the laws of Nebuchadnezzar, on the ground that a higher moral law was at stake. It was practiced superbly by the early Christians, who were willing to face hungry lions and the excruciating pain of chopping blocks rather than submit to certain unjust laws of the Roman Empire. To a degree, academic freedom is a reality today because Socrates practiced civil disobedience. In our own nation, the Boston Tea Party represented a massive act of civil disobedience.

We should never forget that everything Adolf Hitler did in Germany was "legal" and everything the Hungarian freedom fighters did in Hungary was "illegal." It was "illegal" to aid and comfort a Jew in Hitler's Germany. Even so, I am sure that, had I lived in Germany at the time, I would have aided and comforted my Jewish brothers. If today I lived in a Communist country where certain principles dear to the Christian faith are suppressed, I would openly advocate disobeying that country's antireligious laws.

I must make two honest confessions to you, my Christian and Jewish brothers. First, I must confess that over the past few years I have been gravely disappointed with the white moderate. I have almost reached the regrettable conclusion that the Negro's great stumbling block in his stride toward freedom is not the White Citizen's Counciler or the Ku Klux Klanner, but the white moderate, who is more devoted to "order" than to justice; who prefers a negative peace which is the presence of tension to a positive peace which is the presence of justice; who constantly says: "I agree with you in the goal you seek, but I cannot agree with your methods of direct action"; who paternalistically believes he can set the timetable for another man's freedom; who lives by a mythical concept of time and who constantly advises the Negro to wait for a "more convenient season." Shallow understanding from people of good will is more frustrating than absolute misunderstanding from people of ill will. Lukewarm acceptance is much more bewildering than outright rejection.

I had hoped that the white moderate would understand that law and order exist for the purpose of establishing justice and that when they fail in this purpose they become the dangerously structured dams that block the flow of social progress. I had hoped that the white moderate would understand that the present tension in the South is a necessary phase of the transition from an obnoxious

negative peace, in which the Negro passively accepted his unjust plight, to a substantive and positive peace, in which all men will respect the dignity and worth of
human personality. Actually, we who engage in nonviolent direct action are not
the creators of tension. We merely bring to the surface the hidden tension that is
already alive. We bring it out in the open, where it can be seen and dealt with.
Like a boil that can never be cured so long as it is covered up but must be opened
with all its ugliness to the natural medicines of air and light, injustice must be
exposed, with all the tension its exposure creates, to the light of human conscience
and the air of national opinion before it can be cured.

In your statement you assert that our actions, even though peaceful, must be   25
condemned because they precipitate violence. But is this a logical assertion? Isn't
this like condemning a robbed man because his possession of money precipitated
the evil act of robbery? Isn't this like condemning Socrates because his unswerving
commitment to truth and his philosophical inquiries precipitated the act by the
misguided populace in which they made him drink hemlock? Isn't this like condemning Jesus because his unique God-consciousness and never-ceasing devotion
to God's will precipitated the evil act of crucifixion? We must come to see that, as
the federal courts have consistently affirmed, it is wrong to urge an individual to
cease his efforts to gain his basic constitutional rights because the quest may precipitate violence. Society must protect the robbed and punish the robber.

I had also hoped that the white moderate would reject the myth concerning
time in relation to the struggle for freedom. I have just received a letter from a
white brother in Texas. He writes: "All Christians know that the colored people
will receive equal rights eventually, but it is possible that you are in too great a
religious hurry. It has taken Christianity almost two thousand years to accomplish
what it has. The teachings of Christ take time to come to earth." Such an attitude
stems from a tragic misconception of time, from the strangely irrational notion
that there is something in the very flow of time that will inevitably cure all ills.
Actually, time itself is neutral; it can be used either destructively or constructively.
More and more I feel that the people of ill will have used time much more effectively than have the people of good will. We will have to repent in this generation
not merely for the hateful words and actions of the bad people but for the appall-
ing silence of the good people. Human progress never rolls in on wheels of inev-
itability; it comes through the tireless efforts of men willing to be coworkers with
God, and without this hard work, time itself becomes an ally of the forces of social
stagnation. We must use time creatively, in the knowledge that the time is always
ripe to do right. Now is the time to make real the promise of democracy and
transform our pending national elegy into a creative psalm of brotherhood. Now
is the time to lift our national policy from the quicksand of racial injustice to the
solid rock of human dignity.

You speak of our activity in Birmingham as extreme. At first I was rather disappointed that fellow clergymen would see my nonviolent efforts as those of an
extremist. I began thinking about the fact that I stand in the middle of two opposing forces in the Negro community. One is a force of complacency, made up in
part of Negroes who, as a result of long years of oppression, are so drained of

self-respect and a sense of "somebodiness" that they have adjusted to segregation; and in part of a few middle-class Negroes who, because of a degree of academic and economic security and because in some ways they profit by segregation, have become insensitive to the problems of the masses. The other force is one of bitterness and hatred, and it comes perilously close to advocating violence. It is expressed in the various black nationalist groups that are springing up across the nation, the largest and best-known being Elijah Muhammad's Muslim movement. Nourished by the Negro's frustration over the continued existence of racial discrimination, this movement is made up of people who have lost faith in America, who have absolutely repudiated Christianity, and who have concluded that the white man is an incorrigible "devil."

I have tried to stand between these two forces, saying that we need emulate neither the "do-nothingism" of the complacent nor the hatred and despair of the black nationalist. For there is the more excellent way of love and nonviolent protest. I am grateful to God that, through the influence of the Negro church, the way of nonviolence became an integral part of our struggle.

If this philosophy had not emerged, by now many streets of the South would, I am convinced, be flowing with blood. And I am further convinced that if our white brothers dismiss as "rabble-rousers" and "outside agitators" those of us who employ nonviolent direct action, and if they refuse to support our nonviolent efforts, millions of the Negroes will, out of frustration and despair, seek solace and security in black-nationalist ideologies—a development that would inevitably lead to a frightening racial nightmare.

Oppressed people cannot remain oppressed forever. The yearning for freedom 30 eventually manifests itself, and that is what has happened to the American Negro. Something within has reminded him of his birthright of freedom, and something without has reminded him that it can be gained. Consciously or unconsciously, he has been caught up by the *Zeitgeist,* and with his black brothers of Africa and his brown and yellow brothers of Asia, South America, and the Caribbean, the United States Negro is moving with a sense of great urgency toward the promised land of racial justice. If one recognizes this vital urge that has engulfed the Negro community, one should readily understand why public demonstrations are taking place. The Negro has many pent-up resentments and latent frustrations, and he must release them. So let him march; let him make prayer pilgrimages to the city hall; let him go on freedom rides—and try to understand why he must do so. If his repressed emotions are not released in nonviolent ways, they will seek expression through violence; this is not a threat but a fact of history. So I have not said to my people: "Get rid of your discontent." Rather, I have tried to say that this normal and healthy discontent can be channeled into the creative outlet of nonviolent direct action. And now this approach is being termed extremist.

But though I was initially disappointed at being categorized as an extremist, as I continued to think about the matter I gradually gained a measure of satisfaction from the label. Was not Jesus an extremist for love: "Love your enemies, bless them that curse you, do good to them that hate you, and pray for them which despitefully use you, and persecute you." Was not Amos an extremist for justice:

"Let justice roll down like waters and righteousness like an ever-flowing stream." Was not Paul an extremist for the Christian gospel: "I bear in my body the marks of the Lord Jesus." Was not Martin Luther an extremist: "Here I stand; I cannot do otherwise, so help me God." And John Bunyan: "I will stay in jail to the end of my days before I make a butchery of my conscience." And Abraham Lincoln: "This nation cannot survive half slave and half free." And Thomas Jefferson: "We hold these truths to be self-evident, that all men are created equal. . . ." So the question is not whether we will be extremists, but what kind of extremists we will be. Will we be extremists for hate or for love? Will we be extremists for the preservation of injustice or for the extension of justice? In that dramatic scene on Calvary's hill three men were crucified. We must never forget that all three were crucified for the same crime—the crime of extremism. Two were extremists for immorality, and thus fell below their environment. The other, Jesus Christ, was an extremist for love, truth and goodness, and thereby rose above his environment. Perhaps the South, the nation and the world are in dire need of creative extremists.

I had hoped that the white moderate would see this need. Perhaps I was too optimistic; perhaps I expected too much. I suppose I should have realized that few members of the oppressor race can understand the deep groans and passionate yearnings of the oppressed race, and still fewer have the vision to see that injustice must be rooted out by strong, persistent, and determined action. I am thankful, however, that some of our white brothers in the South have grasped the meaning of this social revolution and committed themselves to it. They are still all too few in quantity, but they are big in quality. Some—such as Ralph McGill, Lillian Smith, Harry Golden, James McBride Dabbs, Anne Braden, and Sarah Patton Boyle—have written about our struggle in eloquent and prophetic terms. Others have marched with us down nameless streets of the South. They have languished in filthy, roach-infested jails, suffering the abuse and brutality of policemen who view them as "dirty nigger-lovers." Unlike so many of their moderate brothers and sisters, they have recognized the urgency of the moment and sensed the need for powerful "action" antidotes to combat the disease of segregation.

Let me take note of my other major disappointment. I have been so greatly disappointed with the white church and its leadership. Of course, there are some notable exceptions. I am not unmindful of the fact that each of you has taken some significant stands on this issue. I commend you, Reverend Stallings, for your Christian stand on this past Sunday, in welcoming Negroes to your worship service on a nonsegregated basis. I commend the Catholic leaders of this state for integrating Spring Hill College several years ago.

But despite these notable exceptions, I must honestly reiterate that I have been disappointed with the church. I do not say this as one of those negative critics who can always find something wrong with the church. I say this as a minister of the gospel, who loves the church; who was nurtured in its bosom; who has been sustained by its spiritual blessings and who will remain true to it as long as the cord of life shall lengthen.

When I was suddenly catapulted into the leadership of the bus protest in 35 Montgomery, Alabama, a few years ago, I felt we would be supported by the white church. I felt that the white ministers, priests, and rabbis of the South would be among our strongest allies. Instead, some have been outright opponents, refusing to understand the freedom movement and misrepresenting its leaders; all too many others have been more cautious than courageous and have remained silent behind the anesthetizing security of stained-glass windows.

In spite of my shattered dreams, I came to Birmingham with the hope that the white religious leadership of this community would see the justice of our cause and, with deep moral concern, would serve as the channel through which our just grievances could reach the power structure. I had hoped that each of you would understand. But again I have been disappointed.

I have heard numerous southern religious leaders admonish their worshipers to comply with a desegregation decision because it is the law, but I have longed to hear white ministers declare: "Follow this decree because integration is morally right and because the Negro is your brother." In the midst of blatant injustices inflicted upon the Negro, I have watched white churchmen stand on the sideline and mouth pious irrelevancies and sanctimonious trivialities. In the midst of a mighty struggle to rid our nation of racial and economic injustice, I have heard many ministers say: "Those are social issues, with which the gospel has no real concern." And I have watched many churches commit themselves to a completely otherworldly religion which makes a strange, un-Biblical distinction between body and soul, between the sacred and the secular.

I have traveled the length and breadth of Alabama, Mississippi, and all the other southern states. On sweltering summer days and crisp autumn mornings I have looked at the South's beautiful churches with their lofty spires pointing heavenward. I have beheld the impressive outlines of her massive religious-education buildings. Over and over I have found myself asking: "What kind of people worship here? Who is their God? Where were their voices when the lips of Governor Barnett dripped with words of interposition and nullification? Where were they when Governor Wallace gave a clarion call for defiance and hatred? Where were their voices of support when bruised and weary Negro men and women decided to rise from the dark dungeons of complacency to the bright hills of creative protest?"

Yes, these questions are still in my mind. In deep disappointment I have wept over the laxity of the church. But be assured that my tears have been tears of love. There can be no deep disappointment where there is not deep love. Yes, I love the church. How could I do otherwise? I am in the rather unique position of being the son, the grandson, and the great-grandson of preachers. Yes, I see the church as the body of Christ. But, oh! How we have blemished and scarred that body through social neglect and through fear of being nonconformists.

There was a time when the church was very powerful—in the time when the early Christians rejoiced at being deemed worthy to suffer for what they believed. In those days the church was not merely a thermometer that recorded the ideas and principles of popular opinion; it was a thermostat that transformed the mores of society. Whenever the early Christians entered a town, the people in power became disturbed and immediately sought to convict the Christians for being "disturbers of the peace" and "outside agitators." But the Christians pressed on, in the

40

conviction that they were "a colony of heaven," called to obey God rather than man. Small in number, they were big in commitment. They were too God-intoxicated to be "astronomically intimidated." By their effort and example they brought an end to such ancient evils as infanticide and gladiatorial contests.

Things are different now. So often the contemporary church is a weak, ineffectual voice with an uncertain sound. So often it is an archdefender of the status quo. Far from being disturbed by the presence of the church, the power structure of the average community is consoled by the church's silent—and often even vocal—sanction of things as they are.

But the judgment of God is upon the church as never before. If today's church does not recapture the sacrificial spirit of the early church, it will lose its authenticity, forfeit the loyalty of millions, and be dismissed as an irrelevant social club with no meaning for the twentieth century. Every day I meet young people whose disappointment with the church has turned into outright disgust.

Perhaps I have once again been too optimistic. Is organized religion too inextricably bound to the status quo to save our nation and the world? Perhaps I must turn my faith to the inner spiritual church, the church within the church, as the true *ekklesia* and the hope of the world. But again I am thankful to God that some noble souls from the ranks of organized religion have broken loose from the paralyzing chains of conformity and joined us as active partners in the struggle for freedom. They have left their secure congregations and walked the streets of Albany, Georgia, with us. They have gone down the highways of the South on tortuous rides for freedom. Yes, they have gone to jail with us. Some have been dismissed from their churches, have lost the support of their bishops and fellow ministers. But they have acted in the faith that right defeated is stronger than evil triumphant. Their witness has been the spiritual salt that has preserved the true meaning of the gospel in these troubled times. They have carved a tunnel of hope through the dark mountain of disappointment.

I hope the church as a whole will meet the challenge of this decisive hour. But even if the church does not come to the aid of justice, I have no despair about the future. I have no fear about the outcome of our struggle in Birmingham, even if our motives are at present misunderstood. We will reach the goal of freedom in Birmingham and all over the nation, because the goal of America is freedom. Abused and scorned though we may be, our destiny is tied up with America's destiny. Before the pilgrims landed at Plymouth, we were here. Before the pen of Jefferson etched the majestic words of the Declaration of Independence across the pages of history, we were here. For more than two centuries our forebears labored in this country without wages; they made cotton king; they built the homes of their masters while suffering gross injustice and shameful humiliation—and yet out of a bottomless vitality they continued to thrive and develop. If the inexpressible cruelties of slavery could not stop us, the opposition we now face will surely fail. We will win our freedom because the sacred heritage of our nation and the eternal will of God are embodied in our echoing demands.

Before closing I feel impelled to mention one other point in your statement 45 that has troubled me profoundly. You warmly commended the Birmingham police force for keeping "order" and "preventing violence." I doubt that you would have so warmly commended the police force if you had seen its dogs sinking their teeth into unarmed, nonviolent Negroes. I doubt that you would so quickly commend the policemen if you were to observe their ugly and inhumane treatment of Negroes here in the city jail; if you were to watch them push and curse old Negro women and young Negro girls; if you were to see them slap and kick old Negro men and young boys; if you were to observe them, as they did on two occasions, refuse to give us food because we wanted to sing our grace together. I cannot join you in your praise of the Birmingham police department.

It is true that police have exercised a degree of discipline in handling the demonstrators. In this sense they have conducted themselves rather "nonviolently" in public. But for what purpose? To preserve the evil system of segregation. Over the past few years I have consistently preached that nonviolence demands that the means we use must be as pure as the ends we seek. I have tried to make clear that it is wrong to use immoral means to attain moral ends. But now I must affirm that it is just as wrong, or perhaps even more so, to use moral means to preserve immoral ends. Perhaps Mr. Connor and his policemen have been rather nonviolent in public, as was Chief Pritchett in Albany, Georgia, but they have used the moral means of nonviolence to maintain the immoral end of racial injustice. As T. S. Eliot has said: "The last temptation is the greatest treason: To do the right deed for the wrong reason."

I wish you had commended the Negro sit-inners and demonstrators of Birmingham for their sublime courage, their willingness to suffer and their amazing discipline in the midst of great provocation. One day the South will recognize its real heroes. They will be the James Merediths, with the noble sense of purpose that enables them to face jeering and hostile mobs, and with the agonizing loneliness that characterizes the life of the pioneer. They will be old, oppressed, battered Negro women, symbolized in a seventy-two-year-old woman in Montgomery, Alabama, who rose up with a sense of dignity and with her people decided not to ride segregated buses, and who responded with ungrammatical profundity to one who inquired about her weariness: "My feets is tired, but my soul is at rest." They will be the young high school and college students, the young ministers of the gospel and a host of their elders, courageously and nonviolently sitting in at lunch counters and willingly going to jail for conscience's sake. One day the South will know that when these disinherited children of God sat down at lunch counters, they were in reality standing up for what is best in the American dream and for the most sacred values in our Judaeo-Christian heritage, thereby bringing our nation back to those great wells of democracy which were dug deep by the founding fathers in their formulation of the Constitution and the Declaration of Independence.

Never before have I written so long a letter. I'm afraid it is much too long to take your precious time. I can assure you that it would have been much shorter if I had been writing from a comfortable desk, but what else can one do when he is alone in a narrow jail cell, other than write long letters, think long thoughts, and pray long prayers?

If I have said anything in this letter that overstates the truth and indicates an unreasonable impatience, I beg you to forgive me. If I have said anything that understates the truth and indicates my having a patience that allows me to settle for anything less than brotherhood, I beg God to forgive me.

I hope this letter finds you strong in faith. I also hope that circumstances will 50 soon make it possible for me to meet each of you, not as an integrationist or a civil-rights leader but as a fellow clergyman and a Christian brother. Let us all hope that the dark clouds of racial prejudice will soon pass away and the deep fog of misunderstanding will be lifted from our fear-drenched communities, and in some not too distant tomorrow the radiant stars of love and brotherhood will shine over our great nation with all their scintillating beauty.

Yours for the cause of Peace and Brotherhood

Martin Luther King, Jr.

King's Analysis of His Audience: Identification and Overcoming Difference

King's letter is worth studying for the resources of identification alone. For example, he appeals in his salutation to "My Dear Fellow Clergymen," which emphasizes at the outset that he and his readers share a role. Elsewhere he calls them "my friends" (paragraph 12) and "my Christian and Jewish brothers" (paragraph 23). In many other places, King alludes to the Bible and to other religious figures; these references put him on common ground with his readers. King's letter also deals with that which separates him from his readers. We can use the list in the Concept Close-Up on page 251 to analyze how he addressed those differences:

Assumptions: King's readers assumed that if black people waited long enough, their situation would inevitably grow better. King, in paragraph 26, questions "the strangely irrational notion that . . . the very flow of time . . . will inevitably cure all ills." Against this common assumption that "time heals," King offers the view that "time . . . can be used either destructively or constructively."

Principles: King's readers believed in always obeying the law, a principle blind to intent and application. King substitutes another principle: Obey just laws, but disobey, openly and lovingly, unjust laws (paragraphs 15–22).

Hierarchy of Values: King's readers elevated reducing racial tension over securing racial justice. In paragraph 10, King's strategy is to talk about "constructive, nonviolent tension," an effort to get his readers to see tension as not necessarily a bad thing.

Ends and Means: King's audience seems to disagree with him not about the ends for which he was working but about the means. King focuses not on justifying civil rights but on justifying civil disobedience.

Interpretation: King's audience interpreted extremism as always negative. King counters by showing, first, that he is actually a moderate, neither a "do-nothing" nor a militant (paragraph 28). But then he redefines extremism, arguing that extremism for good causes is justified and citing historical examples to support his point (paragraph 31).

Consequences: King's readers doubtless feared the consequences of supporting civil rights too strongly—losing the support of conservative members of their congregations. But as King warns, "If today's church does not recapture the sacrificial spirit of the early church, it will . . . be dismissed as an irrelevant social club" (paragraph 42). King's strategy is to emphasize long-term consequences—the church's loss of vitality and relevance.

◎◎ FOLLOWING THROUGH

As a class, look closely at one of the essays from an earlier chapter, and do an audience analysis. What audience did the writer attempt to reach? How did the writer connect or fail to connect with the audience's experience, knowledge, and concerns? What exactly divides the author from his or her audience, and how did the writer attempt to overcome the division? How effective were the writer's strategies for achieving identification? What can you suggest that might have worked better?   •

USING THE FORMS OF APPEAL

We turn now to the forms of appeal in persuasion, noting how King used them. For a summary of the forms, see the Concept Close-Up on page 248.

The Appeal to Reason

Persuasion uses the same appeal to reason as convincing. King chose to respond to the clergymen's statement with a personal letter, organized around their criticisms. Most of King's letter amounts to self-defense and belongs to the genre called *apologia*. An **apologia** is an effort to explain and justify what one has done, or chosen not to do, in the face of disapproval or misunderstanding.

Rather than making a single case, King uses a series of short arguments, occupying from one to as many as eight paragraphs, to respond to the criticisms. These include

Refutation of the "outside agitator" concept (paragraphs 2–4)

Defense of nonviolent civil disobedience (paragraphs 5–11)

Definitions of "just" versus "unjust" laws (paragraphs 15–22)

Refutation and defense of the label "extremist" (paragraphs 27–31)

Rejection of the ministers' praise for the conduct of the police during the Birmingham demonstration (paragraphs 45–47)

In addition to defending himself and his cause, King advances his own criticisms, most notably of the "white moderate" (paragraphs 23–26) and the "white church and its leadership" (paragraphs 33–44). This concentration on rational appeal confirms King's character as a man of reason.

King also cites evidence that his readers must respect. In paragraph 16, for example, he cites St. Thomas Aquinas, Martin Buber, and Paul Tillich—representing, respectively, the Catholic, Jewish, and Protestant traditions—to defend his position on just and unjust laws. He has chosen these authorities so that each of his eight accusers has someone from his own tradition with whom to identify.

◎◎ FOLLOWING THROUGH

1. Look at paragraphs 2–4 of King's letter. What reasons does he give to justify being in Birmingham? How does he support each reason? Do his reasons and evidence indicate a strategy aimed at his clergy audience?

2. King's argument for civil disobedience (paragraphs 15–22) is based on one main reason. What is it, and how does he support it?

3. What are the two reasons King gives to refute his audience's charge of extremism (paragraphs 27–31)?

4. Think about a time in your life when you did (or did not do) something for which you were unfairly criticized. Choose one or two of the criticisms, and defend yourself in a short case of your own. Remember to persuade *your accusers,* not yourself. Ask, as King did, How can I appeal to them? What will they find reasonable?　　　　　•

The Appeal to Character

In Chapter 8, our concern was how to make a good case. We did not discuss self-presentation there, but when you make a good case you are also creating a positive impression. A good argument will always reveal the writer's values, intelligence, and knowledge. We respect and trust a person who reasons well, even when we do not agree.

The appeal to character in persuasion differs from convincing only in degree. In convincing, the appeal is implicit and diffused throughout the argument; in persuading, the appeal is often explicit and concentrated in a specific section of the essay. The effect on readers is consequently different: In convincing, we are seldom aware of the writer's character; in persuading, the writer's character assumes a major role.

Perception of character was a special problem for King when he wrote his letter. He was not a national hero in 1963 but rather a controversial civil rights leader whom many viewed as a troublemaker. Furthermore, he wrote this now celebrated document while in jail—hardly a condition that inspires respect and trust. Self-presentation, then, was something he concentrated on, especially at the beginning and end.

In his opening paragraph, King acknowledges that he is currently in jail. But he goes on to establish himself as a professional person like his readers, with secretaries, correspondence, and important work to do.

Just prior to his conclusion, King offers a strongly worded critique of the white moderate and the mainstream white church, taking the offensive in a way that his readers are certain to perceive as an attack. In paragraph 48, however, he suddenly becomes self-deprecating: "Never before have I written so long a letter." As unexpected as it is, this sudden shift of tone disarms the reader. Then, with gentle irony (the letter, he says, would have been shorter "if I had been writing from a comfortable desk"), King explains the length of his letter as the result of his having no other outlet for action. What can one do in jail but "write long letters, think long thoughts, and pray long prayers?" King turns the negative of jail into a positive, an opportunity rather than a limitation.

His next move is equally surprising, especially after the assertive tone of his critique of the church. He begs forgiveness—from his readers if he has overstated his case, from God if he has understated it. This daring, dramatic move is just the right touch, the perfect gesture of reconciliation. Because he asks so humbly, his readers *must* forgive him. What else can they do? The subordination of his own will to God's is the stance of the sufferer and martyr in both Jewish and Christian traditions.

Finally, King sets aside that which divides him from his readers—integration and civil rights—in favor of that which unifies them: All are men of God, brothers in faith. Like an Old Testament prophet, he envisions a time when the current conflicts will be over, when "the radiant stars of love and brotherhood will shine over our great nation." In other words, King holds out the possibility for transcendence, for rising above racial prejudice to a new age. In the end, his readers are encouraged to soar with him into hope for the future.

The key to identification is to reach beyond the individual self, associating one's character with something larger—the Christian community, the history of the struggle for freedom, national values, "spaceship Earth," or any appropriate cause or movement in which readers can also participate.

◎◎ FOLLOWING THROUGH

Look at the list of questions for creating audience identification on page 249. Other than in the conclusion, find some examples in King's letter in which he employs some of these resources of identification. What methods does King use that any persuader might use? •

The Appeal to Emotion

Educated people aware of the techniques of persuasion are often deeply suspicious of emotional appeal. Among college professors this prejudice can be especially strong because all fields of academic study claim to value reason, dispassionate inquiry, and critical analysis. Many think of emotional appeal as the opposite of sound thinking.

We can all cite examples of the destructive power of emotional appeal. But to condemn it wholesale, without qualification, exhibits lack of self-awareness. Most scientists will concede, for instance, that they are passionately committed to their methods, and mathematicians say that they are moved by the elegance of certain equations. All human activity has some emotional dimension, a strongly felt adherence to a common set of values.

Moreover, we ought to have strong feelings about certain things: revulsion at the horrors of the Holocaust, pity and anger over the abuse of children, happiness when a war is concluded or when those kidnapped by terrorists are released, and so on. We cease to be human if we are not responsive to emotional appeal.

Clearly, then, we must distinguish between legitimate and illegitimate emotional appeals. Distinguishing the two is not always easy, but answering certain questions can help:

Do the emotional appeals substitute for knowledge and reason?

Do they employ stereotypes and pit one group against another?

Do they offer a simple, unthinking reaction to a complex situation?

Whenever the answer is yes, our suspicions should be aroused.

Perhaps an even better test is to ask yourself, If I act on the basis of how I feel, who will benefit and who will suffer? You may be saddened, for example, to see animals used in medical experiments, but an appeal showing only the animals and ignoring the benefits for humans panders to emotions.

In contrast, legitimate emotional appeal *supplements* argument, drawing on knowledge and often firsthand experience. At its best, it can bring alienated groups together and create empathy or sympathy. Many examples could be cited from King's letter, but the most effective passage is surely paragraph 14:

> We have waited for more than 340 years for our constitutional God-given rights. The nations of Asia and Africa are moving with jetlike speed toward gaining political independence, but we still creep at horse-and-buggy pace toward gaining a cup of coffee at a lunch counter. Perhaps it is easy for those who have never felt the stinging darts of segregation to say, "Wait." But when you have seen vicious mobs lynch your mothers and fathers at will and drown your sisters and brothers at whim; when you have seen hate-filled policemen curse, kick, and even kill your black brothers and sisters; when you see the vast majority of your twenty million Negro brothers smothering in an airtight cage of poverty in the midst of an affluent society; when you suddenly find your tongue twisted and your speech stammering as you seek to explain to your six-year-old daughter why she can't go to the public amusement park that has just been advertised on television, and see tears welling up in her eyes when she is told that Funtown is closed to colored children, and see ominous

clouds of inferiority beginning to form in her little mental sky, and see her beginning to distort her personality by developing an unconscious bitterness toward white people; when you have to concoct an answer for a five-year-old son who is asking: "Daddy, why do white people treat colored people so mean?"; when you take a cross-country drive and find it necessary to sleep night after night in the uncomfortable corners of your automobile because no motel will accept you; when you are humiliated day in and day out by nagging signs reading "white" and "colored"; when your first name becomes "nigger," your middle name becomes "boy" (however old you are), and your last name becomes "John," and your wife and mother are never given the respected title "Mrs."; when you are harried by day and haunted by night by the fact that you are a Negro, living constantly at tiptoe stance, never quite knowing what to expect next, and are plagued with inner fears and outer resentments; when you are forever fighting a degenerating sense of "nobodiness"—then you will understand why we find it difficult to wait. There comes a time when the cup of endurance runs over, and men are no longer willing to be plunged into the abyss of despair. I hope, sirs, you can understand our legitimate and unavoidable impatience.

Just prior to this paragraph, King has concluded an argument justifying the use of direct action to dramatize social inequities and to demand rights and justice denied to oppressed people. Direct-action programs are necessary, he says, because "freedom is never voluntarily given by the oppressor; it must be demanded by the oppressed." It is easy for those not oppressed to urge an underclass to wait. But "[t]his 'Wait' has almost always meant 'Never'."

At this point, King creates a sense of outrage in his readers. Having ended paragraph 13 by equating "wait" with "never," King next refers to a tragic historical fact: For 340 years, since the beginning of slavery in the American colonies, black people have been waiting for their freedom. He sharply contrasts the "jetlike speed" with which Africa is overcoming colonialism with the "horse-and-buggy pace" of integration in the United States. In African homelands, black people are gaining their political independence; but here, in the land of the free, they are denied even "a cup of coffee at a lunch counter." Clearly, this is legitimate emotional appeal, based on fact and reinforcing reason.

In the long and rhythmical sentence that takes up most of the rest of the paragraph, King unleashes the full force of emotional appeal in a series of concrete images designed to make his privileged white readers feel the anger, frustration, and humiliation of the oppressed. In rapid succession, King alludes to mob violence, police brutality, and economic discrimination—the more public evils of racial discrimination—and then moves to the personal, everyday experience of segregation, concentrating especially on what it does to innocent children. For any reader with even the least capacity for sympathy, these images strike home, creating identification with the suffering of the oppressed and impatience with the evil system that perpetuates it. In sum, through the use of telling detail drawn from his own experience, King succeeds in getting his audience to feel what he feels.

What have we learned from King about the available means of emotional appeal? Instead of telling his audience what they should feel, he has evoked that emotion using five specific rhetorical techniques:

Concrete examples

Personal experiences

Metaphors and similes

Sharp contrasts and comparisons

Sentence rhythm, particularly the use of intentional repetition

We next consider how style contributes to persuasion.

◎◎ FOLLOWING THROUGH

1. Emotional appeals need to be both legitimate and appropriate—honest and suitable for the subject matter and the audience. Find examples of arguments from books, newspapers, magazines, and professional journals and discuss the use or avoidance of emotional appeal in each. On the basis of this study, generalize about what subjects and audiences allow direct emotional appeal.

2. Write an essay analyzing the tactics of emotional appeal in editorials in your campus or local newspaper. Compare the strategies with those used by King. Evaluate the appeals. How effective are they? How well do they reinforce the reasoning offered? Be sure to discuss their legitimacy and appropriateness.   ●

The Appeal through Style

Style refers to the choices a writer makes at the level of words, phrases, and sentences. Style is not merely a "dressing up" of an argument. Ideas and arguments do not get expressed apart from style, and all the appeals involve stylistic choices. Style works hand-in-hand with reason, character, and emotion.

Furthermore, style makes what we say memorable. Because persuasive impact depends largely on what readers remember, style matters as much as any of the other appeals.

Style means choice from options. One choice involves the degree of formality. King strikes a formal and professional tone through most of his letter, choosing words like *cognizant* (paragraph 4) rather than the more common *aware*. Writers also choose words based on **connotation** (what a word implies or what we associate with it) as much as on **denotation** (a word's literal meaning). For example, King opens his letter with "While confined here in the Birmingham city jail." The word *confined* denotes the same condition as *incarcerated* but has more favorable connotations, because people can be *confined* in ways that evoke sympathy.

Memorable writing often appeals to sight and sound. Concrete words paint a picture; in paragraph 45, for example, King tells about "dogs sinking their teeth" into nonviolent demonstrators. Writers may also evoke images through metaphor and simile. King's "the stinging darts of segregation" (paragraph 14) is an example of metaphor. In this same paragraph, King refers to the "airtight cage of poverty," the "clouds of inferiority" forming in his young daughter's "mental sky," and the "cup of endurance" that has run over for his people—each a powerful metaphor.

Even when read silently, language has sound. Style also includes variety in sentence length and rhythms. For example, writers may emphasize a short, simple sentence by placing it at the end of a series of long ones, as King does in paragraph 14. Or they may repeat certain phrases to emphasize a point. In the fourth sentence of paragraph 14, King repeats "when you" a number of times, piling up examples of racial discrimination and creating a powerful rhythm that carries readers through this unusually long sentence. Another common rhythmic pattern is parallelism. Note the following phrases, again from the fourth sentence of paragraph 14:

"lynch your mothers and fathers at will"

"drown your sisters and brothers at whim"

Here King uses similar words in the same places, even the same number of syllables in each phrase. The parallelism is further emphasized by *alliteration,* repetition of consonant sounds. In yet another passage from paragraph 14, King suggests violence when he describes police who "curse, kick, and even kill" black citizens. Repetition of the hard *k* sound, especially in one-syllable words, makes the violence sound as brutal as it was.

◎◎ FOLLOWING THROUGH

1. Analyze King's style in paragraphs 6, 8, 23, 24, 31, and 47. Compare what King does in these paragraphs with paragraph 14. How are they similar? How are they different? Why?

2. To some extent, style is a gift or talent. But it is also learned by imitating authors we admire. Use your writer's notebook to increase your stylistic options; whenever you hear or read something stated well, copy it down and analyze why it's effective. Make up a sentence of your own using the same techniques with different subject matter. In this way, you can begin to use analogy, metaphor, repetition, alliteration, parallelism, and other stylistic devices. Begin by imitating six or so sentences or phrases that you especially liked in King's letter.

3. Write an essay analyzing your own style in a previous essay. What would you do differently now? Why?

DRAFTING A PERSUASIVE ESSAY

Persuasion addresses real needs and moves people to act. Begin, therefore, by conceiving the need you want to address and the audience you want to reach.

Establishing Need

Sometimes the need for action is so widely and well understood that saying much about it isn't necessary. We need a cure for cancer, for instance. Everybody knows this, so a paper about it would at most remind readers of how many people die annually from various types of cancer.

Most of the time, however, need has to be established—or if you are arguing against taking action proposed by someone else, arguing that no need exists that requires action. *Establishing need depends on the extent of common knowledge about your subject and the common attitudes toward it.* By now, for instance, everyone has heard about global warming. You can assume general awareness. However, knowledge of the science is not widespread. You'll need to explain what global warming is and how it's related to human activities. Because attitudes toward it range from casual dismissal to taking it as the biggest problem we face, you must be clear about your own attitude and communicate it forcefully. You can't assume that your audience either understands global warming or is willing to take action that requires self-sacrifice or even inconvenience. Consequently, a substantial portion of your paper will be devoted to establishing need.

In contrast, sometimes there's general acceptance of the need to act when you think no compelling need exists. This situation is common. Politicians and news media, for instance, often pump up minor nuisances into major problems. Soon many people are saying, "We've got to do something." Sometimes the action they want or can be persuaded to accept will do more damage than doing nothing at all. When you write about such a topic, obviously your paper will be devoted to showing that no need exists.

No matter what situation your topic requires you to face, thinking about need—the motivation for action—comes first. The temptation is to think that everyone sees the need as you do, which is rarely the case. Take the time to think through need. It will always be time well spent.

Choosing a Readership

Because we have to consider common knowledge and attitudes about our topic in thinking about need, readers are already in the picture. Such thinking, however, isn't specific enough to envision a readership.

Begin by eliminating the vague, nearly useless concept of "general public." Even when people say they are writing for the general public, they are actually writing for a more limited readership. Also ignore readers who agree with you already. There's nothing to gain by persuading the already persuaded. Finally, you can eliminate readerships so strongly opposed to your position that nothing you could say has a chance of reaching them.

Writing Persuasively: Key Points

The following list summarizes pages 273–281, "Drafting a Persuasive Essay."

1. Choose a **specific** audience whose characteristics you **know well** and who have some capacity for **taking action** or **influencing events.**

2. Identify your audience early in the process.

3. In your case, show **need** and emphasize **urgency.**

4. Your readers must feel that you are **well-informed, confident, fair, honest,** and have their **interests** and **values** in mind. Avoid ridicule of other positions. Recognize and respond to the main objections your readers are likely to have to your proposal.

5. Arouse emotions you genuinely feel. Concentrate on those feelings your audience may lack or not feel strongly enough.

6. Favor a **middle style** for persuasion, conversational without being too familiar or informal.

There's nothing to gain by wasting effort trying to persuade those who won't listen.

What's left? Readerships that are

- *uncommitted*—On most topics, there are people who have not yet formed an opinion.

- *weakly supportive*—There will also be people inclined toward your position but who lack sufficient knowledge and arguments to agree strongly enough to take action.

- *opposed but still open to reason*—For most topics and most efforts to persuade, this is the prime target group. King, for instance, did not try to appeal to white racists but to church leaders who opposed his methods but not his goals.

These categories are useful for thinking about readerships but still not specific enough. Consider two other criteria. First, who is best able to take action or influence outcomes? If you want some change in a local public school policy, for example, parents, especially those active in parent-teacher organizations, may be the best target. But if you want change in public school policy at the state level, probably legislators should be your target readership. Second, among the groups that can take action or influence those that can, which group do you know the best? Obviously, you can appeal most effectively to people you know well.

Selecting a readership demands at least as much careful thought as pondering the need for action. *People who want to persuade go wrong most often by not identifying the most appropriate readership or by not keeping an appropriate readership firmly in mind as they compose.* Therefore, try to identify your readership early in the process. Of course, you can change your mind later, but doing so will require rewriting. Devoting time to discovering your intended audience early in the process can save time and effort later.

◎◎ FOLLOWING THROUGH

For a persuasive argument you are about to write, determine your audience; that is, decide who can make a difference with respect to this issue and what they can do to make a difference. In your writer's notebook, respond to the questions "Who is my audience?" and "What are our differences?" (refer to the lists of questions on pages 248–249 to help formulate answers). Use your responses to write an audience profile.   •

STUDENT SAMPLE Need and Audience

Elizabeth Baxley's persuasive essay, "Be a Parent, Not a Friend," appears on pages 281–284 of this chapter. At the time the paper was assigned, local newspapers were covering the resolution of a dispute that had taken place at her high school while she was in her senior year. Her notebook entry shows her exploring the need for action prompted by the incident behind the dispute.

Elizabeth's notebook entry:

My high school has been in the news because of an incident that took place while I was a senior on the cheerleading squad. Several members of the squad were acting wild and even posed for pictures at a condom store while wearing their cheerleading outfits. Then our coach was fired because she tried to discipline them. It's been in the news lately because the fired coach sued the principal. I feel ashamed about the bad publicity for my school. I would like to write to keep this kind of thing from happening again—at any school. You could say it is the girls' fault for acting out, but I know these girls and I think the problem is a lack of parenting. Too many parents are allowing kids to get away with too much. Guidance isn't happening because parents want to be friends rather than parents.

Elizabeth's audience profile:

The audience for this paper will be parents of high school children. Readers could be both mothers and fathers, but I'll aim the paper more toward the mothers because I've observed them firsthand. The readers for my paper are typical mothers in my upper-middle-class suburb. They are into looking young, buying fashionable clothes, and shopping with their daughters. They want a close relationship with their daughters; they want their daughters to confide in them as if they were peers. They think that their children will love them if they are permissive and will hate them if they discipline them. Many of these mothers don't work; they are in an upper-level bracket because of their husbands' income. Having money they don't earn might make them think that they don't have to worry about preparing their children for the hard realities of life. These mothers know that they should be good parents, but they need more motivation to actually do what needs to be done.

Discovering the Resources of Appeal

Before and during drafting, you will be making choices about

How to formulate a case and support it with research

How to present yourself

How to arouse your readers' emotions

How to make the style of your writing contribute to the argument's effectiveness

All these decisions will be influenced by the audience you want to persuade.

Appealing through Reason

One difference between convincing and persuading is that persuasion argues for a course of action. Therefore, (1) show that there is a need for action; (2) show urgency—we must act and act now; and show that what you're proposing satisfies the need.

Sometimes your goal will be to persuade your audience *not* to act because what they want to do is wrong or inappropriate. Need is still the issue. The difference, obviously, is to show that no need exists or that awaiting further developments will enable a proposed action to work better.

◎◎ FOLLOWING THROUGH

Prepare a brief of your argument (see Chapter 8). Be ready to present an overview of your audience and to defend your brief, either before the class or in small groups. Pay special attention to how well the argument establishes a need to act (or shows that there is no need). •

Appealing through Character

Readers should feel that you are

Well-informed

Confident, honest, and sincere

Fair and balanced in dealing with other positions

Sensitive to their concerns and objections

Sympathetic to what they value

What can you do to communicate these impressions? You must earn them. There are no shortcuts.

To seem well-informed, you must be well-informed. This requires digging into the topic, thinking about it carefully, researching it thoroughly, and taking good notes. This work will enable you to

Make passing references to events and people connected with the issue now or recently

Create a context or provide background information, which may include comments on the history of the question or issue

Produce sufficient high-quality evidence to back up contentions

Draw upon personal experience when it has played a role in determining your position, and don't be reluctant to reveal your own stake in the issue. Make your case boldly, qualifying it as little as possible.

Represent other positions accurately and fairly; then present evidence that refutes those positions or show that the reasoning is inadequate or inconsistent. Indicate agreement with parts of other opinions when they are consistent with your own. Partial agreement can play a major role in overcoming reader resistance.

STUDENT SAMPLE Elizabeth Baxley's Brief

Claim: Parents must take an active role in disciplining their children.

Reason: Children actually want parents to make and enforce rules.

Evidence: "Everyday Rules" from PBS Web site

Evidence: My own family

Reason: When parents don't assume authority, kids will have unrealistic ideas about their own power at home and at school.

Evidence: Twenge on kids with too much power in decisions.

Evidence: The incident at my high school.

Reason: Children suffer the consequence when parents don't act like parents.

Evidence: Girls from my high school

Evidence: Levine on how kids will not be able to meet demands of adult life.

Note that Elizabeth's brief "blocks out" (separates into clear, distinct points) what she intends to say. No matter how closely related they are, *don't allow your points to run together.* If they do, your reader won't be able to detect or follow a sequence of reasons that justify the claim you're defending. Note also that Elizabeth uses both statements from experts and personal experience as evidence, mixing the two well. The experts confirm her outlook, whereas the personal experience makes her stance more concrete and shows her firsthand knowledge of the consequences of bad parenting.

FOLLOWING THROUGH

The "Following Through" assignment on page 275 asked you to prepare an audience profile and explore your key areas of difference. Now use the results to think through how you can appeal to these readers. Use the questions on page 249 to help establish commonality. •

Appealing to Emotion

As in King's essay, argument is the star performer, and emotional appeal plays a supporting role, taking center stage only occasionally. Consequently, you need to decide

What emotions to arouse and by what means

How frequent and intense the appeals should be

Where to include them

The first of these decisions is usually the easiest. Arouse emotions that you genuinely feel; what moved you should move your readers. If your emotions come from direct experience, use it for concrete descriptive detail, as King did.

Deciding how often, at what length, and how intensely to make emotional appeals presents a greater challenge. Much depends on the topic, the audience, and your own range and intensity of feeling.

As always in persuasion, your audience matters most. What attitudes and feelings do they have already? Which of these help your case? Which hinder it? Emphasize those feelings consistent with your position.

Ask also, What does my audience not feel or not feel strongly enough? King decided that his readers' greatest emotional deficit was their inability to feel what victims of racial discrimination feel—hence paragraph 14, the most intense emotional appeal in the letter.

How often and where to include emotional appeals are important considerations. Take your shots sparingly, getting as much as you can each time. Use them to lead into or clinch a point.

◎◎ FOLLOWING THROUGH

After you have a first draft of your essay, reread it with an eye to emotional appeal. Highlight the places where you have sought to arouse the audience's emotions.

Decide if you need more attention to emotional appeal. Consider how you could make each appeal more effective and whether each appeal is located well.   •

Strategies of Appeal in the Student Sample Essay "Be a Parent, Not a Friend"

We wager that you found Elizabeth Baxley's essay persuasive. Most people do because common sense tells them that parents must be parents. But did she reach her target audience, those parents who want to be their children's friends? If so, how did she do it?

As we've seen, Elizabeth had no problem identifying need or audience. The difficulty, rather, was how she viewed the audience she hoped to persuade.

In notebook entries and a first draft, the challenge became clear: How could she reach a readership she saw as almost unreachable—an audience whose behavior seemed to her so completely irrational and misguided that nothing she could say would make any difference?

She began with satire, using a movie that exposes the Mrs. Georges of the world to ridicule. She hoped to accomplish several purposes this way. First, she wanted parents not living up to their role to recognize themselves. Second, she wanted them to admit that how they behave is indefensible. And third, because the purpose of satire is to move deviant behavior toward a desired norm, she saw her opening as strongly implying the action she wanted from her audience.

Undeniably, as she realized, the opening is risky. It's not usually good strategy to ridicule the audience you're trying to persuade. However, she could discover no better way to appeal initially. Furthermore, she followed it with a case that relies on evidence drawn from expert opinion and her own experience, a case that shows erring parents the serious damage they are doing to the children they profess to love. So the ridicule stops after the opening, and rational appeal dominates the rest of the essay.

Insofar as Elizabeth's audience can be reached at all, we think her approach has a chance. Do you agree? If not, how would you try to appeal to her audience?

Appealing through Style

Stylistic choices are part of drafting, but refining them belongs to revision. In the first draft, set an appropriate level of formality. Most persuasive prose is like dignified conversation—the way people talk when they respect one another but do not know each other well. We can see some of the hallmarks of persuasive prose in King's letter:

- It uses *I, you,* and *we.*
- It avoids technical jargon and slang.
- It inclines toward strong action verbs.
- It chooses examples and images familiar to the reader.

These and other features characterize the **middle style.**

As we discovered, King varies his style from section to section, depending on his purpose. He sounds formal in his introduction (paragraphs 1–5), where he wants to establish authority, but more informal when he narrates the difficulties he and other black leaders had in their efforts to negotiate with city leaders (paragraphs 6–9).

Just as King matches style with function, so you need to vary your style based on what each part of your essay is doing. This variation creates *pacing,* the sense of overall rhythm. As you write your first draft, concern yourself with matching style to purpose from section to section, depending

Reader's Checklist for Revising a Persuasive Essay

The following list will direct you to specific features of good persuasion. Exchange drafts with another student and help each other. After you have revised your draft, use the suggestions in the appendix to edit for style and check for errors at the sentence level.

- Read the audience profile. Then read the draft, taking the role of the target audience. Mark the essay's divisions. You may also want to number paragraphs so that you can refer to them easily.

- Inspect the case first. Underline the thesis and mark the reasons. Note any reasons that need more evidence or other support, such as examples.

- Evaluate the plan. Are the reasons well ordered? Does the argument build to a strong conclusion? Can you envision a better arrangement? Make suggestions, referring to paragraphs by number.

- Persuasion requires the writer to present him- or herself as worthy of the reader's trust and respect. Reread the draft, marking specific places where the writer has sought identification from the target audience. Has the writer made an effort to find common ground with readers by using any of the ideas listed on page 249? Suggest improvements.

- Persuasion also requires emotional appeal through concrete examples and imagery, analogies and metaphors, first-person reporting, quotations, and so on. Locate the emotional appeals. Are they successful? What improvements can you suggest?

- Examine the draft for any instances of

  Poor transitions between sentences or paragraphs

  Wordy passages, especially those containing the passive voice (see "Editing for Clarity and Conciseness" in the appendix)

  Awkward sentences

  Poor diction—that is, incorrect or inappropriate words

- After studying the argument, ask whether you are sure what action the writer wants or expects from the audience. Has he or she succeeded in persuading the audience? Why or why not?

on whether you are providing background information, telling a story, developing a reason in your case, mounting an emotional appeal, and so on. Save detailed attention to style for editing a second or third draft.

FOLLOWING THROUGH

When you have completed your draft, select one paragraph which you think is stylistically effective. Share the paragraph with your class, describing your choices as we have done with passages from King's letter. •

 **FOLLOWING THROUGH**

Read the student essay that begins below, and be ready to discuss its effectiveness as persuasion. Build your evaluation around the suggestions listed in the "Reader's Checklist for Revising a Persuasive Essay," opposite.

www.mhhe.com/**crusius**   For further writing coverage, including information on writing in the traditional modes, visit:

Writing > Writing Tutors

STUDENT SAMPLE: An Essay to Persuade

Be a Parent, Not a Friend
Elizabeth Baxley

Many moms are dropping the parenting role for a much more glamorous one—a role full of Juicy Couture track suits accessorized with a mini-Chihuahua. They lack the ability to act their age, which means being a parent. Instead, they live through their children's social life. The recent movie <u>Mean Girls</u> makes fun of these irritating mothers with the character Mrs. George, who thinks that she is one of the gang.

"Hey, hey, hey. How are my best girlfriends?" asks Mrs. George shortly after serving mocktails to her daughter's friends. "Hey, you guys! Happy hour is from four to six!"

Cady, one of her daughter's friends, asks, "Um, is there alcohol in this?"

Mrs. George replies, "Oh, God, honey, no! What kind of mother do you think I am? Why, do you want a little bit? Because if you're going to drink, I'd rather you do it in the house."

The scene worsens when Mrs. George assures her daughter's friends: "There are <u>no</u> rules in the house. I'm not like a regular mom—I'm a cool mom. . . . I'm a cool mom! Right, Regina?"

However, Mrs. George's desperate attempt to be one of the gang only irritates Regina, who has no respect for her mother. Why should she? Mrs. George doesn't deserve it. Regina should be the kid, not Mrs. George.

Although this scene is amusing, the growing problem is not a laughing matter. As a recent high school graduate from an affluent neighborhood, I have witnessed too many of these instances. Many

5

www.mhhe.com/**crusius**

For many additional examples of student writing, go to:

Writing

parents nowadays don't know how to handle their role. Rather than instill values, they just want to be their child's friend. Robert Billingham, an associate professor of human development and family studies at Indiana University, says the problem occurs when "parents are no longer eager to be 'parents.' They want to love and guide their children as a trusted friend" (Twenge 30).

Many parents don't understand that their child wants a parent—one that enforces rules. The Web site of <u>Mr. Rogers' Neighborhood</u>, a show known for its dedication to teaching young children important lessons, discusses this desire for structure: "Even though children may test the limits, they really do feel safer when they know what the rules are—when they've been told by people they love what to do" (Hooper). They want to be part of a family that has traditional roles, one with structure, because structure brings security.

I was thankful (and often envied) for my parents, who were able to provide the guidance I needed. Rules are a part of that process. Ever since I was a little girl, I have loved my parents (despite my resentment at times) because they always knew what I needed even when I didn't. I was taught what is right and wrong. My house had curfews, discipline, and non-negotiable rules. Boundaries allowed me to grow up safely. The kids my age who were also brought up well come from homes with this sort of structure. I am thankful because my parents have prepared me and kept me safe. They always had my best interests at heart.

My view isn't shared by everyone. A group of teens and their 10 families were surveyed for a recent newspaper article. The survey found that "forty percent of teens see their opinions as 'very important' in making family decisions." There was one teenage girl who had actually helped her father select his new job (Twenge 30-31). How can someone in their teens make such a decision? Her father was allowing her to have authority he should assert.

I am dismayed by the frequent encounters I have had with out-of-control teenagers because their parents simply exerted no authority. I was a member of the varsity cheerleading squad throughout high school. Each new year brought a different coach. The school joked that the position was cursed, but the truth was that no one could deal with the insubordination from the girls. Although many of my fellow teammates showed no disrespect to our coach, the second the coach attempted to discipline us, all hell broke loose among some who were not used to being disciplined. Many of the girls had never had to follow any rules in their homes, so they did not know how to follow rules at school. The word "no" was incomprehensible—even listening wasn't necessary.

This year's coach, Mrs. Ward, resigned after being told by the principal, who happened to have a daughter on the team, that she was not allowed to discipline the squad. Mrs. Ward was the first coach to enforce a demerit system. It included punishment for misconduct ranging from skipping classes to representing the school poorly. Mrs. Ward suspended one group of girls for taking sexually suggestive pictures in their cheerleading uniforms in front of the Condom Sense store and then posting them on the Net. However, these attempts at punishment were overturned by the principal, whose daughter was one of the offenders.

It got to the point where there were no rules for our squad. The UIL contracts stating that we would not drink or do drugs were violated without penalty. In the case of the Condom Sense photographs, the guilty party's suspension was reduced from 30 days to only 15. The girls only had to sit out one game. One girl's mother even hired a lawyer to sue Mrs. Ward. Although she agreed that what her daughter did was wrong, she didn't think that it was the coach's job to discipline her daughter. What kind of message was she sending her daughter? These parents were not teaching their children that actions have consequences. They shielded them from the punishment they deserved.

The time will come when parents can't shield their children any longer. Eventually, the girls will pay for their parents' poor job. Of the girls on my squad, some didn't even want to go to college because they had never had the discipline to excel in school. One girl hoped to attend SMU but didn't even apply because of poor grades. She also worked at the country club tennis shop with me, but she was fired because she couldn't follow a few simple rules. For instance, she would leave work while still on the clock. Other cheerleaders were into alcohol, drugs, and sex. None of them understood why any of this was unacceptable because their parents never taught them.

Children need to learn how to live in the real world. Mel Levine, 15 M.D., a child and adolescent development expert, says, "The adult world is full of nonnegotiable expectations. Grown-ups, for example, must fulfill the demands of their jobs and pay their bills on time" (Asnes 97). There will be penalties for careless, irresponsible behavior. So, do your kids a favor and teach them how to be successful. "Teens gain the tools they need to meet [real world] demands by living up to their parents' expectations at home, where people who love them can help them when they fail," says Dr. Levine (Asnes 97). If not for that reason, then do it for your child's protection. You only get one chance with a precious life. It is in your hands. Teens are going to try to push the limits to get away with as much as possible. It is your job to make sure that they are making healthy decisions. Don't just ignore a problem because it is easier than dealing with it.

It is up to parents to instill respect in their children. You must take an active role in your children's lives. Most importantly, you must be their parent, not their friend. Be a role model, someone your kids can look up to. Be someone they can learn from. Do it for your child's safety. Do it for your child's future.

www.mhhe.com/**crusius**

For an electronic tool that helps create properly formatted works-cited pages, go to:

Research > Bibliomaker

Works Cited

Asnes, Marion. "When Your Teen Wants You to Say No." <u>Good Housekeeping</u>. Apr. 2005: 94–97.

"Everyday Rules and Limits." <u>PBS Kids.com</u>. 13 November 2006 <http://pbskids.org/rogers/parentsteachers/theme/1541_t_art.html>.

"Memorable Quotes from Mean Girls (2004)." <u>Internet Movie Database</u>. 15 November 2006 <http://www.imdb.com/title/tt0377092/quotes>.

Twenge, Jean M. <u>Generation Me: Why Today's Young Americans Are More Confident, Assertive, Entitled—And More Miserable Than Ever Before</u>. New York: Free Press, 2006.

Resolving Conflict: Arguing to Mediate

Private citizens can avoid the big conflicts that concern politicians and activist groups: debates over gay marriage, abortion, taxes, foreign policy, and so on. However, we cannot hide from all conflict. Family members have different preferences about budgeting, major purchases, where to go on vacation, and much else. Furthermore, if you care about what goes on beyond your front door, you will find conflict close to home. The school down the street, for example, wants to expand its athletic stadium. Some parents support the decision because their children play sports at the school. Others oppose it because they think the expansion will bring more traffic, noise, and bright lights to the neighborhood.

One way to resolve conflict is through reasoned arguments. The chapters on convincing and persuading show how appeals to logic and emotion can change minds. But what if we cannot change someone's mind and can't impose our will in other ways?

Some conflicts don't have to be resolved. The Republican husband can live happily with the Democratic wife. Other conflicts are resolved by compromise. We can go to the mountains this year, the seashore the next. Compromise is better than shouting matches, but it does not result in a common understanding.

Characteristics of Mediation

1. Aims to **resolve conflict** between opposing and usually **hardened** positions, often because action of some kind must be taken.

2. Aims to reduce hostility and promote understanding between or among conflicting parties; **preserving human relationships and promoting communication** are paramount.

3. Like inquiry, mediation **involves dialogue** and requires that one understand all positions and strive for an **open mind.**

4. Like convincing, mediation involves making a case that **appeals to all parties in the controversy.**

5. Like persuasion, mediation depends on the **good character** of the negotiator and on sharing **values and feelings.**

6. Mediation depends on conflicting parties' desire to **find solutions to overcome counterproductive stalemates.**

Essentially, mediation comes into play when convincing and persuading have resulted in sharply differing viewpoints. The task is first to understand the positions of all parties involved and second to uncover a mediating position capable of producing consensus and a reduction in hostility.

This chapter presents mediation as argument whose aim is to resolve conflict by thinking more critically about it. People too often see disputes uncritically by simplifying them to their extreme positions, pro and con. The news media does little to help us see conflicts as complex and many-sided, with related issues and shades of gray. *Mediation aims to move disputants beyond the polarized thinking that makes conflicts impossible to resolve.*

MEDIATION AND THE OTHER AIMS OF ARGUMENT

Mediation uses the other three aims of argument: inquiry, convincing, and persuading. Like inquiry, it open-mindedly examines the range of positions on an issue. Mediation requires knowledge of case structure. The mediator must scrutinize the arguments offered by all sides. A mediatory essay must also present a well-reasoned case of its own. Finally, like persuasion, mediation considers the values, beliefs, and assumptions of the people who hold the conflicting positions. Mediators must appeal to all sides and project a character all sides will trust and find attractive.

President Ronald Reagan and Premier Mikhail Gorbachev at the Reykjavik summit, 1986. They met to negotiate about arms control and human rights.

In short, mediation requires the mediator to rise above a dispute, including his or her own preferences, to see what is reasonable and right in conflicting positions. The mediator's best asset is wisdom.

THE PROCESS OF MEDIATION

Mediation takes place more often in conversation, through dialogue with the opposing sides, than in writing. But essays can mediate by attempting to argue for middle ground in a conflict. Whether it eventually takes the form of an essay or a dialogue, mediation begins where all arguments should—with inquiry.

MEDIATION AND ROGERIAN ARGUMENT

Arguing to mediate resembles an approach to communication developed by a psychologist, Carl Rogers (1902–1987). In "Communication: Its Blocking and Its Facilitation," he urged people in conflict to listen carefully and with empathy to each other as a first step toward resolving differences. The second step is to go beyond listening in an effort to understand one another's background, the context in which viewpoints take root and grow into hardened positions. Finally, a third step is for each person involved in a dispute to state the position of his or her opponents in a way the opponents can agree is accurate and fair. The total approach reduces misunderstanding and helps to clarify what the genuine points of difference are, thus opening up the potential to resolve conflict.

In their textbook *Rhetoric: Discovery and Change* (1970), Richard Young, Alton Becker, and Kenneth Pike outlined four stages for Rogerian argument:

1. An introduction to the problem and a demonstration that the opponent's position is understood

2. A statement of the contexts in which the opponent's position may be valid

3. A statement of the writer's position, including the contexts in which it is valid

4. A statement of how the opponent's position would benefit if he were to adopt elements of the writer's position. If the writer can show that the positions complement each other, that each supplies what the other lacks, so much the better.[1]

Our approach to mediation draws on Rogerian argument. As a mediator, rather than a participant in a dispute, you'll need to consider the validity of opposing positions, including the personal backgrounds of the people involved. In light of these backgrounds, you look for what is good and right in each position.

Rather than face-to-face verbal arguments, in this chapter you will be reading written arguments on a controversial issue and exploring these arguments to uncover exactly how and why their authors disagree. Instead of sitting around a table with parties in conflict as mediators do, you'll write a mediatory essay proposing a point of view designed to appeal to both sides.

A Conflict to Mediate

The United States is a nation of immigrants, but recently the immigrant population includes a wider array of races, ethnicities, religions, and cultures than in the past. The result is a population less white and less Protestant. Should we become a multicultural nation or maintain a single culture based on the original northern European settlers?

Some people argue that the influx of diverse people should have no impact on the traditional Eurocentric identity of America. According to this position, America has a distinctive and superior culture, traceable to the Puritan settlers and based more broadly on Western civilization. This culture is the source of our nation's strength. To keep it strong, newcomers need to assimilate, adopting its values and beliefs. In other words, people holding this position advocate the melting-pot metaphor. Because they believe cultural differences should dissolve as new immigrants become "true Americans," they oppose multiculturalism. We have chosen a recent essay by Roger Kimball,

---

[1]This summary of the four stages comes from Douglas Brent, "Rogerian Rhetoric: An Alternative to Traditional Rhetoric," *Argument Revisited, Argument Redefined: Negotiating Meaning in the Composition Classroom,* ed. Barbara Emmel, Paula Resch, and Deborah Tenney (Thousand Oaks, CA: Sage, 1996) <http://www.acs.ucalgary.ca/~dabrent/art/rogchap.html>.

an art critic and editor at the conservative journal *The New Criterion,* to represent the assimilationist position.

Opponents argue that newcomers should preserve their distinctive cultures, taking pride in being Mexican, Chinese, African, and so on. Their metaphor is the mosaic, with each culture remaining distinct but contributing to the whole, like the tiles in a mosaic. We have chosen an essay by Elizabeth Martínez to represent the multiculturalist perspective. Martínez is a Chicana writer and an activist on issues of social justice, including racism and women's rights.

Understanding the Positions

Any attempt to mediate positions requires an understanding of opposing cases. Printed below are the two arguments, followed by our analyses.

Institutionalizing Our Demise: America vs. Multiculturalism

ROGER KIMBALL

The following abridged article appeared in *The New Criterion* (June 2004). Roger Kimball's books include *The Long March: How the Cultural Revolution of the 1960s Changed America* (Encounter, 2000) and *Tenured Radicals: How Politics Has Corrupted Our Higher Education* (HarperCollins, 1990).

There is no room in this country for hyphenated Americanism. When I refer to hyphenated Americans, I do not refer to naturalized Americans. Some of the very best Americans I have ever known were naturalized Americans, Americans born abroad. But a hyphenated American is not an American at all. This is just as true of the man who puts "native" before the hyphen as of the man who puts German or Irish or English or French before the hyphen.

—Theodore Roosevelt, 1915

It is often said that the terrorist attacks of September 11 precipitated a new resolve throughout the nation. There is some truth to that. Certainly, the extraordinary bravery of the firefighters and other rescue personnel in New York and Washington, D.C., provided an invigorating spectacle—as did Todd "Let's roll" Beamer and his fellow passengers on United Airlines Flight 93. Having learned from their cell phones what had happened at the World Trade Center and the Pentagon, Beamer and his fellows rushed and overpowered the terrorists who had hijacked their plane. As a result, the plane crashed on a remote Pennsylvania farm instead of on Pennsylvania Avenue. Who knows how many lives their sacrifice saved?

The widespread sense of condign outrage—of horror leavened by anger and elevated by resolve—testified to a renewed sense of national purpose and identity after 9/11. Attacked, many Americans suddenly (if temporarily) rediscovered the virtue of patriotism. At the beginning of his remarkable book *Who Are We? The Challenges to America's National Identity* (2004), the Harvard political scientist

Samuel Huntington recalls a certain block on Charles Street in Boston. At one time, American flags flew in front of a U.S. Post Office and a liquor store. Then the Post Office stopped displaying the flag, so on September 11, 2001, the flag was flying only in front of the liquor store. Within two weeks, seventeen American flags decorated that block of Charles Street, in addition to a huge flag suspended over the street close by. "With their country under attack," Huntington notes, "Charles Street denizens rediscovered their nation and identified themselves with it."

Was that rediscovery anything more than a momentary passion? Huntington reports that within a few months, the flags on Charles Street began to disappear. By the time the first anniversary rolled around in September 2002, only four were left flying. True, that is four times more than were there on September 10, 2001, but it is less than a quarter of the number that populated Charles Street at the end of September 2001.

There are similar anecdotes from around the country—an access of flag-waving followed by a relapse into indifference. Does it mean that the sudden upsurge of patriotism in the weeks following 9/11 was only, as it were, skin deep? Or perhaps it merely testifies to the fact that a sense of permanent emergency is difficult to maintain, especially in the absence of fresh attacks. Is our sense of ourselves as Americans patent only when challenged? "Does it," Huntington asks, "take an Osama bin Laden . . . to make us realize that we are Americans? If we do not experience recurring destructive attacks, will we return to the fragmentation and eroded Americanism before September 11?"

One hopes that the answer is No. . . . But I fear that for every schoolchild 5
standing at attention for the National Anthem, there is a teacher or lawyer or judge or politician or ACLU employee militating against the hegemony of the dominant culture, the insupportable intrusion of white, Christian, "Eurocentric" values into the curriculum, the school pageant, the town green, etc., etc. . . .

The threat shows itself in many ways, from culpable complacency to the corrosive imperatives of "multiculturalism" and political correctness. . . . In essence, as Huntington notes, multiculturalism is "anti-European civilization. . . . It is basically an anti-Western ideology.". . . [W]herever the imperatives of multiculturalism have touched the curriculum, they have left broad swaths of anti-Western attitudinizing competing for attention with quite astonishing historical blindness. Courses on minorities, women's issues, the Third World proliferate; the teaching of mainstream history slides into oblivion. "The mood," Arthur Schlesinger wrote in *The Disuniting of America* (1992), his excellent book on the depredations of multiculturalism, "is one of divesting Americans of the sinful European inheritance and seeking redemptive infusions from non-Western cultures."

A profound ignorance of the milestones of American culture is one predictable result of this mood. The statistics have become proverbial. Huntington quotes one poll from the 1990s showing that while 90 percent of Ivy League students could identify Rosa Parks, only 25 percent could identify the author of the words "government of the people, by the people, for the people." (Yes, it's the Gettysburg Address.) In a 1999 survey, 40 percent of seniors at fifty-five top colleges could not say within half a century when the Civil War was fought. Another study found that more high school students knew who Harriet Tubman was than knew that Washington commanded the American army in the revolution or that Abraham Lincoln wrote the Emancipation Proclamation. Doubtless you have your own favorite horror story.

But multiculturalism is not only an academic phenomenon. The attitudes it fosters have profound social as well as intellectual consequences. One consequence has been a sharp rise in the phenomenon of immigration without—or with only partial—assimilation: a dangerous demographic trend that threatens American identity in the most basic way. These various agents of dissolution are also elements in a wider culture war: the contest to define how we live and what counts as the good in the good life. Anti-Americanism occupies such a prominent place on the agenda of the culture wars precisely because the traditional values of American identity—articulated by the Founders and grounded in a commitment to individual liberty and public virtue—are deeply at odds with the radical, de-civilizing tenets of the "multiculturalist" enterprise.

To get a sense of what has happened to the institution of American identity, compare Robert Frost's performance at John F. Kennedy's inauguration in 1961 with Maya Angelou's performance thirty-two years later. As Huntington reminds us, Frost spoke of the "heroic deeds" of America's founding, an event, he said, that with "God's approval" ushered in "a new order of the ages." By contrast, Maya Angelou never mentioned the words "America" or "American." Instead, she identified twenty-seven ethnic or religious groups that had suffered repression because of America's "armed struggles for profit," "cynicism," and "brutishness.". . .

A favorite weapon in the armory of multiculturalism is the lowly hyphen. When 10 we speak of an African-American or Mexican-American or Asian-American these days, the aim is not descriptive but deconstructive. There is a polemical edge to it, a provocation. The hyphen does not mean "American, but hailing at some point in the past from someplace else." It means "only provisionally American: my allegiance is divided at best.". . . The multicultural passion for hyphenation is not simply a fondness for syntactical novelty. It also bespeaks a commitment to the centrifugal force of anti-American tribalism. The division marked by the hyphen in African-American (say) denotes a political stand. It goes hand-in-hand with other items on the index of liberal desiderata—the redistributive impulse behind efforts at "affirmative action," for example. . . .

Multiculturalism and "affirmative action" are allies in the assault on the institution of American identity. As such, they oppose the traditional understanding of what it means to be an American—an understanding hinted at in 1782 by the French-born American farmer J. Hector St. John de Crèvecoeur in his famous image of America as a country in which "individuals of all nations are melted into a new race of men." This crucible of American identity, this "melting pot," has two aspects. The negative aspect involves disassociating oneself from the cultural imperatives of one's country of origin. One sheds a previous identity before assuming a new one. One might preserve certain local habits and tastes, but they are essentially window-dressing. In essence one has left the past behind in order to become an American citizen.

The positive aspect of advancing the melting pot involves embracing the substance of American culture. The 1795 code for citizenship lays out some of the formal requirements.

> I do solemnly swear (1) to support the Constitution of the United States; (2) to renounce and abjure absolutely and entirely all allegiance and fidelity to any foreign prince, potentate, state, or sovereignty of whom or which the applicant was before a subject or citizen; (3) to support and defend the Constitution and the laws of the United States against all enemies, foreign and domestic; (4) to bear true faith and allegiance to the same; and (5) (A) to bear arms on behalf of the United States when required by law, or (B) to perform noncombatant service in the Armed Forces of the United States when required by law. . . .

For over two hundred years, this oath had been required of those wishing to become citizens. In 2003, Huntington tells us, federal bureaucrats launched a campaign to rewrite and weaken it.

I shall say more about what constitutes the substance of American identity in a moment. For now, I want to underscore the fact that this project of Americanization has been an abiding concern since the time of the Founders. "We must see our people more Americanized," John Jay declared in the 1780s. Jefferson concurred. Teddy Roosevelt repeatedly championed the idea that American culture, the "crucible in which all the new types are melted into one," was "shaped from 1776 to 1789, and our nationality was definitely fixed in all its essentials by the men of Washington's day."

It is often said that America is a nation of immigrants. In fact, as Huntington points out, America is a country that was initially a country of *settlers*. Settlers precede immigrants and make their immigration possible. The culture of those mostly English-speaking, predominantly Anglo-Protestant settlers defined American culture. Their efforts came to fruition with the generation of Franklin, Washington, Jefferson, Hamilton, and Madison. The Founders are so denominated because they founded, they inaugurated a state. Immigrants were those who came later, who came from elsewhere, and who became American by embracing the Anglophone culture of the original settlers. The English language, the rule of law, respect for individual rights, the industriousness and piety that flowed from the Protestant work ethic—these were central elements in the culture disseminated by the Founders. And these were among the qualities embraced by immigrants when they became Americans. "Throughout American history," Huntington notes, "people who were not white Anglo-Saxon Protestants have become Americans by adopting America's Anglo-Protestant culture and political values. This benefited them and the country."

Justice Louis Brandeis outlined the pattern in 1919. Americanization, he said, means that the immigrant "adopts the clothes, the manners, and the customs generally prevailing here . . . substitutes for his mother tongue the English language" and comes "into complete harmony with our ideals and aspirations and cooperate[s] with us for their attainment." Until the 1960s, the Brandeis model mostly prevailed. Protestant, Catholic, and Jewish groups, understanding that assimilation was the best ticket to stability and social and economic success, eagerly aided in the task of integrating their charges into American society. 15

The story is very different today. In America, there is a dangerous new tide of immigration from Asia, a variety of Muslim countries, and Latin America, especially from Mexico. The tide is new not only chronologically but also in substance. First, there is the sheer matter of numbers. More than 2,200,000 legal immigrants came to the U.S. from Mexico in the 1990s alone. The number of illegal Mexican immigrants is staggering. So is their birth rate. Altogether there are more than 8 million Mexicans in the U.S. Some parts of the Southwest are well on their way to becoming what Victor Davis Hanson calls "Mexifornia," "the strange society that is emerging as the result of a demographic and cultural revolution like no other in our times." A professor of Chicano Studies at the University of New Mexico gleefully predicts that by 2080 parts of the Southwest United States and Northern Mexico will join to form a new country, "La Republica del Norte."

The problem is not only one of numbers, though. Earlier immigrants made—and were helped and goaded by the ambient culture to make—concerted efforts to assimilate. Important pockets of these new immigrants are not assimilating, not learning English, not becoming or thinking of themselves primarily as Americans. The effect of these developments on American identity is disastrous and potentially irreversible.

Such developments are abetted by the left-wing political and educational elites of this country, whose dominant theme is the perfidy of traditional American values. Hence the passion for multiculturalism and the ideal of ethnic hyphenation that goes with it. This has done immense damage in schools and colleges as well as in the population at large. By removing the obligation to master English, multiculturalism condemns whole subpopulations to the status of permanent second-class citizens. . . .

As if in revenge for this injustice, however, multiculturalism also weakens the social bonds of the community at large. The price of imperfect assimilation is imperfect loyalty. Take the movement for bilingualism. Whatever it intended in theory, in practice it means *not* mastering English. It has notoriously left its supposed beneficiaries essentially monolingual, often semi-lingual. The only *bi* involved is a passion for bifurcation, which is fed by the accumulated resentments instilled by the anti-American multicultural orthodoxy. Every time you call directory assistance or some large corporation and are told "Press One for English" and "Para español oprime el numero dos" it is another small setback for American identity. . . .

We stand at a crossroads. The future of America hangs in the balance. Huntington outlines several possible courses that the country might take, from the loss of our core culture to an attempt to revive the "discarded and discredited racial and ethnic concepts" that, in part, defined pre-mid-twentieth century America. Huntington argues for another alternative. If we are to preserve our identity as a nation we need to preserve the core values that defined that identity. This is a point that the political philosopher Patrick, Lord Devlin made in his book *The Enforcement of Morals* (1965):

> [S]ociety means a community of ideas; without shared ideas on politics, morals, and ethics no society can exist. Each one of us has ideas about what is good and what is evil; they cannot be kept private from the society in which we live. If men and

women try to create a society in which there is no fundamental agreement about good and evil they will fail; if having based it upon a common set of core values, they surrender those values, it will disintegrate. For society is not something that can be kept together physically; it is held by the invisible but fragile bonds of common beliefs and values. . . . A common morality is part of the bondage of a good society, and that bondage is part of the price of society which mankind must pay.

What are those beliefs and values? They embrace several things, including religion. You wouldn't know it from watching CNN or reading *The New York Times,* but there is a huge religious revival taking place now, affecting just about every part of the globe except Western Europe, which slouches towards godlessness almost as fast as it slouches towards bankruptcy and demographic collapse. (Neither Spain nor Italy are producing enough children to replace their existing populations, while the Muslim birthrate in France continues to soar).

Things look different in America. For if America is a vigorously secular country—which it certainly is—it is also a deeply religious one. It always has been. Tocqueville was simply minuting the reality he saw around him when he noted that "[o]n my arrival in the United States the religious aspect of the country was the first thing that struck my attention." As G. K. Chesterton put it a century after Tocqueville, America is "a nation with the soul of a church." Even today, America is a country where an astonishing 92 percent of the population says it believes in God and 80 to 85 percent of the population identifies itself as Christian. Hence Huntington's call for a return to America's core values is also a call to embrace the religious principles upon which the country was founded, "a recommitment to America as a deeply religious and primarily Christian country, encompassing several religious minorities adhering to Anglo-Protestant values, speaking English, maintaining its cultural heritage, and committed to the principles" of political liberty as articulated by the Founders. . . . Huntington is careful to stress that what he offers is an "argument for the importance of Anglo-Protestant culture, not for the importance of Anglo-Protestant people." That is, he argues not on behalf of a particular ethnic group but on behalf of a culture and set of values that "for three and a half centuries have been embraced by Americans of all races, ethnicities, and religions and that have been the source of their liberty, unity, power, prosperity, and moral leadership."

American identity was originally founded on four things: ethnicity, race, ideology, and culture. By the mid-twentieth century, ethnicity and race had sharply receded in importance. Indeed, one of America's greatest achievements is having eliminated the racial and ethnic components that historically were central to its identity. Ideology—the package of Enlightened liberal values championed by the Founders—[is] crucial but too thin for the task of forging or preserving national identity by themselves. ("A nation defined only by political ideology," Huntington notes, "is a fragile nation.") Which is why Huntington, like virtually all of the Founders, explicitly grounded American identity in religion. . . .

Opponents of religion in the public square never tire of reminding us that there is no mention of God in the Constitution. This is true. Neither is the word "virtue" mentioned. But both are presupposed. For the American Founders, as the historian

Gertrude Himmelfarb points out, virtue, grounded in religion, was presumed "to be rooted in the very nature of man and as such . . . reflected in the *moeurs* of the people and in the traditions and informal institutions of society." It is also worth mentioning that if the Constitution is silent on religion, the Declaration of Independence is voluble, speaking of "nature's God," the "Creator," "the supreme judge of the world," and "divine Providence.". . . Benjamin Rush, one of the signers of the Declaration of Independence, summed up the common attitude of the Founders toward religion when he insisted that "[t]he only foundation for a useful education in a republic is to be laid in religion. Without it there can be no virtue, and without virtue there can be no liberty, and liberty is the object of all republican governments." George Washington concurred: "Reason and experience both forbid us to expect that national morality can prevail in exclusion of religious principles."

No nation lasts forever. An external enemy may eventually overrun and subdue it; internal forces of dissolution and decadence may someday undermine it, leaving it prey to more vigorous competitors. Sooner or later it succumbs. The United States is the most powerful nation the world has ever seen. Its astonishing military might, economic productivity, and political vigor are unprecedented. But someday, as Huntington reminds us, it too will fade or perish as Athens, Rome, and other great civilizations have faded or perished. Is the end, or the beginning of the end, at hand?

So far, the West—or at least the United States—has disappointed its self- 25 appointed undertakers. How do we stand now, at the dawn of the twenty-first century? It is worth remembering that besieged nations do not always succumb to the forces, external or internal, that threaten them. Sometimes, they muster the resolve to fight back successfully, to renew themselves. Today, America faces a new external enemy in the form of militant Islam and global terrorism. That minatory force, though murderous, will fail in proportion to our resolve to defeat it. Do we still possess that resolve? Inseparable from resolve is self-confidence, faith in the essential nobility of one's regime and one's way of life. To what extent do we still possess, still practice that faith?

Reinventing "America": Call for a New National Identity

ELIZABETH MARTÍNEZ

Elizabeth Martínez has written six books, including one on Chicano history. This essay comes from her 1998 book, *De Colores Means All of Us: Latina Views for a Multi-Colored Century.*

For some 15 years, starting in 1940, 85 percent of all U.S. elementary schools used the Dick and Jane series to teach children how to read. The series starred Dick, Jane, their white middle-class parents, their dog Spot and their life together in a home with a white picket fence.

"Look, Jane, look! See Spot run!" chirped the two kids. It was a house full of glorious family values, where Mom cooked while Daddy went to work in a suit and mowed the lawn on weekends. The Dick and Jane books also taught that you should do your job and help others. All this affirmed an equation of middle-class with whiteness with virtue.

In the mid-1990s, museums, libraries and 80 Public Broadcasting Service (PBS) stations across the country had exhibits and programs commemorating the series. At one museum, an attendant commented, "When you hear someone crying, you know they are looking at the Dick and Jane books." It seems nostalgia runs rampant among many Euro-Americans: a nostalgia for the days of unchallenged White Supremacy—both moral and material—when life was "simple."

We've seen that nostalgia before in the nation's history. But today it signifies a problem reaching a new intensity. It suggests a national identity crisis that promises to bring in its wake an unprecedented nervous breakdown for the dominant society's psyche.

Nowhere is this more apparent than in California, which has long been on the 5 cutting edge of the nation's present and future reality. Warning sirens have sounded repeatedly in the 1990s, such as the fierce battle over new history textbooks for public schools, Proposition 187's ugly denial of human rights to immigrants, the 1996 assault on affirmative action that culminated in Proposition 209, and the 1997 move to abolish bilingual education. Attempts to copycat these reactionary measures have been seen in other states.

The attack on affirmative action isn't really about affirmative action. Essentially it is another tactic in today's war on the gains of the 1960s, a tactic rooted in Anglo resentment and fear. A major source of that fear: the fact that California will almost surely have a majority of people of color in 20 to 30 years at most, with the nation as a whole not far behind.

Check out the February 3, 1992, issue of *Sports Illustrated* with its double-spread ad for *Time* magazine. The ad showed hundreds of newborn babies in their hospital cribs, all of them Black or brown except for a rare white face here and there. The headline says, "Hey, whitey! It's your turn at the back of the bus!" The ad then tells you, read *Time* magazine to keep up with today's hot issues. That manipulative image could have been published today; its implication of shifting power appears to be the recurrent nightmare of too many potential Anglo allies.

Euro-American anxiety often focuses on the sense of a vanishing national identity. Behind the attacks on immigrants, affirmative action and multiculturalism, behind the demand for "English Only" laws and the rejection of bilingual education, lies the question: with all these new people, languages and cultures, what will it mean to be an American? If that question once seemed, to many people, to have an obvious, universally applicable answer, today new definitions must be found. But too often Americans, with supposed scholars in the lead, refuse to face that need and instead nurse a nostalgia for some bygone clarity. They remain trapped in denial.

An array of such ostriches, heads in the sand, began flapping their feathers noisily with the publication of Allan Bloom's 1987 best-selling book, *The Closing of the American Mind.* Bloom bemoaned the decline of our "common values" as a society, meaning the decline of Euro-American cultural centricity (shall we just call it cultural imperialism?). Since then we have seen constant sniping at "diversity" goals across the land. The assault has often focused on how U.S. history is taught. And with reason, for this country's identity rests on a particular narrative about the historical origins of the United States as a nation.

THE GREAT WHITE ORIGIN MYTH

Every society has an origin narrative that explains that society to itself and the world 10 with a set of stories and symbols. The origin myth, as scholar-activist Roxanne Dunbar Ortiz has termed it, defines how a society understands its place in the world and its history. The myth provides the basis for a nation's self-defined identity. Most origin narratives can be called myths because they usually present only the most flattering view of a nation's history; they are not distinguished by honesty.

Ours begins with Columbus "discovering" a hemisphere where some 80 million people already lived but didn't really count (in what became the United States, they were just buffalo-chasing "savages" with no grasp of real estate values and therefore doomed to perish). It continues with the brave Pilgrims, a revolution by independence-loving colonists against a decadent English aristocracy and the birth of an energetic young republic that promised democracy and equality (that is, to white male landowners). In the 1840s, the new nation expanded its size by almost one-third, thanks to a victory over that backward land of little brown people called Mexico. Such has been the basic account of how the nation called the United States of America came into being as presently configured.

The myth's omissions are grotesque. It ignores three major pillars of our nation-hood: genocide, enslavement and imperialist expansion (such nasty words, who wants to hear them?—but that's the problem). The massive extermination of indigenous peoples provided our land base; the enslavement of African labor made our economic growth possible; and the seizure of half of Mexico by war (or threat of renewed war) extended this nation's boundaries north to the Pacific and south to the Rio Grande. Such are the foundation stones of the United States, within an economic system that made this country the first in world history to be born capitalist.

Those three pillars were, of course, supplemented by great numbers of dirt-cheap workers from Mexico, China, the Philippines, Puerto Rico and other countries, all of them kept in their place by White Supremacy. In history they stand alongside millions of less-than-supreme white workers and sharecroppers.

Any attempt to modify the present origin myth provokes angry efforts to repel such sacrilege. In the case of Native Americans, scholars will insist that they died from disease or wars among themselves, or that "not so many really did die." At worst it was a "tragedy," but never deliberate genocide, never a pillar of our nationhood. As for slavery, it was an embarrassment, of course, but do remember that Africa also had slavery and anyway enlightened white folk finally did end the practice here.

In the case of Mexico, reputable U.S. scholars still insist on blaming that coun- 15 try for the 1846–48 war. Yet even former U.S. President Ulysses Grant wrote in his memoirs that "[w]e were sent to provoke a fight [by moving troops into a disputed border area] but it was essential that Mexico should commence it [by fighting back]" (*Mr. Lincoln's General: Ulysses S. Grant, an illustrated autobiography*). President James Polk's 1846 diary records that he told his cabinet his purpose in declaring war as "acquiring California, New Mexico, and perhaps other Mexican lands" (*Diary of James K. Polk 1845–49*). To justify what could be called a territorial drive-by, the Mexican people were declared inferior; the U.S. had a "Manifest Destiny" to bring them progress and democracy.

Even when revisionist voices expose particular evils of Indian policy, slavery or the war on Mexico, they remain little more than unpleasant footnotes; the core of the dominant myth stands intact. PBS's eight-part documentary series of 1996 titled "The West" is a case in point. It devoted more than the usual attention to the devastation of Native Americans, but still centered on Anglos and gave little attention to why their domination evolved as it did. The West thus remained the physically gorgeous backdrop for an ugly, unaltered origin myth.

In fact, "The West" series strengthens that myth. White Supremacy needs the brave but inevitably doomed Indians to silhouette its own inevitable conquest. It needs the Indian-as-devil to sustain its own holy mission. Remember Timothy Wight, who served as pastor to Congress in the late 1700s and wrote that, under the Indians, "Satan ruled unchallenged in America" until "our chosen race eternal justice sent." With that self-declared moral authority, the "winning of the West" metamorphosed from a brutal, bloody invasion into a crusade of brave Christians marching across a lonely, dangerous landscape.

RACISM AS LINCHPIN OF THE U.S. NATIONAL IDENTITY

A crucial embellishment of the origin myth and key element of the national identity has been the myth of the frontier, analyzed in Richard Slotkin's *Gunfighter Nation,* the last volume of a fascinating trilogy. He describes Theodore Roosevelt's belief that the West was won thanks to American arms, "the means by which progress and nationality will be achieved." That success, Roosevelt continued, "depends on the heroism of men who impose on the course of events the latent virtues of their 'race.'" Roosevelt saw conflict on the frontier producing a species of virile "fighters and breeders" who would eventually generate a new leadership class. Militarism thus went hand in hand with the racialization of history's protagonists.

No slouch as an imperialist, Roosevelt soon took the frontier myth abroad, seeing Asians as Apaches and the Philippines as Sam Houston's Texas in the process of being seized from Mexico. For Roosevelt, Slotkin writes, "racial violence [was] the principle around which both individual character and social organization develop." Such ideas have not remained totally unchallenged by U.S. historians, nor was the frontier myth always applied in totally simplistic ways by Hollywood and other media. (The outlaw, for example, is a complicated figure, both good and bad.) Still, the frontier myth traditionally spins together virtue and violence, morality and war, in a convoluted, Calvinist web. That tortured embrace defines an essence of the so-called American character—the national identity—to this day.

The frontier myth embodied the nineteenth-century concept of Manifest Destiny, a doctrine that served to justify expansionist violence by means of intrinsic racial superiority. Manifest Destiny saw Yankee conquest as the inevitable result of 20 a confrontation between enterprise and progress (white) versus passivity and backwardness (Indian, Mexican). "Manifest" meant "God-given," and the whole doctrine is profoundly rooted in religious conviction going back to the earliest colonial times. In his short, powerful book *Manifest Destiny: American Expansion and the Empire of Right,* Professor Anders Stephanson tells how the Puritans reinvented the Jewish notion of chosenness and applied it to this hemisphere so that territorial expansion became God's will. . . .

MANIFEST DESTINY DIES HARD

The concept of Manifest Destiny, with its assertion of racial superiority sustained by military power, has defined U.S. identity for 150 years. Only the Vietnam War brought a serious challenge to that concept of almightiness. Bitter debate, moral anguish, images of My Lai and the prospect of military defeat for the first time in U.S. history all suggested that the long-standing marriage of virtue and violence might soon be on the rocks. In the final years of the war the words leaped to mind one day: this country is having a national nervous breakdown.

Perhaps this is why the Vietnam War continues to arouse passions today. Some who are willing to call the war "a mistake" still shy away from recognizing its immorality or even accepting it as a defeat. A few Americans have the courage to conclude from the Vietnam War that we should abandon the idea that our identity rests on being the world's richest, most powerful and indeed *best* nation. Is it possible that the so-called Vietnam syndrome might signal liberation from a crippling self-definition? Is it possible the long-standing belief that "American exceptionalism" had made freedom possible might be rejected someday?

The Vietnam syndrome is partly rooted in the fact that, although other societies have also been based on colonialism and slavery, ours seems to have an insatiable need to be the "good guys" on the world stage. That need must lie at least partially in a Protestant dualism that defines existence in terms of opposites, so that if you are not "good" you are bad, if not "white" then Black, and so on. Whatever the cause, the need to be seen as virtuous, compared to someone else's evil, haunts U.S. domestic and foreign policy. Where on earth would we be without Saddam Hussein, Qaddafi, and that all-time favorite of gringo demonizers, Fidel Castro? Gee whiz, how would we know what an American really is?

Today's origin myth and the resulting concept of national identity make for an intellectual prison where it is dangerous to ask big questions about this society's superiority. When otherwise decent people are trapped in such a powerful desire not to feel guilty, self-deception becomes unavoidable. To cease our present falsification of collective memory should, and could, open the doors of that prison. When together we cease equating whiteness with Americanness, a new day can dawn. As David Roediger, the social historian, has said, "[Whiteness] is the empty and therefore terrifying attempt to build an identity on what one isn't, and on whom one can hold back."

Redefining the U.S. origin narrative, and with it this country's national identity, [25] could prove liberating for our collective psyche. It does not mean Euro-Americans should wallow individually in guilt. It does mean accepting collective responsibility to deal with the implications of our real origin. A few apologies, for example, might be a step in the right direction. In 1997, the idea was floated in Congress to apologize for slavery; it encountered opposition from all sides. But to reject the notion because corrective action, not an apology, is needed misses the point. Having defined itself as the all-time best country in the world, the United States fiercely denies the need to make a serious, official apology for anything. . . . To press for any serious, official apology does imply a new origin narrative, a new self-image, an ideological sea change.

Accepting the implications of a different narrative could also shed light on today's struggles. In the affirmative-action struggle, for example, opponents have said that that policy is no longer needed because racism ended with the Civil Rights Movement. But if we look at slavery as a fundamental pillar of this nation, going back centuries, it becomes obvious that racism could not have been ended by 30 years of mild reforms. If we see how the myth of the frontier idealized the white male adventurer as the central hero of national history, with the woman as sunbonneted helpmate, then we might better understand the dehumanized ways in which women have continued to be treated. A more truthful origin narrative could also help break down divisions among peoples of color by revealing common experiences and histories of cooperation.

A new origin narrative and national identity could help pave the way to a more livable society for us all. A society based on cooperation rather than competition, on the idea that all living creatures are interdependent and that humanity's goal should be balance. Such were the values of many original Americans, deemed "savages." Similar gifts are waiting from other despised peoples and traditions. We might well start by recognizing that "America" is the name of an entire hemisphere, rich in a stunning variety of histories, cultures and peoples—not just one country.

The choice seems clear, if not easy. We can go on living in a state of massive denial, affirming this nation's superiority and virtue simply because we need to believe in it. We can choose to believe the destiny of the United States is still manifest: global domination. Or we can seek a transformative vision that carries us forward, not backward. We can seek an origin narrative that lays the groundwork for a multicultural, multinational identity centered on the goals of social equity and democracy. We do have choices.

There is little time for nostalgia. Dick and Jane never were "America," they were only one part of one community in one part of one country in one part of one continent. Yet we have let their image define our entire society and its values. Will the future be marked by ongoing denial or by steps toward a new vision in which White Supremacy no longer determines reality? When on earth will we transcend the assumptions that imprison our minds?

At times you can hear the clock ticking.   30

Analysis of the Writers' Positions

The first step in resolving conflict is to understand what the parties are claiming and why. Below is our paraphrase of Kimball's and Martínez's arguments.

Kimball's Position He opposes multiculturalism and wants to preserve an American identity based in Anglo-Protestant culture.

> *Thesis:* Multiculturalism weakens America by keeping people of different cultures from assimilating to the core values of America's Anglo-Protestant identity.
>
>> *Reason:* Educational multiculturalism degrades traditional American values and ignores mainstream history and culture.
>>
>>> *Evidence:* Opinions of Samuel Huntington and Arthur Schlesinger, Jr. Examples of college students' ignorance about history. Maya Angelou's speech at Clinton's inauguration.
>>
>> *Reason:* Multiculturalism "weakens the social bond" by denying that immigrants need to assimilate to the language and values of the dominant culture.
>>
>>> *Evidence:* Rise of hyphenization. Rise of non-English-speaking communities. Calls for affirmative action, which violates the idea of success based on merit.
>>
>> *Reason:* America should be defined by one culture and nationality, not many.
>>
>>> *Evidence:* Quotations from de Crèvecoeur on the "new race of men." Quotations from Theodore Roosevelt, John Jay, Thomas Jefferson, Benjamin Franklin. The 1795 oath of allegiance for citizenship.
>>
>> *Reason:* The single, unifying identity of America should be based in Anglo-Saxon Protestant Christianity.
>>
>>> *Evidence:* Religious beliefs of original settlers. Historian Himmelfarb on American virtue as deeply rooted in religion. Quotes from Founding Fathers on relation of virtue to religion. Huntington on the need for national identity based in religion.

Martínez's Position She wants to replace traditional Anglo-American identity with a multicultural one.

> *Thesis:* The United States needs to discard its "white supremacist" identity.
>
>> *Reason:* It's based on racism, genocide, and imperialist expansion.
>>
>>> *Evidence:* The "origin myth" in common accounts of U.S. history. The historical record of slavery, takeover of Native American land, wars of expansion. Primary sources such as Presidents Grant and Polk. Theodore Roosevelt's statements about racial superiority. Historian Richard Slotkin's analysis of frontier myth.

Reason: It's based on a false sense of moral superiority and favor in the eyes of God.

> *Evidence:* Professor Anders Stephanson on the concept of Manifest Destiny. Protestant moral dualism—seeing the world in terms of good and evil. Social historian David Roediger on the Anglo sense of superiority.

Reason: America will be a more fair and democratic country if we revise our identity to acknowledge Anglo faults and adopt the values of non-Anglo cultures.

> *Evidence:* Racism and sexism not eliminated. The valuable gifts of other cultures, such as cooperation over competition.

◎◎ FOLLOWING THROUGH

If you and some of your classmates have written arguments taking opposing views on the same issue, prepare briefs of your respective positions to share with one another. (You might also create briefs of your opponents' positions to see how well you have understood one another's written arguments.)

Alternatively, write briefs summarizing the opposing positions offered in several published arguments as a first step toward mediating these viewpoints.   •

Locating the Areas of Agreement and Disagreement

Differences over Facts

Most conflicts result from interpreting facts differently rather than disagreement about the facts themselves. For example, in the arguments of Kimball and Martínez, we see agreement on many factual points:

- Whites are becoming the minority in some parts of the United States.
- Assimilation has meant conformity to a culture defined by Anglo-Protestant values.
- Christianity has played a large role in America's sense of identity.

If a mediator finds disagreement over facts, he or she needs to look into it and provide evidence from credible sources that would resolve these details. Or the problem might be that one or both sides are arguing without enough information. The mediator can help here by doing the needed research or advising the parties to find out more about what they are arguing over. If they know each other personally, doing the research jointly is a good idea.

◎◎ FOLLOWING THROUGH

For the arguments you are mediating, make a list of facts that the authors both accept. Note facts offered by one side but denied or not considered by the other. Where your authors don't agree on the facts, do research to decide how valid the facts cited on both sides are. Explain the discrepancies. If your class is mediating the same conflict, compare your findings.   •

Differences over Interests, Values, and Interpretations

Facts alone cannot resolve entrenched disputes such as the debate over multiculturalism. For example, a history lesson about white settlers' treatment of Native Americans would not change Kimball's mind. Nor would a lesson in Enlightenment philosophy alter what Martínez thinks. When we attempt to mediate, *we have to look into why people hold the positions they do.* Like persuasion, mediation looks at the contexts of a dispute.

To identify these differences, we can ask questions similar to those that are useful in persuasion for identifying what divides us from our audience (see "Questions for Understanding Difference," page 304). We apply below the questions about difference to Kimball's and Martínez's positions.

Is the Difference a Matter of Assumptions?　Every argument has assumptions—unstated assertions that the audience must share to find the reasoning valid and persuasive. Kimball assumes that Anglo-Protestant culture is moral; therefore, he does not show how Christianity has made America a moral nation. Martínez disputes the very assumption that America is moral. But she also makes assumptions. She assumes that the "origin narrative" of the white man's conquest and exploitation is the sole basis for the nation's past and present identity. This assumption allows her to argue that the culture of the United States is simply white supremacist.

These two assumptions show polarized thinking—one assumes that Anglo-Protestant values are all good, the other that Anglo-Protestant values are all evil. Such polarized assumptions are common in disputes because, as philosopher of ethics Anthony Weston explains, we polarize not just to simplify but to justify: "We polarize . . . to be able to picture ourselves as totally justified, totally right, and the 'other side' as totally unjustified and wrong."[2] It's precisely this tactic that mediation must resist and overcome.

Is the Difference a Matter of Principle?　By principles, we mean informal rules that guide our actions, like the "rule" in sales: "The customer is always right." Kimball's principle is patriotism: Americans should be undivided in loyalty and allegiance to the United States. Martínez's principle is fairness and justice for all, which means rewriting the origin narrative, admitting past mistakes, and recognizing the richness and morality of all the cultures that make up America. A mediator might ask: Can we be patriotic *and* self-critical? Must we repudiate the past entirely to fashion a new national identity?

Is the Difference a Matter of Values or Priorities?　The principles just discussed reflect differing priorities. In the post–9/11 world, Kimball is concerned with America's strength on the world stage, whereas Martínez concentrates more on America's compassion in its domestic policies. This is a significant difference because Martínez supports programs like affirmative action and

---

[2]Anthony Weston, *A Practical Companion to Ethics* (New York: Oxford, 2005) 50.

Questions for Understanding Difference

1. Is the difference a matter of *assumptions?* As we discussed in Chapter 3 on the Toulmin method of analysis and in Chapter 7 on inquiry, all arguments are based on some assumptions.

2. Is the difference a matter of *principle?* Are some parties to the dispute following different principles, or general rules, from others?

3. Is the difference a matter of *values* or a matter of having the same values but giving them different *priorities?*

4. Is the difference a matter of *ends* or *means?* That is, do people want to achieve different goals, or do they have the same goals in mind but disagree on the means to achieve them?

5. Is the difference a matter of *interpretation?*

6. Is the difference a matter of *implications* or *consequences?*

7. Is the difference a result of *personal background, basic human needs,* or *emotions?*

To our list of questions about difference in persuasive writing, we add this last question because mediators must look not just at the arguments but also at the disputants as people with histories and feelings. It is not realistic to think that human problems can be solved without taking human factors into consideration. Mediators must take into account such basic human needs as personal security, economic well-being, and a sense of belonging, recognition, and people's control over their own lives. If you are mediating among printed texts, you must use the texts themselves as evidence of these human factors.

---

multicultural education, the very policies Kimball claims weaken our social bonds (paragraph 10). Once we see this difference, we can see the dispute in the context of liberal and conservative opinion in general. Kimball is arguing for a national identity acceptable to conservatives, Martínez for one acceptable to liberals. But what we need, obviously, is something that can cross this divide and appeal to all or most Americans.

Is the Difference a Matter of Ends or Means? Martínez and Kimball have different ends in mind, so they also have different means to achieve the ends. For Martínez, a multicultural identity is the means to a more fair and livable society for all. For Kimball, a common identity in Anglo-Protestant culture is the means to remaining "the most powerful nation the world has ever seen." A mediator could reasonably ask: Couldn't we have both? Couldn't the United States be a powerful nation that is also fair and livable for all its citizens?

Is the Difference a Matter of Implications or Consequences? The mediator has to consider what each side fears will happen if the other side prevails. Kimball fears that multiculturalism will lead Americans to self-doubt, loss of confidence. He also forecasts a large population of "permanent second-class citizens" if subgroups of the population do not assimilate. Martínez fears continuing oppression of minorities if our national self-conception doesn't change to fit our country's actual diversity. The mediator must acknowledge the fears of both sides while not permitting either to go unquestioned. Fear is a powerful motivator that must be confronted squarely.

Is the Difference a Matter of Interpretation? A major disagreement here is over how to interpret the values of Anglo-Protestant culture. To Kimball, these values are "individual liberty and public virtue" (paragraph 8), "the rule of law" (paragraph 14), "respect for individual rights" (paragraph 14), devotion to God and a strong work ethic (paragraph 14). In contrast, Martínez interprets Anglo-Protestant values as a belief in whites' moral superiority and favor in the eyes of God (paragraph 20) that enabled them to see their own acts of "genocide, enslavement, and imperialist expansion" (paragraph 12) as morally acceptable and even heroic (paragraph 19). These interpretations stem from the different backgrounds of the writers, which we consider next.

Is the Difference a Matter of Personal Background, Basic Human Needs, or Emotions? When mediating between positions in written arguments such as these, it's a good idea to go to the library or an online source for biographical information about the authors. It will pay off with insight into why they disagree.

Kimball and Martínez obviously come from very different backgrounds that are representative of others who hold the same positions they do. For example, as a white male with the financial means to have attended Yale, Kimball represents the group that has benefited most from the traditional national identity. His conservative views have pitted him against liberal academics and social activists.

Martínez identifies herself as a Chicana, an American woman of Mexican descent (her father was an immigrant). She is an activist for social justice and heads the Institute for MultiRacial Justice in San Francisco and has taught women's studies and ethnic studies in the California State University system. She knows the burden of discrimination from personal experience and from her work and research. As a proponent of bilingual and multicultural education, she sees people like Kimball as the opposition.

◎◎◉ FOLLOWING THROUGH

If you are mediating among printed arguments, write an analysis based on applying the questions in the Best Practices box on page 304 to two or more arguments. You could write out your analysis in list form, as we did in analyzing the differences between Kimball and Martínez, or you could treat it as an exploratory essay.

As a creative variation for your analysis, write a dialogue with yourself as mediator, posing questions to each of the opposing parties. Have each side respond to your questions just as we demonstrated in our sample dialogue on pages 182–183.

Finding Creative Solutions: Exploring Common Ground

Using critical thinking to mediate means looking closely at what people want and why they want it. It also means seeing the dispute in larger contexts. For example, the dispute over national identity is part of a larger debate between liberals and conservatives over politics, social policy, and education.

Mediation won't and shouldn't try to reach everyone. Some people hold extreme views that reason cannot touch. An example would be the professor Kimball cites who predicts that the southwestern United States and northern Mexico will eventually become a new and separate country. Mediation between this person and Kimball is about as likely as President Bush and Osama bin Laden having dinner together. But mediators can bring reasonable people closer together by trying to arrive at creative solutions that appeal to some of the interests and values of all parties.

Taking a simple example of conflicting interests, consider the family divided about their vacation destination, mountains or seashore. If the seashore lovers go for swimming and sunbathing and the mountain enthusiasts hiking and mountain biking, why not look for places that have both—mountains *and* seashore?

In complex conflicts, such as the one over multiculturalism and national identity, creative solutions are possible if people can move beyond polarized to cooperative thinking. The ethicist Anthony Weston suggests trying to see conflict in terms of what each side is right about. He says, "If both sides (or all sides) are to some extent right, then we need to try to honor what is right in each of them."[3]

Weston points to the debate over saving owls in old-growth forests versus logging interests that employ people. Preserving the environment and endangered species is good, but so is saving jobs. If jobs could be created that use wood in craft-based ways, people could make a living without destroying massive amounts of timber. This solution is possible if the parties cooperate—but not if greedy corporations are deadlocked with radical environmentalists, neither willing to concede anything or give an inch.

Mediators should aim for "win-win" solutions, which resolve conflict by dissolving it. The challenge for the mediator is keeping the high ground and looking for the good and reasonable in what each side wants. Perfect neutrality isn't necessary and mediators do have to expose bad thinking or factual errors, but they must not fall into advocating one side over the other.

---

[3]Weston, *Practical Companion* 56.

Exploring Common Ground in the Debate over National Identity

To find integrative solutions for the national identity–multiculturalism dispute, we analyzed our list of questions for understanding difference to find interests and values Kimball and Martínez might share or be persuaded to share. Here's what we found.

Both want Americans to know their history. Kimball is right. It's a disgrace that college students can't recognize a famous phrase from the Gettysburg Address. But they need to know that *and* the relevance of Harriet Tubman to those words. Martínez is right also that history should not be propaganda for one view of events. The history of all nations is a mix of good and bad.

Neither Kimball nor Martínez wants a large population of second-class citizens, living in isolated poverty, not speaking English, not seeing themselves as Americans, and not having a say in the democratic process. Martínez's multiculturalism would "break down divisions among peoples of color by revealing common experiences and histories of cooperation" with the goal of "social equity and democracy." She would be more likely, however, to achieve her goal if she considered white men and women *as participants* in this multicultural discussion. To exclude whites keeps people of color where they too often are—on the margins, left out. Kimball needs to be reminded that failure to assimilate is not typically a choice. First-generation immigrants usually learn little English partly because they work several jobs to survive. Living in segregated neighborhoods with others like them provides security and support and can make success easier for their children. Studies show that children who assimilate to the culture of America's poor neighborhoods do less well in school than those whose parents raise them in traditional ways. As in the past, assimilation works only when educational and economic opportunities exist. Kimball needs to look into solutions to the problem of poverty among immigrants.

There is agreement too on the need for a national identity. Martínez calls for "a new identity," implying that we need something deep to define us as Americans. But asking what culture should provide it is the wrong question. Concentrating on the values themselves will help everyone see that most values are shared across races and cultures. For example, Martínez takes Anglo-Protestant culture as competitive, not cooperative. While competition drives capitalism, we need to recall that early Protestant settlers also valued community. The Puritans tried to establish utopian communities devoted to charity; John Winthrop almost went bankrupt making himself an example of generosity to his neighbors. Kimball's "Protestant" work ethic can be found in every ethnic group—for example, in the predominantly Catholic Mexican laborers who do backbreaking work in agriculture and construction. Instead of getting hung up on which religion or ethnic group provided the values, those arguing for a strong American identity can agree on the values themselves: justice, equality, democracy, productivity, charity toward one another, respect for human rights, and love of country.

Finally, what agreement could be reached about assimilation? What does it mean to become "Americanized"? Kimball suggests that immigrants follow Justice Louis Brandeis's advice—adopting "the clothes, the manners, and the customs generally prevailing here." But would such advice mean that what "prevails" here is based in Protestantism and Anglo-Saxon culture? A more realistic idea of "Americanization" comes from our third writer, Bharati Mukherjee, who suggests in her mediatory essay that "assimilation" is a two-way transformation, with immigrants and mainstream culture interacting, influencing each other. Such a conception *requires* both the preservation of tradition Kimball wants and the respect for diversity Martínez wants.

Mediating any controversy involves opening up the thinking of all parties by questioning assumptions, checking facts, and searching for what pulls together rather than tears apart.

FOLLOWING THROUGH

Either in list form or as an informal exploratory essay, explore possible areas of agreement between the various positions you have been analyzing. End your list or essay with a summary of a position that all sides might be willing to acknowledge has some validity.   •

THE MEDIATORY ESSAY

The natural human tendency in argument is to polarize—to see conflict as simply "us" versus "them," like children choosing up sides in a game. Modern media, often striving only for ratings by playing up the dramatic and the sensational, can make matters worse by featuring representatives of extreme positions locked in verbal combat. The result is rarely arguments intended to persuade but rather arguments aimed at solidifying the support of those already in agreement with one or the other sides.

That's why mediation is necessary and matters so much as a way of moving beyond polarized thinking. An example of mediation in the multi-culturalism debate appears below. The essay's author is the novelist Bharati Mukherjee. She was born into a wealthy family in Calcutta but became an American citizen. She is now Distinguished Professor of English at the University of California at Berkeley.

She has been faulted by some Indians and other South Asians for depicting India and its culture too harshly in her fiction; her characters are immigrants who embrace, rather than resist, American culture. These critics, whom Mukherjee denounces near the end of her essay, are part of the academic multiculturalists Kimball describes as anti-American. Obviously, Mukherjee is not writing to them nor to "rabid Eurocentrists" on the other side, people she mentions who want to close our borders and stop even legal immigration. She's writing to people who accept either Kimball's position—

preserve the Euro-Protestant "core" of American identity—or Martínez's—create a new national identity based on the multicultural mosaic.

There's no single model for a mediatory essay. In this case, Mukherjee's essay mediates by making a case against both radical extremes, one way of seeking to bring people together on the remaining middle ground.

Beyond Multiculturalism:
A Two-Way Transformation

BHARATI MUKHERJEE

The United States exists as a sovereign nation with its officially stated Constitution, its economic and foreign policies, its demarcated, patrolled boundaries. "America," however, exists as image or idea, as dream or nightmare, as romance or plague, constructed by discrete individual fantasies, and shaded by collective paranoias and mythologies.

I am a naturalized U.S. citizen with a certificate of citizenship; more importantly, I am an American for whom "America" is the stage for the drama of self-transformation. I see American culture as a culture of dreamers, who believe material shape (which is not the same as materialism) can be given to dreams. They believe that one's station in life—poverty, education, family background—does not determine one's fate. They believe in the reversal of omens; early failures do not spell inevitable disaster. Outsiders can triumph on merit. All of this happens against the backdrop of the familiar vicissitudes of American life.

I first came to the United States—to the state of Iowa, to be precise—on a late summer evening nearly thirty-three years ago. I flew into a placid, verdant airport in Iowa City on a commercial airliner, ready to fulfill the goals written out in a large, lined notebook for me by my guiltlessly patriarchal father. Those goals were unambiguous: I was to spend two years studying Creative Writing at Paul Engle's unique Writers Workshop; then I was to marry the perfect Bengali bridegroom selected by my father and live out the rest of a contented, predictable life in the city of my birth, Calcutta. In 1961, I was a shy, pliant, well-mannered, dutiful young daughter from a very privileged, traditional, mainstream Hindu family that believed women should be protected and provided for by their fathers, husbands, sons, and it did not once occur to me that I might have goals of my own, quite distinct from those specified for me by my father. I certainly did not anticipate then that, over the next three decades, Iowans—who seemed to me so racially and culturally homogeneous—would be forced to shudder through the violent paroxysms of a collective identity in crisis.

When I was growing up in Calcutta in the fifties, I heard no talk of "identity crisis"—communal or individual. The concept itself—of a person not knowing who she or he was—was unimaginable in a hierarchical, classification-obsessed society. One's identity was absolutely fixed, derived from religion, caste, patrimony, and mother tongue. A Hindu Indian's last name was designed to announce his or her forefathers' caste and place of origin. A Mukherjee could *only* be a Brahmin from Bengal. Indian tradition forbade inter-caste, inter-language, inter-ethnic marriages.

Bengali tradition discouraged even emigration; to remove oneself from Bengal was to "pollute" true culture.

Until the age of eight, I lived in a house crowded with forty or fifty relatives. We 5 lived together because we were "family," bonded by kinship, though kinship was interpreted in flexible enough terms to include, when necessary, men, women, children who came from the same *desh*—which is the Bengali word for "homeland"—as had my father and grandfather. I was who I was because I was Dr. Sudhir Lal Mukherjee's daughter, because I was a Hindu Brahmin, because I was Bengali-speaking, and because my *desh* was an East Bengal village called Faridpur. I was encouraged to think of myself as indistinguishable from my dozen girl cousins. Identity was viscerally connected with ancestral soil and family origins. I was first a Mukherjee, then a Bengali Brahmin, and only then an Indian.

Deep down I knew, of course, that I was not quite like my girl cousins. Deeper down, I was sure that pride in the purity of one's culture has a sinister underside. As a child I had witnessed bloody religious riots between Muslims and Hindus, and violent language riots between Bengalis and Biharis. People kill for culture, and die of hunger. Language, race, religion, blood, myth, history, national codes, and manners have all been used, in India, in the United States, are being used in Bosnia and Rwanda even today, to enforce terror, to "otherize," to murder.

I do not know what compelled my strong-willed and overprotective father to risk sending us, his three daughters, to school in the United States, a country he had not visited. In Calcutta, he had insisted on sheltering us from danger and temptation by sending us to girls-only schools, and by providing us with chaperones, chauffeurs, and bodyguards.

The Writers Workshop in a quonset hut in Iowa City was my first experience of coeducation. And after not too long, I fell in love with a fellow student named Clark Blaise, an American of Canadian origin, and impulsively married him during a lunch break in a lawyer's office above a coffeeshop.

That impulsive act cut me off forever from the rules and ways of upper-middle-class life in Bengal, and hurled me precipitously into a New World life of scary improvisations and heady explorations. Until my lunchtime wedding, I had seen myself as an Indian foreign student, a transient in the United States. The five-minute ceremony in the lawyer's office had changed me into a permanent transient.

Over the last three decades the important lesson that I have learned is that in this 10 era of massive diasporic movements, honorable survival requires resilience, curiosity, and compassion, a letting go of rigid ideals about the purity of inherited culture.

The first ten years into marriage, years spent mostly in my husband's *desh* of Canada, I thought myself an expatriate Bengali permanently stranded in North America because of a power surge of destiny or of desire. My first novel, *The Tiger's Daughter,* embodies the loneliness I felt but could not acknowledge, even to myself, as I negotiated the no-man's-land between the country of my past and the continent of my present. Shaped by memory, textured with nostalgia for a class and culture I had abandoned, this novel quite naturally became my expression of the *expatriate consciousness.*

It took me a decade of painful introspection to put the smothering tyranny of nostalgia into perspective, and to make the transition from expatriate to immigrant. I have found my way back to the United States after a fourteen-year stay in Canada. The transition from foreign student to U.S. citizen, from detached onlooker to committed immigrant, has not been easy.

The years in Canada were particularly harsh. Canada is a country that officially—and proudly—resists the policy and process of cultural fusion. For all its smug rhetoric about "cultural mosaic," Canada refuses to renovate its national self-image to include its changing complexion. It is a New World country with Old World concepts of a fixed, exclusivist national identity. And all through the seventies when I lived there, it was a country without a Bill of Rights or its own Constitution. Canadian official rhetoric designated me, as a citizen of non-European origin, one of the "visible minority" who, even though I spoke the Canadian national languages of English and French, was straining "the absorptive capacity" of Canada. Canadians of color were routinely treated as "not real" Canadians. In fact, when a terrorist bomb, planted in an Air India jet on Canadian soil, blew up after leaving Montreal, killing 329 passengers, 90 percent of whom were Canadians of Indian origin, the prime minister of Canada at the time, Brian Mulroney, cabled the Indian prime minister to offer Canada's condolences for India's loss, exposing the Eurocentricity of the "mosaic" policy of immigration.

In private conversations, some Canadian ambassadors and External Affairs officials have admitted to me that the creation of the Ministry of Multiculturism in the seventies was less an instrument for cultural tolerance, and more a vote-getting strategy to pacify ethnic European constituents who were alienated by the rise of Quebec separatism and the simultaneous increase of non-white immigrants.

The years of race-related harassments in a Canada without a Constitution have 15 politicized me, and deepened my love of the ideals embedded in the American Bill of Rights.

I take my American citizenship very seriously. I am a voluntary immigrant. I am not an economic refugee, and not a seeker of political asylum. I am an American by choice, and not by the simple accident of birth. I have made emotional, social, and political commitments to this country. I have earned the right to think of myself as an American.

But in this blood-splattered decade, questions such as who is an American and what is American culture are being posed with belligerence and being answered with violence. We are witnessing an increase in physical, too often fatal, assaults on Asian Americans. An increase in systematic "dot-busting" of Indo-Americans in New Jersey, xenophobic immigrant-baiting in California, minority-on-minority violence during the south-central Los Angeles revolution.

America's complexion is browning daily. Journalists' surveys have established that whites are losing their clear majority status in some states, and have already lost it in New York and California. A recent *Time* magazine poll indicated that 60 percent of Americans favor limiting *legal* immigration. Eighty percent of Americans polled favor curbing the entry of undocumented aliens. U.S. borders are too extensive and too porous to be adequately policed. Immigration, by documented and undocumented aliens, is less affected by the U.S. Immigration and Naturalization Service, and more by wars, ethnic genocides, famines in the emigrant's own country.

Every sovereign nation has a right to formulate its immigration policy. In this decade of continual, large-scale diasporic movements, it is imperative that we come to some agreement about who "we" are now that the community includes old-timers, newcomers, many races, languages, and religions; about what our expectations of happiness and strategies for its pursuit are; and what our goals are for the nation.

Scapegoating of immigrants has been the politicians' easy instant remedy. Hate 20 speeches fill auditoria, and bring in megabucks for those demagogues willing to profit from stirring up racial animosity.

The hysteria against newcomers is only minimally generated by the downturn in our economy. The panic, I suspect, is unleashed by a fear of the "other," the fear of what Daniel Stein, executive director of the Federation for American Immigration Reform, and a champion of closed borders, is quoted as having termed "cultural transmogrification."

The debate about American culture has to date been monopolized by rabid Eurocentrists and ethnocentrists; the rhetoric has been flamboyantly divisive, pitting a phantom "us" against a demonized "them." I am here to launch a new discourse, to reconstitute the hostile, biology-derived "us" versus "them" communities into a new *consensual* community of "we."

All countries view themselves by their ideals. Indians idealize, as well they should, the cultural continuum, the inherent value system of India, and are properly incensed when foreigners see nothing but poverty, intolerance, ignorance, strife, and injustice. Americans see themselves as the embodiments of liberty, openness, and individualism, even when the world judges them for drugs, crime, violence, bigotry, militarism, and homelessness. I was in Singapore when the media was very vocal about the case of an American teenager sentenced to caning for having allegedly vandalized cars. The overwhelming local sentiment was that caning Michael Fay would deter local youths from being tempted into "Americanization," meaning into gleefully breaking the law.

Conversely, in Tavares, Florida, an ardently patriotic school board has legislated that middle school teachers be required to instruct their students that American culture—meaning European-American culture—is inherently "superior to other foreign or historic cultures." The sinister, or at least misguided, implication is that American culture has not been affected by the American Indian, African American, Latin American, and Asian American segments of its population.

The idea of "America" as a nation has been set up in opposition to the tenet 25 that a nation is a collection of like-looking, like-speaking, like-worshiping people. Our nation is unique in human history. We have seen very recently, in a Germany plagued by anti-foreigner frenzy, how violently destabilizing the traditional concept of nation can be. In Europe, each country is, in a sense, a tribal homeland. Therefore, the primary criterion for nationhood in Europe is homogeneity of culture, and race, and religion. And that has contributed to blood-soaked balkanization in the former Yugoslavia and the former Soviet Union.

All European Americans, or their pioneering ancestors, gave up an easy homogeneity in their original countries for a new idea of Utopia. What we have going for us in the 1990s is the exciting chance to share in the making of a new American culture, rather than the coerced acceptance of either the failed nineteenth-century model of "melting pot" or the Canadian model of the "multicultural mosaic."

The "mosaic" implies a contiguity of self-sufficient, utterly distinct culture. "Multiculturism" has come to imply the existence of a central culture, ringed by peripheral cultures. The sinister fallout of official multiculturism and of professional multiculturists is the establishment of one culture as the norm and the rest as aberrations. Multiculturism emphasizes the differences between racial heritages. This emphasis on the differences has too often led to the dehumanization of the different. Dehumanization leads to discrimination. And discrimination can ultimately lead to genocide.

We need to alert ourselves to the limitations and the dangers of those discourses that reinforce an "us" versus "them" mentality. We need to protest any official rhetoric or demagoguery that marginalizes on a race-related and/or religion-related basis any segment of our society. I want to discourage the retention of cultural memory if the aim of that retention is cultural balkanization. I want to sensitize you to think of culture and nationhood *not* as an uneasy aggregate of antagonistic "them" and "us," but as a constantly re-forming, transmogrifying "we."

In this diasporic age, one's biological identity may not be the only one. Erosions and accretions come with the act of emigration. The experiences of violent unhousing from a biological "homeland" and rehousing in an adopted "homeland" that is not always welcoming to its dark-complected citizens have tested me as a person, and made me the writer I am today.

I choose to describe myself on my own terms, that is, as an American without 30 hyphens. It is to sabotage the politics of hate and the campaigns of revenge spawned by Eurocentric patriots on the one hand and the professional multiculturists on the other, that I describe myself as an "American" rather than as an "Asian-American." Why is it that hyphenization is imposed only on non-white Americans? And why is it that only non-white citizens are "problematized" if they choose to describe themselves on their own terms? My outspoken rejection of hyphenization is my lonely campaign to obliterate categorizing the cultural landscape into a "center" and its "peripheries." To reject hyphenization is to demand that the nation deliver the promises of the American Dream and the American Constitution to *all* its citizens. I want nothing less than to invent a new vocabulary that demands, and obtains, an equitable power-sharing for all members of the American community.

But my self-empowering refusal to be "otherized" and "objectified" has come at tremendous cost. My rejection of hyphenization has been deliberately misrepresented as "race treachery" by some India-born, urban, upper-middle-class Marxist "green card holders" with lucrative chairs on U.S. campuses. These academics strategically position themselves as self-appointed spokespersons for their ethnic communities, and as guardians of the "purity" of ethnic cultures. At the same time, though they reside permanently in the United States and participate in the capitalist economy of this nation, they publicly denounce American ideals and institutions.

They direct their rage at me because, as a U.S. citizen, I have invested in the present and the future rather than in the expatriate's imagined homeland. They condemn me because I acknowledge erosion of memory as a natural result of emigration; because I count that erosion as net gain rather than as loss; and because I celebrate racial and cultural "mongrelization." I have no respect for these expatriate fence-straddlers who, even while competing fiercely for tenure and promotion within the U.S. academic system, glibly equate all evil in the world with the United States, capitalism, colonialism, and corporate and military expansionism. I regard the artificial retentions of "pure race" and "pure culture" as dangerous, reactionary illusions fostered by the Eurocentric and the ethnocentric empire builders within the academy. I fear still more the politics of revenge preached from pulpits by some minority demagogues. . . .

As a writer, my literary agenda begins by acknowledging that America has transformed *me.* It does not end until I show that I (and the hundreds of thousands of recent immigrants like me) am minute by minute transforming America. The transformation is a two-way process; it affects both the individual and the national cultural identity. The end result of immigration, then, is this two-way transformation: that's my heartfelt message.

Others often talk of diaspora, of arrival as the end of the process. They talk of arrival in the context of loss, the loss of communal memory and the erosion of an intact ethnic culture. They use words like "erosion" and "loss" in alarmist ways. I want to talk of arrival as gain. . . .

What excites me is that we have the chance to retain those values we treasure 35 from our original cultures, but we also acknowledge that the outer forms of those values are likely to change. In the Indian American community, I see a great deal of guilt about the inability to hang on to "pure culture." Parents express rage or despair at their U.S.-born children's forgetting of, or indifference to, some aspects of Indian culture. Of those parents, I would ask: What is it we have lost if our children are acculturating into the culture in which we are living? Is it so terrible that our children are discovering or inventing homelands for themselves? Some first-generation Indo-Americans, embittered by overt anti-Asian racism and by unofficial "glass ceilings," construct a phantom more-Indian-than-Indians-in-India identity as defense against marginalization. Of them I would ask: Why not get actively involved in fighting discrimination through protests and lawsuits?

I prefer that we forge a national identity that is born of our acknowledgment of the steady de-Europeanization of the U.S. population; that constantly synthesizes—fuses—the disparate cultures of our country's residents; and that provides a new, sustaining, and unifying national creed.

Analyzing Mukherjee's Essay

Let's see what we can learn about how to appeal to audiences in mediatory essays. We'll look at *ethos* (how Mukherjee projects good character), *pathos* (how she arouses emotions favorable to her case), and *logos* (how she wins assent through good reasoning).

Ethos: Earning the Respect of Both Sides

Mediatory essays are not typically as personal as this one. But the author is in an unusual position, which makes the personal relevant. By speaking in the first person and telling her story, Mukherjee seeks the goodwill of people on both sides. She presents herself as patriotic, a foreigner who has assimilated to American ways, clearly appealing to those on Kimball's side. But she is also a "person of color," who's been "tested" by racial prejudices in the United States, clearly appealing to Martínez's side. She creates negative ethos for the radical extremists in the identity debate, depicting them as lacking morality and/or honesty. That's why she cites the violence committed by both whites and minorities, the scapegoating by politicians pandering to voter fears, the hypocrisy of professors who live well in America while denouncing its values. She associates her own position with words like *commitment, compassion, consensus, equality,* and *unity.*

By including her own experiences in India and Canada and her references to Bosnia, Rwanda, Germany, and the former Soviet Union, Mukherjee is able to place this American debate in a larger context—parts of the world in which national identity incites war and human rights violations.

Pathos: Using Emotion to Appeal to Both Sides

Appealing to the right emotions can help to move parties in conflict to the higher ground of consensus. Mukherjee displays a range of emotions, including pride, anger, and compassion. In condemning the extremes on both sides, her tone becomes heated. She uses highly charged words like *rabid, demagogues, scapegoaters, fence-straddlers,* and *reactionaries* to describe them. Her goal is to distance the members of her audience who are reasonable from those who aren't, so her word choice is appropriate and effective.

Patriotism is obviously emotional. Mukherjee's repeated declaration of devotion to her adopted country stirs audience pride. So does the contrast with India and Canada and the celebrating of individual freedom in the United States.

Her own story of arrival, nostalgia, and transformation arouses compassion and respect because it shows that assimilation is not easy. She understands the reluctance of Indian parents to let their children change. This shows her ability to empathize.

Finally, she appeals through hope and optimism. Twice she describes the consensus she proposes as *exciting*—and also fresh, new, vital, alive—in contrast to the rigid and inflexible ethnic purists.

Logos: Integrating Values of Both Sides

Mukherjee's thesis is that the opposing sides in the national identity debate are two sides of the wrong coin: the mistaken regard for ethnic purity. Making an issue of one's ethnicity, whether it be Anglo, Chicano, Indian-American, or whatever, is not a means to harmony and equality. Instead, America needs a unifying national identity that blends the ever-changing mix of races and cultures that make up our population.

Mukherjee offers reasons to oppose ethnic "purity":

Violence and wars result when people divide according to ethnic and religious differences. It creates an "us" versus "them" mentality.

The multicultural Canadian program created second-class, marginal populations.

Hyphenization in America makes a problem out of non-whites in the population.

We said that mediation looks for the good in each side and tries to show what they have in common. Mukherjee shows that her solution offers gains for both sides, a "win-win" situation. She concedes that her solution would mean some loss of "cultural memory" for immigrants, but these losses are offset by the following gains:

The United States would be closer to the strong and unified nation that Kimball wants because *everyone's* contributions would be appreciated.

The cultural barriers between minorities would break down, as Martínez wants. This would entail speaking to each other in English, but being free to maintain diverse cultures at home.

The barriers between "Americans" and hyphenated Americans would break down, as both Kimball and Martínez want. In other words, there would be assimilation, as Kimball wants, but not assimilation to one culture, which Martínez strongly resists.

By removing the need to prove one's own culture superior, we could all recognize the faults in our past as well as the good things. We would have no schools teaching either the superiority or the inferiority of any culture.

Emphasizing citizenship instead of ethnicity is a way of standing up for and demanding equal rights and equal opportunity, helping to bring about the social justice and equality Martínez seeks.

The new identity would be "sustaining," avoiding future conflicts because it would adapt to change.

Mukherjee's essay mediates by showing that a definition of America based on either one ethnic culture or many ethnic cultures is not satisfactory. By dropping ethnicity as a prime concern, both sides can be better off and freer in pursuit of happiness and success.

◎◎ FOLLOWING THROUGH

Look over the essays by Elizabeth Martínez and Roger Kimball. Do you think either of them would find Bharati Mukherjee's essay persuasive? What does Mukherjee say that might cause either of them to relax their positions about American identity? Do you think any further information might help to bring either side to Mukherjee's consensus position? For example, Kimball mentions the "Letter from an American Farmer" by de Crèvecoeur, who describes Americans as a new "race" of blended nationalities, leaving behind their ties and allegiances to former lands. How is Crèvecouer's idea of the "new race" similar to Mukherjee's?

Writing a Mediatory Essay

Prewriting

If you have been mediating the positions of two or more groups of classmates or two or more authors of published arguments, you may be assigned to write a mediatory essay in which you argue for a compromise position, appealing to an audience of people on all sides. In preparing to write such an essay, you should work through the steps of mediation as described on pages 302–305. In your writer's notebook, prepare briefs of the various conflicting positions, and note areas of disagreement; think hard about the differing interests of the conflicting parties, and respond to the questions about difference on page 304.

If possible, give some thought to each party's background—age, race, gender, and so forth—and how it might contribute to his or her viewpoint on the issue. For example, in a debate about whether *Huckleberry Finn* should be taught and read aloud in U.S. high schools, an African-American parent whose child is the only minority student in her English class might well have a different perspective from that of a white teacher. Can the white teacher be made to understand the embarrassment that a sole black child might feel when the white characters speak with derision about "niggers"?

In your writer's notebook, describe the conflict in its full complexity, not just its polar opposites. For example, considering the controversy over *Huckleberry Finn,* you might find some arguments in favor of teaching it anytime, others opposed to teaching it at all, others suggesting that it be an optional text for reading outside of class, and still others proposing that it be taught only in twelfth grade, when students are mature enough to understand Twain's satire. Try to find the good values in each position: a desire to teach the classics of American literature for what they tell us about the human condition and our country's history and values; a desire to promote respect for African-American students; a desire to ensure a comfortable learning climate for all students; and so on. You may be able to see that people's real interests are not as far apart as they might seem. You may be able to find common ground. For example, those who advocate teaching *Huckleberry Finn* and those who are opposed may both have in mind the goal of eliminating racial prejudice.

At this point in the prewriting process, think of some solutions that would satisfy at least some of the interests on all sides. It might be necessary for you to do some additional research. What do you think any of the opposing parties might want to know more about in order to accept your solution?

Finally, write up a clear statement of your solution. Can you explain how your solution appeals to the interests of all sides? In the *Huckleberry Finn* debate, we might propose that the novel be taught at any grade level provided that it is presented as part of a curriculum to educate students about the African-American experience with the involvement of African-American faculty or visiting lecturers.

Drafting

There is no set form for the mediatory essay. In fact, it is an unusual, even somewhat experimental, form of writing. As with any argument, the important thing is to have a plan for arranging your points and to provide clear signals to your readers. One logical way to organize a mediatory essay is in three parts:

Overview of the conflict. Describe the conflict and the opposing positions in the introductory paragraphs.

Discussion of differences underlying the conflict. Here your goal is to make all sides more sympathetic to one another and to sort out the important real interests that must be addressed by the solution.

Proposed solution. Here you make a case for your compromise position, giving reasons why it should be acceptable to all—that is, showing that it does serve at least some of their interests.

Revising

When revising a mediatory essay, you should look for the usual problems of organization and development that you would be looking for in any essay to convince or persuade. Be sure that you have inquired carefully and fairly into the conflict and that you have clearly presented the cases for all sides, including your proposed solution. At this point, you also need to consider how well you have used the persuasive appeals:

The appeal to character. Think about what kind of character you have projected as a mediator. Have you maintained neutrality? Do you model open-mindedness and genuine concern for the sensitivities of all sides?

The appeal to emotions. To arouse sympathy and empathy, which are needed in negotiation, you should take into account the emotional appeals discussed on pages 268–271. Your mediatory essay should be a moving argument for understanding and overcoming difference.

The appeal through style. As in persuasion, you should put the power of language to work. Pay attention to concrete word choice, striking metaphors, and phrases that stand out because of repeated sounds and rhythms.

www.mhhe.com/**crusius**

For help editing your essay, go to:

Editing

For suggestions about editing and proofreading, see Appendix A.

STUDENT SAMPLE An Essay Arguing to Mediate

The following mediatory essay was written by Angi Grellhesl, a first-year student at Southern Methodist University. Her essay examines opposing written views on the institution of speech codes at various U.S. colleges and its effect on freedom of speech.

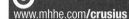

www.mhhe.com/**crusius**

For many additional examples of students writing, go to:

Writing

Mediating the Speech Code Controversy
Angi Grellhesl

The right to free speech has raised many controversies over the years. Explicit lyrics in rap music and marches by the Ku Klux Klan are just some examples that test the power of the First Amendment. Now, students and administrators are questioning if, in fact, free speech ought to be limited on university campuses. Many schools have instituted speech codes to protect specified groups from harassing speech.

Both sides in the debate, the speech code advocates and the free speech advocates, have presented their cases in recent books and articles. Columnist Nat Hentoff argues strongly against the speech codes, his main reason being that the codes violate students' First Amendment rights. Hentoff links the right to free speech with the values of higher education. In support, he quotes Yale president Benno Schmidt, who says, "Freedom of thought must be Yale's central commitment. . . . [U]niversities cannot censor or suppress speech, no matter how obnoxious in content, without violating their justification for existence . . . " (qtd. in Hentoff 223). Another reason Hentoff offers against speech codes is that universities must teach students to defend themselves in preparation for the real world, where such codes cannot shield them. Finally, he suggests that most codes are too vaguely worded; students may not even know they are violating the codes (216).

Two writers in favor of speech codes are Richard Perry and Patricia Williams. They see speech codes as a necessary and fair limitation on free speech. Perry and Williams argue that speech codes promote multicultural awareness, making students more sensitive to the differences that are out there in the real world. These authors do not think that the codes violate First Amendment rights, and they are suspicious of the motives of those who say they do. As Perry and Williams put it, those who feel free speech rights are being threatened "are apparently unable to distinguish between a liberty interest on the one hand and, on the other, a quite specific interest in being able to spout racist, sexist, and homophobic epithets completely unchallenged—without, in other words, the terrible inconvenience of feeling bad about it" (228).

Perhaps if both sides trusted each other a little more, they could see that their goals are not contradictory. Everyone agrees that students' rights should be protected. Hentoff wishes to ensure that students have the right to speak their minds. He and others on his side are concerned about freedom. Defenders of the codes argue that students have the right not to be harassed, especially while they are getting an education. They are concerned about opportunity. Would either side really deny that the other's goal had value?

Also, both sides want to create the best possible educational environment. Here the difference rests on the interpretation of what benefits the students. Is the best environment one most like the real world, where prejudice and harassment occur? Or does the university have an obligation to provide an atmosphere where potential victims can thrive and participate freely without intimidation?

I think it is possible to reach a solution that everyone can agree on. Most citizens want to protect constitutional rights; but they also agree that those rights have limitations, the ultimate limit being when one person infringes on the rights of others to live in peace. All sides should agree that a person ought to be able to speak out about his or her convictions, values, and beliefs. And most people can see a difference between that protected speech and the kind that is intended to harass and intimidate. For example, there is a clear difference between expressing one's view that Jews are mistaken in not accepting Christ as the son of God, on the one hand, and yelling anti-Jewish threats at a particular person in the middle of the night, on the other. Could a code not be worded in such a way as to distinguish between these two kinds of speech?

Also, I don't believe either side would want the university to be an artificial world. Codes should not attempt to ensure that no one is criticized or even offended. Students should not be afraid to say controversial things. But universities do help to shape the future of the real world, so shouldn't they at least take a stand against harassment? Can a code be worded that would protect free speech and prevent harassment?

The current speech code at Southern Methodist University is a compromise that ought to satisfy free speech advocates and speech code advocates. It prohibits hate speech at the same time that it protects an individual's First Amendment rights.

First, it upholds the First Amendment by including a section that reads, "[D]ue to the University's commitment to freedom of speech and expression, harassment is more than mere insensitivity or offensive conduct which creates an uncomfortable situation for certain members of the community" (Peruna 92). The code therefore

5

should satisfy those, like Hentoff, who place a high value on the basic rights our nation was built upon. Secondly, whether or not there is a need for protection, the current code protects potential victims from hate speech or "any words or acts deliberately designed to disregard the safety or rights of another, and which intimidate, degrade, demean, threaten, haze, or otherwise interfere with another person's rightful action" (Peruna 92). This part of the code should satisfy those who recognize that some hurts cannot be overcome. Finally, the current code outlines specific acts that constitute harassment: "Physical, psychological, verbal and/or written acts directed toward an individual or group of individuals which rise to the level of 'fighting words' are prohibited" (Peruna 92).

The SMU code protects our citizens from hurt and from unconstitutional censorship. Those merely taking a position can express it, even if it hurts. On the other hand, those who are spreading hatred will be limited as to what harm they may inflict. Therefore, all sides should respect the code as a safeguard for those who use free speech but a limitation for those who abuse it. 10

Works Cited

Hentoff, Nat. "Speech Codes on the Campus and Problems of Free Speech." Debating P.C. Ed. Paul Berman. New York: Bantam, 1992. 215–24.

Perry, Richard, and Patricia Williams. "Freedom of Speech." Debating P.C. Ed. Paul Berman. New York: Bantam, 1992. 225–30.

Peruna Express 1993–1994. Dallas: Southern Methodist U, 1993.

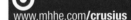
www.mhhe.com/**crusius**

For an electronic tool that helps create properly formatted works-cited pages, go to:

Research > Bibliomaker

A Short Guide to Editing and Proofreading

Editing and proofreading are the final steps in creating a finished piece of writing. Too often, however, these steps are rushed as writers race to meet a deadline. Ideally, you should distinguish between the acts of revising, editing, and proofreading. Because each step requires that you pay attention to something different, you cannot reasonably expect to do them well if you try to do them all at once.

Our suggestions for revising appear in each of Chapters 7–10 on the aims of argument. *Revising* means shaping and developing the whole argument with an eye to audience and purpose; when you revise, you are ensuring that you have accomplished your aim. *Editing,* on the other hand, means making smaller changes within paragraphs and sentences. When you edit, you are thinking about whether your prose will be a pleasure to read. Editing improves the sound and rhythm of your voice. It makes complicated ideas more accessible to readers and usually makes your writing more concise. Finally, *proofreading* means eliminating errors. When you proofread, you correct everything you find that will annoy readers, such as misspellings, punctuation mistakes, and faulty grammar.

In this appendix, we offer some basic advice on what to look for when editing and proofreading. For more detailed help, consult a handbook on grammar and punctuation and a good book on style, such as Joseph Williams's *Ten Lessons in Clarity and Grace* or Richard Lanham's *Revising Prose.* Both of these texts guided our thinking in the advice that follows.

EDITING

Most ideas can be phrased in a number of ways, each of which gives the idea a slightly distinctive twist. Consider the following examples:

> In New York City, about 74,000 people die each year.

> In New York City, death comes to one in a hundred people each year.

www.mhhe.com/**crusius**

For a wealth of online editing resources, check out the tools grouped under:

Editing

www.mhhe.com/**crusius**

To Take a diagnostic test covering editing skills, go to:

Editing > Diagnostic Test

Death comes to one in a hundred New Yorkers each year.

To begin an article on what becomes of the unknown and unclaimed dead in New York, Edward Conlon wrote the final of these three sentences. We can only speculate about the possible variations he considered, but because openings are so crucial, he almost certainly cast these words quite deliberately.

For most writers, such deliberation over matters of style occurs during editing. In this late stage of the writing process, writers examine choices made earlier, perhaps unconsciously, while drafting and revising. They listen to how sentences sound, to patterns of rhythm both within and among sentences. Editing is like an art or craft; it can provide you the satisfaction of knowing you've said something gracefully and effectively. To focus on language this closely, you will need to set aside enough time following the revision step.

In this section, we discuss some things to look for when editing your own writing. Don't forget, though, that editing does not always mean looking for weaknesses. You should also recognize passages that work well just as you wrote them, that you can leave alone or play up more by editing passages that surround them.

Editing for Clarity and Conciseness

Even drafts revised several times may have wordy and awkward passages; these are often places where a writer struggled with uncertainty or felt less than confident about the point being made. Introductions often contain such passages. In editing, you have one more opportunity to clarify and sharpen your ideas.

Express Main Ideas Forcefully

Emphasize the main idea of a sentence by stating it as directly as possible, using the two key sentence parts (*subject* and *verb*) to convey the two key parts of the idea (*agent* and *act*).

As you edit, first look for sentences that state ideas indirectly rather than directly; such sentences may include (1) overuse of the verb *to be* in its various forms (*is, was, will have been,* and so forth), (2) the opening words "There is . . ." or "It is . . . ," (3) strings of prepositional phrases, or (4) many vague nouns. Then ask, "What is my true subject here, and what is that subject's action?" Here is an example of a weak, indirect sentence:

It is a fact that the effects of pollution are more evident in lower-class neighborhoods than in middle-class ones.

The writer's subject is pollution. What is the pollution's action? Limply, the sentence tells us its "effects" are "evident." The following edited version makes pollution the agent that performs the action of a livelier verb, "fouls." The edited sentence is more specific—without being longer.

Pollution more frequently *fouls* the air, soil, and water of lower-class neighborhoods than of middle-class ones.

Editing Practice   The following passage about a plan for creating low-income housing contains two weak sentences. In this case, the weakness results from wordiness. (Note the overuse of vague nouns and prepositional phrases.) Decide what the true subject is for each sentence, and make that word the subject of the verb. Your edited version should be much shorter.

> As in every program, there will be the presence of a few who abuse the system. However, as in other social programs, the numbers would not be sufficient to justify the rejection of the program on the basis that one person in a thousand will try to cheat.

Choose Carefully between Active and Passive Voice

Active voice and passive voice indicate different relationships between subjects and verbs. As we have noted, ideas are usually clearest when the writer's true subject is also the subject of the verb in the sentence—that is, when it is the agent of the action. In the passive voice, however, the agent of the action appears in the predicate or not at all. Rather than acting as agent, the subject of the sentence *receives* the action of the verb.

www.mhhe.com/**crusius**

For more coverage of voice, go to:

Editing > Verb and Voice Shifts

The following sentence is in the passive voice:

> The air of poor neighborhoods is often fouled by pollution.

There is nothing incorrect about the use of the passive voice in this sentence, and in the context of a whole paragraph, passive voice can be the most emphatic way to make a point. (Here, for example, it allows the word *pollution* to fall at the end of the sentence, a strong position.) But, often, use of the passive voice is not a deliberate choice at all; rather, it's a vague and unspecific way of stating a point.

> Consider the following sentences, in which the main verbs have no agents:
>
> It *is believed* that dumping garbage at sea is not as harmful to the environment as *was* once *thought.*
>
> Ronald Reagan *was considered* the "Great Communicator."

Who thinks such dumping is not so harmful? environmental scientists? industrial producers? Who considered former president Reagan a great communicator? speech professors? news commentators? Such sentences are clearer when they are written in the active voice:

> Some environmentalists believe that dumping garbage at sea is not as harmful to the environment as they used to think.
>
> Media commentators considered Ronald Reagan the "Great Communicator."

In editing for the passive voice, look over your verbs. Passive voice is easily recognized because it always contains (1) some form of *to be* as a helping verb and (2) the main verb in its past participle form (which ends in *-ed, -d, -t, -en,* or *-n,* or in some cases may be irregular: *drunk, sung, lain,* and so on).

When you find a sentence phrased in the passive voice, decide who or what is performing the action; the agent may appear after the verb or not at all. Then decide if changing the sentence to the active voice will improve the sentence as well as the surrounding passage.

Editing Practice

1. The following paragraph from a student's argument needs to be edited for emphasis. It is choking with excess nouns and forms of the verb *to be,* some as part of passive constructions. You need not eliminate all passive voice, but do look for wording that is vague and ineffective. Your edited version should be not only stronger but shorter as well.

   Although emergency shelters are needed in some cases (for example, a mother fleeing domestic violence), they are an inefficient means of dealing with the massive numbers of people they are bombarded with each day. The members of a homeless family are in need of a home, not a temporary shelter into which they and others like them are herded, only to be shuffled out when their thirty-day stay is over to make room for the next incoming herd. Emergency shelters would be sufficient if we did not have a low-income housing shortage, but what is needed most at present is an increase in availability of affordable housing for the poor.

2. Select a paragraph of your own writing to edit; focus on using strong verbs and subjects to carry the main idea of your sentences.

Editing for Emphasis

When you edit for emphasis, you make sure that your main ideas stand out so that your reader will take notice. Following are some suggestions to help.

Emphasize Main Ideas by Subordinating Less Important Ones

Subordination refers to distinctions in rank or order of importance. Think of the chain of command at an office: the boss is at the top of the ladder, the middle management is on a lower (subordinate) rung, the support staff is at an even lower rung, and so on.

In writing, subordination means placing less important ideas in less important positions in sentences in order to emphasize the main ideas that should stand out. Writing that lacks subordination treats all ideas equally; each idea may consist of a sentence of its own or may be joined to another idea by a coordinator (*and, but,* and *or*). Such a passage follows with its sentences numbered for reference purposes.

(1) It has been over a century since slavery was abolished and a few decades since lawful, systematic segregation came to an unwilling halt.

(2) Truly, blacks have come a long way from the darker days that lasted for more than three centuries. (3) Many blacks have entered the mainstream, and there is a proportionately large contingent of middle-class blacks. (4) Yet an even greater percentage of blacks are immersed in truly pathetic conditions. (5) The inner-city black poor are enmeshed in devastating socioeconomic problems. (6) Unemployment among inner-city black youths has become much worse than it was even five years ago.

Three main ideas are important here—that blacks have been free for some time, that some have made economic progress, and that others are trapped in poverty—and of these three, the last is probably intended to be the most important. Yet, as we read the passage, these key ideas do not stand out. In fact, each point receives equal emphasis and sounds about the same, with the repeated subject-verb-object syntax. The result seems monotonous, even apathetic, though the writer is probably truly disturbed about the subject. The following edited version, which subordinates some of the points, is more emphatic. We have italicized the main points.

> *Blacks have come a long way* in the century since slavery was abolished and in the decades since lawful, systematic segregation came to an unwilling halt. Yet, although many blacks have entered the mainstream and the middle class, *an even greater percentage is immersed in truly pathetic conditions*. To give just one example of these devastating socioeconomic problems, *unemployment among inner-city black youths is much worse now than it was even five years ago.*

Although different editing choices are possible, this version plays down sentences 1, 3, and 5 in the original so that sentences 2, 4, and 6 stand out.

As you edit, look for passages that sound wordy and flat because all the ideas are expressed with equal weight in the same subject-verb-object pattern. Then single out your most important points, and try out some options for subordinating the less important ones. The key is to put main ideas in main clauses and modifying ideas in modifying clauses or phrases.

Modifying Clauses Like simple sentences, modifying clauses contain a subject and verb. They are formed in two ways: (1) with relative pronouns and (2) with subordinating conjunctions.

Relative pronouns introduce clauses that modify nouns, with the relative pronoun relating the clause to the noun it modifies. There are five relative pronouns: *that, which, who, whose,* and *whom.* The following sentence contains a relative clause:

> Alcohol advertisers are trying to sell a product *that is by its very nature harmful to users.*
>
> —Jason Rath (student)

Relative pronouns may also be implied:

I have returned the library book [that] *you loaned me.*

Relative pronouns may also be preceded by prepositions, such as *on, in, to,* or *during:*

Drug hysteria has created an atmosphere *in which civil rights are disregarded.*

Subordinating conjunctions show relationships among ideas. It is impossible to provide a complete list of subordinating conjunctions in this short space, but here are the most common and the kinds of modifying roles they perform:

To show time: *after, as, before, since, until, when, while*

To show place: *where, wherever*

To show contrast: *although, though, whereas, while*

To show cause and effect: *because, since, so that*

To show condition: *if, unless, whether, provided that*

To show manner: *how, as though*

By introducing it with a subordinating conjunction, you can convert one sentence into a dependent clause that can modify another sentence. Consider the following two versions of the same idea:

Pain is a state of consciousness, a "mental event." It can never be directly observed.

Since pain is a state of consciousness, a "mental event," it can never be directly observed.

—Peter Singer, *"Animal Liberation"*

Modifying Phrases Unlike clauses, phrases do not have a subject and a verb. Prepositional phrases and infinitive phrases are most likely already in your repertoire of modifiers. (Consult a handbook if you need to review these.) Here, we remind you of two other useful types of phrases: (1) participial phrases and (2) appositives.

Participial phrases modify nouns. Participles are created from verbs, so it is not surprising that the two varieties represent two verb tenses. The first is present participles ending in *-ing:*

Hoping to eliminate harassment on campus, many universities have tried to institute codes for speech and behavior.

The desperate Haitians fled here in boats, *risking all.*

—Carmen Hazan-Cohen (student)

The second is past participles ending in *-ed, -en, -d, -t,* or *-n:*

> Women themselves became a resource, *acquired by men much as the land was acquired by men.*
>
> —Gerda Lerner

> *Linked more to the Third World and Asia than to the Europe of America's racial and cultural roots,* Los Angeles and Southern California will enter the 21st century as a multi-racial and multicultural society.
>
> —Ryszard Kapuscinski

Notice that modifying phrases should immediately precede the nouns they modify.

An *appositive* is a noun or noun phrase that restates another noun, usually in a more specific way. Appositives can be highly emphatic, but more often they are tucked into the middle of a sentence or added to the end, allowing a subordinate idea to be slipped in. When used like this, appositives are usually set off with commas:

> Rick Halperin, *a professor at Southern Methodist University,* noted that Ted Bundy's execution cost Florida taxpayers over six million dollars.
>
> —Diane Miller (student)

Editing Practice

1. Edit the following passage as needed for emphasis, clarity, and conciseness, using subordinate clauses, relative clauses, participial phrases, appositives, and any other options that occur to you. If some parts are effective as they are, leave them alone.

   The monetary implications of drug legalization are not the only reason it is worth consideration. There is reason to believe that the United States would be a safer place to live if drugs were legalized. A large amount of what the media has named "drug-related" violence is really prohibition-related violence. Included in this are random shootings and murders associated with black-market transactions. Estimates indicate that at least 40 percent of all property crime in the United States is committed by drug users so they can maintain their habits. That amounts to a total of 4 million crimes per year and $7.5 billion in stolen property. Legalizing drugs would be a step toward reducing this wave of crime.

2. Edit a paragraph of your own writing with an eye to subordinating less important ideas through the use of modifying phrases and clauses.

Vary Sentence Length and Pattern

Even when read silently, your writing has a sound. If your sentences are all about the same length (typically fifteen to twenty words) and all structured according to a subject-verb-object pattern, they will roll along with the monotonous rhythm of an assembly line. Obviously, one solution to this problem is to open some of your sentences with modifying phrases and clauses, as we discuss in the previous section. Here we offer some other strategies, all of which add emphasis by introducing something unexpected.

1. Use a short sentence after several long ones.

   [A] population's general mortality is affected by a great many factors over which doctors and hospitals have little influence. For those diseases and injuries for which modern medicine can affect the outcome, however, which country the patient lives in really matters. Life expectancy is not the same among developed countries for premature babies, for children born with spina bifida, or for people who have cancer, a brain tumor, heart disease, or chronic renal failure. *Their chances of survival are best in the United States.*

   —John Goodman

2. Interrupt a sentence.

   The position of women in that hippie counterculture was, *as a young black male leader preached succinctly,* "prone."

   —Betty Friedan

   Symbols and myths—*when emerging uncorrupted from human experience*—are precious. Then it is the poetic voice and vision that informs and infuses—*the poet-warrior's, the prophet-seer's, the dreamer's*—reassuring us that truth is as real as falsehood. And ultimately stronger.

   —Ossie Davis

3. Use an intentional sentence fragment. The concluding fragment in the previous passage by Ossie Davis is a good example.
4. Invert the order of subject-verb-object.

   Further complicating negotiations is the difficulty of obtaining relevant financial statements.

   —Regina Herzlinger

   This creature, with scarcely two thirds of man's cranial capacity, was a fire user. Of what it meant to him beyond warmth and shelter, we know nothing; with what rites, ghastly or benighted, it was struck or maintained, no word remains.

   —Loren Eiseley

Use Special Effects for Emphasis

Especially in persuasive argumentation, you will want to make some of your points in deliberately dramatic ways. Remember that just as the crescendos stand out in music because the surrounding passages are less intense, so the special effects work best in rhetoric when you use them sparingly.

Repetition Deliberately repeating words, phrases, or sentence patterns has the effect of building up to a climactic point. In Chapter 9, we noted how Martin Luther King, Jr., in the emotional high point of his "Letter from Birmingham Jail," used repeated subordinate clauses beginning with the phrase "when you" to build up to his main point: " . . . then you will understand why we find it difficult to wait" (paragraph 14, pages 256–257). Here is another example, from the conclusion of an argument linking women's rights with environmental reforms:

> Environmental justice goes much further than environmental protection, a passive and paternalistic phrase. *Justice requires that* industrial nations pay back the environmental debt incurred in building their wealth by using less of nature's resources. *Justice prescribes that* governments stop siting hazardous waste facilities in cash-poor rural and urban neighborhoods and now in the developing world. *Justice insists that* the subordination of women and nature by men is not only a hazard; it is a crime. *Justice reminds us that* the Earth does not belong to us; even when we "own" a piece of it, we belong to the Earth.
>
> —H. Patricia Hynes

Paired Coordinators Coordinators are conjunctions that pair words, word groups, and sentences in a way that gives them equal emphasis and that also shows a relationship between them, such as contrast, consequence, or addition. In grade school, you may have learned the coordinators through the mnemonic *FANBOYS*, standing for *for, and, nor, but, or, yet, so.*

Paired coordinators emphasize the relationship between coordinated elements; the first coordinator signals that a corresponding coordinator will follow. Some paired coordinators are:

both _____ and _____

not _____ but _____

not only _____ but also _____

either _____ or _____

neither _____ nor _____

The key to effective paired coordination is to keep the words that follow the marker words as grammatically similar as possible. Pair nouns with nouns, verbs with verbs, prepositional phrases with prepositional phrases, and whole sentences with whole sentences. (Think of paired coordination as a variation on repetition.) Here are some examples:

> Feminist anger, or any form of social outrage, is dismissed breezily—*not* because it lacks substance *but* because it lacks "style."
>
> —Susan Faludi

> Alcohol ads that emphasize "success" in the business and social worlds are useful examples *not only* of how advertisers appeal to people's envy *but also* of how ads perpetuate gender stereotypes.
>
> —Jason Rath (student)

Emphatic Appositives   While an appositive (a noun or noun phrase that restates another noun) can subordinate an idea, it can also emphasize an idea if it is placed at the beginning or the end of a sentence, where it will command attention. Here are some examples:

> *The poorest nation in the Western hemisphere,* Haiti is populated by six million people, many of whom cannot obtain adequate food, water, or shelter.
>
> —Sneed B. Collard III

> [Feminists] made a simple, though serious, ideological error when they applied the same political rhetoric to their own situation as women versus men: too *literal an analogy with class warfare, racial oppression.*
>
> —Betty Friedan

Note that at the end of a sentence, an appositive may be set off with a colon or a dash.

Emphatic Word Order   The opening and closing positions of a sentence are high-profile spots, not to be wasted on weak words. The following sentence, for example, begins weakly with the filler phrase "there are":

> *There are* several distinctions, all of them false, that are commonly made between rape and date rape.

A better version would read:

> My opponents make several distinctions between rape and date rape; all of these are false.

Even more important are the final words of every paragraph and the opening and closing of the entire argument.

Editing Practice

1. Select one or two paragraphs from a piece of published writing you have recently read and admired. Be ready to share it with the class, explaining how the writer has crafted the passage to make it work.

2. Take a paragraph or two from one of your previous essays, perhaps even an essay from another course, and edit it to improve clarity, conciseness, and emphasis.

Editing for Coherence

Coherence refers to what some people call the "flow" of writing; writing flows when the ideas connect smoothly, one to the next. In contrast, when writing is incoherent, the reader must work to see how ideas connect and must infer points that the writer, for whatever reason, has left unstated.

Incoherence is a particular problem with writing that contains an abundance of direct or indirect quotations. In using sources, be careful always to lead into the quotation with some words of your own, showing clearly how this new idea connects with what has come before.

Because finding incoherent passages in your own writing can be difficult, ask a friend to read your draft to look for gaps in the presentation of ideas. Here are some additional suggestions for improving coherence.

Move from Old Information to New Information

Coherent writing is easy to follow because the connections between old information and new information are clear. Sentences refer back to previously introduced information and set up reader expectations for new information to come. Notice how every sentence fulfills your expectations in the following excerpts from an argument on animal rights by Steven Zak.

> The credibility of the animal-rights viewpoint . . . need not stand or fall with the "marginal human beings" argument.

Next, you would expect to hear why animals do not have to be classed as "marginal human beings"—and you do:

> Lives don't have to be qualitatively the same to be worthy of equal respect.

At this point you might ask upon what else we should base our respect. Zak answers this question in the next sentence:

> One's perception that another life has value comes as much from an appreciation of its uniqueness as from the recognition that it has characteristics that are shared by one's own life.

Not only do these sentences fulfill reader expectations, but each also makes a clear connection by referring specifically to the key idea in the sentence before it, forming an unbroken chain of thought. We have italicized the words that accomplish this linkage and connected them with arrows.

> The credibility of the animal-rights viewpoint . . . need not stand or fall with the *"marginal human beings"* argument.
>
> Lives don't have to be *qualitatively the same* to be worthy of *equal respect.*
>
> One's perception that *another life has value* comes as much from an *appreciation of its uniqueness* as from the recognition that it has characteristics that are shared by one's own life.
>
> One can imagine that the lives of various kinds of animals *differ radically.* . . .

In the following paragraph, reader expectations are not so well fulfilled:

> We are presently witness to the greatest number of homeless families since the Great Depression of the 1930s. The cause of this phenomenon is a shortage of low-income housing. Mothers with children as young as two weeks are forced to live on the street because there is no room for them in homeless shelters.

Although these sentences are all on the subject of homelessness, the second leads us to expect that the third will take up the topic of shortages of low-income housing. Instead, it takes us back to the subject of the first sentence and offers a different cause—no room in the shelters.

Looking for ways to link old information with new information will help you find problems of coherence in your own writing.

Editing Practice

1. In the following paragraph, underline the words or phrases that make the connections back to the previous sentence and forward to the next, as we did earlier with the passage from Zak.

> The affluent, educated, liberated women of the First World, who can enjoy freedoms unavailable to any women ever before, do not feel as free as they want to. And they can no longer restrict to the subconscious their sense that this lack of freedom has something to do with—with apparently frivolous issues, things that really should not matter. Many are ashamed to admit that such trivial concerns—to do with physical appearance, bodies, faces, hair, clothes—matter so much. But in spite of shame, guilt, and denial, more and more women are wondering if it isn't that they are entirely neurotic alone but rather that something important is indeed at stake that has to do with the relationship between female liberation and female beauty.
>
> —Naomi Wolf

2. The following student paragraph lacks coherence. Read through it, and put a slash (/) between sentences expressing unconnected ideas. You may try to rewrite the paragraph, rearranging sentences and adding ideas to make the connections tighter.

Students may know what AIDS is and how it is transmitted, but most are not concerned about AIDS and do not perceive themselves to be at risk. But college-age heterosexuals are the number-one high-risk group for this disease (Gray and Sacarino 258). "Students already know about AIDS. Condom distribution, public or not, is not going to help. It just butts into my personal life," said one student surveyed. College is a time for exploration and that includes the discovery of sexual freedom. Students, away from home and free to make their own decisions for maybe the first time in their lives, have a "bigger than life" attitude. The thought of dying is the farthest from their minds. Yet at this point in their lives, they are most in need of this information.

Use Transitions to Show Relationships between Ideas

Coherence has to be built into a piece of writing; as we discussed earlier, the ideas between sentences must first cohere. However, sometimes readers need help in making the transition from one idea to the next, so you must provide signposts to help them see the connections more readily. For example, a transitional word like *however* can prepare readers for an idea in contrast to the one before it, as in the second sentence in this paragraph. Transitional words can also highlight the structure of an argument ("These data will show three things: first . . . , second . . . , and third . . ."), almost forming a verbal path for the reader to follow. Following are examples of transitional words and phrases and their purposes:

To show order: *first, second, next, then, last, finally*

To show contrast: *however, yet, but, nevertheless*

To show cause and effect: *therefore, consequently, as a result, then*

To show importance: *moreover, significantly*

To show an added point: *as well, also, too*

To show an example: *for example, for instance*

To show concession: *admittedly*

To show conclusion: *in sum, in conclusion*

The key to using transitional words is similar to the key to using special effects for emphasis: Don't overdo it. To avoid choking your writing with these words, anticipate where your reader will genuinely need them, and limit their use to these instances.

Editing Practice   Underline the transitional words and phrases in the following passage of published writing:

When people believe that their problems can be solved, they tend to get busy solving them.

On the other hand, when people believe that their problems are beyond solution, they tend to position themselves so as to avoid blame. Take the woeful inadequacy of education in the predominantly black central cities. Does the black leadership see the ascendancy of black teachers, school administrators, and politicians as an asset to be used in improving those dreadful schools? Rarely. You are more likely to hear charges of white abandonment, white resistance to integration, conspiracies to isolate black children, even when the schools are officially desegregated. In short, white people are accused of being responsible for the problem. But if the youngsters manage to survive those awful school systems and achieve success, leaders want to claim credit. They don't hesitate to attribute that success to the glorious Civil Rights movement.

—William Raspberry

PROOFREADING

www.mhhe.com/**crusius**

For some advice and practice related to spelling, go to:

Editing > Spelling

Proofreading is truly the final step in writing a paper. After proofreading, you ought to be able to print your paper out one more time; but if you do not have time, most instructors will be perfectly happy to see the necessary corrections done neatly in ink on the final draft.

Following are some suggestions for proofreading.

Spelling Errors

If you have used a word processor, you may have a program that will check your spelling. If not, you will have to check your spelling by reading through again carefully with a dictionary at hand. Consult the dictionary whenever you feel uncertain. You might consider devoting a special part of your writer's notebook to your habitual spelling errors: some students always misspell *athlete,* for example, whereas others leave the second *n* out of *environment.*

Omissions and Jumbled Passages

Read your paper out loud. Physically shaping your lips around the words can help locate missing words, typos (*saw* instead of *was*), or the remnants of some earlier version of a sentence that did not get fully deleted. Place a caret (∧) in the sentence and write the correction or addition above the line, or draw a line through unnecessary text.

Punctuation Problems

Apostrophes and commas give writers the most trouble. If you have habitual problems with these, you should record your errors in your writer's notebook.

Apostrophes

Apostrophe problems usually occur in forming possessives, not contractions, so here we discuss only the former. If you have problems with possessives, you may also want to consult a good handbook or seek a private tutorial with your instructor or your school's writing center.

Here are the basic principles to remember.

1. Possessive pronouns—*his, hers, yours, theirs, its*—never take an apostrophe.

2. Singular nouns become possessive by adding *-'s.*

   A single parent's life is hard.

   A society's values change.

   Do you like Mr. Voss's new car?

3. Plural nouns ending in *-s* become possessive by simply adding an apostrophe.

   Her parents' marriage is faltering.

   Many cities' air is badly polluted.

   The Joneses' house is up for sale.

4. Plural nouns that do not end in *-s* become possessive by adding *-'s.*

   Show me the women's (men's) room.

   The people's voice was heard.

If you err by using apostrophes where they don't belong in nonpossessive words ending in *-s*, remember that a possessive will always have a noun after it, not some other part of speech such as a verb or a preposition. You may even need to read each line of print with a ruler under it to help you focus more intently on each word.

Commas

Because commas indicate a pause, reading your paper aloud is a good way to decide where to add or delete them. A good handbook will elaborate on the following basic principles. The example sentences have been adapted from an argument by Mary Meehan, who opposes abortion.

1. Use a comma when you join two or more main clauses with a coordinating conjunction.

   Main clause, conjunction (and, but, or, nor, so, yet) *main clause.*

   Feminists want to have men participate more in the care of children, but abortion allows a man to shift total responsibility to the woman.

2. Use a comma after an introductory phrase or dependent clause.

   Introductory phrase or clause, main clause.

   To save the smallest children, the Left should speak out against abortion.

www.mhhe.com/**crusius**

For some additional help using apostrophes, go to:

Editing > Apostrophes

www.mhhe.com/**crusius**

For some additional coverage of comma use, go to:

Editing > Commas

3. Use commas around modifiers such as relative clauses and appositives unless they are essential to the noun's meaning. Be sure to put the comma at both ends of the modifier.

    _____, *appositive,* _____

    _____, *relative clause,* _____

    One member of the 1972 Presidential commission on population growth was Graciela Olivarez, a Chicana who was active in civil rights and anti-poverty work. Olivarez, who later was named to head the Federal Government's Community Services Administration, had known poverty in her youth in the Southwest.

4. Use commas with a series.

    ___x___, ___y___, and ___z___,

    The traditional mark of the Left has been its protection of the underdog, the weak, and the poor.

Semicolons

Think of a semicolon as a strong comma. It has two main uses.

www.mhhe.com/**crusius**

For more coverage of semicolons, go to:

Editing > Semicolons

1. Use a semicolon to join two main clauses when you choose not to use a conjunction. This works well when the two main clauses are closely related or parallel in structure.

    Main clause; main clause.

    Pro-life activists did not want abortion to be a class issue; they wanted to end abortion everywhere, for all classes.

    As a variation, you may wish to add a transitional adverb to the second main clause. The adverb indicates the relationship between the main clauses, but it is not a conjunction, so a comma preceding it would not be correct.

    Main clause; transitional adverb (however, therefore, thus, moreover, consequently), *main clause.*

    When speaking with counselors at the abortion clinic, many women change their minds and decide against abortion; however, a woman who is accompanied by a husband or boyfriend often does not feel free to talk with the counselor.

2. Use semicolons between items in a series if any of the items themselves contain commas.

    ___,___ ; ___,___ ; ___,___

    A few liberals who have spoken out against abortion are Jesse Jackson, a civil rights leader; Richard Neuhaus, a theologian; the comedian Dick Gregory; and politicians Mark Hatfield and Mary Rose Oakar.

Colons

The colon has two common uses.

1. Use a colon to introduce a quotation when both your own lead-in and the words quoted are complete sentences that can stand alone. (See the section in Chapter 5 entitled "Incorporating and Documenting Source Material" for more on introducing quotations.)

www.mhhe.com/**crusius**

For some additional help using colons, go to:

Editing > Colons

   Main clause in your words: "Quoted sentence(s)."

   Mary Meehan criticizes liberals who have been silent on abortion: "If much of the leadership of the pro-life movement is right-wing, that is due largely to the default of the Left."

2. Use a colon before an appositive that comes dramatically at the end of a sentence, especially if the appositive contains more than one item.

   Main clause: appositive, appositive, and appositive.

   Meehan argues that many pro-choice advocates see abortion as a way to hold down the population of certain minorities: blacks, Puerto Ricans, and other Latins.

Grammatical Errors

Grammatical mistakes can be hard to find, but once again we suggest reading aloud as one method of proofing for them; grammatical errors tend not to "sound right" even if they look like good prose. Another suggestion is to recognize your habitual errors and then look for particular grammatical structures that lead you into error.

Introductory Participial Phrases

Constructions such as these often lead writers to create dangling modifiers. To avoid this pitfall, see the discussion of participial phrases earlier in this appendix. Remember that an introductory phrase dangles if it is not immediately followed by the noun it modifies.

   Incorrect: Using her conscience as a guide, our society has granted each woman the right to decide if a fetus is truly a "person" with rights equal to her own.

(Notice that the implied subject of the participial phrase is "each woman," when in fact the subject of the main clause is "our society"; thus, the participial phrase does not modify the subject.)

   Corrected: Using her conscience as a guide, each woman in our society has the right to decide if a fetus is truly a "person" with rights equal to her own.

Paired Coordinators

If the words that follow each of the coordinators are not of the same grammatical structure, then an error known as nonparallelism has occurred. To correct this error, line up the paired items one over the other. You will see that the correction often involves simply adding a word or two to, or deleting some words from, one side of the paired coordinators.

not only _____ but also _____

Incorrect: Legal abortion not only protects women's lives, but also their health.

Corrected: Legal abortion protects not only women's lives but also their health.

Split Subjects and Verbs

www.mhhe.com/**crusius**

For additional coverage of agreement, go to:

Editing > Subject/Verb Agreement

If the subject of a sentence contains long modifying phrases or clauses, by the time you get to the verb you may make an error in agreement (using a plural verb, for example, when the subject is singular) or even in logic (for example, having a subject that is not capable of being the agent that performs the action of the verb). Following are some typical errors:

The *goal* of the courses grouped under the rubric of "Encountering Non-Western Cultures" *are* . . .

Here the writer forgot that *goal,* the subject, is singular.

During 1992, *the Refugee Act of 1980,* with the help of President Bush and Congress, *accepted* 114,000 immigrants into our nation.

The writer here should have realized that the agent doing the accepting would have to be the Bush administration, not the Refugee Act. A better version would read:

During 1992, the Bush administration accepted 114,000 immigrants into our nation under the terms of the Refugee Act of 1980.

Proofreading Practice Proofread the following passage for errors of grammar and punctuation.

The citizens of Zurich, Switzerland tired of problems associated with drug abuse, experimented with legalization. The plan was to open a central park, Platzspitz, where drugs and drug use would be permitted. Many European experts felt, that it was the illegal drug business rather than the actual use of drugs that had caused many of the cities problems. While the citizens had hoped to isolate the drug problem, foster rehabilitation, and curb the AIDS epidemic, the actual outcome of the Platzspitz experiment did not create the desired results. Instead, violence increased. Drug-related deaths doubled. And drug users were drawn from not only all over

Switzerland, but from all over Europe as well. With thousands of discarded syringe packets lying around, one can only speculate as to whether the spread of AIDS was curbed. The park itself was ruined and finally on February 10, 1992, it was barred up and closed. After studying the Swiss peoples' experience with Platzspitz, it is hard to believe that some advocates of drug legalization in the United States are urging us to participate in the same kind of experiment.

Fallacies—and Critical Thinking

Arguments, like [people], are often pretenders.

—Plato

Throughout this book we have stressed how to argue well, accentuating the positive rather than dwelling on the negative, poor reasoning and bad arguments. We'd rather say "do this" than "don't do that." We'd rather offer good arguments to emulate than bad arguments to avoid. In stressing the positive, however, we haven't paid enough attention to an undeniable fact. Too often unsound arguments convince too many people who should reject them. This appendix addresses a daily problem—arguments that succeed when they ought to fail.

Traditionally, logicians and philosophers have tried to solve this problem by exposing "fallacies," errors in reasoning. About 2,400 years ago, the great ancient Greek philosopher Aristotle was the first to do so in *Sophistical Refutations.* "Sophistry" means reasoning that *appears* to be sound. Aristotle showed that such reasoning only seems sound and therefore shouldn't pass critical scrutiny. He identified thirteen common errors in reasoning. Others have since isolated dozens more, over a hundred in some recent treatments.

We respect this ancient tradition and urge you to learn more about it. Irving M. Copi's classic textbook, *Introduction to Logic,* offers an excellent discussion. It's often used in beginning college philosophy courses. However, our concern is not philosophy but arguments about public issues, where a different notion of fallacy is more useful. Let's start, then, with how we define it.

WHAT IS A FALLACY?

Our concern is arguing well, both skillfully and ethically, and arguments have force through *appeals to an audience.* Therefore, we define *fallacy* as "the misuse of an otherwise common and legitimate form of appeal."

A good example is the appeal to authority, common in advancing evidence to defend reasons in an argument. If I'm writing about flu epidemics, for instance, I may cite a scientist studying them at the national Centers for Disease Control to support something I've said. As long as I report what he or she said accurately, fully, and without distortion, I've used the appeal to authority correctly. After all, I'm not a flu expert and this person is—it only makes sense to appeal to his or her authority.

But let's suppose that my authority's view does not represent what most experts believe—in fact most leading authorities reject it. Perhaps I just don't know enough to realize that my authority is not in the mainstream. Or perhaps I do know, but for reasons of my own I want my audience to think a minority view is the majority view. It doesn't matter whether I intend to deceive or not—if I present my authority in a misleading way, I have misused the appeal to authority. I have committed a fallacy in the meaning we're giving it here.

There are other ways of misusing the appeal to authority—for instance, citing someone as an authority on a subject unrelated to the person's field or citing an authority likely to be biased because of his or her affiliation. Stephen Hawking is a genuine expert on physics but probably not on American policy in the Middle East. Scientists employed by an oil company are suspect when they talk about global warming.

Here's the point of our definition of fallacy: There's nothing wrong with the appeal to authority itself. Everything depends on how it's used in a particular case. That's why fallacies must be linked with critical thinking. Studying fallacies can lead to mindless "fallacy hunts" and to labeling all instances of a kind of appeal as fallacious. Fallacies are common, but finding them requires *thinking through any appeal that strikes us as suspect for some reason*. We have to decide in each case whether to accept or reject the appeal—or more often, how much we should let it influence our thinking.

WHY ARE FALLACIES SO COMMON?

Fallacies are common because they are deeply rooted in human nature. We must not imagine that we can eliminate them. But we can understand some of their causes and motivations and, with that understanding, increase our critical alertness. The following account is far from complete; we offer it to stimulate your own thinking about why fallacies occur.

We've distinguished unintended fallacies from intentional ones. We think most fallacies are not meant to deceive, so let's deal with this bigger category first. Unintentional fallacies can result from not knowing enough about the subject, which we may not realize for a number of reasons:

- *Inaccurate reporting or insufficient knowledge.* Arguments always appeal to the facts connected with a controversial question. Again, as with the appeal to authority, there's nothing wrong with appealing to what's known about something. It's hard to imagine how we'd argue without doing so. But we have to get the facts right and present them in a context of other relevant information.

So, for example, experts think that about 300,000 undocumented, foreign-born people immigrate to the United States each year. Not 3,000 or 30,000, but 300,000, and not per month or decade, but annually. The first way we can misuse the appeal to facts is not to report the information accurately. Mistakes of this kind occur often. Even magazines and newspapers frequently acknowledge errors in their stories from previous issues.

If we cite the correct figure, 300,000 per year, to support a contention that the Border Patrol isn't doing its job, we'd be guilty of a fallacy if we didn't know that about half of these immigrants come legally, on visas, and simply stay. They are not the Border Patrol's problem. So, even if we cite information accurately, we can still misrepresent what it means or misinterpret it. Accuracy is important but not enough by itself to avoid fallacies. We have to double-check our facts and understand what the facts mean. Because many people don't, fallacies of fact are common.

- *Holding beliefs that aren't true.* If what we don't know can hurt us, what we think we know that's false does more damage. We pick up such beliefs from misinformation that gets repeated over and over in conversation and the media. For example, many Americans equate Islam with Arabs. But most Muslims aren't Arabs, and many Arabs aren't Muslims. The linkage is no more than a popular association. Furthermore, many terrorists are neither Arabs nor Muslims—we just don't hear about them much. Unfortunately, even when informed people point out the facts just mentioned, they tend not to register or be forgotten quickly. Such is the hold of incorrect beliefs on the minds of many people.

  We have to read deeply in good sources to overcome mistaken associations in our minds; we have to allow ourselves to be corrected when what we thought was true turns out to be false; and we have to be alert not to slip back into old habits of thought. Because this requires more intellectual discipline than many people are willing to exert, fallacies abound.

- *Stubbornly adhering to a belief despite massive counterevidence.* At one time most climate scientists resisted the notion that human activities could influence the weather, much less cause global warming. But as more and more evidence accumulated, the overwhelming majority eventually came to agree that carbon dioxide emissions, especially from vehicles and power-generating plants, are the major cause of global warming. But dissenters still exist, and not all of them are being paid by oil companies. Some may sincerely feel that natural variation in the Earth's climate is the real cause of global warming. Some may enjoy the role of outsider or maverick. Some may say that often the majority opinion turns out to be wrong, which is true enough, and somebody needs to play the skeptic. Whatever the motivation may be, the dissenters are brushing aside an enormous amount of evidence. Their fallacious arguments have helped to convince too many Americans that we don't have a problem when we do. We cite this example to show that fallacies are not restricted to popular arguments. Scientists can be as stubborn as anyone. It's human nature, against which no degree of expertise can protect us.

- *Dodging issues we don't understand or that disturb or embarrass us.* The issues that immigration, both legal and illegal, raises, for example, are more often avoided or obscured than confronted. People talk about immigrants becoming "good Americans" and worry about whether the latest wave can or will "assimilate." But what is a "good American"? The question is rarely posed. Exactly what does "assimilate" involve? Again, few ask the question. Thus, arguments about this subject often dodge the important questions connected with it. In many cases those making these arguments do so while thinking they are confronting it.

  Just as often, we deliberately dodge issues that we understand very well. We know, for example, that most SUVs use more gas than cars, and because of their high center of gravity, they are more prone to flip over. Furthermore, we know that the United States uses too much gasoline and diesel and is therefore dependent on uncertain foreign supplies of crude oil. We also know that burning hydrocarbons releases massive amounts of greenhouse gases, especially carbon dioxide. Yet only high gasoline prices have reduced SUV sales, and people come up with all sorts of bad arguments designed to justify or excuse continuing to drive them. Perhaps a few people, because of large families or their work, really need SUVs, but most who drive them don't and they know this too. They just like them and dodge the issues connected with driving them.

If you recognize yourself and people you know in some or all of these causes and motivations that drive fallacious arguments, welcome to the club. We are all guilty. Without meaning to, we all get the facts wrong; we all pick up notions we take to be true that aren't; and we all are at times stubborn and evasive.

Fortunately, unintended fallacies usually have telltale signs we can learn to detect, such as these:

- the reported fact that seems unlikely or implausible
- the interpretation that reduces a complex problem to something too simple to trust
- the belief that doesn't fit what we know of the world and our own experience
- the argument that strains too hard to downplay or explain away data that would call it into question
- the argument that dances around issues rather than confronting them

The good news is that unintended fallacies are seldom skillful enough to fool us often or for long. They tend to give themselves away once we know what to look for and care enough to exercise our natural critical capacity.

The bad news is that arguments coldly calculated to deceive, although less common than arguments that mislead unintentionally, are often much harder to detect. What makes the problem especially tough is that deceit comes too often from people we want and even need to trust: people in authority, with power, people who are talented, intelligent, charming, sophisticated, connected, and well-educated. Why? Why do people sometimes set out to deceive others? We think the philosopher and brilliant fallacy hunter Jeremy Bentham had the best answer. He called the motivation "interest-begotten prejudice." What did he mean?

He meant that all human beings have interests they consider vital—status, money, and power they either have and seek to protect or strive to acquire. As a direct result of these interests, their outlook, thinking, and of course their arguments are shot through with prejudices, unexamined judgments about what is good, desirable, worthwhile, and so on. For example, through much of American history, Native Americans had something the American government wanted—land. When it didn't take it by force, it took it by treaty, by persuading Native Americans to make bad bargains that often the government never intended to keep anyway. The whole process rode on prejudices: Native Americans were savages or children in need of protection by the Great Father in Washington; besides that, they didn't "do anything" with the land they had. Because the deceit paid off handsomely for its perpetrators, it went on until there was little land remaining to take.

We'd like to tell you that deliberate deceit in argument doesn't work—that deceivers are exposed and discredited at least, if not punished for what they do. We'd like to endorse Abraham Lincoln's famous statement: "You can fool all of the people some of the time, and some of the people all the time, but you can't fool all of the people all of the time." Maybe so—many Native Americans and some independent-thinking white people weren't fooled by the false promises of the treaties. But the humorist James Thurber's less famous observation is probably closer to the truth: "You can fool too many of the people too much of the time." This is so because the interest-begotten prejudices of the powerful coincide with or cooperate with the prejudices of a large segment of the audience addressed. That's why Hitler and his propaganda machine was able to create the disastrous Third Reich and why Joseph Stalin, who murdered more Russians than Hitler did, remains a national hero for many Russians even now, after his brutal regime's actions have long been exposed.

So, what can be done about the fallacious arguments of deliberate deceivers, backed as they often are by the power of the state or other potent interests? The most important thing is to examine our own interest-begotten prejudices, because that's what the deceivers use to manipulate us. They won't be able to push our buttons so easily if we know what they are and realize we're being manipulated. Beyond that, we need to recognize the interests of others, who may be in the minority and largely powerless to resist when too many people are fooled too much of the time. We can call attention to the fallacies of deliberate deceivers, exposing their game for others to see. We can make counterarguments, defending enlightened stances with all our skill. There's no guarantee that what should prevail will, but at least we need not lend support to exploiters nor fall into silence when we ought to resist.

SOME COMMON FALLACIES

For reasons that should be clearer now, people often misuse legitimate forms of appeal. We've mentioned two examples already—the misuse of the appeal to authority and the misuse of the appeal to facts. All legitimate appeals can be misused, and because there are too many to discuss them all, we'll confine our attention to those most commonly turned into fallacies.

In Chapter 9, "Motivating Action: Arguing to Persuade," we described and illustrated all the forms of appeal at length (pages 266–272). In sum, we are persuaded by

- *ethos:* the character of the writer as we perceive him or her
- *pathos:* our emotions and attitudes as the argument arouses them
- *style:* how well something is said
- *logos:* our capacity for logic, by the force of reasons and evidence advanced for a thesis

You'll encounter people, including many professors, who hold that only *logos,* rational appeal, *should* persuade. Anything else from their point of view is irrelevant and probably fallacious. We say in response that, regardless of what should be the case, people *are* persuaded by all four kinds of appeal—that we always have been and always will be. It therefore doesn't help to call appeals to *ethos, pathos,* and style fallacious. It *can* help to understand how these legitimate forms of appeal can be misused or abused. That's what we're trying to do in pointing to common fallacies.

The Appeal to *Ethos*

We don't know many people well whose arguments we encounter in print or in cyberspace. Typically, we don't know them at all. Consequently, we ordinarily rely on their qualifications and reputation as well as our impression of their character from reading what they've written. If *ethos* isn't important or shouldn't matter, we wouldn't find statements about an author's identity and background attached to articles and books they've written. Speakers wouldn't be introduced by someone providing similar information. But *ethos* does matter; as Aristotle said long ago, it's probably the most potent form of appeal. If we don't trust the person we're hearing or reading, it's highly unlikely we'll be persuaded by anything said or written. If we do, we're inclined to assent to all of it. Consequently, appeals to ethos are often misused. Here are some of the common ways.

Personal Attack

There are people we ought never to trust—confidence men who bilk people out of their life savings, pathological liars, and so on. There's nothing wrong with exposing such people, destroying the *ethos* they often pretend very persuasively to have, thereby rendering their arguments unpersuasive.

But too often good arguments by good people are undermined with unjustified personal attacks. The most common is name-calling. Someone offers an argument opponents cannot see how to refute, so instead of addressing the argument, they call him or her "a liberal," a "neocon," or some other name the audience equates with "bad."

This fallacy is so common in politics that we now refer to it as "negative ads" or "negative campaigning." We ought not to dismiss it because experience and studies show that it often works. It works because once a label is attached to someone it's hard to shake.

Common Opinion

It's hard to find any argument that doesn't appeal to commonly accepted beliefs, many of which are accurate and reliable. Even scientific argument, which extols the value of skepticism, assumes that some knowledge is established beyond question and that some ways of doing things, like experimental design, are the right ways. When we indicate that we share the common opinions of our readers, thinking and behaving as they do, we establish or increase our *ethos*.

Used fallaciously, a writer passes off as commonly accepted either a belief that isn't held by many informed people or one that is held commonly but is false or highly doubtful. "Of course," the writer says, and then affirms something questionable as if it was beyond question. For example, "Everybody knows that AIDS is spread by promiscuous sexual behavior." Sometimes it is, but one sexual act with one person can transmit the virus, and infection need not be transmitted sexually at all—babies are born with it because their mothers have AIDS, and addicts sharing needles is another common way AIDS is spread. Furthermore, health care workers are at higher risk because they often are exposed to bodily fluids from infected people. The common opinion in this and many other instances is no more than a half-truth at best.

Tradition

Few can see the opening of the musical *Fiddler on the Roof* and not be at least temporarily warmed by the thought of tradition. Tradition preserves our sense of continuity, helps us maintain stability and identity amid the often overwhelming demands of rapid change. No wonder, then, that writers appeal to it frequently to enhance their *ethos* and often in ways that are not fallacious at all. It was hardly a fallacy after 9/11, for instance, to remind

Americans that part of the price we pay for liberty, our supreme traditional value, is greater relative vulnerability to terrorism. A closed, totalitarian society like North Korea can deal with terrorism much more "efficiently" than we can, but at the price of having no liberty.

Many of the abuses of tradition as a source of ethical appeal are so obvious as to need no discussion: politicians wrapping themselves in the flag (or at least red, white, and blue balloons), television preachers oozing piety to get donations. You can easily provide your own examples. Much more difficult to discern is invoking tradition not to dupe the naïve but to justify resisting constructive change. Tradition helped to delay women's right to vote in the United States, for example, and plays a major role in the high illiteracy rate for women in India and many other countries now.

Like all fallacious uses of legitimate appeals, ethical fallacies can be revealed by asking the right questions:

> For *personal attack,* ask, "Are we dealing with a person whose views we should reject out of hand?" "Is the personal attack simply a means to dismiss an argument we ought to listen to?"

> For *common opinion,* ask, "Is this belief really held by well-informed people?" If it is, ask, "Does the common belief hold only in some instances or in every case?"

> For *tradition,* ask, "Have we always really done it that way?" If so, ask, "Have conditions changed enough so that the old way may need to be modified or replaced?"

The Appeal to *Pathos*

After people understand the indispensable role *ethos* plays in persuasion, few continue to view it only negatively, as merely a source of fallacies. *Pathos* is another matter. In Western culture, the heart is opposed to the head, feeling and emotion contrasted with logic and clear thinking. Furthermore, our typical attitudes toward *pathos* affect *ethos* as well: Emotional people can't be trusted. Their arguments betray a disorganized and unbalanced mind.

With cause, we are wary of the power of emotional appeal, especially when passionate orators unleash it in crowds. The result often enough has been public hysteria and sometimes riots, lynchings, and verbal or physical abuse of innocent people. We know its power. Should it, then, be avoided? Are emotional appeals always suspect?

Let's take a brief look at a few of them.

Fear

"We have nothing to fear but fear itself," Franklin Roosevelt declared, at a time when matters looked fearful indeed. The Great Depression was at its height; fascism was gaining ground in Europe. The new president sought to reduce the fear and despair that gripped the United States and much of the world at the time.

About a year later, in 1933, Hitler came to power, but the authorities in Britain, France, and other countries failed to realize the threat he represented soon enough, despite warnings from Winston Churchill and many others. As a result, the Allied powers in Europe fell to the Nazis, and Britain came to the brink of defeat. Fear can paralyze, as Roosevelt knew, but lack of it can result in complacency when genuine threats loom.

How can we tell the difference? With appeals to fear, as with all appeals to any emotion, this hard-to-answer question is the key: *Does reality justify the emotion a speaker or writer seeks to arouse or allay?* Recently, for instance, it's been easy to play on our fear of terrorists. But the odds of you or me dying in a terrorist plot are very low. The risk of death is greater just driving a car. Far more Americans will die prematurely from sedentary ways than Osama bin Laden and his associates are ever likely to kill. 9/11 has taught us yet again that "eternal vigilance is the price of liberty," but the sometimes nearly hysterical fear of terrorism isn't justified.

The appeal to fear is fallacious when fear is trumped up, manufactured to scare people into doing unwise things. But playing down fear when we should be afraid is also fallacious and can do just as much damage. We should be more afraid, for instance, of the effects of global warming than most Americans appear to be. The fallacy is not the appeal to fear but the lack of justification or evidence for the fear we're attempting to arouse or reduce.

Pity

Fear has its roots in the body, in the fight-or-flight rush of adrenaline that helps us to survive. Pity, the ability to feel sorry for people suffering unjustly, has social roots. Both are fundamental emotions, part of being human.

Like the appeal to fear, the appeal to pity can be used fallaciously, to mislead us into, for example, contributing to a seemingly worthy cause which is really just a front for con artists. A favorite human ploy is attempting to dodge the consequences for irresponsible behavior by appealing to pity. Children do this well, learning at an early age to avoid punishment by pulling at the heartstrings of their parents. And some adults are pity-addicts, always ready with a tale of woe, in extreme cases even faking illness or making themselves sick to get attention—it's called Munchausen syndrome.

But if pity can be used to manipulate us, we can also fail to respond when pity is warranted. Or we can substitute the emotion for action. The suffering in Darfur in recent years has been acute but the response of the rest of the world has usually been too little, too late. Like fear, then, we can fail to respond to appeals for pity when they are warranted.

Which is worse? To be conned sometimes or to be indifferent in the face of unjust suffering? Surely the latter. Because fear can lead to hysteria and violence, we should meet appeals to it skeptically. Because unjust suffering is so common, we should meet appeals to pity in a more receptive frame of mind. But with both emotions we require critical thinking. "I just feel what

I feel" is not good enough. We have to get past that to distinguish legitimate emotional appeals from fallacious ones.

Ridicule

We mention ridicule because student writers are often advised to avoid it. "Don't ridicule your opponents in an argument" is the standard advice, advice you'll find elsewhere in this book. So, is ridicule always fallacious, always a cheap shot, always a way to win points without earning them?

Well, not always. With most positions on most issues, we're dealing with points of view we may not agree with but must respect. But what if a position makes no sense, has little or no evidence to support its contentions, and yet people persist in holding it? What then? Is ridicule justified, at least sometimes?

If it isn't, then satire isn't justified, for satire holds up for scorn human behavior the satirist considers irrational and destructive. We all enjoy political cartoons, which thrive on ridicule of the absurd and the foolish. How many stand-up comedians would have far less material if ridicule was never justified?

Like pity, ridicule is a social emotion. It tries to bring individuals who have drifted too far away from social norms back into the fold. It allows us to discharge our frustration with stupid or dishonest positions through largely harmless laughter—far better than "let's beat some sense into old So-and-So." Ridicule, then, has its place and its functions.

But it also has its fallacies. Most commonly an intelligent, well-reasoned, and strongly supported position suffers ridicule simply because it is unpopular, because most people have difficulty getting their minds around it. Some arguments are ahead of their time and fly in the face of commonly held prejudices. Only a half century ago, the arguments against segregating blacks and whites in our schools were ridiculed. Now the quite cogent arguments for recognizing some gay relationships as legal unions are likewise ridiculed. Clearly, the fact that an argument has been dismissed as ridiculous or absurd doesn't mean that it is, and we must be especially careful when we unthinkingly join in the ridicule. Maybe we need to rethink our prejudices. In any case, we need to think through the argument that's been scorned or dismissed with laughter. We may find an intelligent, well-reasoned, and strongly supported position that challenges us to change our minds.

Like the fallacies related to *ethos,* pathetic fallacies can be revealed with the right questions:

1. Is the emotion appropriate to the situation, in proportion to what we know about what's going on in the world?

2. What are the consequences of buying into a particular emotional appeal? Where will it take us?

3. Does the emotional appeal *substitute* for reason, for a good argument, or does it reinforce it in justified ways?

4. What is the relation of the appeal to unexamined and possibly unjustified prejudice or bias? Are we being manipulated or led for good reasons to feel something?

The Appeal to Style

Most experienced and educated people are aware of the seductions of *ethos* and *pathos*. They know how easy it is to be misled by people they trust or manipulated by emotion into doing something they ordinarily wouldn't and shouldn't do. They've been fooled enough to be wary and therefore critical. However, even experienced and educated people often aren't alert to the power of style, to the great impact that something can have *just because it is stated well*. One of the great students of persuasion, the American critic Kenneth Burke, explained the impact of style. He said that when we like the *form* of something said or written, it's a small step to accepting the *content* of it as well. We move very easily from "Well said" to "I agree," or even "It must be true." It's almost as if we can't distrust at a deep level language that appeals to our sense of rhythm and sound.

Yet fallacies of style are a major industry. It's called advertising. People are paid handsomely to create slogans the public will remember and repeat. From some time ago, for instance, comes this one: "When guns are outlawed, only outlaws will have guns." Has a nice swing to it, doesn't it? The play on words is pleasing, hard to forget, and captures in a powerful formula the fears of the pro-gun lobby. Of course, in reality there's never been a serious movement to outlaw guns in the United States. In some states, gun owners must register their weapons. Other laws may restrict gun ownership under certain circumstances or forbid carrying a concealed weapon in certain places. But no one is going to take away your guns, so the slogan is nothing more than scaremongering at best.

Now compare this slogan with another memorable phrase: "Justice too long delayed is justice denied." Martin Luther King used it to characterize the situation of black Americans in 1963 in his classic essay "Letter from Birmingham Jail." He got the phrase from a Supreme Court justice, but its appeal has less to do with the source of the statement than with its formula-like feeling of truth. It stuck in King's mind so he used it in his situation, and once you read it, you won't forget it either. In other words, it works in much the same way that the fallacious slogan works. But King's use of it isn't at all fallacious. As a matter of undisputed fact, black Americans were denied their civil rights legally and illegally for more than a century after the Emancipation Proclamation.

The point, of course, is that the form of a statement says nothing about its truth value or whether it's being used to deceive. If form pushes us toward unthinking assent, then we must exert enough resistance to permit critical thought. Even "justice too long delayed is justice denied" may require some careful thought if it is applied to some other situation. Many people who favor the death penalty, for example, are outraged by the many years it usually takes to move a murderer from conviction to execution. They could well apply the phrase to this state of affairs. How much truth should it contain for someone who has no legal, moral, or religious objections to capital punishment? It's true that often the relatives of a victim must wait a decade or more for justice. It's true that sometimes, for one reason or another, the execution never happens. Is that justice denied? But it's also true that convicted felons on death row have been found innocent and released. Some innocent ones have been executed. Has justice been too long delayed or not? Would it be wise to shorten the process? These are serious questions critical thought must address.

The appeal of style goes well beyond slogans and formulas. We have not offered a list of common stylistic devices and how they may be misused because there are far too many of them. All can be used to express the truth; all can be used to package falsehood in appealing rhythm and sound. Separating ourselves from appeals of language long enough to think about what is being said is the only solution.

The Appeal to *Logos*

Before we present a short list of common errors in reasoning, the traditional focus of fallacy research, let's review a fundamental point about logic: An argument can be free of errors in reasoning, be logically compelling, and yet be false. Logic can tell us whether an argument makes sense but not whether it is true. For example, consider the following statements:

> Australia began as a penal colony, a place where criminals in England were sent.

> Modern Australians, therefore, are descendents of criminals.

There's nothing wrong with the logical relation of these two statements. But its truth value depends on the *historical accuracy* of the first statement. It depends also on the *actual origins* of all modern Australians. As a matter of fact, Australia was used by the English as a convenient place to send certain people the authorities considered undesirable, but they weren't all criminals. Furthermore, native Australians populated the country long before any European knew it existed. And most modern Australians immigrated long after the days of the penal colony. So the truth value of these perfectly logical statements is low. It's true enough for Australians to joke about sometimes, but it's not really true.

Here's a good rule of thumb: *The reality of things reasoned about is far more varied and complex than the best reasoning typically captures.* Sometimes errors in reasoning lead us to false conclusions. But false conclusions result much more often from statements not being adequate to what's known about reality. Furthermore, there's always a lot about reality we don't know yet, and things we think we know that in time prove false. We should care a great deal about the logic of an argument but not jump to the conclusion it's true just because it's logical.

With that in mind, let's look at a few fallacies of logical appeal.

False Cause

We've defined *fallacy* as the misuse of a legitimate form of appeal. There's nothing more common or reasonable than identifying the cause of something. We're not likely to repair a car without knowing what's causing that wobble in the steering, or treat a disease effectively, or come up with the right solution to almost any problem without knowing the cause.

The difficulty is that just because "a" follows "b," "b" didn't necessarily cause "a." Yet we tend to think so, especially if "a" always follows "b." Hence, the possibility of "false cause," reasoning that misleads by confusing sequence with cause. If we flip a light switch and the light doesn't go on, we immediately think, "The bulb's burned out." But if we then replace the bulb, and it still doesn't work, we think the problem must be the switch. We may tinker with that for a while before we realize that none of the lights are working: "Oh, the breaker's cut off." By a process of trial and error, we eliminate the false causes to find the real one.

But if we're reasoning about more complex problems, trial and error usually isn't an option. For example, a recent newspaper article attributed the decline in the wages of Americans despite increased productivity to the influx of illegal aliens, especially from Mexico. Because they are paid less than most American citizens are, attributing the cause of lower wages to them may seem plausible. But actually some groups of Americans have endured a steady decline for some time, as high-paying industrial jobs were lost and lower-paying service work took their place. Globalization has allowed companies to force wages down and reduce the power of labor unions by taking advantage of people in other countries who will work for much less. It's highly unlikely that depressed wages are caused by illegal aliens alone. But if we don't like them, it's especially tempting to blame them for a more complex problem with which they are only associated. That's called *scapegoating,* and false cause is how the reasoning works that justifies it.

As a rule of thumb, let's assume that complex problems have multiple causes, and let's be especially suspicious when common prejudices may motivate single-cause thinking.

Straw Man

Nothing's more common in argument than stating an opponent's position and then showing what's wrong with it. As long as we state our opponent's position fully and accurately and attack it intelligently, with good reasons and evidence, there's nothing fallacious about such an attack.

The temptation, however, is to seek advantage by attributing to our opponents a weak or indefensible position they don't hold but which resembles their position in some respects. We can then knock it down easily and make our opponents look dumb or silly in the process. That's called "creating a straw man," and it's a common ploy in politics especially. It works because most people aren't familiar enough with the position being distorted to realize that it's been misrepresented, and so they accept the straw man as if it was the real argument. Often people whose views have been caricatured fight an uphill battle, first to reestablish their genuine position and then to get it listened to after an audience has accepted the distorted one as genuine. Thus, many fallacies succeed because of ignorance and ill will on the part of both the fallacious reasoner and the audience.

It's all very well to say, "Be fair. Don't say somebody thinks something she or he doesn't." Indeed, we shouldn't. It's just sophisticated lying that lowers the quality of public discussion. But the real challenge is to be critical when someone misrepresents a person or a position we didn't like beforehand. Being fair despite our own prejudice is very difficult, more perhaps than we can expect from most people.

Slippery Slope

Human experience offers many examples of "one thing leading to another." We decide to have a baby, for instance, and one thing follows another from the first diaper change all the way to college graduation, with so much in between and beyond that a parent's life is altered forever and fundamentally. Furthermore, it's always prudent to ask about any decision we face, "If I do *x*, what consequent *y* am I likely to face? And if *y* happens, where will that lead me?" We also know that what we do often sets in motion actions on the part of other people, sometimes with unforeseen results. The Bush administration invaded Iraq to remove an apparently dangerous dictator, succeeded in doing that, but also unleashed the forces that may well result in civil war in that country.

The slippery-slope fallacy takes advantage of our commonsense notion that actions have consequences, that one thing leads to another. The difference between the truth and the fallacy is that the drastic consequences the arguer envisions could not or are not likely to happen. Those who opposed making the so-called morning-after pill available without a prescription sometimes warned of a wholesale decline in sexual morality, especially among young adults. That hasn't happened, and in any case, technology is one thing, morality another. What makes sex right or wrong has little to do with the method of contraception.

The slippery-slope fallacy plays on fear, indicating one of the many ways that one kind of appeal—in this case, to logic, or reasoning about consequences—connects with other kinds of appeal—in this case, to emotion. Working in tandem, such appeals can be powerfully persuasive. All the more reason, then, to stand back and analyze any slope an argument depicts critically. Is the predicted slide inevitable or even probable? In many cases, the answer will be no, and we can see through the appeal to what it often is: a scare tactic to head off doing something that makes good sense.

Hasty Generalization

We can't think and therefore can't argue without generalizing. Almost any generalization is vulnerable to the charge of being hasty. All that's required for what some logicians label as "hasty generalization" is to find a single exception to an otherwise true assertion. So "SUVs waste gas." But the new hybrid SUVs are relatively gas efficient. "Since 9/11 American Muslims have felt that their loyalty to the United States has been in doubt." Surely we can find individual Muslims who haven't felt insecure at all.

The problem with hasty generalization is not exceptions to statements that are by and large true. The problem, rather, is generalization based on what's called a biased (and hence unrepresentative) sample, which results in a generalization that is false. If you visit an institution for the criminally insane, you'll probably encounter some schizophrenics. You may conclude, as many people have, that schizophrenics are dangerous. Most of them, however, are not, and the relatively few who are don't pose a threat when they stay on their meds. The common fear of "schizo street people" results from a hasty generalization that can do real harm.

With hasty generalization, then, we face the problem we face with all fallacies—distinguishing the legitimate appeal from its illegitimate misuse. The best attitude we can take is to be open to correction. We will make hasty generalizations based on a too-limited range of experience. That's just human. The question is, Will we allow additional experience or the greater experience of others to revise the generalizations that are more often false than true? If not, our minds have closed down and learning has stopped. We will victimize ourselves and others with actions based on hasty generalizations.

Begging the Question

We end with this because it is especially tricky. Every argument makes assumptions that haven't been and in some cases can't be proven. We simply couldn't argue at all if we had to prove everything our position assumes. Hence virtually all arguments can be said to "beg the question," to assume as true that which hasn't been shown definitively as true. Furthermore, we can never tell when an assumption that almost no one doubts can turn out to be very doubtful as new information emerges. Assumptions we used to make routinely can become hot issues of controversy.

Not long ago, for example, medicine assumed that increased environmental pollutants caused the higher incidence of allergies among recent generations of people who otherwise enjoy generally better health than their ancestors did. But now a competing theory is getting a lot of attention—that our homes are too clean, not contaminated enough for our immune system to react appropriately when we encounter ordinary levels of pollen and other allergens. So now, older arguments about how to prevent and treat allergies seem to beg the question, and the cause of allergies, once considered settled, is now at issue again.

Consequently, we should confine "begging the question" to *taking as settled the very question that's currently at issue.* Someone is charged with a crime, and the press gives it much ink and air time. Inevitably, some people jump to the conclusion that the accused is guilty. This can be such a big problem that it's hard to impanel a jury that hasn't been hopelessly biased by all the coverage.

We beg the question whenever we assume something that can't be assumed because it's the very thing we must prove. Fallacies of this kind are usually no harder to spot than the juror who thinks the defendant is guilty simply because he or she has been charged with a crime. Pro-lifers, for example, argue in ways that depend on the fetus having the legal status of a person. Of course, if the fetus is a person, there is no controversy. Abortion would be what pro-lifers say it is, murder, and thus prohibited by law. The personhood of the fetus is *the* issue; assuming the fetus is a person is begging the question.

No doubt we'd all prefer a simpler world, where everything is either this or that, black or white, yes or no, where we could say, "This kind of appeal is always fallacious, but this kind you can always rely on." That's not how it is. Sorting out the good from the bad in reasoning requires critical thinking, the results of which may not be certain either.

The following exercise does not include what many such exercises offer—fallacies so obvious they would fool no one over the age of ten. You'll have to think them through, discuss them at length. In some cases, rather than flatly rejecting or accepting the arguments, you may want to give them "partial credit," a degree of acceptance. That's fine, part of learning to live with shades of gray.

EXERCISE

The following examples come from instances of persuasion that appeared in the fifth edition of this book. Some may not be fallacious in any way. Assess them carefully and be prepared to defend the judgment you make.

1. From an ad depicting the VW Beetle: "Hug it? Drive it? Hug it? Drive it?"

2. From a cartoon depicting a man holding a pro-life sign, above which appear two specimen jars, one containing "a dead abortion doctor," the other "a dead fetus." The man is pointing at the jar with the dead fetus. The caption reads "We object to this one."

3. From an essay called "The End of Life," James Rachels offers the following interpretation of the Biblical prohibition against taking human life: "The sixth commandment does not say, literally, 'Thou shalt not *kill*'—that is a bad translation. A better translation is, Thou shalt not commit *murder,* which is different, and which does not obviously prohibit mercy killing. Murder is by definition *wrongful killing;* so, if you do not think that a given kind of killing is wrong, you will not call it murder" [author's emphasis].

4. From a panel discussion in *Newsweek* about violence in the media: The moderator asks a representative of the movie industry why the rating NC-17 is not applied to "gratuitously violent movies." The response is "because the definition of 'gratuitous' is shrouded in subjectivity. . . . Creative people can shoot a violent scene a hundred

different ways. Sex and language are different, because there are only a few ways [you can depict them on screen]. . . . Violence is far more difficult to pin down."

5. From an essay critical of multiculturalism comes the following quotation from the political scientist Samuel B. Huntington, whose view the essay's author endorses: "Does it take an Osama bin Laden . . . to make us realize that we are Americans? If we do not experience recurrent destructive attacks, will we return to the fragmentation and eroded Americanism before September 11?"

6. From an essay advocating multiculturalism: "The attack on affirmative action isn't really about affirmative action. Essentially it is another tactic in today's war on the gains of the 1960's, a tactic rooted in Anglo resentment and fear. A major source of that fear: the fact that California will almost surely have a majority of people of color in 20 to 30 years at most, with the nation as a whole not far behind."

7. From an essay urging us to move beyond the multiculturalism debate, written by a naturalized American citizen who was born in India: "I take my American citizenship very seriously. I am a voluntary immigrant, and not a seeker of political asylum. I am an American by choice, and not by the simple accident of birth. I have made emotional, social, and political commitments to this country. I have earned the right to think of myself as an American."

8. From an article arguing that militant Islam and Islamic terrorism is like Nazism: "Once again, the world is faced with a transcendent conflict between those who love life and those who love death both for themselves and their enemies. Which is why we tremble."

9. From an article arguing that American foreign policy provokes terrorism and that the root of it all is "our rampant militarism": "Two of the most influential federal institutions are not in Washington but on the south side of the Potomac River: the Defense Department and the Central Intelligence Agency. Given their influence today, one must conclude that what the government outlined in the Constitution of 1787 no longer bears much relationship to the government that actually rules from Washington. Until that is corrected, we should probably stop talking about 'democracy' and 'human rights.'"

10. From an article that attempts to explain human mating in evolutionary terms: "Feelings and acts of love are not recent products of particular Western views. Love is universal. Thoughts, emotions, and actions of love are experienced by people in all cultures worldwide—from the Zulu in the southern tip of Africa to the Eskimos in the north of Alaska."

For additional examples of fallacies for analysis, see "Stalking the Wild Fallacy" <http://www.fallacyfiles.org/examples.html>.

GLOSSARY

allusion: Reference to a person, event, or text, usually not explained.

annotation: A brief critical commentary on a text or section of text.

apologia: An effort to explain and justify what one has done, or chosen not to do, in the face of condemnation or at least widespread disapproval or misunderstanding.

argument: Mature reasoning; a considered opinion backed by a reason or reasons.

bibliography: A list of works on a particular topic.

brief: Outline of a case, including thesis, reasons, and evidence.

case strategy: The moves a writer makes to shape a particular argument, including selecting reasons, ordering them, developing evidence, and linking the sections of the argument for maximum impact.

case structure: A flexible plan for making any argument to any audience; it consists of one or more theses, each of which is supported by one or more reasons, each of which is supported by evidence. See also *brief.*

claim: In argument, what the author wants the audience to believe or to do.

connotation: What a word implies or what we associate it with; see also *denotation.*

conviction: An earned opinion achieved through careful thought, research, and discussion.

convincing: One of the four aims of argument; to use reasoning to secure the assent of people who do not share the author's conviction.

critical reading: A close reading involving analyzing and evaluating a text.

denotation: A word's literal meaning; see also *connotation.*

dialectic: Dialogue or serious conversation; the ancient Greeks' term for argument as inquiry.

graphics: Visual supplements to a longer text such as an essay, article, or manual.

identification: A strong linking of the readers' interests and values with an image, which represents something desired or potentially desirable.

implied question: A question that is inherent in an argument but not explicitly stated; all statements of opinion are answers to questions, usually implied ones.

inquiry: One of the four aims of argument; to use reasoning to determine the best position on an issue.

issue: An aspect of a topic that presents a problem, the solution to which people disagree about.

mediation: One of the four aims of argument; using reason and understanding to bring about consensus among disagreeing parties or positions.

middle style: A style of persuasive writing that is neither stiff and formal nor chatty and familiar.

paraphrase: To restate someone else's writing or speech in one's own words.

persuasion: One of the four aims of argument; persuasion uses both rational and emotional appeals to influence not just thinking but also behavior.

plagiarism: The act of presenting someone else's words and/or ideas as one's own, without acknowledging the source.

position: An overall, summarizing attitude or judgment about some issue.

rhetoric: The art of argument as mature reasoning.

rhetorical context: The circumstances surrounding the text as an act of communication: the time and place in which it was written; its place of publication; its author and his or her values; the ongoing, historical debate to which it contributes.

rhetorical prospectus: A plan for proposed writing that includes a statement of the thesis, aim, audience, speaker's persona, subject matter, and organizational plan.

sampling: A fast, superficial, not necessarily sequential reading of a text, not to learn all that a text has to say but to get a feeling for the territory it covers.

thesis: In argumentation, a very specific position statement that is strategically designed to appeal to readers and to be consistent with available evidence.

topic: A subject or aspect of a subject; see also *issue.*

visual rhetoric: The use of images, sometimes coupled with sound or appeals to the other senses, to make an argument or persuade one's audience to act as the image-maker would have them act.

CREDITS

Text and Illustration Credits

THE AMERICAN HERITAGE DICTIONARY OF THE ENGLISH LANGUAGE, excerpts from definitions of "mature" and "critical." Copyright © 2006 by Houghton Mifflin Company. Reproduced by permission from *The American Heritage Dictionary of the English Language, Fourth Edition*.

SISSELA BOK, "Media Literacy" from *Mayhem: Violence as Public Entertainment* by Sissela Bok. Copyright © 1998 by Sissela Bok. Reprinted by permission of Da Capo Press, a member of Perseus Books Group.

JAMES FORMAN, JR., "Arrested Development: The Conservative Case against Racial Profiling." From *The New Republic*, September 10, 2001. Reprinted by permission of The New Republic. Copyright © 2001 The New Republic, L.L.C.

PAT JOSEPH, "Start by Arming Yourself with Knowledge: Al Gore Breaks Through with His Global-Warming Message," *Sierra*, September/October 2006. Reprinted with permission from *Sierra*, the magazine of The Sierra Club.

DANIEL M. KAMMEN, "The Rise of Renewable Energy," *Scientific American*, September 2006. Text: Reprinted with permission. Copyright © 2006 by Scientific American, Inc. All rights reserved. Illustrations: Illustration of wind turbines by Kenn Brown/Mondolithic Studios. Reprinted with perission. "Growing Fast, but Still a Sliver" by Jen Christiansen (Sources: *PV News*, BTM Consult, AWEA, EWEA, F. O. Licht and *BP Statistical Review of World Energy 2006*), originally printed in *Scientific American*; "Wind Power" (map) by Jen Christiansen (Source: National Renewable Energy Laboratory), originally printed in *Scientific American*; "R&D Is Key" by Jen Christiansen (Source: Reversing the Incredible Shrinking Energy R&D Budget, D. M. Kammen and G. Nemet, in *Issues in Science and Technology*, Fall 2005), originally printed in *Scientific American*. Reprinted by permission of Jen Christiansen.

ROGER KIMBALL, "Institutionalizing Our Demise: America vs. Multiculturalism" from *Lengthened Shadows: America and Its Institutions in the Twenty-First Century*, edited by Roger Kimball and Hilton Kramer. San Francisco: Encounter Books, 2004. First published by Encounter Books. Reprinted by permission of the author.

MARTIN LUTHER KING, JR., "Letter from Birmingham Jail." Reprinted by arrangement with The Heirs to the Estate of Martin Luther King Jr., c/o Writers House as agent for the proprietor, New York, NY. Copyright 1963 Dr. Martin Luther King Jr.; Copyright renewed 1991 Coretta Scott King.

ELIZABETH MARTÍNEZ, "Reinventing 'America': Call for a New National Identity" from *De Colores Means All of Us: Latina Views for a Multi-Colored Century* by Elizabeth Martínez. Copyright © 1998 by Elizabeth Martínez. Reprinted by permission of South End Press.

WILLIAM F. MAY, "Rising to the Occasion of Our Death." Copyright © 1990 by the *Christian Century*. Reprinted by permission from the July 11–18, 1990, issue of the *Christian Century*.

RICHARD MOE, "Battling Teardowns, Saving Neighborhoods." Speech given to the Commonwealth Club, San Francisco, California, June 28, 2006. © 2006 National Trust for Historic Preservation. Reprinted with permission.

BHARATI MUKHERJEE, "Beyond Multiculturalism: A Two-Way Transformation," in *MultiAmerica: Essays on Cultural Wars and Cultural Peace*, ed. Ishmael Reed. Viking, 1997. Copyright © 1997 by Bharati Mukherjee. Reprinted with permission of author.

RICHARD RHODES, "Hollow Claims about Fantasy Violence." From *New York Times*, September 17, 2000. Copyright © 2000 The New York Times. Reprinted by permission.

Photo Credits

Page 4: Fig. 1.1, The J. Paul Getty Museum, Villa Collection, Malibu, California; © The J. Paul Getty Museum; **6:** © The Art Archive/Corbis; **25:** © Bill Aron/Photo Edit; **39** (top & bottom), © Chris Rainer/Getty Images; **48:** © Reuters/Corbis; **Color Insert:** C-1 © Image courtesy of The Advertising Archives; C-2 © U.S. Postal Service/AP/Wide World Photos; C-3 Holzman & Kaplan Worldwide, Bret Wills, photographer; C-4 © Louis Vuitton; C-5 © Geek Squad/Best Buy Inc.; C-6 By permission of Leagas Delaney, Inc., for Adidas. Adidas has not authorized, sponsored, endorsed, or approved this publication and is not responsible for it's contents; C-7 © AP Photo/Seth Wenig; C-8 © Frances Fife/AFP/Getty Images; **68:** Courtesy of the Department of Defense; **69** (top): © Barbara Alper/Stock Boston; **69** (bottom): © Richard Pasley/Stock Boston; **70:** © Bruce Young/Reuters/Corbis; **72** (top): © Anthony Suau 2006; **72** (bottom): © Marco Di Lauro/Getty Images; **144, 145, and 149:** © Carolyn Channell; **162:** © John Engstead/Hulton Archive/Getty Images; **195:** © Tim Boyle/Getty Images; **213:** © Kathy Willens/AP/Wide World Photos; **245:** © Liz Mangelsdorf/San Francisco Chronicle/Corbis; **252:** © Gene Herrick/AP/Wide World Photos; **253:** © Flip Schulke/Corbis; **287:** © Bettmann/Corbis.

INDEX

Note: Pages on which a term is defined are in bold type.